1995

Professional
and Technical
Writing
Strategies

SECOND EDITION

Professional and Technical Writing Strategies

Judith S. VanAlstyne
Broward Community College

PRENTICE HALL, Englewood Cliffs, New Jersey 07632

Library of Congress Cataloging-in-Publication Data

VanAlstyne, Judith S. (date)
   Professional and technical writing strategies / Judith S.
VanAlstyne. — 2nd ed.
      p.   cm.
   ISBN 0-13-728882-4
   1. English language—Rhetoric.   2. English language—Business
English.   3. English language—Technical English.   4. Technical
writing.   5. Business writing.   I. Title.
PE1479.B87V36   1990
808′.0666—dc20   89-25538
                                                        CIP

Editorial/production supervision: Virginia Rubens
Interior design: Virginia Rubens and Linda J. Den Heyer Rosa
Cover design: Linda J. Den Heyer Rosa
Manufacturing buyer: Mary Ann Gloriande

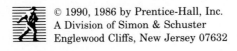

© 1990, 1986 by Prentice-Hall, Inc.
A Division of Simon & Schuster
Englewood Cliffs, New Jersey 07632

Printed in the United States of America

10 9 8 7 6 5 4 3 2 1

ISBN 0-13-728882-4

PRENTICE-HALL INTERNATIONAL (UK) LIMITED, *London*
PRENTICE-HALL OF AUSTRALIA PTY. LIMITED, *Sydney*
PRENTICE-HALL CANADA INC., *Toronto*
PRENTICE-HALL HISPANOAMERICANA, S.A., *Mexico*
PRENTICE-HALL OF INDIA PRIVATE LIMITED, *New Delhi*
PRENTICE-HALL OF JAPAN, INC., *Tokyo*
SIMON & SCHUSTER ASIA PTE. LTD., *Singapore*
EDITORA PRENTICE-HALL DO BRASIL, LTDA., *Rio de Janeiro*

Contents

152,807

Chapter 8   **Longer Reports, Proposals   174**

Chapter 9   **Professional Papers   220**

Chapter 10   **Accessing Information   248**

Chapter 11   **Documenting Reports   289**

Preface

The second edition of *Professional and Technical Writing Strategies* is designed for students making the transition from freshman composition courses into advanced levels of writing for the professions. Although the book is designed primarily for students in the first two years of study, it is comprehensive and flexible, suitable for college and university students at any level, professional and technical writers, and business people seeking a guideline and model text. The materials have been tested in academic classes and in training workshops in a variety of businesses and industries. The book has won two professional awards: the Award of Distinction from the Everglades Chapter of the Society for Technical Communication, and the Award of Achievement from the International Society of Technical Communication.

College students of the 1990s are a heterogeneous group with a myriad of interests and needs. They range from 17 to over 70 (average age, 28) and major in every field from aviation to zoology. The text includes writing samples which illustrate actual writing demands in a cross-section of career fields: allied health professions, architecture, criminal justice, data processing, electronic technology, fire science, landscape technology, pest control technology, insurance, and real estate, to name a few. These samples have been culled from students as well as from professionals in business and industry.

The emphasis is on practical writing and its applications, rather than on rhetoric and theory, although this edition reviews expository writing skills. The book covers strategies for effective general communications (written and oral), computer-assisted composing, editing, correspondence, professional reports, technical papers, and technical manual components. This edition expands on accessing research information and collection data by surveys as well as focusing on the writing of both technical articles and professional papers (employing the MLA, author/year, and number styles of documentation).

Although the organization of the text is intended to offer cumulative skills—moving from general considerations, to composing and editing, to correspondence and reports, to technical articles, and, finally, to specialized technical writing strategies—individuals may move about the text as freely as their audience and purpose dictate. Each chapter provides a list of skills which should be obtained, writing strategy guidelines, samples, exercises to reinforce the strategies, and writing options.

The second edition of *Professional and Technical Writing Strategies* is divided into four parts.

Part 1 contains four chapters on General Communication Strategies:

1. Professional/Technical Communications
2. The Writing Process
3. Graphics
4. Computer-assisted Writing

Part 2 contains seven chapters on The Professional Strategies:

5. Correspondence
6. Resumes, Cover Letters, and Interviews
7. Brief Reports
8. Longer Reports, Proposals
9. Professional Papers
10. Accessing Information
11. Documenting Reports

Part 3 contains five chapters on The Technical Strategies:

12. Preparing Manuals
13. Defining Terms
14. Describing Mechanisms
15. Giving Instructions
16. Analyzing a Process

Part 4 contains one chapter on Oral Strategies:

17. Verbal Communcations

Finally, there are two appendixes:

Appendix A. Conventions of Construction, Grammar, and Usage
Appendix B. Punctuation and Mechanical Conventions

The Instructor's Manual offers general notes to the instructor, student preparation guidelines, and sample syllabi for a variety of class situations. In addition, the manual discusses approaches to each chapter, provides exercise answers, and illustrates solutions to the writing options.

ACKNOWLEDGMENTS

I wish to thank Neil Linger for his research assistance, Bill Senior, Gordon Maddison, and Dave Shaw for patiently teaching me word processing and other computer intricacies, and Chas Howard for caring support.

I particularly thank Virginia Rubens, Production Editor, whose professional assistance throughout the writing and production process made this book possible. I am deeply indebted to Henry W. Pels for his rigorous editing of the copy. I am also grateful to Phil Miller, Editor in Chief for Humanities, who has encouraged me throughout both editions of the text; and to Nancy Perry, Executive Editor for English; Ann Knitel, Editorial Assistant; Kathy Hursh, Humanities Marketing Assistant; Jane Baumann; Lynne F. Rosenfeld; and many others who have played a part in the production of this edition. A sincere word of appreciation is due Marilyn Conner, Chemeketa Community College; Joseph T. Barwick, Central Piedmont Community College; and John Christie, Indiana State University, for their rigorous reviews of the manuscript and invaluable suggestions for the second edition.

A special thanks to my contributors: students in both my academic classes and professional workshops, business and industrial professionals, and the companies that so willingly gave me permission to reproduce their correspondence, reports, and manual materials.

Judith S. VanAlstyne

PART 1

General Communication Strategies

CHAPTER 1

Professional and Technical Communications

by Bruce Hammond

© 1982 Universal Press Syndicate. By permission.

Skills:

After studying this chapter, you should be able to

1. Define *audience, message, purpose, tone, style, jargon, shoptalk, gobbledygook, wordiness, redundancy,* and *voice.*

2. Recognize that the anticipated audience determines the manner in which the message should be written.

3. Organize an attractive message by using short paragraphs, visuals, and graphics.

4. State the purpose of a message quickly and clearly.

5. Avoid an emotional, flowery, judgmental, or pompous tone.

6. Write brief messages in factual, objective, impersonal style.

7. Recognize and eliminate jargon, shoptalk, and gobbledygook.

8. Recognize and eliminate wordiness.

9. Recognize and eliminate redundancies.

10. Recognize and revise sluggish passive-voice constructions.

INTRODUCTION

Television, computers, movies, advertising flyers, sales promotion letters, highway signs, and shop marquees bombard our sense of sight and literate ability. Word processors and copy machines spew out language in mind-boggling quantity. The transactions of all occupations (business, industry, services) depend largely upon written correspondence and reports—concise, orderly messages which elicit results, not confusion.

Even the entry-level employee—the clerk, the firefighter, the pest control technician, the physical therapist—must contribute to the written record of the company. Frequently, the employee who writes well is the one who is noticed by management and marked for promotion. Your ability to write reveals your organizational skills, your persuasiveness, and your logic. Your writing may even suggest your commitment to your occupation or profession.

Surveys show that employees at all levels spend approximately 25 percent of their time at work writing. Further, another significant percentage of time is spent dealing with the writing of others. And finally, despite the diversity of careers in the nation, writing demands are more similar than dissimilar. On-the-job writing includes a variety of special-purpose letters, memorandums, long and short reports, sets of instructions, and explanations of procedures and mechanisms.

The professional writer is faced with a number of questions:

- Who will read my message? (Audience)
- What is my message supposed to accomplish? (Purpose)
- Just exactly what shall I write? (Message)
- What emphasis shall I choose? (Tone)
- What language level shall I use? (Style)

Sorting out the answers to these questions is the key to effective professional and technical communications.

AUDIENCE

"Different strokes for different folks" is a wise adage. Anticipating your audience is a major key to writing well. Your audience is the reader or readers to whom your written message is directed. You must ask yourself still more questions to determine audience:

- Is my audience informed or uninformed on the subject?
- Does my audience have a grasp of the specialized vocabulary of my field or not?
- Is my audience singular or a group?
- Is my audience a subordinate, a peer, or a superior in my occupation?

Just as you would make natural adjustments in vocabulary, sentence structure, and overall message in explaining the operation of a toaster to a child or to an adult, so will you make subtle changes in written instructions of any sort to a potential customer or to a group of factory assemblers. Consider the differences in the following two excerpts—one written for an advanced audience and the other for a novice audience:

> The buccal cavity is abounded laterally by the cheeks, anteriorly by the lips, superiorly by the hard and soft palates, inferiorly by the tongue and associated muscles, and posteriorly by the pharynx and uvula. It contains the teeth, which masticate food; the tongue, which aids in mastication and deglutition; and the salivary glands, which manufacture and excrete salivary amylase, an enzyme that attacks starch and hydrolyzes it into maltose and mucin, a very sticky substance that mixes with the food to form the bolus.

The vocabulary and sentence structure are, perhaps, too sophisticated for a novice reading audience. The following rewrite is more appropriate for an uninformed audience.

> The mouth cavity is bounded on the sides by the cheeks, in front by the lips, on top by the roof of the mouth, on the bottom by the tongue, and in the back by the throat. It contains teeth to chew food, and a tongue which helps to chew food and to swallow. There are also salivary glands which produce a chemical that attacks starch and breaks it down into a sugar, forming a sticky substance that holds food in a ball.

If your reading audience has received preliminary information on a subject, you may eliminate details which are old information. If your audience is uninformed about the subject, you must be alert to include definitions, descriptions, background data, and other pertinent information.

Determine ahead of time if your reading audience has specialized training and vocabulary. If the audience's background is similar to your own, you may include technical terms, abbreviations, and graphics which an expert understands. If, however, your expected audience has little training in your field, you must remember to include synonyms, explanations, and details in plain English.

Some memorandums, letters, and reports are addressed to a single individual while others are intended for groups. The number of potential readers determines the style and tone in which the message is written. When you write for a single individual, you may be more personal, but when you write for a group, such as members of your department or all employees of an organization, or even potential readers of a manual or a professional journal article, a more objective and detailed report will be necessary. You need to identify the *lowest* level of understanding within the group and write to that level.

Whether your audience consists of subordinates, peers, or superiors should have a bearing on your presentation also. You must determine whether you should be familiar, supportive, or gracious.

Consider that you are often communicating in a political and bureaucratic environment. Occasionally you must think like a lawyer to protect yourself or your organization. Channel your memorandums and reports through the levels of hierarchy to keep others informed, to provide a clear record of your activities in a certain situation, and sometimes to avoid confrontation.

Use a "you" perspective in all of your writing. A "you" perspective does not mean that you use the second person pronoun, but that you keep your audience's needs in mind throughout your correspondence or report. Put yourself in the reader's place and write naturally, concisely, and objectively. Audience consideration is so important that it is discussed separately in the following chapters for each type of writing strategy.

PURPOSE

By keeping one clear-cut purpose in mind, you will write a better letter or report. Purpose is your intention, aim, or plan. Is your purpose to query? to explain? to analyze? or to persuade? Not only should your purpose be clear to you, but you should also establish your purpose as quickly as possible in your writing. Begin your writing with such statements as:

I am seeking additional information on your IBM Selectric II Typewriter.

This pamphlet has been prepared to help you use your Ace microwave oven safely and efficiently.

The feasibility of purchasing an Apple II computer for use in our three flower shops is presented in this study.

The purpose of this proposal, regarding a salary index scale, is to provide incentive to our employees to remain with the company and to eliminate the charge of "favoritism" which has contributed to low employee morale.

Knowing and establishing your purpose will keep your message "on track" and will give your reader a clear sense of how to handle your information.

MESSAGE

Once you have identified your audience and purpose, you are ready to consider your message. Your message is the explanation, response, set of instructions, recommendations, or questions which will accomplish your transaction. But before you write, you should consider your organization, format, and other special features, such as visuals and graphics.

The reader probably has piles of paperwork to handle—letters requiring a response, memos giving instructions for action, bulletins and reports imparting information to be retained, and more. The last thing the beleaguered reader wants to read is a "gray" message, a page or pages of uninterrupted type. To avoid the "gray" look:

- Be as brief as possible.
- Divide your message into an introduction, body, and closing.
- Write in short paragraphs (4 to 5 typed lines).
- Use headings (Completed Work, Work In Progress, Work To Be Completed).
- Use numbers for key points or chronological steps (1., 2., 3.).
- Use capital letters for section headings (COSTS, PERSONNEL).
- Use underlining, v a r i a b l e   s p a c i n g, and asterisks (*) to indicate divisions and headings.
- Use bullets (●) for lists of items.
- Insert graphics (bar charts, line graphs, drawings) such as those discussed in Chapter 3.

Although a message may be as brief as two sentences, it may also be many pages. Careful attention to visuals will make your message more readable. They will divide the text into logical units, add emphasis to essential points, and help the reader to relocate quickly passages requiring action.

TONE

Almost all professional writing demands a factual and objective tone. Tone is the word choice and phrasing which expresses your attitude toward the subject. Professional writing is marked by its lack of emotionalism, editorializing, sarcasm, or even overt enthusiasm. Good writers avoid humor, satire, anger, irony, and bitterness. Consider this partial text of an incident report illustrating inappropriate tone:

> On Wednesday, May 26, 199X, at 10:42 A.M., I had the misfortune of witnessing Keypunch Operator Polly Black take a nasty fall in the 5A West office area.
> While not looking where she was going, Polly clumsily caught her heel on a CRT tri-stand and crashed to the floor. The paramedic on call at security rendered first aid and transported her to Mercy Hospital. The accident was due to sheer carelessness.

The tone in this report is sarcastic (*had the misfortune*), judgmental (*while not looking where she was going, clumsily*), emotional (*a nasty fall, crashed*), and pompous (*CRT tri-stand, rendered, transported*). The following, a revised version of the same incident, illustrates an objective tone:

> On Wednesday, May 26, 199X, at 10:42 A.M., I witnessed Keypunch Operator Polly Black fall in the 5A West Office area.
> While approaching the door, Ms. Black caught her heel on an equipment stand and fell on her left side. The paramedic on call at Security treated her bruised knee and took her to Mercy Hospital.

The tone of professional communication should be factual and impartial.

STYLE

Professional writing usually uses an impersonal and simple style. Style is the manner or mode of expression in language, your way of putting thoughts into words. Unless your audience is technically sophisticated, you will want to use simple words, uncomplicated sentences, and short paragraphs. Avoid technical terms, jargon, shoptalk, gobbledygook, and overblown language. You will also want to avoid wordiness, redundancy, and unnecessary passive-voice constructions. Inappropriate style presents more problems in professional writing than does any other consideration. If a reader cannot understand your language, your message is lost. This chapter will emphasize stylistic problems and how to overcome them.

CONCRETENESS

Guard against unfounded assumptions about your audience. Even though you think your reader or readers *should* know why you are writing, *should* have a grasp of the situation, *should* be familiar with the language you are using, or *should* be able to act upon your message, you may be wrong. People are busy and preoccupied with their own work. Do not be vague. Use concrete language to eliminate any possible questions in the mind of the reader.

Vague   As we discussed recently, I have the figures on the project.

Concrete   I have the comparative costs of three word processing computers which you requested in our telephone conversation last Friday.

Vague   The policy change will affect us adversely.

Concrete   New Policy 1204.05 (Leaves) will decrease our allowable sick days from 10 to 8 per year.

Vague   We will fill your order within the next few weeks.

Concrete   We will ship C.O.D. your order for three, 4-drawer, 36 in. high by 45 in. deep by 14 in. wide, beige filing cabinets September 2, 199X. You should receive them no later than September 30.

JARGON, SHOPTALK, AND GOBBLEDYGOOK

Jargon is the specialized vocabulary and idiom of those in the same work. The jargon of one field often spreads to the professional world at large. Other words and phrases are intelligible only to those in the same line of work and may be classified as *shoptalk*. Another type of jargon, which may be called *gobbledygook*, is characterized by unintelligible, pompous, or stiff language. General jargon and shoptalk may be acceptable in very personal oral communication, but a competent writer eliminates all jargon from written communication.

General Jargon

The following list of words and phrases is used rather widely in informal professional communications:

ballpark figure	interface
bottom line	optimization
finalized	output
game plan	parameters
impacted	time frame
input	viable

Moderate use of such terms is common in verbal transactions but should be revised for written messages. The following sentences demonstrate typical jargon exchanges and suggested written revisions:

Jargon　　Give me a ballpark figure on the new office furniture.

Written　　Give me a price estimate on the new office furniture.

Jargon　　We'll use the input of each department to finalize our game plan.

Written　　We will consider the suggestions of each department to complete our programming.

Jargon　　The bottom line is that the recession has impacted on our hiring time frame.

Written　　The key point is that the recession has affected our hiring schedule.

Jargon　　The parameters for departmental interfacing must be viable.

Written　　The guidelines for departmental boundaries must be realistic.

Jargon　　His running mate is a heavyweight debater, and if he doesn't dribble around in circles or suffer a late-inning letdown, he is sure to deliver the knockout punch.

Written　　His vice-presidential candidate is a fine debater, and if he doesn't include too many details nor get discouraged, he will win the debate.

Shoptalk

The use of shoptalk, the more technical slang of those in the same profession, becomes second nature to the users but should never be used in writing. Every occupation has its own shoptalk.

Television shoptalk	He shot the bridge with a minicam and then bumped up the tape.
Translation	He filmed the connecting segment between the news items with a small camera and then machine-processed the videotape to a larger size.
Aviation shoptalk	He checked the pax list, activated the SATCOM, and prepared the PIREP.
Translation	He checked the passenger list, turned on the satellite communication system, and prepared the pilot's report on meteorological conditions.
Academic shoptalk	The increase in FTE's is probably due to so many students' having clepped math.
Translation	The increase in the number of full-time equivalency students is probably due to many students' having waived the mathematics requirement by passing the College Level Examination Program test.

Gobbledygook

Besides avoiding jargon and shoptalk, the skillful writer should avoid gobbledygook—unintelligible, pompous, and stiff language. Gobbledygook may sound more official or important but rarely states the message clearly.

Gobbledygook	At this juncture, the aforementioned procedure should be utilized.
Plain English	The plan which we discussed should be used now.
Gobbledygook	We should commence operational capabilities in systematic increments.
Plain English	We should begin the project step-by-step.
Gobbledygook	It would be prudent to consider expeditiously the provision of instrumentation that would provide an unambiguous indication of the level of fluid in the reactor vessel.
Plain English	We need a more accurate device to measure radioactivity.

WORDINESS

Effective professional writing is characterized by its brevity. The concise writer avoids roundabout phrases, redundancies, and sluggish passive-voice constructions.

Following is a checklist of shorter words and phrases to replace wordy, roundabout phrases:

Roundabout Phrases	Concise Expressions
a downward adjustment	cut, decrease
a great deal of	much
a majority of	most
accounted for the fact that	because
affix a signature to	sign
after the conclusion of	after
as a result	so, therefore
as a result of	because
as per your request	as you requested
as soon as	when
at which time	when
at all times	always
at an early date	soon
at a much greater rate than	faster
at the present time at this time	now
at the time of	during
avail yourself of	use
based on the fact that	because
be acquainted with	know
be of assistance to	assist, help
brief in duration	short, quick
by way of	by, to
came to an end	ended
consensus of opinion	opinion, everyone thinks
despite the fact that	although, though
due to the fact that in view of the fact that	because
enclosed please find	here is
for the purpose of	for, to
for this reason	so
for the reason that	since, because
give encouragement to	encourage
he was instrumental in	he helped
higher degree of	higher, more
in a manner similar to	like
in a position to	can
in accordance with	by, under
in favor of	for, to

Roundabout Phrases	*Concise Expressions*
in lieu of	instead
in reference to / in relation to	on, about
in the amount of	of
in the nature of	like
in the vicinity	near, around
is dependent upon	depends on
is situated in	is in
it is necessary that	you must
it is recommended	we recommend
miss out on	miss
not infrequently	often
on account of	because, due to
on the part of	from, of
preparatory to / prior to	before
provided that	if
pursuant to	under, with, following
referred to as	called
so as to	to
through the use of	by, with
to the extent that	as far as
until such time as	until
with reference to / with regard to	on, about
with the exception of	except
with the result that	so that

Avoid "Due to the fact that your reader has a great amount of other work to account for, it is necessary that you write so as to eliminate wordiness in your writing, through the use of concise words." Write "Because your reader is busy, write concisely."

REDUNDANCY

A *redundancy* is a phrase which says the same thing twice (*repeat again*), contains obvious expansion (*square in shape*), or doubles the idea (*each and every*). Such repetition is pointless, wordy, and distracting. Consider the redundancies in the following sentences:

Redundant   It is *absolutely essential* in *this day and age* to *completely eliminate bigotry and prejudice.*

Revision   Bigotry must be eliminated now.

Redundant   The sheriff's department and the city police *cooperated together* in *the month of May* to *devise and develop* a *totally unique drug and narcotics* control program.

Revision   The sheriff's department and the city police cooperated in May to develop a unique narcotics control program.

Redundant   There are *many in number* who consider the *total understanding* of *basic fundamentals* a *good asset.*

Revision   Many consider the understanding of basics an asset.

VOICE

Verbs have two voices: active and passive. In an active-voice expression the subject of the sentence performs the action stated by the verb.

Mr. Jones *conducts* the plant tours.

The president *presented* the budget.

The firm *is spending* $50 million this year to promote the new beer.

The new price *will increase* our profit.

In passive-voice expressions the subject is acted upon.

The plant tours *are conducted* by Mr. Jones.

The budget *was presented* by the president.

Fifty million dollars *will be spent* this year by the firm to promote the new beer.

Our profit *will be increased* by the new prices.

Generally, the active voice suggests immediacy and emphasizes the subject. Because the passive-voice verb is always at least two words (the verb plus a form of *to be*), passive-voice expressions tend to be wordy. The passive voice may bury your main idea in sluggish sentences.

Edit your writing to determine which voice permits your desired emphasis in the fewest number of words.

The secretary typed the report. (Emphasis on secretary)

The report was typed by the secretary. (Emphasis on report)

EXERCISES

1. Concreteness

Eliminate *assumptions*. Remove all vagueness in the following sentences by inventing as many concrete details as necessary to answer any possible questions the reader might have.

    a. The work is now quite a bit behind schedule.

    b. We need frequent inspections at critical checkpoints despite the cost suggested by your representative during her recent visit.

    c. The typewriters in our department are frequently not as efficient as those in yours.

    d. We will implement your proposal provided that the requisite labor can be found.

    e. Those letters should be attended to properly.

2. Jargon/Gobbledygook

Eliminate *jargon* and *gobbledygook*. Rewrite these sentences into simply expressed, intelligible sentences.

    a. At this juncture, the bottom line depends on sales output.

    b. In a nutshell we failed to finalize our conceptualized contingencies in the proper time frame.

    c. We require in-depth communication to determine why our game plan was defunded.

    d. During the implementation phase the recession impacted upon our employment levels.

    e. Research indicates that the distinction of critical sociocultural parameters rendered the project nonviable.

3. Wordiness

Eliminate *wordiness*. Rewrite these sentences to eliminate wordy and roundabout phrases.

    a. We are inclined to make the recommendation to utilize the room for the purpose of training.

    b. Due to the fact that the seat belt broke, the passenger sustained a high degree of injury.

    c. Pursuant to our discussion, we decided to let go some forty technicians until such time as the economy picks up.

    d. If we plan on showing a profit of three percent, we will need to make a downward adjustment in travel expenditure.

    e. As per your request, I have affixed my signature to the reports at this time.

4. Redundancy

Eliminate *redundancies*. Rewrite these sentences to eliminate repetitions, unnecessary expansions, and doublets.

    a. Either one or the other of the copy machines is totally acceptable.

    b. It is absolutely essential that each and every secretary employ the use of new typewriter ribbons.

    c. The troops advanced forward in close proximity to the enemy territory.

    d. Through mutual cooperation we can stamp out and eliminate crime in this day and age.

    e. During the month of May we will begin to package our product in boxes square in shape and red in color.

5. Passive Voice

Eliminate sluggish *passive-voice* expressions. Rewrite these passive constructions into the active voice.

    a. A report on the salary increases was requested by the union officers.

    b. Graphic construction is discussed in the next chapter.

    c. For the final report a cover letter was used.

    d. At our corporate headquarters decisions are made.

    e. Jargon is in the chapter in which style and tone are discussed.

WRITING OPTIONS

1. *Audience*. Rewrite a short (3–4 paragraph) article from your field. Select an article or textbook explanation which is as technical and complex as you can understand and then translate the material for a different audience, such as a junior high school student or a layperson who has no knowledge of your field. Submit a copy of the original along with your rewrite.

2. *Message*. Reorganize the following report to make the message more readable. Divide the material into logical paragraphs; add section headings, numbers, bullets, and any other appropriate visual device to make the proposal more readable.

Here is a proposal to introduce a standard format for sales proposals in order to avoid inconsistent layout, to improve secretarial productivity, and to save the company money. Because the sales force has been relocated from headquarters into the field, the system of preparing the sales proposals has presented the following problems: salespersons must dictate all proposals by costly telephone calls, each dictation suggests a different format which is confusing, the salespersons require a mailed copy for approval and editing; each then mails the proposal back with format changes, an inefficient procedure. To cut costs, eliminate inconsistent proposal formats, and to improve efficiency, I propose that we should develop a form for each salesperson to fill in with the particular prices, routing, and dates for each sales proposal. Secondly, we should create a printed sample proposal format for each salesperson to use consistently. The information sheet may be mailed or phoned to the office, and inserted into the standard format for immediate mailing to the client. Attached are the two sample forms. The advantages of this system are long distance telephone calls will be eliminated or shortened, sales persons will have a checklist which will eliminate mistakes and omissions of details, all proposals will be consistent, and the preparation of the sales proposals will be faster and more efficient. I am available to discuss this proposal with you Monday through Thursday.

3. *Style*

   a. Rewrite the following memorandum in an appropriate style and tone. Divide the message into brief, logical paragraphs. Eliminate jargon, gobbledygook, wordiness, redundancies, and awkward passive-voice expressions.

     As per your request, here is the finalized report of the Incentive Award Committee. The bottom line of our in-depth investigation is that the continuation of our issuance of incentives is dependent upon the prioritization by employees and company objectives. An extensive list of twenty company objectives has been devised by the committee. However, your input is of primary importance and is needed before we finalize the aims and goals of the company for the better understanding of all employees. Your evaluation and suggestions should be rapidly forwarded to me. We are sorry for any inconvenience this simple request may cause you. Please don't hesitate to contact me for further clarification.

   b. Write a 4- to 5-sentence memo commending a committee chairperson on a job well done. Use one-syllable words only. Avoid jargon, gobbledygook, wordiness, and the like.

CHAPTER 2

The Writing Process

SHOE

by Jeff MacNelly

INTRODUCTION

Writing is a *process* of prewriting, writing, and revision. If your writing is to have clout, it must meet the 4 *Cs* test: Is the paper *clear*, *concise*, *complete*, and *correct*? Careful planning for detail and logical organization, the ability to write a good rough draft, and sharp attention to repair will produce the documents you desire.

From begining to end you need to approach your material from a *global* point of view. Imagine yourself as an astronaut looking down at earth. The entire planet is seen as a globe containing land masses, oceans, rivers, mountains, clouds, and sunlight. Approach your writing with the same viewpoint, with an intent to transmit an overall message with an appropriate format, clear purpose, logical organization, complete and correct detail, and consistent tone.

PREWRITING

Effective writers seldom compose a finished product by merely dictating or typing a message off the tops of their heads. The first global considerations are the audience, the detail list, and the overall organization. Next, the language must be appropriate and nonsexist.

Audience

By targeting your exact audience, you will develop a "you" orientation in your writing. A widespread problem among many writers is the inability to write a letter, memo, or report which appeals to the reader's needs and interests. Picture your reader as a busy person, and you will soon get the habit of coming quickly to the point. Put yourself on the receiving end. Will your writing present a global message? Will the format help to frame the content? Can you state a purpose clearly? What organization is appropriate? Will you answer all possible questions? Do you have correct and complete facts? Will your reader "see" the global aspects of your paper?

Fact List

With your audience and overall purpose in mind, think over the material and consider the ideas and facts you need to present. Research any missing data. List all of the facts and ideas. This list does not need to be elaborate. Brief topic entries will do to get you started in the writing process. This chapter was conceived with the following loose topic list:

introduction	induction/deduction
prewriting	vivid verbs/nouns
global aspects	process steps
emphasis	grammar
organization	spelling
outlines	punctuation
audience	usage
repairs	research
language style	style
sexist language	mechanics
rough drafts	basic sentence errors

Outlines

The third step is to organize the material into a tight presentation. Arrange your topics into an outline which conveys logical order and completeness. As you organize, other important topics as well as logical groupings should emerge. An organized chapter outline with necessary subordination follows:

I. Introduction
   A. Process
   B. Global aspects
II. Prewriting
   A. Audience
   B. Fact list
   C. Outlines
III. Writing the draft
   A. Flow
   B. Inductive/deductive presentation
IV. Revision
   A. Global critique
   B. Sexist language check
   C. Organization check
   D. Modifier check
   E. Basic sentence check
   F. Signal word check
   G. Vivid word check
   H. Usage check
   I. Grammar check
      1. Subject/verb agreement
      2. Pronoun agreement
      3. Pronoun case
      4. Modifier place
      5. Infinitives
   J. Mechanics check
      1. Spelling
      2. Punctuation
      3. Other
V. Exercises
VI. Writing options

Compare the initial topic list with the refinements in the outline. Outline even a brief memo or letter. All effective writers do.

WRITING THE DRAFT

Flow

Writing the rough draft is simply a matter of expanding your outlined topics into sentences and paragraphs. Beyond global considerations of format, tone, and style (Chapter 1) don't worry too much at this step about the refinements of language or mechanical aspects in your draft. Refinements are the task of revision and repair. Try to write with a speedy flow, using simple and conversational words and sentences.

Induction / Deduction

Do decide whether to present the information in a particular paragraph inductively or deductively. *Inductive* presentation cites particular facts or individual cases followed by a general conclusion. *Deductive* presentation cites a general conclusion followed by the supporting facts or individual cases. Modern professional writing leans more and more to the deductive method without, however, entirely abandoning the other.

Draft 1 (*Inductive*)

Gross margins declined from 13.8% in the first quarter of 1990 to 13.1% in the corresponding 1991 quarter. There was a drop of 26% in sales volume between these two periods. At the branch level new unit margins dropped from 15.8% to 12.2%, but 50% of all units sold in the first quarter of 1991 were from inventory made prior to 1990. Profits have been adversely affected by a decline in sales volume and a drop in gross margin.

Draft 2 (*Deductive*)

Company profits have been adversely affected by a decline in sales volume accompanied by a drop in gross margin. Sales in the first quarter of 1991 were 26% below the volume in first quarter 1990. In the same period gross margin decreased from 13.8% to 13.1%. The principal reason for the lower gross margin in 1991 was the fact that 50% of the 1991 sales were from 1990 inventory rather than new production.

The first draft loses the reader in a mass of figures while the second draft presents the key thought in the first sentence. It presents a global purpose first so that the reader is able to understand the statistics quickly.

GLOBAL REVISING

Efficient revision will repair your rough draft and produce a polished product. The first tip is to allow time between your draft writing and your revising. Do something else for a few minutes, hours, or even days for a cooling-off period. You'll find yourself more objective and critical when you return to the writing task. You are not alone in your urge to just get the paper off your desk and off your mind. But take the time to rethink, rewrite, and revise.

This is the time to check the paper for its global message. Again, ask yourself if the message comes across loud and clear. Critique your paper for global unity, coherence, and style. Consider the relationship of the whole to the parts and the parts to the whole. Add what is needed and purge unmercifully what is not. As you scan your material for its global message, put a mark in the margin when you find an awkward or unclear sentence, a questionable usage, uncertain grammatical construction, or a mechanical complexity. But don't worry about these needed repairs until the global revisions are complete. These repairs are largely cosmetic. You need the basics before the shine. Focus on these questions to ensure **global unity:**

- Are the purpose and emphasis immediately clear?
- Does every part of the whole focus on that purpose?
- Is there a clear line of thought?
- Does each paragraph advance the thought?
- Are there digressions that can be eliminated?
- Is the tone consistent?

When you are satisfied that your paper has unity, critique its **global coherence.** Ask yourself these questions:

- Is the organization suitably chronological, spatial, or logical by any other consideration?
- Are the subject and purpose of each paragraph crystal clear?
- Does each paragraph cover related material without extraneous ideas or facts?
- Are there sections of inadequate or excessive facts?
- Are the paragraphs too long or too short?
- Is the information complete?
- Will your reader have to search for details?
- Are there needless repetitions or padding?
- Does your manuscript clearly answer all possible questions, review results, or present conclusions?

Finally, check your manuscript for **global style.** Style considerations should include an examination of your paper for inadvertent sexist language.

Sexist language favors one sex at the expense of the other. Our language tends to emphasize the role and importance of men over women, as in

Sexist   A president sets *his* own agenda.

Sexist   A doctor should always carry *his* beeper.

Professional people are sensitive to this language and edit their writing to eliminate the bias.

Nonsexist   Presidents set *their* own agendas.

Nonsexist   Doctors should always carry *their* beepers.

Sometimes the plural can be unclear.

Unclear	Drivers should study *their* manuals. (Does each driver have more than one manual?)
Clear	Each driver should study *his or her* manual.

In this case *his or her* clarifies the meaning. Overuse of *he or she*, *his or her*, *him and her* can be awkward, but they are, at least, clear and nonsexist. Such words as *chairman, mailman, policeman*, and *stewardess* may be replaced by *chairperson, postal carrier, police officer*, and *flight attendant*. Drop the female suffix *-ess* in *authoress* and similar words. Sexism in language is not a trivial matter. Responsible writers are careful not to be offensive.

In addition to a sexist language check, ask these questions to ensure an appropriate global style:

- Does the paper contain jargon, shoptalk, or gobbledygook?
- Is the information wordy or redundant?
- Are there unnecessary passive-voice constructions?
- Is the writing lively with a variety of sentence patterns (See Appendix A) and lengths?

DETAIL REPAIR

Sentence Construction Check

Next, consider the parts carefully for necessary repairs. Read through slowly for sentence sense. Find the main sentence elements (subject, verb, and object) to ensure that your sentence conveys the idea you intend. Repair sentence fragments, faulty parallel constructions, run-on and run-together sentences. Appendix A discusses basic sentence errors and includes exercises to test your recognition of each error. Some reminders follow:

Fragment	Lithium has many uses in bioengineering. *Especially* in the development of pacemakers.
Repair	Lithium has many uses in *bioengineering. It is especially* useful in the development of pacemakers.
Parallel problem	We need adjuncts *to handle* peak-hour activity, *to free* full time employees from routine duties, *to relieve* assembly workers for lunch breaks, and *for the replacement of* vacationing employees.
Repair	We need adjuncts *to handle* peak-hour activity, *to free* full time employees from routine duties, *to relieve* assembly workers for lunch breaks, and *to replace* vacationing employees.

Run-on   If the Roman government at the height of its power, and at a time when means of communication had been greatly improved, showed anxiety for the food supply of that Italy which was dominant in the Mediterranean world, it may be imagined that in the period preceding the great economic organization introduced by the Roman Principate the peoples of the Mediterranean region peoples no one of which at the height of its power had controlled the visible food supply of the world so widely or so absolutely, had far graver cause for anxiety on the same subject, and this was an anxiety such as would be, under ordinary circumstances, the main factor, or, even under the most favorable circumstances possible in those ages, *a* main factor, in molding the life of the individual and the policy of the state.

Repair   If we understand that the Roman government at the height of its power showed anxiety for the food supply, we can imagine that earlier Mediterranean peoples had far graver cause for anxiety. The Roman Principate had greatly improved communications and economic organization to handle the food supply of Italy, the dominant country in the Mediterranean world. No earlier people in the region had controlled the visible food supply so widely or so absolutely as had the Romans. Under ordinary circumstances the food supply was a main factor of concern. Under even the most favorable circumstances, anxiety over the food supply would be *a* main factor in molding the life of the individual and the policy of the state of those earlier peoples.

Use uncomplicated sentences to state complex ideas.

Signal Word Check

Look again for unity and coherence within paragraphs as well as from paragraph to paragraph. Use signal words to make connections and transitions.

Time Signals	*Addition Signals*	*Results Signals*
soon	again	hence
then	and	therefore
finally	besides	consequently
previously	furthermore	accordingly
first, second, etc.	also	thus
next	additionally	as a result
last	moreover	finally

Summary Signals	*Contrast Signals*	*Comparison Signal*
in brief	however	similarly
finally	nevertheless	likewise
in conclusion	yet, and yet	correspondingly
to conclude	but	equally
summing up	still	equally important
on the whole	on the other hand	in the same manner
lastly	though, although	in the same way

Other Signals

simultaneously	conversely
meanwhile	unfortunately
for example	to begin with
for instance	so
to demonstrate	in the past
indeed	in the future
in other words	eventually

Word Choice Check

The English language offers more synonyms than any other language. A **desk dictionary** and a **word thesaurus** are absolutely necessary tools for the effective writer. Pay particular attention to your verbs; select the word with just the right nuance. As an example, here are two lists of verbs requesting action. Notice how each column increases in intensity.

(would) appreciate	hinted at
(would) suggest, propose	implied, intimated
prefer, would like	suggested
request, ask	indicated
recommend, urge	signified
remind	demonstrated
advise	confirmed
require	substantiated
insist	proved
demand	established

Likewise, noun synonyms can suggest minute shades of meaning.

aid	sketch
assistance	plan
help	program
full support	design
championship	project

Usage Check

English is a complicated language containing homonyms (words which sound alike: *there, their, they're*) and other confusing similar words (*insure/ assure/ensure*). The astute reader is disturbed over common usage errors. Check carefully such words as *its/it's*, *accept/except*, *advice/advise*, and the like. The adverb *hopefully* is frequently misused; the writer usually means "I hope." The best advice is to avoid *hopefully* altogether. Your audience may miss the impact of your message if you fail to edit these problems carefully. Familiarize yourself with the **usage glossary** in Appendix A, and then be alert to repair your own mistakes.

GRAMMAR REPAIR

Read your draft again to spot and repair grammar mistakes. Common errors include subject/verb disagreements, incorrect pronoun usage, improperly placed modifiers, and split infinitives. Appendix A addresses these problems at length, but here are some tips.

Subject / Verb Check

A verb agrees with its subject in number.

Incorrect	*Each* of the insurance companies *are* reviewing the application.
Correct	*Each* of the insurance companies *is* reviewing the application.
Incorrect	The *manager* as well as the supervisor *have* been promoted.
Correct	The *manager* as well as the supervisor *has* been promoted.

Pronoun / Antecedent Check

Similarly, pronouns must agree with their antecedents in number.

Incorrect	*Each* of the women bought *their* own computer software.
Correct	*Each* of the women bought *her* computer software.
Incorrect	*Ace Company* is sending twenty of *their* employees to the seminar.
Correct	*Ace Company* is sending twenty of *its* employees to the seminar.

Pronoun Usage Check

Pronouns are grouped into cases. Case 1, the nominative, is used for sentence subjects and predicate nouns, nouns which follow a linking verb and identify the subject. Appendix A covers pronoun case fully. Some common errors follow:

> It is *I*. (not *me*)
>
> It will be *he* who goes. (not *him*)
>
> *He and she* were appointed to the committee. (not *him and her* or *he and her*)
>
> Ms. Johnson and *I* attended the meeting. (not Ms. Johnson and *me*)

Case 2, the objective, is used for direct objects, indirect objects, and object of prepositions.

Direct object	Catherine's secretary took her boss and *me* to lunch. (not *I*)
Indirect object	Ken sent Charles and *me* the document. (not *I*)
Object of preposition	The plan divides the work between Mr. Howard and *me*. (not *I*)

Avoid using reflexive pronouns (*myself, himself, herself, themselves, ourselves*) as subjects or objects.

Incorrect	Jane and *myself* wrote the manual.
Correct	Jane and *I* wrote the manual.
Incorrect	The work was completed by the secretary and *herself*.
Correct	The work was completed by the secretary and *her*.

Modifier Placement Check

Check the placement of modifying words, phrases, and clauses.

Incorrect	The *little brick doctor's* house.
Correct	The *doctor's little, brick* house.
Incorrect	The accountant *only* comes in on Tuesdays.
Correct	The accountant comes in on Tuesdays *only*.
Incorrect	The computer was broken *in the closet*.
Correct	The computer *in the closet* was broken.
Incorrect	*Speaking before a crowd of people*, my knees shook.
Correct	*Speaking before a crowd of people*, I had shaky knees.

Split Infinitive Check

An infinitive, you remember, is a verb form using *to* (*to work*, *to write*, *to go*). Do not split infinitives with adverbs.

Incorrect   We need *to* further *investigate* safety measures.

Correct   We need *to investigate* safety measures further.

Incorrect   The writer needs *to* thoroughly and accurately *proofread* the report.

Correct   The writer needs *to proofread* the report thoroughly and accurately.

MECHANICS REPAIR

Repair your spelling, punctuation, and other mechanical errors. Familiarize yourself with Appendix B, which reviews the conventions for each.

Spelling Check

A list of frequently misspelled words is at the end of Appendix B. Photocopy the list and tape it near your desk, computer, or typewriter for easy reference. Watch out for *business*, not *bussiness*; *separately*, not *seperately*; *convenience*, not *convenence*; and a host of others.

Punctuation Check

Review apostrophe, comma, semicolon, and hyphen usage in Appendix B. A misplaced or omitted comma or semicolon can change the entire meaning of a sentence:

Woman without her man is nothing. (Who is nothing?)

Woman, without her, man is nothing. (Who is nothing?)

The secretary Caroline Mike the chairperson, Belinda the typist Jerry and I formed a coffee committee. (How many people?)

The secretary, Caroline; Mike; the chairperson, Belinda; the typist, Jerry; and I formed a coffee committee. (How many people are now indicated?)

Hyphens are called for frequently in technical data, as indicated in the following examples:

> The top portion has a centered, 25-millimeter, circular cutout.
>
> The U-shaped, stainless-steel clamp connects to the six-inch-long handle.

Plural abbreviations are usually written in the same form as the singular. Some examples follow:

> We need 17 gal. (not *gals.*) of nonleaded fuel.
>
> The car accelerates to 100 mph (not *mph's*) in 50 sec. (not *secs.*)

Also check your capitalization, italics, number conventions, and technical symbols. Appendix B reviews these standard systems. The more frequently you write and edit your work, the more likely you will recognize and overcome the pitfalls of written communication.

EXERCISES

1. Eliminate the sexist language in the following:

    > Neither the engineer nor the draftsman could do his job until he understood the new concept. Mrs. Janet Barnes appointed a committee chairman to develop a program to explore the concept. Everybody who attended the meeting made his difficulties known.

2. Rewrite the following inductive paragraph to deductive organization format.

    > In Tubatse, South Africa, Union Carbide Company employs about four hundred blacks. In Port Elizabeth the Ford Motor Company has actually encouraged black unionism and is training blacks for supervisory positions. More than a hundred American firms subscribe to the so-called Sullivan principle, which calls for increased pay and opportunities for blacks, integration of black and white workers, and recognition of black unions. American business should be allowed to stay in South Africa.

3. Add at least four transitional signal words to your above revision.

4. Repair the organization in the following paragraph.

We are sending you a new fall line of jeans, slacks, and knit sportwear. The license for the company has been granted to new owners. I am establishing new systems for order, entry, return, shipping, and the like. I am the new Director of Merchandising. Please study the new price list and swatch cards which I am enclosing. You may meet your new directors at the January sales meeting. Destroy all previous price lists and swatch cards.

5. Replace the dull verbs with vivid ones.

a. The comptroller **wanted** his accountant **to work** for excellence.

b. He **went** to the meeting and **drew up** a new sales plan.

6. Select the proper usage.

a. I am not going to (except, accept) your set of instructions.

b. Mr. Shaw gave the following (advise, advice): pay your taxes on time.

c. The rising cost of gas has drastically (effected, affected) the automobile industry.

d. It is (all right, alright) to leave a few minutes before 5:00 P.M.

e. The salesperson was (conscious, conscience) that the computer performed (bad, badly) during (its, it's) initial run, so he went no (further, farther) with the demonstration.

7. Repair the grammatical errors in the following:

The banker along with the stockbrokers agree that another increase in the prime lending rate will seriously harm their major customers. It would keep a borrower from getting their needed capital. Investors will have to carefully weigh whether to borrow more money or cut back services. Mr. Mills and myself will need to postpone purchasing a new house. Keeping the interest rates in mind, the new car purchases will be postponed by Mr. Mills and I also.

8. Correct the punctuation, spelling, and capitalization errors in the following:

After graduating from Ohio State university, my Dad turned his favorite past-time into a full time profession. He became a prominant computer consultant He has written two books: Double Program Merging and Know Your Computer Capabilities. He has in addition engineered twenty one, 6000 component circuit boards. He earns 80000 dollars a year.

WRITING OPTION

Write quickly a 500-word draft on the advantages of a word processor, a copy machine, or a specific automobile for a potential customer. Next, exchange papers with another student to revise and repair his or her draft. Use this checklist:

1. Is the global intent and impression clear, coherent, concise, and complete?
2. Is the purpose clear and the organization logical?
3. Is the inductive or deductive format appropriate?
4. Is the general language appropriate to the audience?
5. Are there any sexist slips?
6. Is the tone objective?
7. Is the sentence pattern varied?
8. Is any sentence too wordy?
9. Are there any errors in sentence construction?
10. Is the word choice vivid?
11. What signal words could improve the unity and coherence of points?
12. Is usage correct throughout?
13. Are there any grammatical errors?
14. Are there any mechanical errors?

NOTES

CHAPTER 3

Graphics

by Parker & Wilder

© 1982. By permission.

Skills:

After studying this chapter, you should be able to

1. Recognize the purpose and function of bar charts, line graphs, circle graphs, flow charts, organization charts, drawings, maps, and photographs.
2. Distinguish the conventions of incorporating tables and figures.
3. Prepare random, continuation, and formal tables.
4. Prepare a bar chart.
5. Prepare a line graph.
6. Prepare a circle graph.
7. Prepare a flow chart.
8. Prepare an organization chart.
9. Prepare a simple, exploded, or cutaway drawing.
10. Incorporate a map or photograph into a brief report.
11. Devise and prepare the appropriate graphics for a specific writing assignment.

INTRODUCTION

In addition to the visuals discussed in Chapter 1 (short paragraphs, headings, numbers, capitals, underlining, bullets, and so forth), graphic illustrations are characteristic of professional and technical report writing. These are referred to as *tables* and *figures*. Tables include randomly incorporated data, continuation tables, and formal tables. All other graphics are referred to as figures. Figures include bar charts, line graphs, circle graphs, flow charts, organization charts, drawings, maps, and photographs.

Large companies may employ graphic artists to assist writers in graphic illustration, but it is the writer's task to decide on appropriate graphics and to provide, at least, a rough idea of the layout and data. Many simple graphics can be handled by the novice without assistance.

Purpose

Graphic incorporations are never merely decorative. They serve to

- Speed up a reader's comprehension
- Add credibility to the material
- Serve as a method of quick reference
- Add to the attractiveness of the report

Each type of graphic serves a distinct purpose. For instance, a table displays data in vertical columns that would otherwise involve lengthy prose sentences which, in turn, might be difficult to comprehend or to interpret. A bar chart illustrates comparisons of parts while a circle graph shows not only comparisons of parts but also the relationship of each part to the whole. Drawings, maps, and photographs can show details that words cannot describe. You must consider not only when to use a graphic illustration, but also which type of graphic will best serve your purpose.

General Conventions

Certain conventions are adhered to for all graphic illustrations:

1. All graphics are inserted as close to their textual reference as possible rather than attached on separate pages. Graphics which are included as supplemental or exhibit materials following a report lose their impact.

2. Graphics are not just "plopped" into a report. An introductory sentence explains the purpose and refers, usually, to the number of the graphic. The introductory sentence is followed by a colon if the graphic can be placed at the exact point of reference, as illustrated:

   Figure 2 shows a line drawing made by tracing a photocopy:

   The available equipment, features of each, prices, and warranties are shown in Table 3:

   A commentary line of interpretation, emphasis, or the like follows a graphic.

3. In addition to the introduction, formal graphics are always numbered and titled. Sometimes the introductory sentence(s) and the titles are very similar, but both should be included for clarity; the titled graphic may be taken out of the report for photocopying and distribution and will obviously require a title line. Formal **tables** are always numbered and titled *above* the data. All other graphics are referred to as **figures** and are numbered and titled *beneath* the graphic. The numbers and titles may be centered or placed flush left to the margin of the report.

4. If more than one table or more than one figure is used in a report or manual, each is numbered in order of its appearance throughout the material. Arabic numbers are used:

   Table 1
   Table 2
   Figure 1
   Table 3
   Figure 2

If the report contains numbered chapters, a decimal numbering system is used to indicate both the chapter and the sequential number of the graphic:

> Figure 7.1
> Table 7.1
> Figure 7.2
> Table 7.2

5. A precise *noun-phrase title* is included with each designation for clarification.

Table 1	Cost Comparison of Transportation Modes
Table 2	Smoke Detector Ratings
Table 3	Characteristics of Whales

TABLE 4
MEAN SALT CONCENTRATION
IN VARIOUS SOURCES OF WATER

Figure 1	Cross section of a typical speed bump before and after modification
Figure 2	Proposed Transit Systems Routes

6. Convention 4 indicates a variety of acceptable uses of periods and capital letters. It is important to be consistent, however. If you decide to use a period after the graphic number, do so for all graphic designations throughout your report. You may capitalize an entire title, capitalize initial letters of each word, or capitalize only the initial letter of the first word. Consistency within a report is the key to effectiveness.

7. Titles which require more than one line are usually single spaced. Second and consecutive lines are aligned under the first word of the title, not under the word *table* or *figure*.

8. Graphics are contained within the margins of your report. No labels, headings, portions of drawings, legends, and so forth should extend left or right of your established margins. It is unconventional to place graphics sidewards on a page. Copy machines with reduction capabilities are helpful for wide graphics. Prepare a graphic with the top on the vertical plane of your paper, reduce it with the copy machine, carefully paste it in the appropriate space of your report, and photocopy the entire page. If reduction is not possible, insert the graphic on a separate page with the top of the graphic on the left-hand-side vertical plane.

9. In the case of tables which require more than one full page, begin the second page with the designation, number, and the word *Continued*:

> Table 4   Continued

10. Explanatory notes, keys, and legends usually appear within the graphic or beneath the graphic in the left-hand position but above the number and title. See Figure 3.5 for an example of this convention.

11. Identify your source of borrowed graphics in parentheses after the title:

Figure 1   Sample formal proposal (Courtesy of Charles E. Smith, Jr., Robert Heller Associates)

Table 7   Average Yearly Salaries by Sex and Race. Source: Catherine Brown, Discrimination in the Work Place, New York: Silver Press, 1980 (8).

Figure 2   Fire ground injuries by cause. From "Fire Ground Injuries in the United States during 1979," Fire Command December 1980 (12). Reprinted by permission.

TABLES

Tables are visual displays of numerical or non-numerical data arranged in vertical columns so that the data may be emphasized, compared, or contrasted. Tables may be *informal* (random and continuation) or *formal*. Figure 3.1 illustrates informal random tables in report texts.

Random Tables

Brief lists of figures, dates, personnel, important points, and the like may be displayed in vertical columns for visual clarity and quick reference.

Random Table Conventions

1. Random tables are used only for brief data.
2. Each is introduced by an explanatory sentence.
3. Each is indented 5 to 10 spaces from the left- and right-hand margins of the page.
4. The tabulated data may contain column headings, numbered data, or bullets.
5. A random table does not include a table designation, number, or title.

Continuation Tables

A continuation table is one that contains prose data in a displayed manner. It reads as a continuation of the text and includes the same punctuation marks which would be required if the data were presented in paragraph form. Figure 3.2 illustrates two informal continuation tables in a brief accident report.

The Training Center announces the beginning of a mini-course, "Write It Right—Write It Well," for senior executive secretaries and administrative assistants. Dates, locations, and purposes follow:

Date	Room	Purpose
May 11	102	to review grammar/usage
May 13	102	to review brief report forms
May 18	101	to review graphics
May 20	102	to review manual components
May 25	103	to review formal reports
May 27	101	to critique individual writing

To register, fill out the attached form and forward it to Julie Wood, Training Specialist, Room 608.

Regardless of what kind of accident is being reported, certain information must be reported objectively and specifically:

- What the accident is
- When and where the accident occurred
- Who was involved
- What caused the accident
- What were the results of the accident (damage, injury, and costs)
- What has been done to correct the trouble or to treat the insured
- What recommendation or suggestions are given to prevent a recurrence

Information required for the accident report has become so standardized that many companies have designed accident report forms.

FIGURE 3.1 *Sample informal random tables*

Our insurance policy All State #17B-445-9100K will cover the cost of the fire damage. Repairs and replacements total $390.00. This price includes

$45.00	for carpet replacement (9 sq ft @ $5.00 per ft; Carl's carpets),
20.00	for labor for removing burned carpet and replacing (5 hr @ $4.00 per hr),
15.00	for cleaning solution for wall (15 sq ft @ $1.00 per ft),
35.00	for paint for wall (70 sq ft @ $0.50 per ft)
80.00	for labor for cleaning and repainting wall (10 hr @ $8.00 per hr),
80.00	for fabric for brown leather armchair (8 yd @ $10.00 per yd),
70.00	for labor for reupholstering armchair (7 hr @ $10.00 per hr),
20.00	for new magazine stand from Pier One, and
25.00	for fire extinguisher replenishment.

In order to prevent fires such as this in the future, I recommend that

a) all ashtrays be removed from the waiting rooms,
b) three "No Smoking" signs be placed on each of the end tables, and
c) the magazine rack be placed next to the receptionist's desk to remove it from hazard.

Should you endorse the second recommendation, I will personally obtain the signs from the Davie Fire Department at no cost and place them by Monday, February 4, 198x.

FIGURE 3.2 *Sample informal continuation tables*

Continuation Table Conventions

1. Each is introduced by a sentence followed by a colon if the last introductory word is *not* a verb.
2. The tabular data is indented 5 to 10 spaces from the left and right margins.
3. The continuation table presents an alignment of figures, dates, or other data.
4. The data is punctuated by standard commas, semicolons, and periods as if the material were presented in paragraph form.

Formal Tables

Formal tables are used to present statistical information or to categorize and tabulate other written information. Tables 3.1 and 3.2 show two types of formal tables and the conventions adhered to in typing such tables. Either the centered or flush-left title is conventional.

TABLE 3.1
TIME/COST FOR AERIAL PHOTOGRAPH SEARCHES

Time Frame	Searches (#)	Time @ 30 min ea (hr)	Cost @ $6.00 per hr wage ($)
Daily	3	1½	9.00
Weekly	15	9	54.00
Monthly	60	30	180.00
Quarterly	180	90	540.00
Yearly	720	360	2160.00

Table 3.2   Troubleshooting Chart for Heath Kits

Difficulty	Possible Cause
Receiver section dead	Check V1, V3, V4, V7, and V8 Wiring error Faulty speaker Faulty receiver crystal Crystal oscillator coil mistuned
Receiver section weak	Check V1, V2, and V3 Antenna, RF or IF coils mistuned Faulty antenna or connecting cable
Transmitter appears dead	Check V5 and V6 Wiring error Recheck oscillator, driver, and final tank coil tuning Dummy load shorted on open

Formal Table Conventions

1. Formal tables contain horizontal lines from margin to margin above the title (optional), below the title, below the body of the table, and between the column headings (the boxhead) and the body of the table.
2. The boxhead of vertical column headings indicates the body figure symbols in parentheses [*i.e.* ($), (rpm), (hr), (ft)].
3. Formal tables are not closed on the sides.
4. The columns are always vertical. The first body column is called the *stub*.
5. In modern practice the body does not contain leaders (spaced periods to aid the eye in following data from column to column).

FIGURES

As previously mentioned, all graphics except tables are referred to as figures both in textual reference and in titling. When you plan figures, you may wish to construct them on separate paper and then photocopy them into the space which you have allowed in your text. Consider making your working graphs 1-½ times as large as you intend for the final chart or drawing; photoreduce the work by 60 percent to obtain the proper proportion for your text. You will find it handy to use rulers, bow compasses, protractors, templates of geometric figures, and possibly transfer letters. Buy Helvetica and Univers type styles because they are the easiest to read.

Bar Charts

Bar charts are used to show differences in quantity visually and instantaneously. They are frequently made from a statistical table source. They are commonly used to show quantities of the same item at different times, quantities of different items for the same time period, or quantities of the different parts of an item that make up the whole.

Bars may be plotted vertically or horizontally. It is conventional to plot bars representing monetary units into vertical graphs.

Use graph paper to plot your chart. The scale you select is critical to the success of your chart. Do not include grids which will not contain some portion of a bar. All grids must be scaled to equal increments, such as 0, 1, 2, 3, or 0, 5, 10, 15, but not 0, 5, 7, 12.

If the order of the bar placement is not controlled by a sequential factor, place the longer bars to the bottom of a horizontal chart or to the right of a vertical chart. This placement avoids a top-heavy or one-sided chart. Figure 3.3 shows a horizontal bar chart where placement is not a factor; therefore, the longest bars have been placed at the bottom. Figure 3.4 shows a vertical bar chart where the bars must be placed in sequential order; however, in this case the largest bars naturally fall to the right side of the chart. A bar chart may illustrate up to three or four comparative bars in groupings. Figure 3.5 illustrates a multiple bar graph.

Shadings and hatchings add interest and emphasis to multiple bar representations. Dimension adds depth, volume, and body.

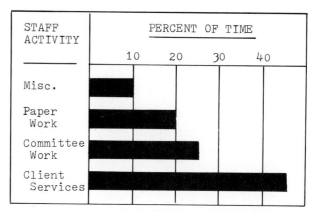

FIGURE 3.3   *Typical horizontal bar chart*

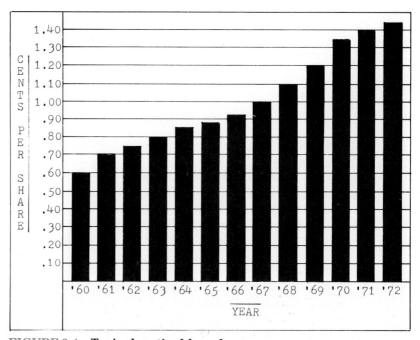

FIGURE 3.4   *Typical vertical bar chart*

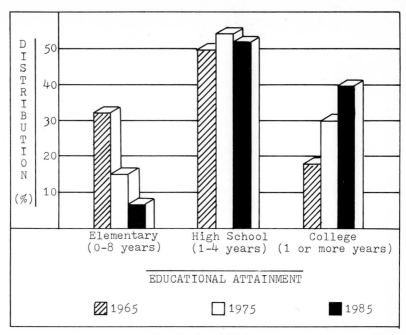

FIGURE 3.5 *Typical multiple bar chart*

Bar Chart Conventions

1. All of the headings, legends, and so forth are contained within a box.
2. Bars of even width should be evenly spread.
3. Partial cut-off lines separate headings from grid notations.
4. The horizontal or vertical grids are usually shown, but not both in a single chart.
5. Grid notations are centered on the grid lines.
6. All headings read horizontally, if possible.

Line Graphs

Line graphs, or curves, are used to show changes in two values. Most commonly, they show a change or trend over a given period or a performance with a variable factor.

Like bar charts they are usually boxed. The curve is always plotted from left to right. Both horizontal and vertical grid lines of equal increments are drawn in or indicated by tick marks. The lower left-hand intersection of the grids is the key point from which both incremental grids begin. The horizontal axis contains the grid notations for the static values (years, months, speeds, or other set units). The vertical axis shows incremental grids for quantity or amount factors. The vertical axis is graduated into equal proportions from the least amount at the bottom to the greatest amount at the top.

Figure 3.6 shows a simple sales curve over a seven-month period. Figure 3.7 illustrates a multiple line graph. Notice that the zero point of the graph is not included because to do so would result in an extraneous, unused grid. Lines which serve both as outline and grid are not labeled; it is obvious to the reader that the increments are equal and sequential.

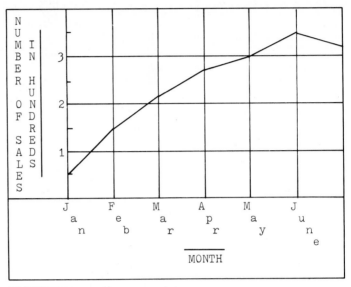

FIGURE 3.6 *Typical line graph*

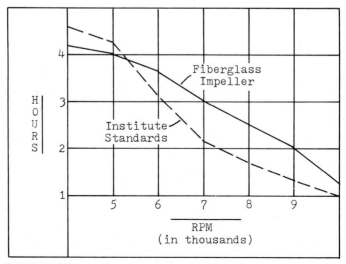

FIGURE 3.7 *Typical multiple line graph*

Line Graph Conventions

1. Usually, all of the information is boxed.
2. Curves are always plotted from left to right.
3. Horizontal and vertical grids are drawn in or indicated by tick marks.
4. Major headings are capitalized; subheadings or grid notations use initial-letter capitals only.
5. Grid notations are centered on the line or tick marks.
6. Usually, partial cut-off lines separate headings from grid notations.
7. All headings read horizontally, if possible.

Circle Graphs

Circle graphs, also known as pie charts, circle charts, pie diagrams, or sector charts, are used to compare the relative proportions of various factors to each other and to the whole. The circle represents 100 percent while the segments indicate the proportionate percentage of each factor to the whole. They are popular for illustrating financial information or survey responses.

Because a circle contains 360 degrees, you must first convert your real data to percentages of the whole and then calculate the number of degrees needed to represent each segment or wedge. Use the following format to calculate the number of degrees for each segment:

	Item	Raw Data	Frac-tion	4 place decimal	3 place decimal	Percent	Percent rounded	Degrees % × 360°	Degrees rounded
Ex:	Rent	$400	400 2300	.1739	.174	17.4%	17%	61.2°	61°
		TOTAL: $2300					TOTAL: 100%	TOTAL: 360°	

There is a quick formula for these calculations, which is to multiply the 4-place decimal by 360 degrees. However, this method is not as accurate, and you will probably have to make arbitrary adjustments to make sure your final calculations total 360 degrees.

A compass or circle template and protractor are needed to draw the circle and to divide it into segments. As a rule of thumb use a 3-in.-diameter circle on standard 8½ by 11 in. paper. This will make your circle large enough for emphasis yet small enough to allow space for labeling the wedges. Think of your circle as a clock, and plot your largest wedge in the upper right-hand quadrant from the 12 o'clock position. The wedges then decrease in size clockwise with proportionately smaller wedges or segments.

A circle graph is effective without shading although you may use shading and hatching to add interest and to differentiate further each segment of the circle. Labels and the percentage are generally shown outside of each wedge to avoid crowding. Center each label on the radius of each wedge or use a tag line to aid the eye. All labels must be contained within the left- and right-hand margins, and all are typed on a horizontal plane. Figure 3.8 shows a simple circle graph with tag lines to center the segment labels. Figure 3.9 shows a circle graph with separated wedges.

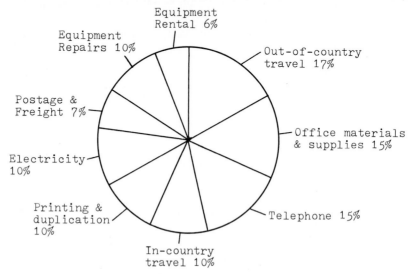

Figure 8   Ace Company's Sales Department budget: 1982-83

FIGURE 3.8   *Typical circle graph*

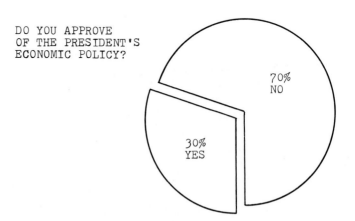

Figure 9   Presidential economic policy poll results—1000 community college students

FIGURE 3.9   *Typical circle graph with separated wedges*

Circle Graph Conventions

1. Circles are usually no larger than 3 inches in diameter.
2. The largest segment is placed in the upper-right-hand quadrant with the segments decreasing in size clockwise.
3. Segment labels and the represented percent are usually typed outside of the segments, centered on the segment radius.

Computer Graphics

A wide array of graphic software programs are now on the market. Samplings of computer-generated graphics are shown in Chapter 4: Computer-assisted Writing.

Flow Charts

A flow chart is used to show pictorially how a series of activities, procedures, operations, events, or other factors are related to each other. It shows the sequence, cycle, or flow of the factors and how they are connected in a series of steps from beginning to end. The information is qualitative rather than quantitative as in bar charts, line, and circle graphs.

The components of a flow chart may be diagrammed in horizontal, vertical, or circular directions. They condense long and detailed procedures into a visual chart for easy comprehension and reference. Computer programmers use templates which contain a variety of shapes symbolizing various activities, such as

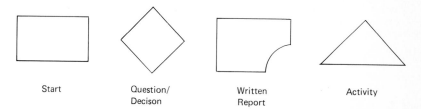

| Start | Question/
Decison | Written
Report | Activity |

Usually boxed steps are arranged in sequence and connected by arrows to show the flow. Flow charts may be simple or pictorial. Figures 3.10 and 3.11 illustrate simple and pictorial flow charts.

Flow Chart Conventions

1. Flow charts employ squares, boxes, triangles, circles, diamonds, and other shapes to enclose each step.
2. Steps naming major activities are typed within the shapes.
3. The flow of steps may be horizontal, vertical, circular, or a combination of directions.
4. Lines or arrows connect the shapes to show the flow of activities.

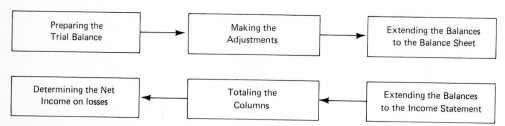

Figure 13   Six steps in preparing a work sheet

FIGURE 3.10   *Typical flow chart*

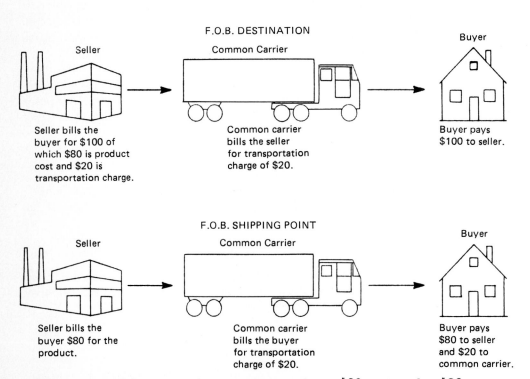

Figure 15   F.O.B. pricing for a product with an $80 cost and a $20
transportation charge

FIGURE 3.11   ***Typical pictorial flow chart*** (From Raymond E. Glos, Richard D. Steade, James R. Lowry, Business: Its Nature and Environment, 9th ed. Cincinnatti, South-Western Publishing Co., 1980: 190.)

Organization Charts

Like flow charts, organization charts show quantitative, rather than qualitative material. The organization chart is used to show the relationship of the organization's staff positions, units, or functions to each other.

A staff organization chart shows the chain of command of the staff positions, such as President, Vice-presidents, Directors, Controller, Personnel Director, Salespersons, and so forth. A unit organization chart depicts the relationships among such units as Public Relations Department, Research Division, Finance Office, Personnel Section, and so forth.

A function chart shows the span of control of such functions as Planning, Marketing, Production, Data Processing, and so forth. These three aspects—staff, unit, functions—should not be mixed together in the same chart.

Either a horizontal or a vertical emphasis can be imparted to an organizational chart by the layout:

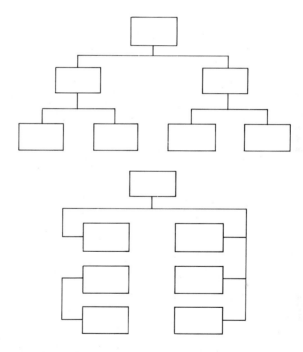

Figure 3.12 shows a staff organization chart for a manufacturing company. Notice within the chart that the Accounting Director is subordinated to the Treasurer by a broken line but to the Comptroller with a solid line. This indicates that the normal chain of command for the Accounting Director is to the Comptroller, but that he or she may route inquiries or important information directly to the Treasurer.

Organization Chart Conventions

1. Organization charts usually use rectangular boxes to enclose staff, unit, or function titles.
2. Solid lines represent the relationship, line of authority, or chain of command between the units; a broken line may represent an open line of communication for reporting out of the chain of authority.
3. A horizontal or vertical emphasis may be suggested by the chart layout.

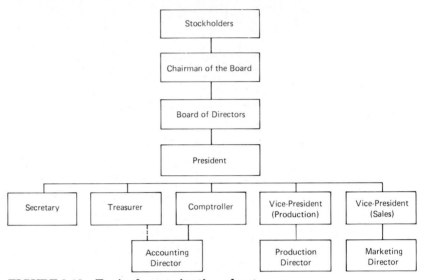

FIGURE 3.12   *Typical organization chart*

Drawings

A variety of simple drawings may be executed by the novice. A simple line drawing is often clearer than a photograph because the former can give emphasis to the major parts. Diagrams of procedures can be useful for clarifying instructions. Exploded-view illustrations show the proper sequence in which parts fit together. A cutaway drawing can show the internal parts of a mechanism or piece of equipment. Electricians and electronic technicians use schematics and wiring diagrams to illustrate concepts.

Drawings should be uncluttered, properly ruled, and carefully labeled. Figures 3.13 through 3.17 show a variety of simple drawings which can clarify descriptions, instructions, definitions, and process analyses.

Drawing Conventions

1. All drawings should be simple and uncluttered.
2. All labels of pertinent parts are typed.
3. Dotted lines are shown to indicate relationships of internal or connecting parts.

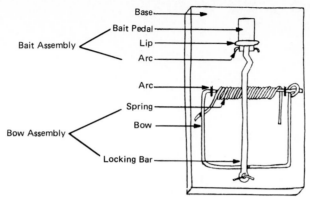

Base
Bait Pedal
Bait Assembly
Lip
Arc

Arc
Spring
Bow Assembly
Bow

Locking Bar

Figure 16   Parts of the Victor Baited Mousetrap, Model #19033

FIGURE 3.13   *Typical line drawing*

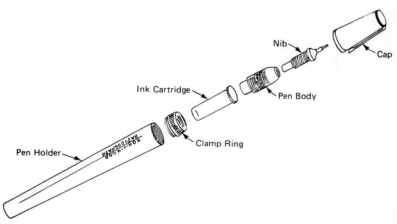

PUSH

Figure 17   Opening the 2 spring clips with a putty knife

FIGURE 3.14   *Typical procedural drawing*

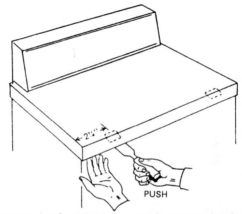

Nib
Cap
Ink Cartridge
Pen Body
Pen Holder
Clamp Ring

FIGURE 3.15   *Typical exploded view illustration*

(Courtesy of student Jennifer Woper)

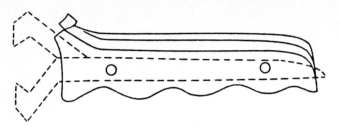

Figure 19   Cross section of Fiberglass casing assembled over steel
brace of Universal Pressure Cooker

FIGURE 3.16   *Typical cutaway drawing*

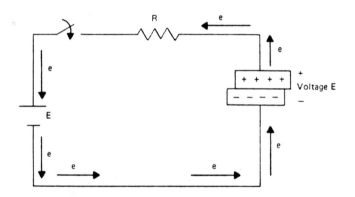

Figure 20   A capacitor and a resistor in a circuit

FIGURE 3.17   *Typical schematic drawing*

Maps and Photographs

Maps may be hand-drawn or photocopied to illustrate such elements as
specific locations, geographical factors, and routes. Photographs are useful
to illustrate complex mechanisms and equipment or to provide evidence
of such important details as damage or injuries to persons, automobiles,
and buildings. Photographs show actual appearance.

Both maps and photographs must be used with care. Both may
show attention-diverting and insignificant detail which detract from the
emphasis you wish to impart. Figures 3.18, 3.19, and 3.20 show maps
and photographs used in a variety of reports.

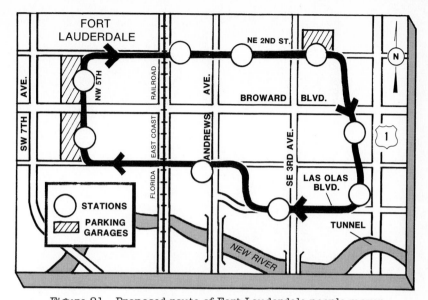

Figure 21   Proposed route of Fort Lauderdale people mover

FIGURE 3.18 *Typical large-scale map* (Fort Lauderdale *News/Sun Sentinel* map by Tom Alston)

Figure 22   Blast site north of Londonderry, Ireland

FIGURE 3.19 *Typical small-scale map* (Fort Lauderdale *News/Sun Sentinel* map by Keith Robinson)

Figure 23   Front end damage to automobile

FIGURE 3.20   *Cropped photograph emphasizing detail*
(Courtesy of George Chillag)

EXERCISES

1. Devise a formal table to present the following data obtained from a college study on sex discrimination:

   Of 215 faculty members 79 or 36.7 percent are women

   Of 36 administrators 3 or 8.3 percent are women

   Of 9 counselors 3 or 33.3 percent are women

   Of 7 librarians 5 or 71 percent are women

   Of 18 standing committee chairpersons 2 or 11.1 percent are women

   Of 207 committee members 52 or 25 percent are women

   Number and title your graphic.

2. Figure out how many hours you spend on a typical Wednesday in each of the following activities:

Travel	Grooming
Study/School	Leisure
Work	Sleep
Meals	

Present this information in a horizontal bar chart. Number and title your graphic.

3. Using an imaginary monthly income of $1,950.00, devise a budget for the following major expenses:

Rent/Housing	Insurance
Utilities	Leisure
Auto Upkeep	Payments
Food/Meals	Miscellaneous

Present the budget in a circle graph.

4. Devise a line graph to show the population of an imaginary town over a thiry-year span:

1955	20 thousand
1960	50 thousand
1965	26 thousand
1970	65 thousand
1975	80 thousand
1980	115 thousand
1985	70 thousand

Number and title your graphic.

5. Devise a flow chart to represent visually the basic steps in ordering and receiving materials in manufacturing.

Step 1	Establishing specifications
Step 2	Recognizing needs and activating purchase
Step 3	Selecting the vendor
Step 4	Preparing the purchase order
Step 5	Receiving the goods
Step 6	Evaluating the vendor's performance
Step 7	Updating the vendor's ratings

This is tricky because Step 7 affects Step 3. Show the relationship. Number and title your graphic.

6. Devise an organizational chart to depict the chain of command of data processing positions in a typical business. A data processing manager oversees all other positions. A systems manager, a programming manager, and an operations manager report to the data processing manager. Under the systems manager's authority are two systems analysts. Two programmers report directly to the programming manager. The operations manager oversees the work of two computer operators and one word processor. Number and title your graphic.

7. Select a small mechanism, hand tool, or kitchen implement and construct a simple or exploded drawing of it. Label all parts including nuts, bolts, rivets, handles, and so forth. Number and title your graphic.

8. Obtain a bus route map or a clear photograph which illustrates a procedure in your field of study. Write a brief paragraph into which it is appropriate to insert the graphic. Introduce, number, title, and comment on the graphic.

WRITING OPTION

You are a marketing specialist at National Motors Corporation. Write a memorandum to the Vice-president of Marketing concerning data on the new-model Econo automobile. Your purpose is to suggest some facts which should be stressed in the new-model Econo sales promotion materials. Use an informal table, a formal table, circle diagram, and a bar chart or curve in the text of your memorandum. Number and title your figures.

The Econo was the most popular car compared to four other competitive mid-sized cars on the market last year. Of total sales 30 percent of buyers chose Econo, 23 percent selected Car A, 20 percent chose car B, 17 percent chose car C, and 10 percent chose car D.

The Econo has doubled its fuel efficiency in five years. Four years ago the Econo was rated at 10.5 miles per gallon (mpg); three years ago the Econo averaged 14 mpg; two years ago the fuel efficiency increased to 17 mpg; a year ago it increased to 20.5 mpg, and this year it has a 21 mpg rating.

Despite base price increases the new Econo is as economical to own and to operate as it was four years ago due to fuel economy. Four years ago the base sticker price was $5801. A 20 percent down payment of $1160 resulted in a $4641 balance to finance. The monthly cost of financing for 48 months was $125 at 13.2 percent. The fuel expense per month for 1250 miles of driving (15,000 miles annually) at $1.30 per gallon was $116 at 14 mpg. The cost per month over 48 months (finance charge plus fuel cost) was $241. The new Econo has a base sticker price of $7301. A 20 percent down payment of $1460 leaves $5841 to finance. The monthly cost of financing over 48 months is $170 at 17.7 percent. But fuel expense is reduced to $77 at 21 mpg. Therefore, the cost of owning a new Econo over 48 months (finance charge plus fuel cost) is only $247.

CHAPTER 4

Computer-assisted Writing

B.C.   by Johnny Hart

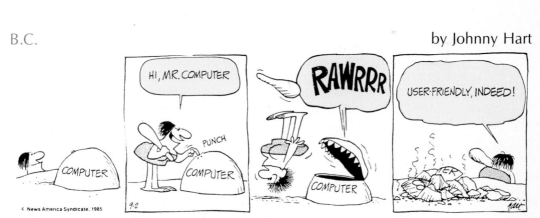

By permission of Johnny Hart and Creators Syndicate, Inc.

Skills:

After studying this chapter, you should be able to

1. List six advantages of writing with a word processor.
2. Be familiar with the basic computer equipment needed for writing assistance.
3. Locate instructional assistance on your campus or place of work.
4. Understand the basic operations of word processing.
5. Apply the writing process using a word processor.
6. Appreciate and/or construct simple graphics on a computer.
7. List four or five new software systems just on the market or about to be produced.
8. Develop a glossary of twenty words or more which are related to word processing.

INTRODUCTION

The late twentieth century is the Information Age. Never before has so much data been generated, processed, and disseminated so widely. The automated work place is here—complete with central and work station computers; graphic, letter quality, and laser printers; high speed copiers which can reduce, enlarge, collate, and staple; fax (facsimile) machines which can transmit detailed pictures over telephone lines; extensive software libraries; and new state-of-the-art options available almost daily.

Not just professionals, but everyone in the work force needs to be "computer fluent." According to Diane Booher, a writing consultant and author of *Cutting Paperwork in the Corporate Culture*, the production, duplicating, and storing of corporate paperwork costs the United States $100 billion annually to produce 30 billion original documents. To cut the costs and speed up the process, the *least* any student should learn about computers is word processing.

Word Processing

Technology has created the instruments to let us write faster, edit at the click of a key, print letter-quality copy, and distribute the finished product by electronic mail. It may be difficult at first to break the habit of outlining and writing drafts by hand, but most people who have made the transition to word processing estimate that it doubles and even triples their productivity.

Advantages

Writing on a word processing computer offers a host of overall advantages over traditional methods of writing such as pen and pencil or the typewriter. It not only shortens the task of writing but also allows a flexibility that a typewriter cannot even begin to offer. Among the advantages are

- **Speed**—A word processing program allows you to alter text at any time by inserting, correcting, and deleting with only a touch of a few control keys.
- **Manipulation**—Whole blocks of text can be cut up and moved from one point of text to another or even temporarily stored in memory until such time as the writer wants to recall the data.
- **Neatness**—The speedy functions of editing and page formatting make a document *look* professional (although the content is still the responsibility of the writer).
- **Play**—Because of word processing capabilities, the writer often feels free to write with a smooth flow and then to "play" with possibilities of layout (margins, headers, footers, and the like.)
- **Confidence**—The drafting of a text on a word processor allows the writer to write different sections in any sequence and then to work on one or more of them as the writer feels comfortable.
- **Flexibility**—The word processor can merge materials, such as graphics or other data bases, into text for viewing and/or printing. Standard formats for a variety of graphics or reports can be recalled instantly.

EQUIPMENT/FEATURES

The equipment needed for effective word processing is probably familiar to modern students. To get started you will need the following items:

1. The **central processing unit** (CPU) is the heart of the computer. It is the hardware with built-in editing functions and the means for storing and retrieving input (text, files, graphics, and the like.)
2. The **keyboard** is like that of a typewriter but with additional keys to perform editing, formatting, and computational functions.
3. The **display screen,** similar to a television picture screen, displays the text, menus (lists) of programs, files, operations, text, and graphic matter.
4. The **software** (program) and the **document** (blank) **disks,** flexible or rigid pieces of magnetic tape, are inserted into the CPU to present a

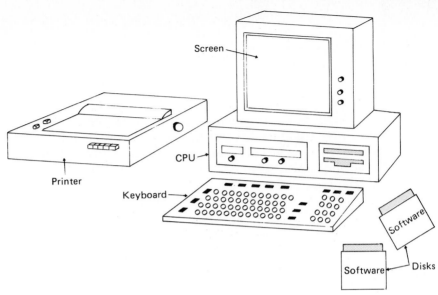

FIGURE 4.1 *Basic word processing computer needs*

new program (data disk) or to store your own material (document disk).
Many computers contain a "hard disk" which is a built-in memory device
holding the software programs and text you enter. Hard disk material
may be "backed up" by copying data onto a soft disk.

5. The **printer** works in tandem with the CPU to print out "hard copy"
of your material. There are, perhaps, over a hundred different printers
from simple to letter quality dot matrix, to top-quality laser machines.
Some offer a wide variety of features such as different character styles,
compressed type, justified lines, and horizontal/vertical print options.
Paper can be inserted into printers by feeding in a continuous roll or
by inserting single pages, such as stationery. Other accessories, such
as multi-pen plotters, can produce color graphics. Figure 4.1 shows the
basic equipment needed to word process material.

Learning to Word Process

If you are unfamiliar with computers, it is very likely that your college
has a computer lab or even a computer-equipped classroom for student
instruction, practice, and production. Take advantage of any equipment
and instruction that are offered. Learning word processing and computer
graphic operations is not difficult. Again, there are dozens of word processing programs, but they offer, essentially, the same options. There are
six tools for learning the process:

1. Instructions from a teacher or other knowledgeable person
2. Manuals which accompany the purchased software
3. Textbooks of instruction
4. Video and audio cassettes
5. Film strips
6. Newsletters to update your information

Any number of periodicals are available for subscription or perusal in libraries. Owners of computers and word processing software receive updates from the manufacturers discussing new products to enhance their capabilities. Among the popular periodicals for you to review are

Byte	*On Computing*
Computing	*Personal Computing*
Creative Computing	*Popular Computing*
Digital Research News	*Seybold Report on W. P.*
Interface Age	*Word Processing News*
Info World	*Words*

Basic Features

Most word processing programs are very similar although each manufacturer will add special editing features or methods of providing help to you. The basic features are the ability to type copy; to change page formats instantly; to scroll through your copy from place to place; to replace, insert, and delete characters at any point and at any time in the process; to mark text for special print features such as boldfacing or italicizing (underlining); to move entire sections from place to place; to save the document copy in the memory as a file for future reference; to merge material from other sources; and to print the material on a compatible printer.

Competitive manufacturers offer special features to enhance their sales and to ensure the writer fast, accurate word processing. These features will be discussed in The Writing Process section below, but among the common options are "windows" or screens which can be accessed for instant help, spelling correctors, thesaurus lists of synonyms, word counters, and merging capabilities to insert addresses, names, mathematical calculations, simple drawings, and graphics.

Figure 4.2 shows a window over a text giving the writer instructions for processing or editing functions.

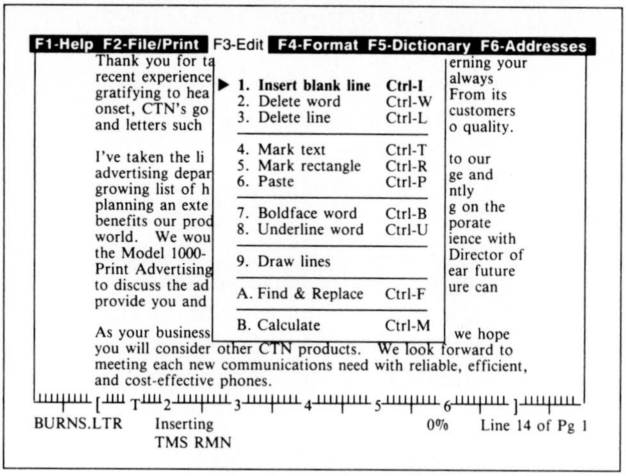

```
 F1-Help F2-File/Print  F3-Edit  F4-Format F5-Dictionary F6-Addresses
  Thank you for ta                          erning your
  recent experience  ▶ 1. Insert blank line  Ctrl-I  always
  gratifying to hea    2. Delete word        Ctrl-W  From its
  onset, CTN's go      3. Delete line         Ctrl-L  customers
  and letters such                                   o quality.

  I've taken the li    4. Mark text           Ctrl-T  to our
  advertising depar    5. Mark rectangle      Ctrl-R  ge and
  growing list of h    6. Paste               Ctrl-P  ntly
  planning an exte                                    g on the
  benefits our prod    7. Boldface word       Ctrl-B  porate
  world.  We wou       8. Underline word      Ctrl-U  ience with
  the Model 1000-                                     Director of
  Print Advertising    9. Draw lines                  ear future
  to discuss the ad                                   ure can
  provide you and      A. Find & Replace      Ctrl-F

                       B. Calculate           Ctrl-M
  As your business                                    we hope
  you will consider other CTN products.  We look forward to
  meeting each new communications need with reliable, efficient,
  and cost-effective phones.

  BURNS.LTR     Inserting                 0%     Line 14 of Pg 1
                TMS RMN
```

FIGURE 4.2 ***Word processing editing window***
(Professional Write is a Trademark of Software
Publishing Corporation, 1989)

THE WRITING PROCESS

Planning with a Word Processor

Chapter 2 discussed planning, drafting, and editing a document. Most of these activities can be enhanced with a computer word processor. For instance, your initial list of topics can be typed onto the screen and then quickly manipulated into clusters in the four corners and center of the screen, thus:

intro	tools to learn
twentieth century	software
Information Age	journals
productivity	

CPU
Keyboard
Disks
Screen
Printer
Accessories

advantages	listing
speed	clustering
manipulation	outlining
flexibility	etc.
play	
confidence	

These clusters of listed topics will help you to brainstorm the necessary ideas, to organize the sequences, and to keep you on track. In addition to your lists you might even jot down phrases or a sentence or two for future reference as if you were making notes on a clipboard note pad. There are some software programs which are idea or thought processors and some which are planning helpers.

It is not a long step to devising a complete and logical outline from your initial lists. Outline programs are available for use with your basic word processing software.

Processing the Draft

The next step is to draft a rough copy or create the working copy. All word processors have standard preset margins and tabs. These formats may be changed at any point in the writing process, but for the most part, use the preset layout for your draft. Chapter 2 urges you to write with a free flow. Try writing a **working copy** with little concern for the refinements which will come later. If watching your imperfect draft unfold on the screen distracts you, turn down the screen brightness and continue with your "invisible" writing. Some beginners claim that this process is not as intimidating as constantly looking at an obviously rough draft; they feel they can concentrate more specifically on content.

Each time a line fills up, the "carriage" will automatically return to the left margin of the next line as you continue typing. What's more, the **wordwrap** feature automatically moves a word that won't fit at the end of one line down to the beginning of the next line. At any time you may **scroll,** or shift the screen contents vertically or horizontally to reveal information beyond the current margins. This process is comparable to the way movie credits "roll" at the end of a film. Keys with directional arrows allow you to move the **cursor** to any word on any line with a few strikes. As you become more comfortable with a particular word processing system, you will insert, or at least tag with an asterisk, changes as you write the draft. But repairing, revising, and editing can be executed at the end of the rough draft writing session. Name your working copy and **save** the draft, errors and all. Later alterations will overwrite the rough draft errors when you revise.

Revising the Working Copy

Chapter 2 discusses the steps for repair and editing of your draft. Your computer will assist you in performing these tasks. Read through your draft several times, perhaps even print a hard copy, to ensure that your purpose, organization, paragraphing, and overall content are logical and complete. Use the **insert, delete, block move,** and other common features to repair the draft. A few computers have speech synthesizers that can read your text to you, offering a different perspective than the written page.

There are any number of features built into particular word processing programs to help you proofread and edit your work. In addition, entire programs may be purchased to assist you. Among the most popular features are built-in dictionaries and synonym finders for hundreds of words. Most dictionary programs will proof anything from a word to an entire document. Other popular aids are style and grammar checkers which will tag jargon, diction errors, active- and passive-voice usage, redundancies, and so forth. Other editing features will give you an immediate word count, number of sentences, average word length, and readability-level assessment. Still others will summarize the number of sentence types (simple, compound, complex, and compound/complex), drawing your attention to sentence subordination patterns.

Proofreading and editing need to be done very carefully. Computer typists tend to hit double letters or forget to delete words and phrases after inserting improved material. Don't be misled by the neatness of the screen text or the hard copy. Just because it *looks* professional doesn't mean it *is* professional.

COMPUTER GRAPHICS

The market offers a range of graphic programs. Some are part of a larger package of computer applications including word processing, paint or graphics, spreadsheet, database files, and so forth. Other graphic software may be purchased separately. Dot matrix printers will actually print your bar charts, circle graphs, and other graphics. The circles will have a rough, but perfectly acceptable, edge as you will notice in Figure 4.6. Multi-pen plotters will do an even better job. With a little practice you can produce excellent graphs and drawings similar to those shown in Figures 4.3 through 4.7.

DESKTOP PUBLISHING

Desktop publishing is revolutionizing communications. Progressive companies are actively looking for desktop publishing experience on student and professional resumes. Desktop publishing is a page-composition software system for personal computers. It offers immense possibilities for producing newsletters, brochures, publicity flyers, quarterly reports, press releases, and other professional-looking documents. You can blend headlines, text, graphics, and photographs into camera-ready copy right at your desk, which is far faster and significantly less expensive than working with an outside printer using traditional production methods.

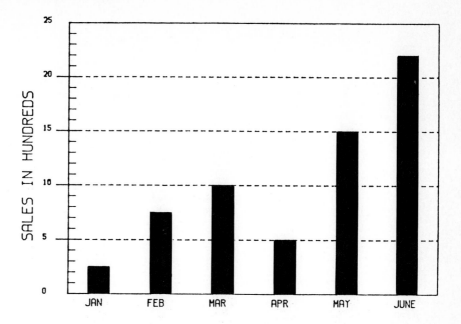

Figure 1 Sales of widgets in a six month period

FIGURE 4.3   *Computer bar chart* (Courtesy of Radio Shack)

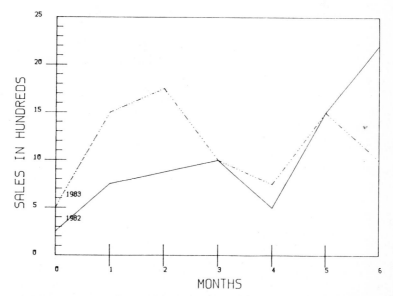

Figure 11   Widget Sales for six month period, 1982 and 1983

FIGURE 4.4   *Computer line graph* (Courtesy of Radio Shack)

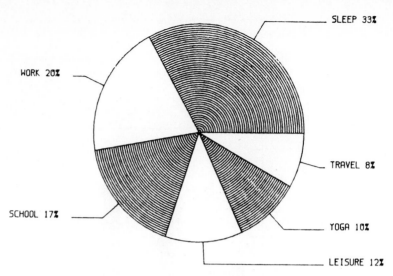

Figure 12   John Doe's typical Wednesday Activities Time Chart

FIGURE 4.5   *Computer circle graph* (Courtesy of Radio Shack)

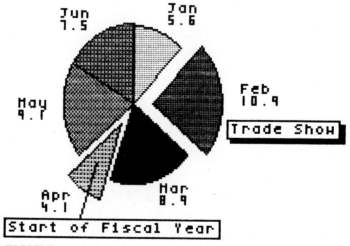

FIGURE 4.6   *Segmented circle chart*

(Courtesy of John Thompson, Etcetera, Inc.)

    Desktop publishing programs are available in prepackaged formats for newsletters, brochures, and so on, or with style sheets which allow you to design and lay out your own page format. Among the capabilities are page banners and article titles in larger or smaller typefaces. Usually options include the sans serif typefaces such as Helvetica, Univers, and Optima, and the more elaborate typefaces with serifs such as Melior, Century, and Times Roman. A touch of a key or a click of a computer mouse will set the text into 3 or 4 columns. You may also block out

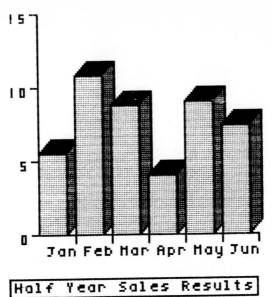

FIGURE 4.7 *Computer block bar chart*
(Courtesy of John Thompson, Etcetera, Inc.)

space for graphics and pictures which can be inserted vertically or at a slant. Watch for and attend demonstrations of desktop publishing applications.

FUTURE COMPUTER-ASSISTED WRITING AIDS

Software companies are competing vigorously to produce new programs. Software is already available which will format and alphabetize all of your research paper bibliography data. Both Modern Language Association (MLA) and American Psychological Association (APA) styles are available. In addition to the voice synthesizers previously mentioned, there are programs which allow you to dictate directly to the screen. Other software translates foreign languages into English, an enormous aid to foreign-language students, speakers of English as a second language, and scholars.

Color-capable printers are improving, as are graphic software programs. Magazine-quality paper is increasingly available for printers. Encyclopedia publishers are printing the entire contents onto disks for accessible reference.

There are even artificial intelligence systems in the works. These systems will examine and analyze your document and rewrite it in a polished style. What significance this is going to have on student writing assignments is not yet clear!

EXERCISES

1. Using the computer journals listed in the Equipment/Features section, develop a glossary of ten or more computer-related words including the following:

bit	interface
byte	icon
microchip	peripheral
cursor	pixel
block move	word-wrap

2. Use a word processor and copy any page of this textbook. Have a peer proofread it for you.

3. Go to a computer center which handles a wide array of software. List at least five word processing systems and note the special features of each (dictionary, style check, and so on).

WRITING OPTIONS

1. Using the data which you collected in Exercise 3 or articles in the special interest journals, write a short (300–500 word) comparison and contrast analysis of two software programs.

2. After completing Exercise 2, write a brief summary of the functions which you used as you copied the page.

3. Think about the ways that computer-assisted writing will benefit the kinds of documents you expect to produce in your career field. Write a brief paper about those applications you foresee.

NOTES

PART 2

The Professional Strategies

CHAPTER 5

Correspondence

DUFFY

by Bruce Hammond

INTRODUCTION

The writing strategies professional persons need first in all career fields are those required for effective correspondence. Memorandums and letters are records which promote action, transact business, and maintain continuity.

A one-page typewritten letter is very costly. Consider salaries and the equipment needed: memory typewriters, word processing software and hardware, paper, copies, envelopes, and postage. Therefore, mastering the strategies of effective correspondence is crucial for cost-effective transactions.

A memorandum, usually called a *memo*, is used for internal (within the company or organization) correspondence. A memo is used to request information, confirm a conversation, announce changes in policy and procedure, congratulate someone, summarize meetings, transmit documents, and report on day-to-day activities.

Letters are used for external (outside of the company or organization) correspondence. A letter may be used to seek employment (see Chapter 6), request information, respond to inquiries, promote sales and services, register complaints, offer adjustments, provide instructions, or report on any other activity.

Both types of correspondence are characterized by a "you" perspective—brevity, clarity, and accuracy.

MEMORANDUMS

Types of memos may vary from a brief, handwritten message which will probably be discarded by the reader after the appropriate action is taken to a carefully typed message which will be filed as part of the permanent record.

Format

Many companies use a preprinted communications memorandum for telephone and caller messages as shown in Figure 5.1:

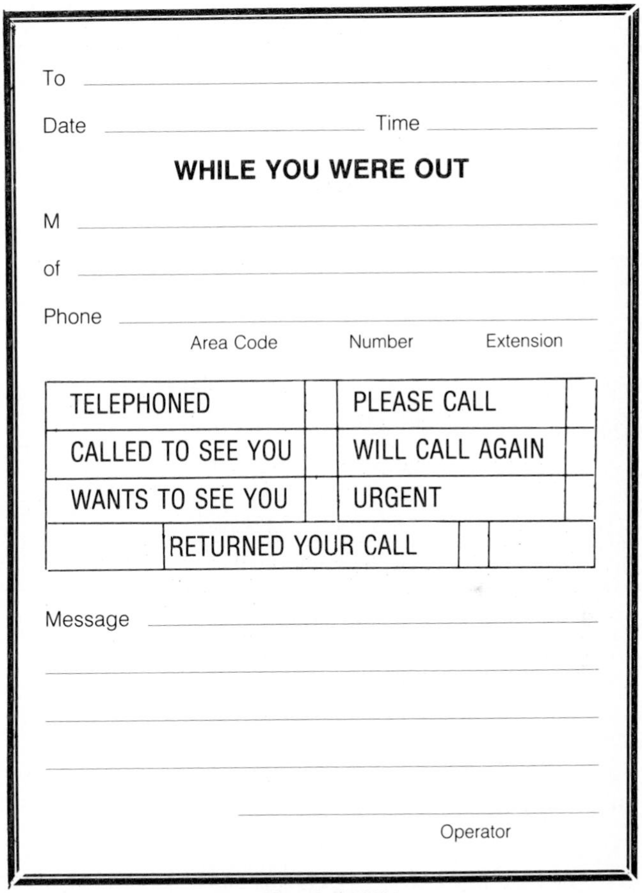

To _____

Date _____ Time _____

WHILE YOU WERE OUT

M _____

of _____

Phone _____
           Area Code   Number   Extension

TELEPHONED	PLEASE CALL
CALLED TO SEE YOU	WILL CALL AGAIN
WANTS TO SEE YOU	URGENT
RETURNED YOUR CALL	

Message _____

_____

_____

_____

                                    Operator

Campbell 09301

FIGURE 5.1 *Preprinted communication memorandum*

Some organizations also use preprinted memo forms on 8½ by 11 in. or half-page paper. These usually include the company name and logo plus the guide words TO, *FROM*, *SUBJECT*, and *DATE*. Some organizations use a "speed memo," one with carbon copies which allow the reader to send the message, retain a copy, and solicit a reply, as shown in Figure 5.2:

R **RYDER** **RYDER TRUCK RENTAL, INC.**   Date _____

TO ▶ _____ At _____ SUBJECT: _____

FROM _____ At _____ LOCATION CODE: _____

M E S S A G E _____

_____

_____

_____

_____

_____

_____

_____ Signed _____

                                          Date_____

R E P L Y _____

_____

_____

_____

_____

_____ Signed _____

S10-01 (1-79)

ADDRESSEE TO RETAIN WHITE COPY — RETURN GREEN COPY TO ORIGINATOR
ORIGINATOR TO RETAIN BLUE COPY — SEND WHITE AND GREEN COPIES WITH
CARBON INTACT TO ADDRESSEE

FIGURE 5.2 *Preprinted speed memorandum* (By permission)

If your company does not have preprinted forms, the model shown in Figure 5.3 is the most common format:

<u>MEMORANDUM</u>
(2 lines)
TO: John Snyder, President
(2 lines)
FROM: Maureen O'Neill, Personnel Specialist *M. O.*
(2 lines)
DATE: January 14, 199X
(2 lines)
SUBJECT: Fire in Reception Area, 1/13/9X
_____

(2 lines)
    _____
    _____
    _____ .

(2 lines)
    _____

    _____ .

(2 lines)
MO:jv
(2 lines)
Enclosures

FIGURE 5.3 *Standard memorandum format*

Notice the capitalization, margins, and spacing. The message paragraphs are usually single spaced with double spacing between paragraphs. The writer's signature or initials appear after the typed name in the *FROM* line for authorization, and for possible legal purposes, too.

Although frequently written in haste, a memo requires careful consideration. The addressee line should contain the full name and title of the person. Most employees wear several hats within an organization. An employee may be the Director of Human Resources, Chairman of the Comptroller Search Committee, and member of the Ad Hoc Committee on Leave Policies. The receiver of a memo wants to know immediately in which capacity he or she is being addressed. Memos may also be addressed to several people.

Examples

TO: John Q. Jones, Secretary, Vacation Committee
TO: Dr. Glen R. Rose, Academic Dean
        Dr. Benjamin Popper, Acting Director, Communications Division
        Dr. Mary Ellen Grasso, Chair, English Department

The sender should also include one's own title, indicating the position from which the memo is written.

Examples

FROM: Susan Long, Professor of English
FROM: Susan Long, Chair, Ways and Means Committee

The subject line should contain a precise, descriptive title indicating the topic of the memorandum.

Imprecise   SUBJECT: Meeting report
  Precise   SUBJECT: Ways and Means Committee
                              Minutes—3/5/9X

Content

A memo is a tool, not a piece of literature. One of the most effective memos ever written was by the famous General David Shoup. When Shoup completed his first inspection upon becoming Marine Corps commandant at Parris Island, he noticed that officers from noncoms to full colonels were carrying swagger sticks, an affectation adopted from the British Royal Marines. Shortly, he posted the following memo: "From the commanding general, regarding swagger sticks: If you need one, carry one." The next day not a swagger stick was to be seen on Parris Island. Shoup had mastered the convention of **brevity.** Most employees read numerous memos each day and must react to each message. Reading and reacting take time.

Memos get **to the point** quickly. Usually the in-house reader is somewhat informed about the general subject. Lengthy background and tactful motivations to act are usually not necessary. Just state your message and exclude irrelevant detail.

Even though you have several messages to convey to the same person, do not confuse your reader. Cover only **one topic,** and write a separate memo for each new subject.

Finally, be **timely.** Announce meetings several days in advance. Respond in writing to the memos you receive as quickly as possible. Interoffice correspondence is designed for efficiency. Figure 5.4 shows a sample of a memorandum which is brief, to-the-point, and timely on a single subject.

MEMORANDUM

TO: Members of the Long-Range Planning Committee

FROM: Kenton Duckham, Chairperson *K.D.*

DATE: April 27, 199X

SUBJECT: Change in May meeting date

The regularly scheduled May 15, 199X meeting of the Long-Range Planning Committee is rescheduled for May 22, 199X, at 3:00 P.M. in the Board Room because President Jean Laird must attend a marketing conference in Atlanta.

Please notify me at extension 6647 if you will be unable to attend.

KD:jv

FIGURE 5.4 *Sample memorandum*

LETTERS

Effective letter writing is the key to successful business operation. Letters are the essential link between you and your business connections and between one organization and another. Letter content promotes and confirms most business transactions. Conventions of format, mechanics, and content regularize and simplify these transactions.

Format

Several acceptable letter formats are in use today. Individual companies tend to adopt a uniform format for use on preprinted letterhead stationery.

If letterhead stationery is not used or if you are writing business letters as an individual, select white, unlined, 8½ by 11-in. bond paper of about 20-lb weight. Cheap, flimsy paper neither feels nor looks important. The quality of the paper may seem like a small point, but it does make a difference in the amount of attention your letter will receive.

Figures 5.5 and 5.6 show the two most widely adopted letter formats: the **full block** and the **modified block.** Study the spacing and indentation. Side margins are 1 to 1½ in. The top margin is a minimum 1 in. but may be deeper if the letter is short. A letter usually has more white space at the bottom than at the top, and it is conventional to type the body, or text, of the letter over the centerfold of the page.

Heading
409 Northeast Twelfth Avenue
Irving, Texas   75060
February 12, 199X

(3–6 lines)

Inside address
Mr. James W. Nelson
General Manager
Ace Equipment Company, Inc.
1092 East Eleventh Street
Seattle, Washington   98122
(2 lines)

Salutation
Dear Mr. Nelson:
(2 lines)

Special element
SUBJECT: Your letter of January 15, 199X
(2 lines)

_____
_____
_____ .

(2 lines)

Body
_____
_____
_____
_____ .

(2 lines)

_____
_____ .

(2 lines)

Complimentary closing
Very truly yours,

(4 lines)

Signature
Carol Hopper
(2 lines)

Notations
CH:cm
(2 lines)
c: David L. Meeks

FIGURE 5.5 *Full block format for business correspondence*

Heading

2107 West New Boulevard
Sterling, VA   22170
August 3, 199X

(3–6 lines)

Inside address

Mr. Ray Adams, Associate
Sun Air Corporation
State Road 7
Auburn, WA   98002
(2 lines)

Salutation

Dear Mr. Adams:
(2 lines)

Body

(2 lines)

(2 lines)

(2 lines)

Complimentary closing

Sincerely,

(4 lines)

Signature

Marcia Jordan
Personnel Specialist

(2 lines)

Notations

MJ:ts
(2 lines)
Enclosures (2)

FIGURE 5.6 *Modified block format for business correspondence*

Parts of Letters

All letters have six major parts: the heading, the inside address, the salutation, the body, the complimentary closing, and the signature. In addition, many letters contain subject, reference, or attention lines; typist's initials; enclosure and distribution notations.

Headings.   If you are using printed letterhead stationery, add only the date two spaces below the letterhead. If you are using plain, white stationery, type your street address, city, state, zip cope, and the date.

Example

1414 Southwest Ninth Street
Florence, South Carolina   29501
November 12, 199X

Do not include your name. Each line begins at the same margin. Refrain from abbreviating. Write out *Street*, *Avenue*, *Boulevard*, *East*, *Northeast*, and so on. Notice also that in street addresses one- and two-digit numbers are written out, but three or more digits are written in Arabic numerals

Examples

One Landmark Plaza
Twenty-two West Third Avenue
123 Forty-second Street
                    but
2134 West 114th Street

Leave two spaces between the state and the zip code. The heading is placed flush left in the block format or flush to the right margin in modified block format.

Inside Address.   The inside address includes the full name, position, company, and address of the recipient of your letter. It is spaced three to six lines below the heading.

Examples

Dr. Mary Jones, President
New Community College
101 South Palm Avenue
Fairmont, West Virginia   26555

Mr. Horacio L. Fernandez
Director of Human Resources
Ace Manufacturing Company, Inc.
Davenport, Iowa   90521

Notice that short titles may be placed on the same line as the name while long titles are placed in a separate, second line. If possible, address your letter to a specific person rather than just to a position within a company. While you may abbreviate titles such as *Dr., Mrs., Mr.,* and *Ms,* do not abbreviate *the Reverend* or *the Honorable* nor titles denoting rank, such as *Lieutenant, Captain, Professor.*

The inside address is always placed flush to the left margin.

You may abbreviate the state using the Postal Service two-letter abbreviations, as shown on page 82.

Salutation. The salutation is your greeting to your reader. It is typed two lines below the inside address and is followed by a colon. Further, it must agree with the addressee of the inside address.

Examples

Dr. Susan Clark, Dean
New Community College
101 South Palm Avenue
Miami, Florida   30212

Dear Dr. Clark: (agreement with person)

Director of Personnel
Ace Manufacturing Company, Inc.
4012 West Grand Street
Hilo, HI   96720

Dear Sir: (agreement with title)

Ace Manufacturing Company, Inc.
4012 West Grand Street
Augusta, GA   30906

Gentlemen: (agreement with corporate body)

League of Women Voters
Ten Northeast Datepalm Drive
Phoenix, AZ   85062

Ladies: (agreement with gender)

Because many women are joining the corporate ranks of business and industry, it is not unusual to see salutations, such as *Ladies and Gentlemen:, Hello:,* or *Dear Director of Training:.* Unless a woman has expressed a desire for *Miss* or *Mrs.,* use *Ms* (optional period) whether she is married or unmarried.

Alabama	AL	Montana	MT
Alaska	AK	Nebraska	NE
Arizona	AZ	Nevada	NV
Arkansas	AR	New Hampshire	NH
California	CA	New Jersey	NJ
Colorado	CO	New Mexico	NM
Connecticut	CT	New York	NY
Delaware	DE	North Carolina	NC
District of Columbia	DC	North Dakota	ND
Florida	FL	Ohio	OH
Georgia	GA	Oklahoma	OK
Guam	GU	Oregon	OR
Hawaii	HI	Pennsylvania	PA
Idaho	ID	Puerto Rico	PR
Illinois	IL	Rhode Island	RI
Indiana	IN	South Carolina	SC
Iowa	IA	South Dakota	SD
Kansas	KS	Tennessee	TN
Kentucky	KY	Texas	TX
Louisiana	LA	Utah	UT
Maine	ME	Vermont	VT
Maryland	MD	Virginia	VA
Massachusetts	MA	Virgin Islands	VI
Michigan	MI	Washington	WA
Minnesota	MN	West Virginia	WV
Mississippi	MS	Wisconsin	WI
Missouri	MO	Wyoming	WY

Avoid *Sir:* (too formal), *My dear Sir:* (too pretentious), *Dear Sirs:* (use *Gentlemen:*), and *To Whom It May Concern:* (too impersonal).
The salutation is always typed flush to the left margin.

Body. The body, the text of your letter, begins two lines below the salutation. Notice in Figures 5.5 and 5.6 that paragraphs are not indented in the block format but are indented five spaces in the modified block. Single space within paragraphs and double space between them. The body should fall over the center of the page.

Complimentary Closing. The complimentary closing is two lines below the body and is followed by a comma. Only the first word is capitalized.

Examples

Very truly yours,	(formal)
Yours truly,	(less formal)
Sincerely,	(emotional)
Respectfully,	(if addressee outranks you)
Cordially,	(warm)

The complimentary closing is flush to the left margin in block format and at the horizontal midpoint or at the heading margin in modified block format.

Signature.   Your full name is typed four lines under the complimentary closing. Sign your name in black ink between the two. If the addressee is known to you, you may sign less formally than the typed signature.

Example

Very truly yours,

Judy VanAlstyne

Judith S. VanAlstyne

Special Elements.   Occasionally, a subject, reference, or attention line is used to alert the reader to the subject, file reference, previous correspondence, account number, or other emphasis.

Examples

Below salutation	Subject: Invoice #20947
Above salutation	ATTENTION: Mr. D. W. Clark
	RE: Your letter of June 12, 199X

Such special elements are typed flush to the left margin two lines below the inside address but above the salutation.

Typist's Initials.   If your letter is typed by someone other than you, place your initials in capital letters and the typist's initials in lower case letters flush to the left margin two lines below the typed signature. use a colon or a virgule between them.

Examples

JSV:mt

or

JSV/mt

Enclosure Notations.   If you send materials or documents with your letter, add an enclosure notation two lines below the typist's initials.

Examples

Enclosure

    or

Enclosures (2)

    or

Enc: Photocopy of Check #1029

Distribution Notation.   If you are sending copies of your letter to other readers, add a distribution notation two lines below the last element.

Examples

pc: Mr. David Little, Chairman

Since most copies are now photocopies rather than carbon copies, *PC* is favored over the traditional *CC*.

Second Pages

If a letter requires a second page, type the recipient's name, the page number, and the date in a block flush to the left margin or across the page.

Examples

Ms Sally Queen
Page 2
July 15, 199X

    or

Ms Sally Queen   –2–   July 15, 199X

ENVELOPES

Your envelope should be $9\frac{1}{2}$ by $4\frac{1}{2}$ in. and of the same quality as your stationery. The recipient's name, title, company, address, city, state, and zip code are centered horizontally and vertically. As a guideline, begin twelve lines down from the top. Single space between lines. Your own name, address, city, state, and zip code are placed in the upper-left-hand corner. Use the Postal Service abbreviations for states.

Dr. Richard Grande
1022 Northeast First Street
La Mesa, CA   92041

                    Ms Julie Maney
                    Director of Personnel
                    Ace Manufacturing Company, Inc.
                    4092 West Grant Street
                    Manchester, CT   06040

CONTENT

Organization

Organize your message into three parts:

1. A brief introduction which states the purpose of the letter immediately unless you are conveying "bad news."
2. One or more body paragraphs which contain specific detail.
3. A conclusion which establishes goodwill or encourages your reader to act.

Introductory Purpose

State your purpose immediately. Do not just fill space until you get around to your purpose.

Vague purpose   It became apparent about five years ago that computerized bookkeeping was to be the answer to the problems which were plaguing our bookkeeping department. Therefore, we would like to investigate your software program . . .

Clear purpose   I am seeking answers to three questions regarding your software program, Computerized Automotive Reporting Service.

Other clear introductory purpose statements follow.

Examples

Here are the instructions for assembling the Ace 1 Trampoline which you requested by phone on September 20.

Please consider my resume and application for a junior management position at your Pompano resort.

This is in answer to your inquiry about leasing our trucks.

Your vacuum cleaner is repaired and is ready to pick up.

Congratulations on your promotion to Director of Affirmative Action.

You are right. You paid your bill exactly when you said you did.

"You"-perspective Body

Provide the details of your correspondence in the body, using a "you" perspective. Put yourself in your recipient's shoes and consider how that person will respond to your words. Be courteous, direct, and confident. Avoid a slangy, abrasive, pompous, or abrupt tone. Consider the abrasiveness of the following phrases:

Examples

Your department should shape up . . .

I demand that . . .

I am appalled at your slow response . . .

I beg to advise you of my intent to . . .

Rush me information on . . .

Much of our correspondence is highly repetitive ("Thank you for your order of July 25." "Our records indicate that your payment is past due."), yet trite and cliché expressions should be avoided.

Cliché Expressions	Plain English
Having received your letter, we . . .	We received your letter . . .
Pursuant to your request . . .	As you requested . . .
Per your memorandum . . .	As you noted . . .
Enclosed please find my report . . .	Here is my report . . .
It is imperative that you write at once . . .	Please write at once . . .
I am cognizant of the fact that my report is tardy . . .	I know that my report is late . . .
At the earliest possible date . . .	As early as possible . . .

I beg to differ with your . . .	I disagree with your . . .
Please be advised that the new policy . . .	The new policy is . . .
I hereby request that . . .	Please consider . . .
I beg to acknowledge receipt of your check . . .	I received your check . . .
We are in hopes that you succeed . . .	Good luck . . .

Every letter you write should sound fresh and conversational.

Purposeful Conclusions

Your conclusion provides an opportunity for you to urge action or establish goodwill. A brief closing should motivate the recipient to follow up on your letter or, at least, to feel favorable to you, as illustrated in these examples.

Examples

May I have your answer by March 12?

If you will call us within the next few days, we can send our sales representative to demonstrate our software capabilities.

I would like an interview and am available weekdays for the rest of this month.

Thank you for pointing out this problem.

I appreciate your services . . .

Do not, however, be obvious or presumptuous. Avoid "I want to thank you in advance for . . ." and "Please feel free to call me if you have further questions." An advance thank-you implies that you may be too lazy to write a proper thank-you when your request is fulfilled. The second closing is unnecessary; the recipient will call you if he or she has questions whether you invite a call or not.

Word Processing

A final word about the "you" perspective should be added. Word processing by computers has removed the drudgery from written correspondence by allowing organizations to create standard text for repetitive form letters. If you are already using a word-processing computer program, you know that you can delete anything from a character to a paragraph or relocate or insert words, phrases, sentences, and entire paragraphs with ease.

The word-processing capability, however, may tend to depersonalize our letters. Great care must be taken to maintain a friendly, "you"-oriented tone.

GOOD NEWS LETTERS

Recipient of many types of letters are happy to receive them. Letters may inquire about merchandise and services to which the recipient is pleased to respond. Other letters offer services or sales, place orders, tender a congratulation or thank-you, or transmit desired information. You will not only receive such letters but will also be called upon to write them in your career field. "Good news" letters include:

- Inquiry and Request letters
- Invitations
- Order letters
- Congratulatory letters
- Thank-you letters
- Sales- or service-offer letters
- Employment application and cover letters
- Transmittal letters

Inquiry and Request Letters

An inquiry or request letter is a "good news" letter in that the recipient stands to benefit from the writer's interest. Nevertheless, an inquiry or request solicits a response which will ask of the recipient time and, perhaps, effort. Therefore, certain strategies will help to motivate the recipient to respond quickly and accurately.

First, your introductory purpose statement may include the suggestion that you need an immediate response.

Example

I am seeking additional information on your TP-I Daisy Wheel printer because I plan to purchase one this month.

Secondly, you may clarify why you need this particular information.

Example

Because I edit our Company's in-house newsletter, it is essential that I purchase a printer which performs proportional spacing.

Third, you may subtly compliment the person or the company.

Example

I am interested in obtaining some additional details about your VID-80 Model III. Your company was the first to advertise such a modification more than six months ago, so I feel that you have the most expertise in this field.

Fourth, if you are asking questions, simplify and separate them into numbered items, make each specific, arrange them in a numerical table, and allow sufficient space between each to allow a jot of answers right on your letter.

Example

I have three questions which will affect whether or not I upgrade my system at this time:

1. What type of format does your CP/M use? Is it compatible with the system Radio Shack computers use?
2. Do schematic diagrams come with the unit? If not, are they available for an extra charge?
3. If the added memory is purchased, is there any way to use the additional memory when operating with TRSDOS or similar operating systems?

You may also consider enclosing a self-addressed, stamped envelope. This double strategy of leaving space to answer on your letter and sending a return envelope will allow the recipient to respond right on your letter and place your response in the outgoing mail immediately.

Finally, if it is appropriate, you may offer to share the results of your inquiry.

Example

Because I am compiling information on the technical writing programs of all Florida community colleges, I will be happy to share with you my final report.

Figure 5.7 shows a poor request letter. It exemplifies a "me" rather than a "you" perspective and is poorly organized and rude. Figure 5.8, however, illustrates a well-written request letter which motivates a quick response.

3072 Southwest Sixth Avenue
Norwich, CT 06360
May 4, 199X

Mr. Fred Mandel
Radio-Electronics
200 Park Avenue
New York, NY 70908

Dear Mr. Mandel:

Demanding and insulting

Please rush me information on how to convert my transistor output voltage to 6VDC usable voltage for my portable radio. I read your article in Radio-Electronics, but it confused me.

Unclear questions

What I need to know is can I use the same 300 Ohm pot or something else for my 9VAC. Can I use the same number rectifier for my radio? Can you recommend a zenior diode? What else do I need to know?

Rude

Thank you in advance for answering my questions.

Very truly yours,

Walt

Walter Matthews

WM:jsv

FIGURE 5.7 ***A poor request letter***

7661 Hood Street
Hollywood, FL   33024
June 29, 199X

Mr. Jerry Diener
Vice-president
Smith-Corona Company
65 Locust Lane
New Canaan, CT   06840

Complimentary [

Dear Mr. Diener:

To-the-point [

I saw your excellent advertisement for a TP-I Daisy Wheel printer in the July 199X issue of 80 Micro on page 95, and I am writing to you to obtain answers to five questions concerning this printer.

Clearly organized questions

1. How many characters per second does this printer print?

2. Can the TP-I printer perform proportional spacing?

3. Can the printer produce copies? If so, how many can it make?

4. Is there an additional charge for the parallel data interface?

5. Are the printer control codes the same as those used on the Diablo 620?

Enabling [

For quick response, you may jot the answers to my questions on this letter. Please also send me any brochures available on your TP-I printer.

Urge to action with good reason [

I would appreciate this information as quickly as possible so that I may take advantage of your rebate offer which ends on July 31. I have enclosed a stamped, self-addressed envelope for your convenience.

Very truly yours,

Sandra J. Burnette

Sandra J. Burnette

SJB:jsv

Enclosure

FIGURE 5.8   *An effective request letter* (Courtesy of student Sandra J. Burnette)

Invitations

An invitation is a type of request letter, too. You may wish to invite a speaker to address your group or organization. Or you may wish to invite members or guests to attend special functions, such as meetings or luncheons. Invitations should be brief, but detailed. First, extend the invitation including the function, date, time, and place. If necessary, mention guest status, fee, honorarium or the like to be expected. Second, elaborate on the purpose and offer any other particulars which the invitee will need such as the number of expected persons, length of a requested speech, or other program components. Finally, urge a response by enclosing a response card requesting a call, or suggesting you will be calling in a few days for an answer. Figure 5.9 shows a typical invitation letter.

Order Letters

Another "good news" letter is the order letter, one that informs a seller that you want to purchase a product or service. Three writing strategies will help you to be clear and accurate about your specific order, shipping instructions, and method of payment. First, accurately describe the product or service by specifying the name, brand, model, stock number, quantity, color, dimensions, unit price, and so on. Include an informal table for multiple product or service orders for easy reader reference. Second, include your shipping instructions, such as first-class or third-class mail, Federal Express, United Parcel, or special mailing address, department, or special attention notation. Third, mention the date needed if this is an issue, and, finally, specify your method of payment: enclosed check or money order, credit card charge number, C.O.D., installment, and so on.

Figure 5.10 illustrates a clear and accurate order letter.

Congratulatory and Thank-you Letters

Both of these "good news" letters are characterized by informality and friendliness. The salutation might address the recipient by a first name. The introduction should mention specifically the occasion for congratulations or appreciation. Add detail to underscore your sincerity and end with a warm complimentary close.

Figures 5.11 and 5.12 illustrate typical congratulatory and thank-you letters.

Sales and Service Offer Letters

Even though a sales or service offer letter is written to persuade the recipient to purchase a product or service, it may be considered a "good news" letter in that it offers to enhance the recipient in some manner. Five writing strategies can aid you in obtaining a favorable response.

First, identify and limit your audience. Determine the needs of this

Meet for Good Fellowship

PROVIDENCE JEWELERS CLUB
P. O. BOX 4350
EAST PROVIDENCE, RHODE ISLAND 02914

September 16, 199X

Ms. Robin Revell
30 Ormsby Avenue
Warwick, Rhode Island   02886

Dear Ms. Revell:

The particulars

Please accept my invitation to attend as my guest the Providence Jewelers Club "Speakers' Luncheon" on October 1, 199X, 12:00 noon, at the Providence Marriott Hotel.

Elaboration

I would like to introduce you to our members and guests as the recipient of the Providence Jewelers Club 1990–1991 scholarship. Your choice of meals should be indicated on the enclosed card and returned as soon as possible.

Urge to action

Should you not be able to attend, please call me at 738-8560 as soon as possible. I look forward to meeting you.

Very truly yours,

Paul J. Austin

Paul J. Austin
President

PJA/eeg

Enclosure

FIGURE 5.9 *An invitation letter* (Courtesy of Paul J. Austin)

Sunshine Aviation School
1701 Rio Vista Boulevard
Fort Lauderdale, Florida   33316
July 30, 199X

Sporty's Pilot Shop
Clermont County Airport
Batavia, Ohio   45103

ATTN: Aviation Department:

Gentlemen:

Specific order

Please send us by first-class mail the following items which are listed in your 198X catalogue:

3128 A	Jumbo Computer	10@$7.95	$79.50
2071 A	Topcomp Runway Computer	10@11.95	119.50
2241 B	Sectional Timescale	10@18.50	185.00
			$384.00

Mailing instructions

Mark the package "ATTN: Instructor Jerry Nordstrom." We will expect this order by next Friday. If there will be a delay, please call me collect (305-491-7702).

Payment details

I am enclosing a check for one-half of the order ($192.00) and will pay the balance on receipt of the materials.

Very truly yours,

Jerry Nordstrom

Jerry Nordstrom
Chief Flight Instructor

JN:dt

Enclosure

FIGURE 5.10   *An effective order letter*

ACE COMPANY, INCORPORATED
2900 Northeast Seventy-ninth Street
Fort Lauderdale, Florida   33301

January 5, 199X

Ms Paula Watkins
Tech Laboratories, Inc.
P.O. Box 37021
Miami, Florida   30321

Dear Paula:

The good news that you were promoted to Director of Personnel was in the Business News section of this morning's <u>Miami Herald</u>. Tech Labs certainly picked the right person for the job. Congratulations!

You've earned this advancement, Paula. Your consistent good work and extra efforts, such as your participation in our Broward County Career Festival, set an example for all of us in the field.

Warmest wishes,

Ben

Informal salutation

Source of knowledge

Specific message

Underscore of sincerity

Friendly closing

FIGURE 5.11   *An effective congratulatory letter*

3502 Southwest Palm Avenue
Athens, GA   30605
March 7, 199X

Professor J. John Jenks
Community Service Division
Broward Community College
1 East Las Olas Boulevard
Fort Lauderdale, Florida   33301

Dear Professor Jenks:

To-the-point, informal   Your generous recommendation of me to Tech Laboratories, Inc. got me the job. Thank you!

Specific details of appreciation   The word processing skills you taught me plus your pep talks on organization have opened new doors of self-confidence for me. I'm truly grateful for your interest.

I'll keep you posted on my advancement.

Thanks again,

Ralph

Ralph Kennery

FIGURE 5.12   *An effective thank-you letter*

group and bear in mind exactly what you want your audience to do after reading your letter. The "you" perspective is critical for your desired response. Keep in mind what you can do for your reader throughout the letter.

Second, begin your letter with an attention-getting statement. You may ask a question, offer a free gift, employ a "how to" statement, or use flattery. In short, hook your reader into reading further.

Examples

You will receive a free vacation for two, a new car, a dream cottage, or other valuable gift simply by making an appointment to inspect our resort.

Here's how to save $100.00 on your next automobile purchase.

You made a smart choice by enrolling at Broward Community College. Now let us help you make a smart choice in selecting your college wardrobe.

Third, call attention to the product or service's appeal. Persuade the reader that your offer is so desirable that he or she can't resist it.

Example

Our time-share condominiums are caressed by gentle ocean breezes and within steps of your very own tennis courts, golf course, and spa. We offer the last word in glamorous vacations.

Ace Motors offers the world-recognized most economical car on the highways—the Ace 400ZT.

Designer jeans, polo shirts, a dazzling array of blouses, dresses, skirts, and accessories are waiting for you.

Fourth, present evidence of your product or service's application. Emphasize its convenience, usefulness, and economy. Endorsements, guarantees, and special features may be highlighted. It is here that you present the facts, but do so in a manner that emphasizes the attractiveness of your offer.

Examples

A member of Time-Share International, Driftwood Resort offers not only the most reasonable prices on the Gold Coast but also opportunity to vacation in 39 countries of the world. Spacious two and three bedroom plus studio accommodations are available to suit your precise requirements. Fully equipped kitchens with modern hottubs allow you the casual lifestyle of a truly refreshing holiday.

Fifty-three motoring journalists from 15 European nations voted this newest Ace "Car of the Year." The 400ZT is aerodynamically designed to accelerate from zero to fifty in only seven seconds. Disc brakes, rack and pinion steering, and a performance-tuned suspension system make this automobile a marvel to drive.

College Corner clothes will make you feel confident and poised. Our College Board representatives make sure we buy the "in" ensembles to fit your classroom, party, and extracurricular needs. We even offer free alterations.

Finally, urge your reader to action. Make it easy for your readers to return a postcard to order your product, suggest an appointment next week, invite them into your store for a free gift, include a phone number to call, and so on.

Examples

Call 305-455-9000 to arrange a tour of our facilities and to find out what valuable gift is yours. You won't be disappointed.

Stop by this weekend to test drive your next car—the Ace 400ZT.

During Orientation Week we will be open until 9:00 P.M. for you to drop in and browse. Free textbook covers are yours with every purchase.

Jane Hansen & Associates
409 East Seventy-second Street
Suite 9001
Los Angeles, CA   90028
May 12, 199X

Mr. Frank Mahoney
Senior Vice-President
City National Bank
100 Northeast First Street
Los Angeles, CA   90066

Dear Mr. Mahoney:

Attention getter

DID YOU KNOW   —it costs $17.50 for each letter
                         your staff types?

                      —your typical employee spends
                         25% of his or her time at work writing?

OF COURSE YOU KNOW—the ability to write well gets the results you
                      want.
                      Contracted training saves your bank money.

Appeal of offer

To upgrade the writing skills of your employees, you may now contract
WRITING SKILLS & STRATEGIES, a training seminar tailored to your
employees. Further, we will conduct the seminar at your bank during
the times most convenient for your busy staff.

Application and appeal

Endorsement

WRITING SKILLS & STRATEGIES reviews troublesome mechanics,
grammar, and usage as well as offers indispensable tips on
correspondence, report writing, and much more. An experienced writing
instructor will tailor the materials to your specific needs. Over 40 banks
in south Florida will attest to the practicality of this training program.

Urge to action

May I make an appointment, Mr. Mahoney, to discuss course content,
prices, and times? I will call your office within the next ten days.

Very truly yours,

Jane Hansen

Jane Hansen
Writing Consultant

JH:jsv

Application

P.S. The enclosed brochure highlights features of WRITING SKILLS &
     STRATEGIES.

FIGURE 5.13 *An effective service offer letter*

Figure 5.13 opposite shows a persuasive service offer letter. The audience consists of busy top executives who may be frustrated by the poor quality and time-consuming writing skills of their employees. The layout is catchy and appealing. The service's application and the desired action is effectively covered, yet the letter is brief.

Employment Application and Cover Letters

Because employment application letters often include a resume, a separate writing strategy, they will be discussed separately in Chapter 6.

Transmittal Letters

Letters of transmittal, sometimes called cover or face letters, announce the enclosure of attached material and reports. Content and samples are covered in Chapters 6 and 8.

BAD NEWS LETTERS

Some letters must, of necessity, convey "bad news." They may inform the recipients that they are not hired, cannot get a refund, are late with a payment, and so on. Again there are writing strategies to convey your "bad news" in a positive, result-producing manner. "Bad news" letters include

- Negative response letters
- Complaints
- Collection letters
- Solicitations

Negative Response Letters

A letter which must say *no* requires a buffer statement before the "bad news." A buffer statement presents a valid reason before the negative response.

Examples

We lease our apartments only through registered real estate brokers; therefore, . . .

Because the criteria for the position of Personnel Specialist requires a college degree in business administration, we can consider only those applicants with that credential.

I have referred your letter to Ms Jane Clifford, assistant to the director of computer services, because only that department is authorized to give you the information you request.

A second strategy is to avoid the word *no*.

Too harsh   I'm sorry to say no, I cannot address your engineers next week.

Buffered   Because I will be in Chicago all of July, I cannot speak before your group.

ACE COMPANY, INCORPORATED
2900 Northeast Seventy-ninth Street
Columbus, Ohio   43219

January 5, 199X

Ms Jane Doe
1107 Northwest Twelfth Street
Dayton, Ohio   33331

Dear Ms Doe:

Buffer statement
Negative response

    We have received your letter and resume, exploring career opportunities at Ace Company. While your education and experience present an interesting background, your qualifications do not fit our particular requirements at this time.

No apology but positive action

    We will place your materials in our potential file. Should a position for which you qualify open, we shall review your file and notify you.

Establishes goodwill

    We appreciate your interest in Ace and wish to extend our wishes for success in the attainment of your career goals.

Sincerely,

Ralph Maran

Ralph Maran

RM:tac

FIGURE 5.14   *An effective negative response to a job applicant*

A third strategy in a negative response letter is to avoid an apology. Your reasons are valid, so eliminate *unfortunately*, *we regret*, *we are sorry*, *we wish we could*, and so on.

Fourth, do not leave the opportunity to reopen discussion or consideration. Avoid "If you wish to discuss this further . . ." and "We wish we could . . ."

Finally, conclude by establishing goodwill. Use "We hope we have an opportunity to serve you in the future," "We appreciate your interest in our organization," and the like. Sincerity is an important consideration. If your effort to establish goodwill appears contrived, forced, or formulistic, it will irritate your reader.

Figure 5.14 illustrates an effective negative response letter to a job applicant. It buffers the bad news, does not apologize, and establishes goodwill.

Complaints

All of us have found it necessary to complain about defective products, delayed orders, billing errors, or inadequate services. Although we usually write complaint letters at a time of anger or frustration, angry tones seldom elicit the action we desire. A complaint letter needs restraint, specificity, and a clear statement of desired action.

The first strategy is to provide a detailed description of the faulty product, service, or suspected error along with the specifics about your purchase or contract.

Example

I am returning for a full refund the U.D.S. Computer Telephone, model 333, for which I sent money order 40920 in the amount of $10.00 on July 15, 199X. I received the defective phone on August 20, 199X.

Secondly, state precisely what is wrong with the product or service.

Example

The phone malfunctions. The beeper activates on the third dialed digit so that dialing cannot be completed. A persistent, loud buzzing interferes with reception on incoming calls.

Third, consider describing the inconveniences you have experienced. This is not always necessary but may help to underscore the seriousness of your complaint.

Example

Because I conduct a great deal of business from my home telephone, I have lost sales and commissions by not having a properly functioning instrument.

1390 Southwest Twentieth Street
Davie, FL   33326
September 17, 199X

The Doubleday Book Club
Customer Service Department
501 Franklin Avenue
Garden City, NY   11530

Re: Account #96–299–38934

Gentlemen:

Details of Complaint

Please review my account for a credit. On July 12, 199X, I received the Pierre Cardin Canvas luggage set from your company. When I received this luggage from your company, it was on a trial basis for 60 days. After examining the luggage, I returned the entire set on August 12, 199X.

Expansion

The charge of $79.95 has continued to be shown on my last two monthly statements. I wrote a note on the statement each time indicating the return of luggage and sent the statement back to your company. Photocopies of these notes are attached to this letter. To date, I have not received an adjusted statement.

Desired action

Would you credit my account for $79.95 and send me an adjusted statement.

I will appreciate your prompt attention to this matter.

Very truly yours,

Ruth Burrows

Ruth Burrows

RB

Enclosures: 2 statement photocopies

FIGURE 5.15   *An effective complaint letter* (Courtesy of student Ruth Burrows)

Finally, state clearly what action you desire. You may want a refund, a replacement, copies of all records, or some other consideration.

Example

I am enclosing the warranty and am requesting a full refund for the purchase price. I will not consider a replacement because I have lost confidence in your merchandise. I shall appreciate a prompt refund check.

Figure 5.15 illustrates a complaint about a credit problem.

Collection Letter

Unfortunately, not all consumers pay their bills on time. Therefore, companies must employ several correspondence strategies to urge payment. Frequently, companies send a series of collection letters, each employing a stronger tone than the former. It is not wise to demand immediate payment in the first collection letter because there may be valid reasons for slow payment, such as misdelivered or misplaced bills, errors in the company's billing, and so on. Further, an early threat to begin legal action may cause the well-intentioned customer to avoid further profitable transactions with the company, or the company may suffer negative word-of-mouth publicity. A tactful "you" perspective is important in maintaining good relationships.

The first letter should make the customer feel valuable, allow the customer to save face, urge prompt payment, but offer to establish a partial payment schedule.

A follow-up letter should refer to the first request for payment and urge partial or full payment by return mail in order to avoid "further action."

A final letter usually refers to the first requests for payment and alerts the customer that the account will be turned over to a collection agency if partial or full payment isn't made immediately.

Figure 5.16 illustrates an initial letter of collection to a customer for an overdue charge account payment.

Solicitations

Although not truly "bad news," a solicitation for money or volunteer activities may be classed here because such solicitations offer nothing in return except, perhaps, the opportunity to further a cause which interests the reader. Alumni groups, political candidates, supporters of various causes, and the like frequently solicit money and volunteers. Such letters

ACE DEPARTMENT STORE
491 East Seventh Way
Peoria, Illinois   61650

August 1, 198X

Mrs. Quentin Adler
2201 West Orange Boulevard
Oak Lawn, Illinois   60454

RE: ACCOUNT #427-010-20

Dear Mrs. Adler:

"You"
perspective
buffer

> Ace Department Store values you as a shopper. Offering you a charge
> account is just one way we try to make your shopping more convenient.

"You"
perspective
urge for
full payment

> Our records indicate that you have missed two payments in June and
> July and that your amount past due as of August 1, 198X, is now $420.00.
> Unless you have a question regarding this figure, we would appreciate
> receiving your full payment. If you are unable to pay the full due amount
> now, won't you please call our Customer Service Department to set up a
> partial payment schedule in order to maintain your credit with us?

Urge for
action

> We will appreciate your prompt attention to this matter.

Very truly yours,

Marian Williams

Marian Williams
Customer Service

MW:jn

FIGURE 5.16   *An effective initial collection letter*

require inventive, eye-catching, persuasive techniques. Among these techniques are those used in advertising: bandwagon appeal, snob appeal,
humor, endorsements, and so on.

The humorous approach is one effective technique, as illustrated
in Figure 5.17, a letter soliciting a contribution from a college alumnus.

MIAMI UNIVERSITY   Miami University Fund

SPRING IS
SPRINKLING AGAIN.

Whoever picks the weathermen for southwestern Ohio must assign the
same one here year after year

. . . and he, or she, must like rain.

So up and down High Street, across the Slant Walk, in and out of the
dorms, apartments, classrooms and libraries, thousands of students, just
like when you were here, are going . . .

. . . drip, drip, drip.

Of course, after the "rainy season" the skies brighten. Oxford gets
breathtakingly beautiful. The dogwoods and redbuds, croci and daffydillies
all pop out . . . to say nothing of the lifelong friendships that seem,
also, to bloom in the Spring.

Then everything seems better than ever. Remember?

The same kind of cycle repeats each Spring for The Miami University
Fund. Around this time of year we begin to experience a heavy sprinkle
of checks from friends like you who know that Miami's bright skies
next year depend a great deal on how many key scholarships we can
offer and on all the other rays of educational sunshine the Fund supports.

And the results do show. Miami stays better than other schools; attracts
finer students; offers them a better experience; keeps an admired faculty;
even reflects favorably on the alumni and friends who make its annual
blossoming possible.

So take a moment now, won't you, to check on the weather and see if
this isn't a good time to help "sprinkle" on the Fund. If you'll put a
check in the mail, we'll put it right to work painting the skies sunny,
just as you'd want us to . . .

                                        Zip, zip, zip.

                                        Doug Wilson

                                        Douglas M. Wilson
                                        Vice President
                                        University Relations

DMW:ehd

FIGURE 5.17 *An effective solicitation letter* (By permission)

EXERCISES

1. Rewrite the following memo subject lines to make them more precise and descriptive:

Test Results	Vacations
Minutes	Training
Meeting	New Personnel
New Policy	Copy Machine
Schedules	Hours

2. Correct the errors in the letter elements of the following block letter format.

Ms. Julie Wilson
2 N. W. Park Ave.
Chicago, Ill.   33302

Mr. Daniel C. Taylor
four-one-two E. 72nd St.
Dayton, Oh,   40727

Dear Sir,

Re: Account #407-201 E

_____
_____
_____

_____
_____
_____

                        Best,

                        Marcia Morris

                        Marcia Morris, Treasurer

                        mm:tc

---

3. Rewrite the body of the following complaint letter by dividing it into
    an introduction, body, and closing and by eliminating "letterese," a
    "me" perspective, and an inappropriate tone.

Dear Sir:

In reference to your lousy iron which I purchased recently, I want my
hard-earned money back. If you don't refund me the price in full, I beg to
inform you that I will take legal action. It spews water all over the clothes I
iron, scorches things even on a low setting, will not stand up on its base, and
the plug broke the last time I plugged it in. If you have any questions, do not
hesitate to call me. I am appalled at the workmanship of this piece of junk.
Get with it.
Cordially,

---

4. Write buffers to the following blunt, negative response statements.

    a. We cannot send you the Ace Wrist Fans because you enclosed
        only one box top.

    b. We're sorry to inform you that we cannot hire you at this time.

    c. I must say no to your request for a writing seminar in June.

WRITING OPTIONS

1. Write a **brief** memo to a subordinate to urge that a previously assigned
    written report be turned in a week earlier than previously scheduled.

2. Write a memo to your employer (real or imaginary) to point out a
    minor problem at your place of work, such as a scheduling mixup,
    inadequate lighting, the need for more storage shelves or files, your
    inability to perform an assigned task, an error in your paycheck,
    and so on. Be brief, to-the-point, and focused.

3. Write a "good news" letter.

    a. Write an inquiry or request letter to a company or other organiza-
        tion in response to an advertisement or article in a professional
        journal in your field. Ask at least four technical questions about
        a product or service. Review the writing strategies which will
        motivate a quick response.

    b. Write an invitation to a professor or an authority in some field
        to make a twenty-minute address at your annual kickoff meeting
        of a special-interest organization. Make up all of the details that
        the invitee will need to know.

    c. Write an order letter for merchandise from a particular company. Specify the stock number, quantity, size, color, unit cost, and total cost as appropriate. Include all details about payment and delivery.

    d. Write a congratulatory or thank-you letter. Some suggested topics are congratulations to a friend who has been hired or promoted, won a professional award, completed a degree or other special training, been elected to public or organizational office, or opened up a business. Thank-you letter topics might be a response to a letter of recommendation, a letter of appreciation to a teacher or counselor whose advice you followed, to a hotel or restaurant which hosted a group function or dinner, or to a person who directed some business opportunity your way.

    e. Write a sales or service offer letter. Consider your audience's age, occupation, geographical location, needs, and interest. Some suggested topics are the merits of a particular automobile, college, restaurant, new store, personal computer, bank, travel bureau, flower shop, or maintenance service for lawn, pool, or snow removal.

4. Write a "bad news" letter.

    a. Write a negative response letter. Some suggested topics are turning down an offered job, declining an invitation to speak, declining to serve on a committee or joining an organization, refusal to volunteer time to an organization, refusal to a job applicant, inability to fulfill a reservation request at a hotel or travel group, declining to refund money for a specific piece of merchandise, or refusal to a sales or service offer.

    b. Write a complaint letter. Some suggested topics are an error in your credit card or telephone bill, rude service you received at a store or restaurant, late delivery of merchandise, poor quality of some product recently purchased, or damaged goods delivered by bus, air, or rail.

    c. Write a series of three collection letters, each firmer than the last. Some suggested topics are late dues payment to a club or organization, late payment for a service you rendered, or late payment for an automobile, credit account, or bank loan.

    d. Write a solicitation letter. Select a cause which interests you— save the whales or manatees, abortion legislation, a political candidate, the equal rights amendment, zoning irregularities, a halfway house for troubled youth, and so on—and solicit donations or appearance at a civic forum to discuss the issue with top policymakers.

CHAPTER 6

Resumes, Cover Letters, and Interviews

SHOE

by Jeff MacNelly

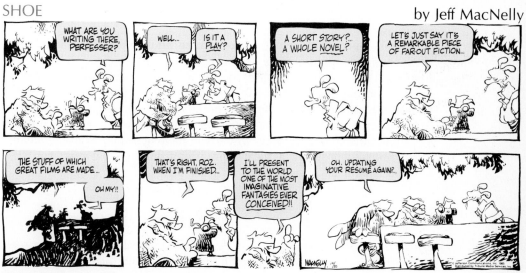

Reprinted by permission: Tribune Media Services.

Skills:

After studying this chapter, you should be able to

1. Define *resume* and *cover letter*.
2. Appreciate the importance of a detailed, letter-perfect resume and cover letter.
3. Compile a personal dossier of educational and employment background materials and reference letters.
4. Compile a dossier of future position prospects.
5. Write a personal resume in an appropriate format, including career objectives, personal data, educational background, employment history, and references.
6. Write a cover letter to a specific prospective employer.

INTRODUCTION

Résumé is a French word which means "summary." A personal resume is a concise summary of pertinent facts about yourself—your employment objectives, your employment and educational history, personal data, and reference lists. Although most dictionaries include the accent marks (résumé), it is common practice to omit them. A resume and its accompanying cover letter are indispensable job-hunting tools which are submitted to employers to "sell" yourself as a prospective employee and to obtain an interview.

Your resume allows you to organize and amplify your data in a manner which highlights your strengths. A job application form (see Figure 6.1) usually restricts you to a mere listing of schools and previous employment names and addresses. Although the resume and cover letter are usually mailed to companies who have advertised for applicants or to those companies where you know an opening exists, you may present a resume during an interview which you have obtained by other means. The summary provides a focal point for discussion between you (the applicant) and the interviewer.

RECORD KEEPING

Long before you seek initial employment in your chosen career or seek to change jobs, it is wise to compile a file of your achievements and employment experiences. This file, or dossier, should also contain all

application for employment

We are an equal opportunity employer, dedicated to a policy of non-discrimination in employment on any basis including race, color, age, sex, religion or national origin.

PERSONAL INFORMATION

Date _____   Social Security Number _____

Name _____
Last   First   Middle

Present Address _____
Street   City   State   Zip

Permanent Address _____
Street   City   State   Zip

Phone No. _____

Referred By _____

Last

First

Middle

EMPLOYMENT DESIRED

Position _____   Date You Can Start _____   Salary Desired _____

Are You Employed Now? _____   If So May We Inquire of Your Present Employer? _____

Ever Applied to this Company Before? _____   Where _____   When _____

EDUCATION

	Name and Location of School	Circle Last Year Completed	Did You Graduate?	Subjects Studied and Degree(s) Received
Grammar School			☐ Yes ☐ No	
High School		1 2 3 4	☐ Yes ☐ No	
College		1 2 3 4	☐ Yes ☐ No	
Trade, Business or Correspondence School		1 2 3 4	☐ Yes ☐ No	

Subjects of Special Study or Research Work _____

Activities Other Than Religious (Civic, Athletic, etc.) _____
EXCLUDE ORGANIZATIONS. THE NAME OR CHARACTER OF WHICH INDICATES THE RACE, AGE, SEX, COLOR OR NATIONAL ORIGIN OF ITS MEMBERS.

Form M660-26NR   Printed in U.S.A
©1985 Wilson Jones Company

(Continued on Other Side)

APPLICATION FOR EMPLOYMENT

FIGURE 6.1 *Sample employment application—continues on next page*

FORMER EMPLOYERS List Below Last Four Employers, Starting With Last One First

Date Month and Year	Name and Address of Employer	Salary	Position	Reason for Leaving
From				
To				
From				
To				
From				
To				
From				
To				

REFERENCES: Give Below the Names of Three Persons Not Related To You, Whom You Have Known At Least One Year.

	Name	Address	Business	Years Acquainted
1				
2				
3				

PHYSICAL RECORD: Do you have any physical condition which may limit your ability to perform the job applied for?   This question is voluntary, and any answers will be kept confidential.

In Case of Emergency Notify

            Name   Address   Phone No

I authorize investigation of all statements contained in this application. I understand that misrepresentation or omission of facts called for is cause for dismissal. Further, I understand and agree that my employment is for no definite period and may, regardless of the date of payment of my wages and salary, be terminated at any time without any previous notice.

Date   Signature

DO NOT WRITE BELOW THIS LINE

Interviewed By   Date

REMARKS:

Neatness		Ability	

Hired	For Dept.	Position	Will Report	Salary Wages

Approved: 1   2.   3.

     Employment Manager   Dept. Head   General Manager

FIGURE 6.1 *continued*

leads you can gather on employment possibilities and a list of personal references. A complete dossier will make your writing tasks easier.

For your file, compile a list of the names and addresses of all educational institutions you have attended (high schools, community colleges, universities, trade and vocational schools, and military schools). Note the inclusive dates (months and years) of your attendance. List your degrees, fields of study, outstanding awards, achievements, and grades. Also include records of your employment history: company names, addresses; position titles, dates, and summaries of your responsibilities.

List names, addresses, and phone numbers of prospective references. These may include present and past employers, teachers and professors of courses in your chosen field, recognized leaders in your field with whom you have been in work-oriented contact, clergy, and other professional and experienced men and women who can attest to your skills, abilities, and personal attributes.

Each time you obtain a new skill, such as mastering a word-processing method, earning a certificate for achieving new typing or dictation skills, learning an emergency medical rescue technique, earning a new license, attending a management workshop or seminar, and so on, drop a note into your file.

Also include in your file a list of all prospective employers. You should be active in searching out all of the companies, agencies, or institutions which might have future openings for which you qualify. Some sources for the job search include

1. **Help-wanted Columns.** Read your newspaper classified section to determine the openings in your field. Note the number of openings, the job descriptions, the qualifications, and salary ranges. List the companies and details.

2. **Classified Telephone Directories.** Thumb through the Yellow Pages and list the names of companies or agencies which might be prospective employers.

3. **Civil Service Offices.** Call federal, state, county, and city civil service offices. These offices list government positions in such fields as engineering, building and construction, technology, law enforcement, and parks and recreation. Some offices offer prerecorded recruitment telephone tapes, listing open positions. Others print lists of local, state, and national positions along with qualifications, salaries, and application details.

4. **Trade Magazines and Newspapers.** Buy or subscribe to magazines or newspapers which specialize in your field. These publications often include Help Wanted sections.

5. **Libraries.** Ask the reference librarian to help you locate occupational handbooks, government publications, and newsletters which contain information on openings and qualification requirements in your field.

6. **College Placement Offices.** Visit your college or university career service center. Most offices offer interest inventory tests, career counseling,

computer-assisted career guidance programs, occupational briefs and recruitment brochures, and job files of local, state, and national full- and part-time positions.

7. **Interviews.** Actively arrange to speak to faculty in your major field and people already employed by companies which interest you. They can offer invaluable, practical advice and employment tips.

8. **Employment Agencies.** Many companies do not advertise openings, but put their employment search tasks in the hands of employment agencies and executive search companies. Some agencies specialize in certain types of employment, such as electronics, money and banking, allied health fields, and so on. Incidentally, employers often pay the fee to the agency at no cost to you. Seek those agencies which can help you.

In summary, be informed and realistic about your job prospects. Learn how your qualifications fit the needs of prospective employers.

THE RESUME

Format

Although there are several acceptable formats for an effective resume, all of them are divided by similar sections to provide a complete inventory of your qualifications and experience. For easy preparation and reading, try to contain your information on no more than two pages. The sections will include

- Name, address, and phone
- Career objectives
- Educational background
- Employment experience
- Personal data
- References

Employers skim resumes, sorting out those which are uninteresting or messy. Therefore, you want to present a letter-perfect resume which, due to overall layout, headings, and white space, not only is readable but also quickly highlights your strengths. Copies should be quick-printed on bond paper rather than photocopied. Figure 6.2 shows a sample resume format. Headings may be centered or placed flush left to the margin. The bracketed items are optional, depending on the position for which you are applying.

Resume of
JANE C. DOE

Street address
City, State   Zip
Phone: 000-000-0000

OBJECTIVE

Name of position or broader statement indicating long-term objective

EDUCATION

Month, year to
present

Name of present institution
Street address
City, State   Zip
- Phrase on degree sought, major, and expected date of graduation
- [Several bulleted listings of high accumulated grade point, honors, activities, organizations, certificates earned]

Month, year—
Month, year

Previous schools
Street address
City, State   Zip
- Types of degrees, diplomas, major achievements

Dates

[Miscellaneous educational experiences, such as company courses, correspondence courses, seminars, home study]

EMPLOYMENT

Month, year to
present

Name of company
Street address
City, State   Zip
- Job title
- [Several bulleted phrases which amplify the duties performed, promotions, awards, and, possibly, the reason for leaving]

FIGURE 6.2 *Sample resume format—continues on next page*

Resume of
JANE C. DOE   page 2

Month, year—   Name of company
Month, year   Street address
                      City, State   Zip
                        • Job title
                        • [Several bulleted phrases of amplification]

PERSONAL

Age: years [Day, month, year; place of birth]
[Appearance: Height: Weight:]
Marital Status: Status [If married, spouse's name, number and ages of
                      children]
[Health: State of, significant limitations; date of last check-up]
[Citizenship: Country; work visas]
[Military Status: Rank; Service; date of discharge]
[Residence: Length of state residence; own, rent, live with parents;
                      will or will not relocate]
[Affiliations: Other than religious, list community, fraternal, etc.]
[Special interests: Travel abroad; languages, skills, *no sports*]

REFERENCES

References available upon request [if sending resume to large number of employers]

                                        or

Name, Title   Name, Title
Company or Institution   Company or Institution
Street address   Street address
City, State   Zip   City, State   Zip
Phone: 000-000-0000   Phone: 000-000-0000

Name, Title   Name, Title
Company or Institution   Company or Institution
Street address   Street address
City, State   Zip   City, State   Zip
Phone: 000-000-0000   Phone: 000-000-0000

FIGURE 6.2   *continued*

Names and Addresses

In the upper left-hand corner type "Resume of" and your full, legal name. In the upper right-hand corner type your street address, city, state, zip code, and phone number. Include your area code. You may wish to include both your home and business phones. See Figures 6.2, 6.3 and 6.4 for examples.

Job Objective

Center the heading "Objective" in capital letters and underline it. Beneath it type the exact desired position you are seeking or a brief phrase which spells out your short- and long-term career objectives. Avoid full sentences.

Examples

Legal Secretary

Position in Customer Service or Sales Field

Position in drafting leading to design responsibilities

Electronic Technician with opportunity for advancement into management

Entry-level position in data processing leading to computer programming

Educational Background

If your educational preparation is stronger than your employment experience, develop this section first. Type the heading "Education." Beneath it begin with your most recent school and list all other schools in reverse chronological order. List the inclusive dates, including the months, in one column. In another column include the names of the institutions, addresses, cities, states, and zip codes. Cite your major field of study, degrees earned or expected, and graduation dates. Highlight your academic record (if high), awards, special activities, organizations, special skills, and job-related courses. Include only those achievements, however, which are slanted towards the job. A prospective employer in banking might be impressed if you were treasurer of your student government association, but would not care if you were on the tennis team.

Employment Experience

If your previous employment is more indicative of your qualifications, place this section before your educational data. Type the heading "Employment" or "Work Experience" in capital letters. Beneath it begin with your present or most recent employment and work backward in time.

Resume of   11701 Southwest Tenth Place
JOANNE L. FATA   Fort Lauderdale, Florida   33325
                                   305-475-9641

OBJECTIVE

Medical laboratory technician at a modern,
expanding hospital laboratory

August 1987—   Broward Community College/Central
  to present   3501 Southwest Davie Road
                                   Fort Lauderdale, Florida 33314
                                   - Majoring in Medical Laboratory Technology;
                                     will receive Associate in Science degree
                                   - Grade-point average: 3.1 of 4.0
                                   - Special Courses: Advanced Instrumentation,
                                     Advanced Medical Laboratory Techniques,
                                     Advanced Mycology, Technical Report Writing

November 1986—   Sheridan Vocational Center
  November 1987   5400 Sheridan Street
                                   Hollywood, Florida 33021
                                   - Completed the NAACLS accredited, 12-month
                                     Certified Laboratory Assistant program

EMPLOYMENT

August 1989—   Florida Medical Center
  to present   5000 West Oakland Park Boulevard
                                   Fort Lauderdale, Florida 33313
                                   - Laboratory Technician in Hematology
                                   - Responsible for early morning start-up
                                     procedures on the Coulter Model S-Plus, Model
                                     S, Coulter Diff 3 System, and Coag-A-Mate
                                   - Perform routine Urinalyses and Serology
                                     procedures
                                   - Experienced in Whole Blood Calibration
                                     procedures
                                   - Experienced in patient blood-drawing
                                     procedures

FIGURE 6.3   *Sample resume of a student*—*continues on next page* (Courtesy of Joanne L. Fata)

Resume of   Page 2
JOANNE L. FATA

February 1978–   Robert G. Talley, M.D.P.A.
  April 1989   912 East Broward Boulevard
                     Fort Lauderdale, Florida 33301

- Responsible for all laboratory procedures including manual chemistry tests for Glucose, BUN, SGOT, Alkaline Phosphatase, Uric Acid, and Cholesterol
- Performed routine urinalysis, manual CBC's, and differentials
- Reason for leaving: Registered as full-time student for three months.

PERSONAL

Age: 24   Health: Excellent   Marital Status: Single
Affiliation: American Society of Clinical Pathologists
                     Willing to relocate

REFERENCES

Ms. Rebecca Meehan, MT (ASCP)   Robert G. Talley, M.D.P.A.
Chief Laboratory Technologist   912 East Broward Boulevard
Florida Medical Center   Fort Lauderdale, Florida   33301
5000 West Oakland Park Boulevard   305-463-5271
Fort Lauderdale, Florida   33313
305-735-6000

Ms. Karen Mead, MT (ASCP)   Ms. Barbara L. Kremp, MT (ASCP)
Hematology Supervisor   Broward Community College
Florida Medical Center   Central Campus
5000 West Oakland Park Boulevard   Allied Health Department
Fort Lauderdale, Florida   33313   3501 Southwest Davie Road
305-735-6000   305-581-8700

FIGURE 6.3   *continued*

Resume of   7661 Hood Street
SANDRA J. BURNETTE   Albuquerque, NM   87123
                                                   305-962-2365

OBJECTIVE

Seeking an entry-level position in your data processing department leading to a
  computer programming position

PERSONAL

Date of birth: June 5, 1970   New Mexico residency: 5 years
Marital status: Married; no children   Health: excellent

EDUCATION

January 198X   Albuquerque Vocational-Technical Institute
  to present   525 Buena Vista SE
                        Albuquerque, NM   87106
                          ● Majoring in Data Processing
                          ● Will earn Associate of Science degree in August 1992
                          ● GPA: 4.0 of possible 4.0
                          ● Major courses: Programming in Basic, Programming
                            in Cobol, Professional Writing, Intermediate Algebra,
                            Fundamentals of Data Processing
                          ● CLEP credit: Introductory Accounting I and II
                          ● Award: President's list

August 198X–   Sheridan Vocational Center
  January 198X   5400 Sheridan Street
                        Hollywood, FL   33020
                          ● Completed Bookkeeping Systems Program
                          ● Completed a two-semester course in one semester
                          ● Major courses: Advanced Accounting, Microcomputer
                            Applications

September 198X–   Cardinal High School
  June 198X   Thompson Avenue
                        Middlefield, OH   44062
                          ● GPA: 3.89 of possible 4.0
                          ● Major courses: Bookkeeping, Typing, Business
                            English and Communications, Shorthand
                          ● Awards: Valedictorian, National Honor Society,
                            Scholastic Team

FIGURE 6.4 *Sample resume of a student—continues on next page* (Courtesy of Sandra J. Burnette)

SANDRA J. BURNETTE continued Page 2

EXPERIENCE

February 198X–
July 198X

D & J Construction, Incorporated
5155 Southwest Sixty-fourth Avenue
Davie, FL 33315
305-587-2360

- Maintained sales, cash receipts, cash payments, journals, accounts payable sub-ledger
- Completed weekly payroll for sixty employees
- Completed associated quarterly payroll tax forms
- Maintained personnel and group insurance records for sixty employees
- Prepared quarterly reports and summaries for use by accounting firm
- Conducted interviews for my replacement

August 198X–
July 198X

Southern Door Company
3600 North Twenty-ninth Avenue
Hollywood, FL 33021
305-922-6747

- Assistant Bookkeeper
- Maintained Accounts Receivable sub-ledger
- Completed weekly payroll for forty employees
- Maintained raw materials inventory
- Performed customer service duties

198X to 198X

Part time secretarial and clerical positions for three insurance companies and a rubber manufacturing firm

REFERENCES

Mrs. Deanna J. Siegel
Controller
Southern Door Company
3600 North Twenty-ninth Avenue
Hollywood, FL 33021
305-922-6747

Mr. Frank Pittnaro
Certified Public Accountant
William Webb and Associates
400 E. Adobe Road
Albuquerque, NM 87107
505-921-9999

Mrs. Eileen Duffie
Bookkeeping Systems Teacher
Sheridan Vocational Center
5400 Sheridan Street
Hollywood, FL 33020
305-963-8600

Mr. Jack Attaway
Vice-president
D & J Construction, Inc.
5115 Southwest 64th Avenue
Davie, FL 33314
305-587-2360

FIGURE 6.4 *continued*

Include the inclusive dates, including months, in one column. Employers are often looking for gaps in both education and employment histories. A continuous record of employment or education suggests that you are a responsible individual with work-oriented goals. In another column include the names of the companies, addresses, cities, states, zip codes, and phone numbers. List your position titles and whether the work was part- or full-time. Using brief phrases ("Responsible for . . . ," "Implemented . . . ," "Maintained . . ."), highlight your duties, achievements, and awards. You may want to list your reason for leaving ("Offered higher-paying position," "Returned to college full-time").

Personal Data

Type the heading "Personal." Consider what data your prospective employer wants to know. At the least include your age, marital status, and general health status. Decide whether to include your place of birth, length of local residency, ownership of home, relocation willingness, military service, community affiliations, and special skills and interests other than sports. You may list these in tabular form as shown in Figures 6.3, 6.4, and 6.5.

References

Type the heading "References." If you are submitting your resume to a large number of employers, it will be wise to write only "References will be furnished upon request." Otherwise each reference may be unduly bothered by spot checks from many companies. If you are selective about your application, list four or five people who can supply strong, positive assessments of your qualifications and character. Obtain permission in advance to list anyone as a reference. Select present or past employers, college instructors, clergy, and other community leaders. Do not include relatives. Type the name, position, company affiliation, street address, city, state, zip code, and phone number of each reference.

Figures 6.3, 6.4, and 6.5 illustrate sample resumes. Figure 6.3 is a resume of a typical college student earning an associate degree in an allied health field. Figure 6.4 is a resume of a mature student with wider experience and training than a recent college graduate. Figure 6.5 illustrates an alternative format.

COVER LETTER

A cover letter, also called a *letter of application* or a *face letter*, accompanies your resume and serves both as an introduction of yourself and as a strategy to interest employers sufficiently to read your resume and to

Resume of   7061 Tyler Street
KENTON L. LAIRD   Hollywood, FL 33055
                                               Hm: 305-962-2365
                                               Bus: 305-472-1212

Objective

Electronic Technician in computer application company

Experience

June 198X to Present

Senior Field Engineer. Field Engineer of the Year Award. Maintained inventory control system for parts and complete units. Controlled expense system for service area. Assigned product responsibility for Beta and Gamma printers, VT-100, and Ace 5600 video terminals.

(Ace Communications Corporation, 201 South Johnson Street, Hollywood, Florida   33051)

June 197X to August 198X

Supervisor of Maintenance and Mechanical Equipment. Supervised 15 machinists. Charged with responsibility of keeping machinery and vehicles running in a plant employing 2000 on each shift. Products: electronic equipment used in modern medical laboratories.

(Greer Corporation, 4000 Palmetto Park Road, Miami, Florida, 31302)

May 197X to May 197X

United States Air Force. Maintained surveillance equipment on reconnaissance aircraft. At fighter base in Thailand assigned both aircraft and in-shop repairs; equipment included multi-channel tape recorders, radar receivers, signal analyzers, direction finders, and radio-jamming devices.

FIGURE 6.5 *Sample alternate resume format*—*continues on next page*

Resume of Kenton L. Laird continued   Page 2

Education

    June 198X to Present   Broward Community College
                                      Fort Lauderdale, FL   33314

    Seeking Associate in Science degree in Electronic Technology with
a GPA of 3.7 out of possible 4.0. Expect to be graduated May 198X.
Member of Association of Computing Machinery.

    August 197X to May 197X   Keesler Air Force Base
                                        Biloxi, MS   50001

    Graduated with honors in Basic Electronics and Electronic
Counter Measures courses.

    August 197X to June 197X   Grant High School
                                        Dayton, Ohio   70012

Personal

Age:	25	Marital Status:	Single
Languages:	Fluent Spanish;	Military:	Staff Sargeant,
	Some Italian		U.S. Air Force;
			Honorably discharged;
			May 198X

References
Business and personal references will be furnished upon request. DO
NOT CONTACT PRESENT EMPLOYER AT THIS TIME.

FIGURE 6.5 *continued*

grant you an interview. The letter should reflect your personality and emphasize your potential. While a model letter may be developed, each letter should be tailored to a particular prospective employer.

Each letter should be individually typed on bond paper of the same quality as your resume. Address your letter to a specific name, if possible.

Your opening paragraph must attract the reader's attention without being overly aggressive or "cute." You must indicate the position or type of employment you are seeking and refer to your enclosed resume. You may want to mention how you learned of the position and subtly praise the company. Consider these opening paragraphs:

> I am an ideal candidate for the electronics technician position which you advertised in the July 2 edition of The Miami Herald. My two years of experience in the field and an Associate of Science degree in Electronic Technology qualify me for employment with your progressive corporation. My enclosed resume amplifies my background.

> Mr. Jack Smith, Chair of the Data Processing Department at Broward Community College, has alerted me that there will be a computer technician opening in your computer maintenance group. As my resume details, my specific qualifications prove that I would be an asset to your organization.

Your body paragraph(s) should summarize and emphasize your specific qualifications and personal qualities as they relate to the position. Use an enthusiastic tone and project self-confidence. Mention your outstanding personal attributes. Consider this sample:

> I can offer you four years of experience in employment and education. I will earn my Associate of Science degree in radiology technology this May and have been employed as a medical assistant to Dr. James E. Perry, radiologist, here in Fort Lauderdale for two years. My personal attributes include determination, courtesy, and attention to detail.

The body material should be short, direct, and persuasive.

Your closing paragraphs should urge action on the part of the reader. Ask for an interview or suggest that you will phone shortly to arrange for an interview. If it is appropriate, seek additional information, applications, and so on. Mention your flexibility and availability. Consider these closings:

> May I have a personal interview to discuss your position and my qualifications? I will call your office on Monday to arrange a convenient date.

> I would welcome your consideration for an entry-level position and can start work any time next month. Any information you may have regarding my prospects with your company will be greatly appreciated. You may reach me after 3:00 P.M. weekdays at the number listed on my resume to arrange an interview.

Figures 6.6 and 6.7 show the complete texts of sample cover letters.

7661 Hood Street
Troy, NY 12181
July 6, 199X

Mr. Jerry Diener
Personnel Director
American Express Company
777 American Expressway
Plantation, FL   33324

Dear Mr. Diener:

I am an applicant for an entry-level position in your data processing
department. Dr. Ted Smith, head of the Data Processing Department at
Queens Community College, South campus, has told me about your
progressive practices, and I believe I can offer a substantial contribution
to American Express Company. My resume highlights my qualifications.

My main experience is in the accounting field. To further my understanding
of the complete accounting cycle, I enrolled in 198X at Hudson Valley
Community College in Troy, New York. At that time I received my first
exposure to computers. I found that I have a natural ability for the logical
thinking that is required for a good computer programmer. Because a career
in computer programming seems the ideal goal for me, I am now working
towards my A.S. degree in data processing and will be graduated this August.

I will call you on Wednesday, July 13, to arrange an appointment for an
interview.

Yours truly,

Sandra J. Burnette

Sandra J. Burnette

SJB

Enc: 1

FIGURE 6.6 *Sample cover letter* (Courtesy of student Sandra J. Burnette)

5000 Griffin Road
Hickory, NC   28603
May 2, 199X

Mr. J.W. Duran
Attorney-at-law
346 North Andrews Avenue
Hickory, NC   28603

Dear Mr. Duran:

Please consider my application for the position of legal secretary which you advertised in the May 1 edition of the Hickory Sentinel. I am the "trained professional who can perform a variety of office duties" you seek. My training in legal techniques, business law, and legal secretary practices plus considerable experience as a general secretary for Ace Construction Company definitely meet your qualifications. My complete resume is attached.

I will be graduated on June 9, 199X, from Catawa Valley Technical College with an associate degree in Legal Secretarial Science. In addition to the required courses of this program, I have studied word processing software techniques. My shorthand rate is 120 words per minute, and I type at 65 words a minute.

In addition to specialized training, I can offer you three years of experience in general office work, bookkeeping, and salesmanship. You will find me to be reliable, efficient, and personable.

I trust you will consider me for your position. May I have a personal interview at your convenience? I may be reached by telephone between noon and 5:00 P.M. at 583-4771.

Very truly yours,

Sharon Cates

Sharon Cates

SC

Enclosure

FIGURE 6.7 *Sample cover letter*

INTERVIEWS

An interview is the final step in job hunting. Here your prospective employer evaluates you—your appearance, your personality, and your ability. Chapter 17 discusses a number of verbal strategies to employ in an interview, but a few tips are timely here.

1. **Be prepared.** In advance, learn as much as you can about the company so that you can project your interest and ask informed questions. Take a copy of your resume along to refresh your memory in response to direct questions about your background.

2. **Dress appropriately.** Although you will generally dress neatly and conservatively (a suit, a tie, a dark dress, hose and heels), wear one article which is eye-catching and memorable. This might be a striped tie, a lapel rose, or an unusual, but not showy, piece of jewelry.

3. **Be on time.** Know the exact time and location of your interview. Arrive a few minutes early and state your name and purpose to the secretary, receptionist, or actual employer.

4. **Don't smoke.** You may be offered a cigarette, but refrain from accepting it. Spilled ashes, clouds of smoke, and ungainly stretches to an ashtray do not create a favorable impression.

EXERCISES

1. Using the following information, type the Employment section of a resume. Use a heading and arrange the data in a readable format. The applicant is seeking a position as an electronics technician with the opportunity for advancement. (1) His first job was as an auto mechanic with Bird Ford Agency, 101 North Federal Highway, Fort Lauderdale, Florida, where he serviced cars and was responsible for all radio repair. He was employed at Bird for two years, January to January. Add zip codes to the addresses. (2) Next, he worked from February 198X to May 198X (1½ years) as a supervisor of mechanical maintenance at Borg Corporation, 6024 Southwest 50th Street, Miami, Florida. There he trained assistants and received The Worker of the Year Award. (3) The applicant is presently employed as a service manager for Ace Automation Company, 1102 Broad Way, Pompano, Florida, where he supervises workers in all aspects of repair and service. He began work at Ace in June 199X.

2. Revise the following cover letter content to make it more assertive, specific, and persuasive. The applicant is seeking a position as a draftsperson with a large, architectural firm.

Pursuant to your recent ad, I am applying for a job with your company. I don't have much experience but am willing to learn. I will be graduated from college this June, and although I changed my major three times, I will earn a degree in drafting technology.

I have studied some very pertinent courses and held a number of part-time jobs with local architects learning about materials, office procedures, and on-site supervision. I think I have a pretty good design ability and am a careful draftsperson.

I realize you want a more experienced person, but I would like to talk to you about myself.

3. Compile an employment dossier on yourself. List all of the companies where you have been employed. Note the inclusive dates, complete address, and your position titles. List all of your responsibilities, promotions, achievements, and awards.

Next, collect your educational records. Obtain the addresses of all schools attended and your final report cards and college transcripts. Figure out your accumulated grade point average. Underline those courses which are job-oriented. Assemble and/or list your extracurricular activities, recognition or reward certificates, and so on.

Clip newspaper and trade magazine Help Wanted ads in your field. Photocopy the Yellow Pages which list companies which might employ you. Arrange an interview with a career counselor, employment agency representative, or someone in your desired line of work. Take notes and file them in your dossier.

List your three greatest character and work-related strengths.

Include your military records, community organization data, and other pertinent records.

4. Speak to four past employers, faculty members, or other community leaders about supplying letters of reference for you. Inform the prospects about the type of employment you are seeking. Ask each to write a general letter addressed to "To Whom It May Concern" attesting to your qualifications and character.

WRITING OPTIONS

1. Using the sample resume format or any of the three sample resumes in this chapter, write a personal resume for a particular position which you could fill immediately while you continue your college education. Include four references.

2. Using the sample resume format or any of the three sample resumes in this chapter, write a personal resume for a full-time position. Assume that you were graduated last month so that you have completed the courses and earned the requisite degree for your chosen career. Include four references.

3. Write a cover letter to a specific person at a specific company, agency, or institution. Be brief, persuasive, and self-confident.

4. Exchange cover letters with another student and write a negative response to the cover letter. Pretend you are a Director of Personnel and that the applicant either lacks the position qualifications, or fulfills the qualifications but no positions are available at this time. Review the strategies for negative response letters which are discussed in Chapter 5.

NOTES

CHAPTER 7

Brief Reports

DUFFY   by Bruce Hammond

© 1983 Universal Press Syndicate. By permission.

INTRODUCTION

In the working world the writing of informal and formal reports is an everyday task. Although your particular job description may not detail your writing responsibilities, helping to keep the written record is everyone's duty.

Reports record the events and progress of work. They assist management in making decisions, or they may become working documents to help employees carry on a program.

Types of Reports

Many companies print forms for the types of reports which are required most often, such as accident report forms, travel expense forms, work logs, leave request forms, and so forth. Figures 7.1, 7.2 and 7.3 show typical printed report forms.

Because the information required for other reports is so variable, you must learn to devise your own written accounts. It is helpful to classify reports. Here is a list of typical reports required in business and industry:

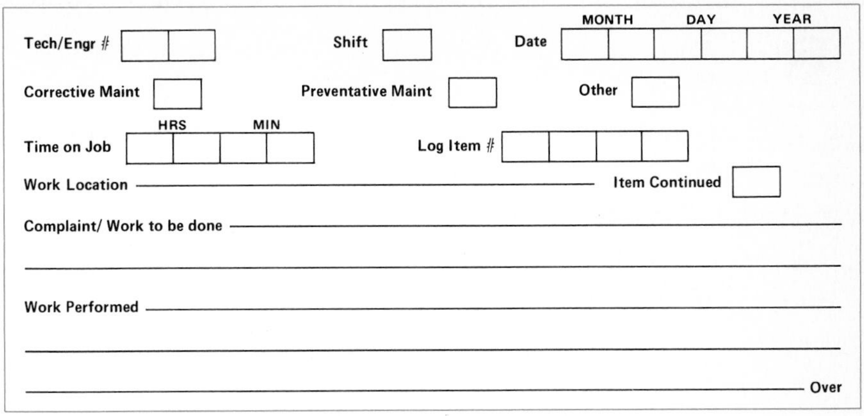

Tech/Engr # Shift Date MONTH DAY YEAR

Corrective Maint Preventative Maint Other

Time on Job HRS MIN Log Item #

Work Location Item Continued

Complaint/ Work to be done

Work Performed

Over

FIGURE 7.1 ***Typical preprinted work log report***

- Expense report (an itemized accounting of all expenses incurred while performing duties, such as promoting sales, attending conferences, or inspecting field progress).
- Feasibility report (sometimes called an *analytical report*; the written evaluation of data to determine the practicality of future products, expansion programs, new equipment or services).
- Field report (the written analysis of data to determine appropriate action, such as estimating real estate value, determining service costs, or establishing claims for damage).
- Incident report (sometimes called an *investigative report*; the written record of an unforeseen occurrence, such as accidents, machine breakdowns, delivery delays, cost overruns, production slowdowns, or personnel problems).
- Laboratory report (sometimes called a *test report*; the written results of laboratory or testing experimentation).
- Periodic or progress report (the written information on the status of a project).

Reports may vary from a few sentences in a memorandum or on a preprinted form to several volumes in bound folders, but all share common elements of organization, format, and presentation. By reviewing these elements in five common types of reports, you should attain the skills which apply to writing short reports. Chapter 8 will discuss longer reports and their special features.

Format

The organization of data in each type of report follows fairly uniform formats. The purpose and audience of your report will determine if you will present your report in a memo or letter, or in a separate, titled report. If the report is lengthy, you will want to consider a cover letter,

RYDER TRUCK RENTAL, INC.

TRAVEL EXPENSE REPORT

VENDOR NUMBER	REFERENCE NUMBER	LOC. CODE	MO. REC.

NAME _____

TITLE _____

WEEK ENDING _____

VEHICLE NUMBER	ACCOUNT NUMBER	AMOUNT

AIR TRAVEL CHARGED TO RYDER (FOR H.Q. AND REGION MANAGER USE ONLY)		
TICKET NUMBER (last 3 digits)	TICKET DATE	TICKET AMOUNT
		$

W/E DATE		TOTAL AMOUNT	

BUSINESS PURPOSE OF EACH TRIP

DATE OF		EXPLANATION (IF NOT CHECKED BELOW)
DEPART.	RETURN	
		☐ VISIT TO COMPANY LOCATION ☐ SALES CALL
		☐ VISIT TO COMPANY LOCATION ☐ SALES CALL
		☐ VISIT TO COMPANY LOCATION ☐ SALES CALL

	DATE	SUN	MON	TUES	WED	THURS	FRI	SAT	TOTAL
DAILY ITINERARY	FROM								
	TO								
	TO								
AIR TRAVEL PAID BY EMPLOYEE									
CAR RENTAL*									
PERSONAL CAR EXPENSE (DETAIL ON REVERSE SIDE)									
ROOM*									
MEALS PLUS TIPS**									
COMPANY CAR EXPENSE (DETAIL ON REVERSE SIDE)*									
MISCELLANEOUS (DETAIL ON REVERSE SIDE)									
ENTERTAINMENT (DETAIL ON REVERSE SIDE)**									
TOTAL									

ACCOUNTING FOR ADVANCES			
ADVANCE RECEIVED			
EXPENSES THIS VOUCHER			
BALANCE DUE COMPANY			
OR BALANCE DUE TRAVELER			

* ATTACH RECEIPTS
** INCLUDE ENTERTAINMENT MEALS ON REVERSE

IN ADDITION TO THE REQUIRED RECEIPTS AS SPECIFIED ABOVE, RECEIPTS FOR EACH EXPENDITURE OF $25.00 OR MORE MUST BE ATTACHED.

TRAVELER'S SIGNATURE

APPROVED BY (SIGNATURE)

6-22 (11/80)   SIDE ONE   10395   Litho By R In U.S.A.

FIGURE 7.2 *Typical preprinted travel expense report* (Courtesy of Ryder Truck Rental, Inc.)

PERSONAL CAR EXPENSE									
DATE	SUN	MON	TUES	WED	THURS	FRI	SAT	TOTAL	
ODOMETER READING-ENDING									
ODOMETER READING – BEGINNING									
MILEAGE									
LESS PERSONAL MILEAGE									
NET COMPANY MILEAGE									
AMOUNT AT _____ ¢ PER MILE									

DATE	AMOUNT	VEHICLE NO.	COMPANY CAR EXPENSE (DETAIL BELOW)

DATE	AMOUNT	MISCELLANEOUS (DETAIL BELOW)

ENTERTAINMENT EXPENSE					
DATE	AMOUNT	TYPE OF ENTERTAIN- MENT	PLACE NAME, ADDRESS, OR LOCATION	BUSINESS RELATIONSHIP OF INDIVIDUALS OR GROUP ENTERTAINED (Give Name, Title, Etc., Include Names of Co. Employees.)	BUSINESS PURPOSE Date, Duration, Place, and Nature of Associated Business Discussion or how otherwise related to active conduct of the business.

SIDE TWO

FIGURE 7.2 *continued*

REQUEST FOR LEAVE OF ABSENCE*
FIRE DEPARTMENT
NAME _____

                               Last   First

DATE _____

*1   Leave requests for vacation and anticipated leaves must be submitted two weeks prior to requested starting date.

*2   Leave requests for sick leave and emergency leave must be submitted by 9:00 A.M. the day before your shift works.

_____

                                                 Signature

<u>LEAVE CODES</u>   Department _____

V   — Vacation   _____ Days _____ from _____ to
S   — Sick with pay   Code
FS   — Family Sick with pay
I   — Job Injury with pay   _____ (inclusive dates).
Z   — Sick without pay
W   — Personal Absence w/o pay   _____ Days pay in advance requested on
A   — Absence w/o leave
PG   — Maternity Leave w/o pay   _____ (last shift worked).
FL   — Funeral Leave with pay (next of kin)   Date
M   — Military Leave (calendar days)
CL   — Conference Leave   Regular pay checks of: _____
JD   — Jury Duty
SV   — Vacation from Sick   _____
MV   — Management Vacation
CT   — Comp Time   Explanation _____

                                   _____

STATION OFFICERS SIGNATURE NECESSARY FOR SICK LEAVE.

                         DISAPPROVED
                         APPROVED   _____
                                          Station Officer

DISAPPROVED   DISAPPROVED
APPROVED   _____   APPROVED   _____
                    Commander   Chief Officer

FORM AA-108 Rev. 4/82

FIGURE 7.3   *Typical preprinted leave request form*
(Courtesy of Fort Lauderdale, Florida, Fire Department)

an abstract, table of contents, and appendixed exhibits. These elements will be discussed in Chapter 8. Chapter 1 lists visual devices which will make your message more readable. Devices such as topical headings, capital letters, underlining, variable spacing, numbers, and bullets can enhance even the briefest report. Make your report convey its message as clearly and concisely as possible.

Graphics

Besides planning your format (organization, headings, and other visuals) you should consider incorporating graphics to present your data. Study your message to determine if informal tables, formal tables, circle graphs, simple drawings, maps, charts, and other graphics will present the information more clearly than lengthy paragraphs of explanation. An incident report detailing a work-related accident might include a brief location diagram and an informal table of repair or replacement costs. A progress report may call for a formal table of materials, costs, or scheduling dates. A lab or test report will best display testing results in tables or performance curves. A feasibility report may include the results of surveys presented in circle graphs, bar charts, or tables. Further, tables comparing features of optional equipment may be appropriate. Be alert to graphic possibilities.

Language

As in all professional writing, your language should be factual and objective. Avoid opinionated or judgmental language. Consider this biased paragraph from an accident report:

> A minor accident occurred at the Central Piedmont Community College Central Campus Library recently. Librarian Neil Springer carelessly overturned a cup of coffee on the microfilm machine which resulted in a massive short circuit when the machine was turned on. Luckily, there were no personal injuries.

The emphasis here is on blame rather than on the incident itself. An improved version would emphasize the facts:

> An explosion occurred on the second floor, east wing of the Central Piedmont Community College Central Campus Library on June 13, 199X, at 3:42 P.M.
>
> The cause of the explosion was an overturned cup of coffee spilled by Librarian Neil Springer onto an Acme 710 microfilm projector (Inventory #703–11201–8). The liquid penetrated the felt light seals and dripped onto the main power supply resulting in an explosive short circuit when the machine was turned on by student Mary Phillips.
>
> Although there were no personal injuries, damages to the machine and surrounding area total $480.00.

The revised version contains more essential facts and presents them in an unbiased manner.

INCIDENT REPORTS

Purpose

No matter where you work, the unexpected frequently occurs. Such digression from normal operating procedure generally requires an incident report to supervisors or others to prevent the incident from recurring. The incident report is a written investigation of accidents, machine breakdowns, delivery delays, cost overruns, production slowdowns, or personnel problems.

The incident report may be reviewed when the next budget is planned if your recommendations involve finances. The report may constitute the basis of a longer proposal to improve procedures. It may even be used as legal evidence in a follow-up investigation. A carefully detailed report becomes part of the written record of what goes on in your place of work.

Organization

The incident report adheres to fairly conventional organization. Its parts cover

- What happened (factual, not opinionated)
- What caused it (detailed and chronological)
- What were the results (injuries, losses, delays, costs)
- What can be done to prevent recurrence (recommendations)

In a lengthy incident report it is a good idea to include topical headings, such as

Incident		Accident Description
Cause	or	Analysis of Causes
Results		Corrective Action
Recommendations		Recommendations

Your reader will be able to cull the appropriate information quickly by glancing at the headings.

Incident Description. In your introductory material, write a concrete statement detailing what happened. Include the exact date, time, and location. Personnel details, such as employees' names, titles, and departments, should be included. If personal injuries occurred, include the name(s) of victim(s), titles, and departments, or in the case of victims who are not employees, include home addresses, phone numbers, and places of employment. Describe the actual injury. If equipment is involved, identify it by including brand names, serial numbers, inventory numbers, or other pertinent descriptive detail.

Analysis of Causes. In this section write a chronological review of what caused the incident. Include what was happening prior to the incident and each step which caused the incident.

Results. In this section, explain what happened due to the incident, such as the action which was taken immediately. If anyone was injured, describe the extent of the injury and how, when, and where the person was treated. Explain who was immediately involved. This may include paramedics, police, repair experts, or extra workers. In the case of equipment failure, explain how it was repaired or replaced, how late deliveries were speeded, or how high costs were curtailed. Detail what was done to settle a personnel problem or to satisfy a customer demand.

The results section may require an actual or estimated expense review. Include a precise breakdown of medical expenses, equipment replacement, repair costs, profit loss, or other applicable costs.

Recommendations. This section should include concrete suggestions to prevent the incident from recurring. Consider what should be done, who should do it, and when it should be done. Include as much detail as your position authorizes.

Figure 7.4 shows a preprinted accident report which illustrates the conventional organizational format.

Figure 7.5 shows the narrative portion of a fire incident report. Page one of the report, which is not included in the sample, is a printed checklist which serves as a record of location, method of alarm, fire origin, extent of damage, and other pertinent details.

Figure 7.6 shows a brief incident report illustrating logical organization and detail. The incident, a fall and supplies breakage, requires a replacement breakdown, which is presented in an easy-to-read continuation table.

Figure 7.7 shows an incident report with topical headings and numbered recommendations. In each the message is complete, objective, and concise.

OCCUPATIONAL INJURY AND ANALYSIS REPORT — EASTERN

ABG 70568 OPR-150 REV. 6/81

CAUTION — NCR PAPER
PLEASE PRINT - COMPLETE IN DETAIL

Refer to SP 52-202

REPORING DIVISION: ☐ MAINTENANCE ☐ SALES & SERVICE ☐ OTHER

EMPLOYEE DATA

EMPLOYEE NAME - LAST	FIRST	M.I.	EMPLOYEE NO.	DATE OF BIRTH	SEX	SOCIAL SECURITY NO.	EMPLOYMENT DATE	BASE STATION

STREET ADDRESS	CITY	STATE	ZIP CODE	HOME PHONE NO./AREA CODE	JOB CLASS	COST CENTER NAME	COST CENTER NO.

NO. DEPENDENTS UNDER 18	MARITAL STATUS ☐ SINGLE ☐ MARRIED ☐ DIVORCED ☐ WIDOWED	CONSECTUIVE DAYS ON DUTY	SCHEDULED DAYS OFF	DATE OF INJURY	TIME OF INJURY

LENGTH OF TIME ON DUTY ☐ 1 HR. OR LESS ☐ 1-4 HRS. ☐ 4-8 HRS. ☐ OVER 8 HRS.	DAY OF WEEK	REPORTED TO SUPERVISOR DATE: ______ TIME: ______	INJURY PAST TWELVE MONTHS ☐ 1st. ☐ 2nd. ☐ 3rd. ☐ 4th. ☐ RECURRENT ☐ MORE

NAME OF IMMEDIATE SUPERVISOR	TITLE	COMAIL ADDRESS	EXTENSION NO.

SUPERVISOR'S INVESTIGATION

1 - PART OF BODY AFFECTED
☐ HEAD/FACE ☐ HAND/FINGERS ☐ FEET/TOES ☐ SHOULDER ☐ BACK ☐ LEG ☐ EYE ☐ WRIST ☐ KNEE ☐ ANKLE ☐ NECK ☐ ELBOW ☐ CHEST ☐ OTHER (specify)

2 - TYPE OF INJURY
☐ BRUISE ☐ BURN ☐ SPRAIN ☐ RASH ☐ HERNIA ☐ FRACTURE ☐ CUT ABRASION ☐ MULTIPLE INJURIES ☐ AMPUTATION ☐ OTHER (specify)

3 - SPECIFIC TASK
☐ PUSHING ☐ PULLING ☐ LIFTING ☐ KNEELING ☐ REACHING ☐ SLIPPING ☐ TRIPPED ☐ FALL FROM ELEVATION ☐ CAUGHT BETWEEN ☐ STRUCK AGAINST OBJECT ☐ STRUCK BY OBJECT ☐ OTHER (specify)

4 - EQUIPMENT INVOLVED
VEHICLE NO. ______
☐ BENT LOADER ☐ LOADER LIFTER ☐ FUEL TRUCK ☐ FUEL PUMPER (Hydrant) ☐ CONTAINER TYPE ______ ☐ V BED CART ☐ LAV TRUCK ☐ PORTABLE STEPS ☐ DOLLIE ☐ CLEANING VAN ☐ POWER CART ☐ JETWAY ☐ TRACTOR ☐ COVERED CART ☐ OTHER (specify)

5 - AIRCRAFT INVOLVED
AIRCRAFT NO. ______
☐ A300 ☐ DC9 ☐ B727 ☐ L1011 ☐ OTHER (specify)

6 - LOCATION OF ACCIDENT
☐ BAG ROOM ☐ BAG ROOM BELT ☐ AIR FREIGHT ☐ LOADING DOCK ☐ RAMP ☐ ACFT GALLEY ☐ CLAIM AREA ☐ TICKET COUNTER ☐ INSIDE VEHICLE/VAN ☐ ACFT REAR STAIRS ☐ ACFT FWD STAIRS ☐ ACFT CABIN ☐ ACFT BELLY ☐ FWD BIN ☐ AFT BIN ☐ BIN 3 ☐ OTHER (specify)

7 - OBJECT INVOLVED
WEIGHT OF OBJECT ______ lbs.
☐ BAGGAGE ☐ COMAT ☐ FREIGHT ☐ MAIL ☐ HUMAN REMAINS ☐ TRASH CONTAINER ______ GAL SIZE ☐ INVALID PSGR. ☐ LIQUOR KITS ☐ LIQUOR PIGS ☐ COST CUTTER WGT. ______ AMT. ______ ☐ OTHER (specify)

8 — NARRATIVE - WHAT WAS EMPLOYEE DOING WHEN INJURED? DESCRIBE EVENTS AND NATURE OF INJURY FULLY. IF EQUIPMENT MALFUNCTIONED, EXPLAIN.

9 — CORRECTIVE ACTION YOU HAVE TAKEN OR WILL TAKE TO PREVENT RECURRENCE OF ACCIDENTS OF THIS TYPE

M.D. OR R.N. REPORT

☐ RETURNED TO WORK ☐ TREATED BY PHYSICIAN ☐ FIRST AID TREATMENT ONLY ☐ NOT RETURNED TO WORK (see remarks) ☐ RETURNED FOR ADDITIONAL TREATMENT DATE: ☐ RETURNED TO WORK WITH LIMITATIONS (see remarks) ☐ ADMITTED TO HOSPITAL

REMARKS:	NAME OF ATTENDING PHYSICIAN OR NURSE ☐ M.D. ☐ R.N.	(AREA CODE) TELEPHONE NO.	DATE

SUPV. FOLLOW-UP

DID EMPLOYEE RETURN TO WORK ON NEXT SCHEDULED SHIFT? ☐ YES ☐ NO	WITH MEDICAL LIMITATIONS ☐ YES ☐ NO	WAS EMPLOYEE TRANSFERRED TO ANOTHER JOB? ☐ YES ☐ NO	IF YES, WAS IT: ☐ TEMPORARY ☐ PERMANENT	☐ I HAVE PERSONALLY INVESTIGATED THIS ACCIDENT AND VERIFY IT OCCURRED AS DESCRIBED

☐ I AM UNABLE TO VERIFY THIS ACCIDENT AS DESCRIBED BY EMPLOYEE FOR THE FOLLOWING REASONS:	REASON(S)

REVIEW

PREPARED BY (SIGNATURE)	TITLE	EXTENSION NO.	DATE
EMPLOYEE'S SIGNATURE	POSITION	EXTENSION NO.	DATE
MANAGER'S SIGNATURE	TITLE	EXTENSION NO.	DATE

DISTRIBUTION: ORIGINAL (white) – Local File (5 years) DUPLICATE (yellow) – Ground Safety, MIAGS TRIPLICATE (pink) – Worker's Compensation, MIAWC

FIGURE 7.4 *Typical preprinted accident report*

REMOVE CARBON

Station __2__ District __k__ Company __E-2__ 10-8 __1407__ 10-10 __1438__ Hi-Rise __No__

Mileage __5__ Code __3__ Out of City __No__ Damage H M L N # Floors __1__

Condition on Arrival: Smoke H M L N   Flames H M L N

APPLIANCES USED	EXTINGUISHING AGENTS USED		HOSE LINES USED
_____ Deluge Gun	_____ Wetwater	_____ Gals.	_____ Booster Line
_____ Deck Turret	_____ Foam	_____ Gals.	__1__ 1½" Pre-Conn.
_____ Snorkel Gun	_____ AFFF	_____ Gals.	_____ 1½"Pre-Conn-SP
_____ Tele-Squirt	__X__ Water	__300__ Gals.	_____ 2½" Wyed Lines
_____ Ladder Pipe	_____ Dry Chemical	_____ Gals.	_____ 2½" Hand Lines
			_____ 2½" Master Str.

ON-SITE EXT. USED   ON-SITE SYSTEMS USED   _____ 3" Master Str.

_____ Pressurized Water _____ Standpipe   __1__ 2½" Supply

_____ Soda Acid   _____ Sprinkler   _____ 3" Supply

_____ Foam   _____ Dry Chemical

_____ Dry Chemical   _____ Carbon Dioxide   LADDERS USED

_____ Carbon Dioxide   _____ Halogenated   _____ Aerial

_____ Halogenated   _____ Ground up-30'

                                                          _____ Ground over 30'

                                                          _____ Squirt

Personnel: Lt. J. Yancey, M. Clarke, W. McGill, D. LeValley
Man Minutes: 124
Operations: While assisting the Fire Prevention Division on a standpipe test at 1625
             Southeast Tenth Avenue, a passerby advised of smoke coming from a building
             at the listed address. I advised dispatch to start a full response, and E-2
             responded to same. Upon arrival, I found the building with heavy fire
             involvement to the north half. E-2 laid a line in and then extinguished the fire
             with our pre-connect. After total extinguishment, I found evidence of two
             separate areas of origin. I-24 and 34 came on the scene and made an
             investigation. E-2 returned to #2 Station.
       Cause: Suspicious; found two origins of fire.
       Damage: Medium fire damage; probable no dollar damage because the south
                half of the building had been gutted by a previous fire.
       Note: For additional information see Alarm #821158, 3/1/8x.

Form AA-271 Rev. 4/81

FIGURE 7.5 *Florida fire incident report* (Courtesy of Fort Lauderdale, Florida, Fire Department; narrative portion only)

MEMORANDUM

TO: James Freidman, Supervisor

FROM: Cathy Venci, Night Manager C.V.

DATE: October 8, 199X

SUBJECT: Busboy Fall Near Kitchen Entrance, 10/6/9X

On Sunday, October 6, 199X, at 8:15 P.M. Mike Sullivan, busboy, fell at the kitchen entrance located in the rear of the dining room. Mr. Sullivan was not injured, but there was considerable breakage of dishes and glassware. Figure 1 shows the exact location of the fall:

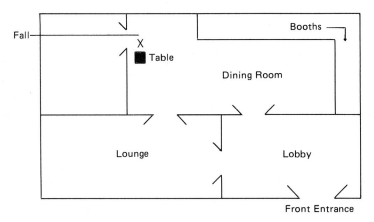

Figure 1   Exact location of incident

Prior to the fall, Mr. Sullivan had cleared dishes from three tables, as is customary. He was returning to the kitchen when his foot caught the leg of the table next to the kitchen. The weight of the dishes he was carrying caused him to lose his balance and to fall forward. As he fell, the tray dropped, and the dishes broke.

As a result, the replacement of the dishes and glassware will cost $133.00, which includes

$36.00   for Anchor Hocking stemware (6 @ $6.00 ea),
25.00   for Whitehall water glasses (5 @ $5.00 ea),
42.00   for Sango dinner plates (6 @ $7.00 ea), and
30.00   for Sango coffee cups (6 @ $5.00 ea).

In order to prevent such a fall from recurring, I recommend that the table next to the kitchen entrance be removed. This will give the busboys more clearance when entering the kitchen area.

CV:jv

FIGURE 7.6   *Brief incident report* (Courtesy of student Cathy Venci)

MEMORANDUM

TO: James Little, Director Administration & Contract

FROM: Jill Fowler, Personnel Specialist *J. F.*

DATE: May 22, 199X

SUBJECT: Assault on Susan Watson, 5/19/9X

INCIDENT

On Wednesday, May 19, 199X, at 9:35 P.M. a female employee of the Benefits Department, Susan Watson, was assaulted in the Ace parking lot by a white male who fled with her purse.

CAUSE

Ms Watson was approaching her car after working overtime when the attack occurred. According to Ms Watson, the suspect approached her from behind as she was nearing her car. Using a blunt object, he struck Ms Watson on the head, and she fell to the ground. The man then ran with her purse in the direction of Northwest Thirty-sixth Street.

RESULTS

Since Ms Watson's car keys were stolen with her purse, she walked back to the lobby. However, she could not gain entrance to the building because her access card was also in her purse. Bleeding profusely from her head wound, Ms Watson pounded on the door to gain entrance; however, the guard, Ralph Murchison, had temporarily left his post. Mr. Murchison returned to find Ms Watson unconscious on the pavement. He immediately called an ambulance, and she was taken to Palmetto General Hospital where she was treated for scalp lacerations and multiple bruises. She was held for observation overnight and was released on May 20. Her insurance will cover all medical payments. Mr. Murchison reported the incident to the police, but because Ms Watson is unable to describe her assailant, no arrest is expected.

FIGURE 7.7   *Brief incident report with headings* (By permission)

RECOMMENDATIONS

Several problems have been spotlighted due to this incident. First, women leaving the building after dark are extremely vulnerable to such attacks. There is no protection afforded to them, and the parking area is not well lighted. The security gates are not functional, and unauthorized persons can easily gain entrance to the grounds. There is no way for an employee in distress to make his or her presence known at the lobby door if the guard is away from the security desk. Therefore,

1. Two security personnel should be stationed outside of the building. One should be situated at the main gate until the card access system is perfected. Unauthorized persons should be turned away at this point. The other guard should patrol the parking lot by buggy and escort employees to their cars when summoned to the main lobby by walkie-talkie.

2. Proposals should be obtained to install better lighting in the parking area.

3. A buzzer or bell should be installed outside the lobby door to summon the inside guard in emergency situations.

4. The main security desk should never be left unattended. Your department should institute a new policy and procedure in this area.

5. Training should be developed in two areas:

   a) CPR and basic emergency medical training for security guards, and

   b) Self-defense training for interested employees developed with the assistance of the police department.

I would like to meet with you to discuss my recommendations as soon as possible.

JF:jmf

FIGURE 7.7   *continued*

PERIODIC AND PROGRESS REPORTS

Purpose

A periodic or progress report provides a record of the status of a project over a specific period of time. The report or reports are issued at regular intervals throughout the life of a project to allow management and workers to keep projects running smoothly. A periodic or progress report states what has been done, what is being done, and what remains to be done. The report usually reviews the expenditures of time, money, and materials; therefore, decisions can be made to adjust schedules, allocate budget, or schedule supplies and equipment. Often a company employs preprinted forms to report routine progress. Employees simply fill in the blanks at the completion of tasks. Figure 7.8 shows a fire department's weekly and monthly Apparatus Report form.

Similar periodic reports may be required daily, weekly, quarterly, semiannually, or annually. They insure uniformity and completeness of data.

Organization

All narrative reports in a series of progress reports should be uniform in organization and format. A progress report covers

- A review of the aims of the project highlighting accomplishments or problems
- A summary or explanation of the work completed
- A summary or explanation of the work in progress
- A summary or explanation of future work
- An assessment of the progress

Headings for the sections, however brief, are usually used. Consider these topical headings:

Introduction	Overall Goal
Work Completed	Work Completed
Work in Progress or	Expenses Incurred
Work Remaining	Present Work
Appraisal	Future Work
	Conclusions

The major factor of a progress report is time. Other features, such as costs, materials, and personnel, may be incorporated into the appropriate sections or attached as support materials. If the reports are being prepared frequently during the course of a project, they are characterized by brevity—phrases rather than sentences and paragraphs. Figures 7.9 and 7.10 show progress reports in memo and letter formats.

APPAR. NO. _____ RADIO NO. _____ MO. _____ YEAR _____ CO. _____ MAKE _____

WEEKLY APPARATUS REPORT

	1st Monday	2nd Monday	3rd Monday	4th Monday	5th Monday
Check pumps—Record vacuum test					
Check pumps—Record pressure test					
Were all drains flushed?					
Did connections or packing glands leak?					
Does relief valve or governor operate satisfactorily?					
Change Hurst Tool Fuel					
Check and flush foam pick-up					

	1st Tuesday	2nd Tuesday	3rd Tuesday	4th Tuesday	5th Tuesday
Resuscitator—Blood pressure of lowest cylinder					
Air Chisel—Record pressure of lowest oxygen cylinder					
Demand Regulator Mask—Record pressure					
Portable Spotlight—Running test					
Wench & Cord—Operating check					
First Aid Kits—Inventory check					
Hurst Tool & Compressor—Running test					
Tires—Record pressure					

Form AA-122 Rev. 8/77

FIGURE 7.8 *Sample periodic report* (Courtesy of Fort Lauderdale, Florida, Fire Department)

MEMORANDUM

TO: Susan Niles, Law Department

FROM: Catherine Robertson, Executive Secretary *C.R.*

DATE: May 12, 199X

SUBJECT: Ace Company, Inc. Acquisition—Progress Report

___

INTRODUCTION

Here is a progress report on the Ace Company, Inc. acquisition.

WORK COMPLETED

- Stock purchase and Non-compete Agreements have been typed in final draft.

- Copies of drafts have been faxed to Seller.

- Hotel and plane reservations have been confirmed by Zeta Travel Agency for arrival in Detroit on June 25 at 3:30 P.M.

WORK IN PROGRESS

- Limousine has been requested for transfer of all parties to Hilton Hotel; awaiting confirmation.

WORK REMAINING

- Meeting with the Seller and lawfirm to take place June 26.

- Drafts of Stock Purchase and Non-compete Agreements to be typed in final form for execution by all parties.

- Upon return, file on acquisition to be completed, and all documents to be filed as previously discussed.

APPRAISAL

Although this acquisition was originally scheduled for a May 1 closing, all work is up to date, all parties have been notified of the delays, and all parties are scheduled for the June 25–26 closing. With the final execution of all documents, this acquisition will be concluded.

CR:js

FIGURE 7.9 *Brief progress report* (By permission)

Acme Advertising, Inc.
206 Lexington Avenue
New York, New York 10112
September 24, 199X

Mr. Bert Campbell
Widget, Inc.
2552 Washington Street
Youngstown, Ohio   37602

Dear Mr. Campbell:

As you requested the following is a progress report on the West Coast advertising campaign of your new product, Super Widget.

WORK COMPLETED
On September 23, 199X, thirty-second radio commercials began appearing in the following markets: Portland, Seattle, San Francisco, Los Angeles, and San Diego. As we agreed, the commercials aired on local sports shows on one station in each of those cities.

WORK IN PROGRESS
On October 1, 199X , full page ads will appear in the Sunday morning sports sections of newspapers in the thirty largest West Coast markets.

Regent Stores has agreed to special promotions for Super Widget at all their retail outlets on October 5, 199X.

WORK REMAINING
Depending on the success of the first few weeks of sales of Super Widget on the West Coast, we will determine our best approach for national advertising. A target date for national television advertising is November 15.

APPRAISAL
So far our surveys reveal that the public is enthusiastic about the new product, and if the West Coast is any indication, Super Widget will be a financial success.

Very truly yours,

Nancy R. Merrell

Nancy R. Merrell
Account Executive

NRM:eq

FIGURE 7.10   *Sample progress report* (By permission)

FEASIBILITY REPORTS

Purpose

You may be assigned to look into a new project—a new product, the development of a new program, a relocation, the purchase of new equipment—to determine the practicality of the project. The feasibility report presents the evidence of your investigation and analysis plus your conclusions and recommendations.

Typically, feasibility reports analyze data to answer specific questions:

- Will a given product, program, service, procedure, or policy work for a specific purpose?
- Is one option better than another option for a specific purpose?
- How can a problem be solved?
- Is an option practical in a given situation?

Figures 7.11 and 7.12 illustrate feasibility reports which address themselves to these various questions.

Organization

The feasibility report usually includes:

- Explanation of the problem
- Preset standards or criteria
- Description of the item(s) or subject(s) to be analyzed
- An examination of the scope of the analysis
- Presentation of the data
- Interpretation of the data
- Conclusions and recommendations

A brief feasibility report does not require headings; however, for a longer report consider these headings:

Background		Introduction
Standards		Problem
Options	or	Criteria
Method		Options
Data		Limitations
Conclusions		Recommendations

MEMORANDUM

TO: J. D. Big, Director, Accounts Department

FROM: Jane White, Secretary, Accounts Department *J.W.*

DATE: May 9, 199X

SUBJECT: Replacing Copy Machine

Inasmuch as we have been experiencing difficulties with our Atlas copy machine, I have investigated the feasibility of our renting a new copier. The Atlas costs $311.00 per month to rent. It does not make two-sided copies. In the past 30 days we have needed seven service calls costing a minimum of $30.00 a call. In April we were without copy capability for three days while a part was being located by the service representative.

Our criteria for a new machine include

- low cost (below $400 a month)
- two-side print capability
- various paper quality capability
- reduction capability
- immediate delivery

Only two copy machines are available within our price range. Table 1 compares the costs, capabilities, and limitations of Brand X and Brand Y:

Table 1   Comparative Features of Brand X and Brand Y Copy Machines

Brand	Rental Cost Per Month ($)	Capabilities	Limitations
X	316.00	• One step operation for two-sided print • Any paper • Reductions • Immediate delivery	• $35.00 base service fee • Reputation for frequent breakdowns
Y	389.00	• One step operation for two-sided print	• $75.00 base service • Reputation for slow

FIGURE 7.11 *Sample feasibility report*

- Any paper
- One-size reductions
- Immediate delivery

Both copiers meet our criteria; the Brand Y one-size reductions are suitable. In order to assess the disadvantages, I surveyed five departments which use the X or Y copiers to determine the number of service calls required in a one year period. Table 2 shows the departments and number of service calls required for each:

Table 2   Service Calls for Brand X and Y Copy Machines in One-Year Period

Department	Brand	# of calls (one year)
Personnel	X	11
Payroll	Y	2
Data Processing	X	25
Records	X	7
Purchasing	Y	0

Both Brand X and Brand Y appear to be more reliable than our Atlas copy machine. Although Brand Y charges more ($75.00) for a base service fee than does Brand X ($35.00), the survey data suggests that Brand Y is the more reliable machine.

Therefore, I recommend that we rent a Brand Y copy machine which will give us a two-side print capability which we do not presently have as well as meet all other criteria.

May I have your authorization by Friday to negotiate a Brand Y rental?

JW:eg

FIGURE 7.11   *continued*

NORTHEAST REGION MCS

BONUS PROGRAM

Feasibility Report

I.   INTRODUCTION

The Northeast Region MCS Partners are considering the feasibility of discontinuing annual bonuses and of paying bonuses to professional staff on an individual basis throughout the year immediately following bonus-worthy events or conditions. In this way the bonus would be kept separate from salary considerations, and the reward would more closely relate to the event or condition.

II.   BACKGROUND

For many years the Northeast Region MCS has had a bonus program for professional staff. Each staff member was eligible for an annual bonus payable September 30. Whether or not he or she was paid a bonus and what the amount would be were determined at the time of the June performance evaluation. When paid, the bonuses ranged up to 15% of annual salary.

The bonus was meant to recognize and reward unusual contribution or difficult conditions during the previous year. It also reflected the economic condition of the practice. In good times, total bonus payments were higher than they were in bad times. In one recent year, when operations were showing a loss, there were no bonuses.

The program was abused in two ways. To some extent partners and staff began to consider bonuses as regular, recurring payments with only the amount subject to annual determination, and they sometimes were used as a substitute for salary increases that were not as permanent as a salary increase. Also, during wage controls, some payments that would have been salary increases in other times were awarded as bonuses.

FIGURE 7.12   *Sample feasibility report* (Courtesy of Charles E. Smith, Jr.)

III.   <u>STANDARDS</u>

An equitable bonus plan must

1.   motivate staff toward desirable activities,

2.   reward unusual contribution,

3.   compensate for difficult conditions, and

4.   make salary adjustments more representative of a staff member's overall performance.

IV.   <u>OPTIONAL BONUS PLAN</u>

Under the new program, bonuses will be awarded for the same reasons as before—unusual, meritorious contribution and undue hardship. Some examples follow:

A. <u>Meritorious Contribution</u>

- For any professional, a contact or other development work leading to securing a new audit client.

- For a manager, a self-conceived practice development program of self-initiated contact leading to a consulting engagement. (Bonuses should not be awarded to managers for an excellent sales record <u>per se</u>.)

- For any professional, the conception and eventual use of a unique approach to an engagement-related work task.

- For any professional, the development of a technique (engagement-related or not) that has wide application in our practice.

- For a staff consultant, completion of a clearly defined engagement work task in significantly less time than had been budgeted by a partner or manager.

- For a staff consultant, a contact or other development work leading to securing a consulting engagement.

FIGURE 7.12   *continued*

B. Undue Hardship

- An extended period of travel away from home, defined as spending more than 75 percent of weekday nights away from home over a six-month period or spending one-half of the weekends in a four-month period away from home.

- A close working relationship for a month or more with intransigent, unreasonable, abusive, or otherwise difficult client personnel.

- Uncomfortable physical working conditions for a month or more, such as at a remote, isolated community or in a noisy, dirty, hot, or cold facility.

- An extended period of weekend or evening work where total hours worked are more than twice normal hours for a month or more.

V. PROBLEMS

This bonus plan option may present some problems. Some members of the staff, both managers and consultants, are apt to direct their efforts towards earning bonuses, and thereby pay less attention to their regular professional work. Furthermore, they may embarrass the Firm in doing so.

For example, a consultant may devote too much time on an engagement looking for a unique approach rather than following the work plan as laid out by the manager or partner. It is also possible that a manager or staff consultant may actively seek new audit clients at the expense of MCS engagements, or his activity in developing an audit client may conflict with plans of the general practice or infringe on professional ethics. There is also a remote possibility that a member of the professional staff might try to encourage rather than allay intransigence in a client.

FIGURE 7.12 *continued*

VI.   <u>RECOMMENDATIONS</u>

1. The optional bonus plan should be adopted for a period of two years because it provides for more equity than the previous bonus plan.

2. The Northeast Region MSC Partners should develop preliminary guidelines listing events and conditions and the amounts of bonus merited by each.

3. To provide initial equity any partner may propose a bonus for any staff member who may warrant a bonus within the next six months. The bonus proposal will be discussed at each scheduled partners' meeting and approved or disapproved by the Regional Director. In this way the guidelines may be further refined, and all of the partners will develop a consistent point of view.

4. Subsequently, bonuses will be approved or disapproved directly by the Regional Director without joint discussion, but the justification for the amounts of all bonuses paid in the preceding period will be presented for informational purposes at each partners' meeting.

CHS:eg

FIGURE 7.12   *continued*

Background.   This section includes all introductory material, such as the purpose of the report, a description or definition of the question, issue, problem, or item(s). You may discuss the scope or extent of the report.

Standards.   Here you present a detailed explanation of the established criteria, aims, or goals of the question being investigated.

Options.   If applicable, present each alternative according to your established criteria. Consider costs, capabilities, procedures, personnel involved, required training, or other appropriate features of each option.

Method.   In this section explain how each option was analyzed to determine its practicality. This may include description of testing methods, survey instruments, research source material, qualifications of consultants, and discussion of limitations to your investigation.

Data.   In this section present the test results, survey results, or research findings.

Recommendations.   Finally, the feasibility report summarizes the investigation, drawing logical conclusions. Discuss the limitations, if any, of your study. Build in a time schedule for action and a review of the results. In short, interpret the data and offer your recommendations.

Figure 7.11 shows a brief feasibility report in a memo format. It analyzes whether product X or product Y is better for the particular needs of a department in a large firm. Although it does not contain headings, the message covers the *background*, the *criteria* established for replacing a copy machine, a review of the *optional equipment* capabilities, the *method* of weighing the alternatives along with the survey data, and a *recommendation for action*.

Figure 7.12 shows another feasibility report. This report addresses itself to solving a problem of abuses in a present bonus program. The organization remains much the same; the report presents the *background* and *problem*, the *standards* for an equitable bonus plan, the details of an *optional plan* along with its possible *limitations*, and the *recommendations* for adopting the new bonus program.

LABORATORY AND TEST REPORTS

Purpose

Students and employees in the fields of chemistry, data processing, fire science, electronics, nursing, and other allied health areas must frequently write laboratory or test reports. The reports present the results of research or testing.

Organization

Typically the report includes

- Statement of purpose
- Review of method or procedure of testing
- Results
- Conclusions and recommendations

Purpose Statement. Here you clarify what is being tested and for what purpose (durability, colorfastness, safety factors, customer preference, and so forth).

Method/Procedure. Explain the particulars of your testing method.

Results. Present the test results. Use graphics for quick comprehension or comparison to preset standards.

Conclusions. Explain the implications of the test results and make recommendations.

A test report is usually less formal than a true laboratory report. The test report may be transmitted in a memorandum or business letter. Figure 7.13 shows a test report from an automotive laboratory which tested the durability of fiberglass impellers for use in automobile water pumps. It is clear that the *purpose* of the tests was to determine the endurance time of the impellers. The *procedure* used to conduct the test is described only to the extent that it would interest the reader. The *results* of the test are presented in graphics for clear comprehension, and the *conclusions and recommendations* are stated with reference to predetermined standards. Use topical headings if they will make your report clearer.

Laboratory reports generally cover the same four considerations, but are more formally structured. Figure 7.14 shows a report on the preparation of aspirin. It includes flow charts of the main chemical reactions, potential side reaction, and the separation scheme. The procedure section of the report details the method used to prepare the aspirin with attention to the equipment used. The results and conclusion are covered under separate headings.

UNIVERSAL TESTING LABORATORIES
1111 North University Drive
Cleveland, OH 44141

October 6, 199X

Mr. Thomas Jones
5445 Northwest Third Court
Columbus, OH 43229

Dear Mr. Jones:

Thank you for the submission of the fiberglass impellers to us for testing as an alternative to cast iron impellers for automobile water pumps. To determine the endurance of your impellers, we destruct tested the impellers under simulated load conditions at various revolutions per minute (RPM). The table indicates the endurance times of the test impellers in comparison to the standards set by the American Automobile Association:

FIBERGLASS IMPELLER ENDURANCE TEST AT VARIABLE RPM			
Test Number	RPM	Endurance Time (Minutes)	American Automobile Standards (Minutes)
1	4000	248	300
2	5000	242	275
3	6000	235	250
4	7000	225	225
5	8000	206	200
6	9000	165	175
7	10000	75	150

This same information is illustrated in a curve:

FIGURE 7.13 *Sample test report* (Courtesy of student Cindy E. Grotsky)

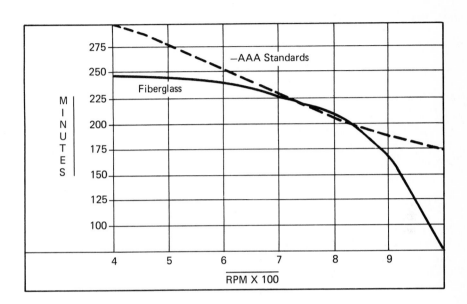

It is apparent from the data that the fiberglass impeller does not meet the minimum standards of endurance set by the American Automobile Association, except at 7000 and 8000 RPM. It would not be practical to produce the fiberglass impeller at this time. We recommend that you reinforce the impeller with steel webbing for further testing.

We look forward to assisting you in your future refinements.

Very truly yours,

Cindy E. Grotsky

Cindy E. Grotsky
President

CEG:eg

FIGURE 7.13 *continued*

THE PREPARATION OF ASPIRIN

Main Reaction

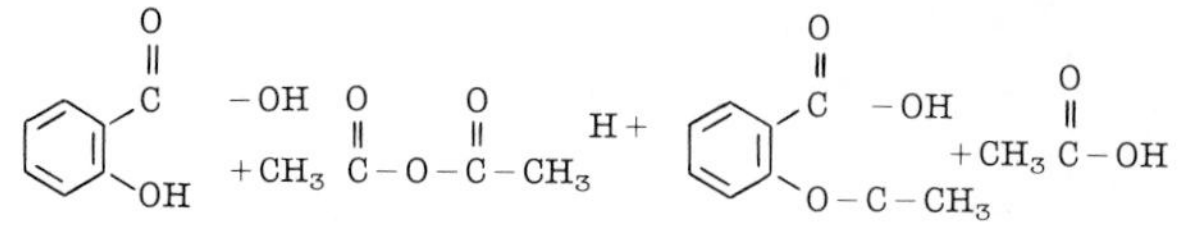

From Literature:

Salicylic Acid M.P.||157@159®

Aspirin (Acetylsalicylic Acid) M.P.||135@136®

Aspirin||C_9 H_8 O_4 M.W.||180

Calculations

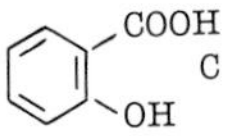

$C_7H_6O_3$ M.W. 138

(2 0g. Salicylic Acid) $\left(\frac{\text{1 mole Salicylic Acid}}{\text{138g. Salicylic Acid}}\right)$ = 0 014 moles Salicylic Acid

$(CH_3CO)_2O$ $C_+H_6O_3$ MW 102 Density = 108 g./ML.

The limiting reagent is salicylic acid.

Side Reaction

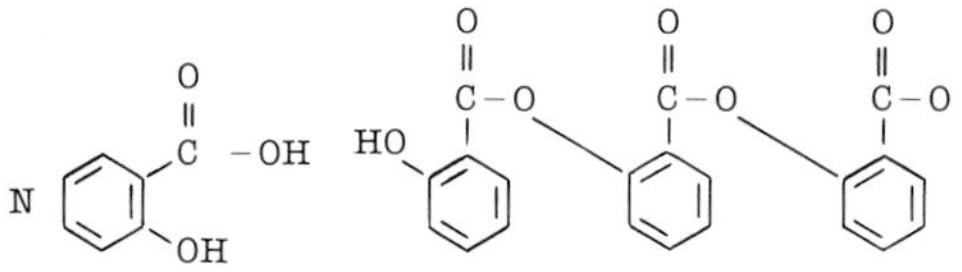

Separation Scheme

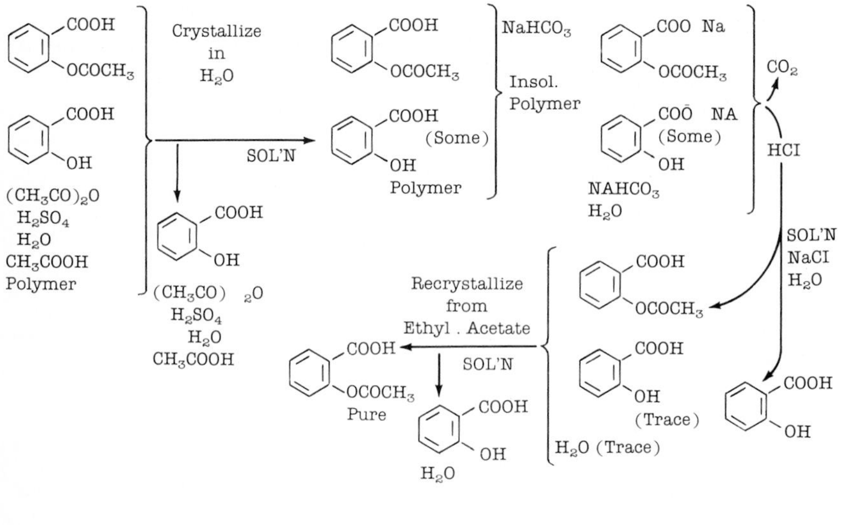

FIGURE 7.14 ***Sample laboratory report*** (From *Laboratory Manual for General Chemistry* by Kenneth D. Whitten and Kenneth D. Gailey. Copyright © 1981 by Saunders College Publishing. Reproduced by permission of the publisher.)

Procedure:

	Salicylic acid:	Sample + Paper 3.12g.	2.00g = 0.014 moles
		Paper 1.12g.	138g./mole
		Sample 2.00g.	salicylic acid

The salicylic acid was placed in a 125 ml Erlenmeyer flask. Acetic anhydride (5 ml) was added along with 5 drops of conc. H_2SO_4. The flask was swirled until the salicylic acid was dissolved. The solution was heated on the steambath for 10 minutes. The flask was allowed to cool to room temperature, and some crystals appeared. Water (50 ml) was added, and the mixture was cooled in an ice bath. The crystals were collected by suction filtration, rinsed three times with cold H_2O, and dried.

Crude yield: Product + paper 3.07g.

                                          paper 1.15g

                                          1.92g. aspirin

Theoretical yield = (0.014 moles) (180g. Aspirin/mole) = 2.52g.

Actual yield   = 1.92g.

Percentage yield = 76%

The crude product gave a faint color with $FeCl_3$. Phenol and salicylic acid gave strong positive tests.

The crude product was placed in a 150 ml beaker, and 25 ml of saturated NaHCO was added. When the reaction had ceased, the solution was filtered by suction. The beaker and funnel were washed with CA. Two ml of H_2O dilute HCI was prepared by mixing 3.5 ml conc. HCI, and 10 ml H_2O in a 150 ml beaker. The filtrate was poured into the dilute acid, and a precipitate formed immediately. The mixture was cooled in an ice bath. The solid was collected by suction filtration, washed three times with cold H_2O, and placed on a watch glass to dry overnight.

Yield: Paper and product: 2.78g.

                    paper: 1.08g.

                    product: 1.70g.

Theoretical yield = 2.52g.

Actual yield   = 1.70g.

Percentage yield = 67% mp. 133–135°C.

The solid did not give a positive $FeCI_3$ test. The final product (CA. 0.75 g) was dissolved in a minimum amount of hot ethyl acetate. Crystals appeared. The crystals were collected by suction and dried. MP. 135–136°C.

FIGURE 7.14 *continued*

FIELD REPORTS

Purpose

A field report presents an analysis of a location, site, or situation to record and determine appropriate action. Realtors prepare field reports on undeveloped, commercial, and industrial properties to determine the value and prospects of such properties. Service people from every field inspect property to determine costs and plans for building on, improving, or repairing the property. Firefighters, health inspectors, and others report their work in the field. Insurance adjustors inspect sites to establish claims for damages.

Organization

Often preprinted forms with space for narrative reporting are used. Many companies devise organization formats in outline form to be followed by their reporting personnel. These regulating outlines list specific topical headings along with brief instructions about the data to be included under each.

Despite the diversity of headings required for any one specific field report, all such reports include

- Essential background data
- Account of the field inspection
- Analysis of findings
- Conclusions and recommendations

Background.   Explain what is being investigated and for what purpose (safety or health factors, cost determination, need for improvement, validity of claims, and so forth).

Account of Inspection.   Clarify what the field investigation found.

Findings Analysis.   Interpret the significance of the findings as related to the purpose of the investigation.

Conclusions/Recommendations.   Detail what action should be taken.

Figure 7.15 shows a fire department company run report. Page one of the report records the essential background data while page two contains a narrative report about what happened in the field.

Figure 7.16 shows a realtor's field inspection report on a parcel of unimproved land. The data includes pertinent information required for a listing.

Figure 7.17 is a lengthier field report filed by an insurance adjustor regarding a claimant seeking medical expenses for an injury sustained while on the premises of an insured fast-food restaurant. The enclosures to the report are not reproduced in the sample.

FORT LAUDERDALE FIRE DEPARTMENT
Secondary Company Run Report

INCIDENT #: 6179	COMPANY: R-5	STN #: 5	FIRE PERSONNEL AT SCENE: (Your Co.) Officers 1 Men 1	MILEAGE: 2	CODE: 3

TIME OF ALARM: 1414	10-8: 1415	10-67: 1420	TIME BACK IN SERV.: 1525	DAY OF WEEK: Mon.	MONTH: 11	DAY: 1	SHIFT: B	1A

CORRECT ADDRESS: 610 Northeast First Avenue	OUT OF CITY: ☐ Yes ☒ No	ROOM OR APT #: --

PROCEDURES EMPLOYED

- ☐ HOLD IN
- ☐ FORCIBLE ENTRY
- ☐ SEARCH
- ☐ RESCUE
- ☐ EVACUATION
- ☐ SALVAGE
- ☐ STAND BY
- ☐ VENTILATION
- ☐ ARSON INVESTIGATION
- ☐ OVERHAUL
- ☐ EXTINGUISHMENT
- ☐ REMOVE HAZARD
- ☐ INVESTIGATION

APPLIANCES USED

- ☐ DELUGE GUN
- ☐ DECK TURRET
- ☐ SNORKEL GUN
- ☐ TELE-SQUIRT
- ☐ LADDER PIPE

HOSE LINES USED

No.		Total Feet
☐	Booster Line	
1	1½" Pre-Conn	
☐	1½" Wyed Lines	
☐	2½" Hand Lines	
☐	2½" Master Stream	
☐	3" Master Stream	
☐	2½" Supply	
☐	3" Supply	
☐	1½" Pre-Conn S.P.	

EXTINGUISHING AGENTS USED

		Amount	
☐	Wetwater		Gals.
☐	Foam		Gals.
☐	AFFF		Gals.
☐	Water		Gals.
☐	Dry Chemical		Lbs.

ON-SITE SYSTEMS USED

- ☐ STANDPIPE
- ☐ SPRINKLER
- ☐ DRY CHEMICAL
- ☐ CARBON DIOXIDE
- ☐ HALOGENATED

ON-SITE EXTINGUISHERS USED

- ☐ PRESSURIZED WATER
- ☐ SODA ACID
- ☐ FOAM
- ☐ DRY CHEMICAL
- ☐ CARBON DIOXIDE
- ☐ HALOGENATED

LADDERS USED

- ☐ AERIAL
- ☐ GROUND UP TO 30'
- ☐ GROUND OVER 30'
- ☐ SQUIRT

EQUIPMENT USED

- ☐ SELF-CONT. UNITS
- ☐ RESUSCITATOR
- ☐ FIRST AID EQUIPMENT
- ☐ STOKES STRETCHER
- ☐ HOUT FOAM MAKER
- ☐ TARGET SAW
- ☐ SCUBA EQUIPMENT
- ☐ HAND LINE
- ☐ GENERATOR
- ☐ PORTABLE LIGHTS
- ☐ WATER VACUUM
- ☐ EXPLOSIMETER
- ☐ ULTRA-VIOLET LIGHT
- ☐ SELF-CONT. SPARE CYL.
- ☐ RESUSCITATOR O2 CYL.
- ☐ BODY BOARD
- ☐ AIR-FOAM BLOWER
- ☐ HURST TOOL
- ☐ HYDRAULIC JACK
- ☐ SMALL TOOLS (Axe-Pick)
- ☐ LIFE LINE
- 2 SMOKE EJECTOR
- ☐ PORTABLE PUMP
- ☐ SALVAGE COVERS
- ☐ PROBEYE
- ☐ PORTA POWER
- ☐ HI-RISE KIT

FORM AA-205 Rev. 3/77   COMPLETE OTHER SIDE

FIGURE 7.15 *Sample field report* (Courtesy of Fort Lauderdale, Florida, Fire Department)

OPERATIONS AND COMPANY AND STORY OF FIRE

      Give a complete account of the work of the company. The sequence of operations and where the company worked (floor of building, for example) should be clearly recorded. To the best of your recollection show where each man worked and what he did. Describe where fire apparently started and from what cause; what material burned; progress of fire upon arrival of company; and, any dangerous condition of the building. List all company personnel responding. List all injury and/or fatality information.

      Condition of doors or windows (locked or open, for example); any unusual presence of flammable or combustibles; or, obstacles placed to hamper the fire department deliberately should be noted. This information should so far as possible be coupled with the name of the man who encountered the condition so that he can be witness to it if necessary in connection with further investigation of the fire.

      Also, utilizing Form 901-J, make sketch to show the relative positions of pumper, hydrant, ladder or other apparatus with respect to the building afire. Show hose lines manned by this company and their approximate lengths.

```
R-5 Crew:    Lts. Sicliri and Ferranti
Man Min:     140
Operation:
```

This unit was dispatched to a reported structure fire at topic
address. Upon arrival on the scene District Commander One told
me to bring a second line to the fire floor. We pulled an inch
and one-half line from engine one S and advanced it to the fire
floor. This line was not needed at this time. Driver Ferranti
brought smoke ejectors and a pike pole to the apartment involved.
DC-1 told me to check for fire extension. I went into the attic
and crawled the length of the building checking for fire. Finding
no fire in the area, I reported back to the Commander. Commander
Zettek then had my unit stand by in reserve. When the area was
safe, we cleared the area and returned to quarters.

By *Howard J. Sicliri Lt.*
Officer in Charge

Checked By _____

(Use Additional Sheet If Needed)

FIGURE 7.15   *continued*

MEMORANDUM

TO: Ken Vordermeier, Vice-president

FROM: Jane Ellyson, Realtor $\mathcal{J} \cdot \mathcal{E}$.

DATE: September 22, 199X

SUBJECT: Unimproved Land Inspection

On Friday, September 20, 199X, I inspected 3.4+ acres of unimproved land fronting on Powerline Road and Northwest Twentieth Street, Boca Raton, Broward County, Florida, to determine its potential and to obtain the seller's listing.

DESCRIPTION

Legal—Hillmont Middle River Vista, Replat of a portion of Plat Book 59, Page 188, Parcel B less pt., Desc. in CRS 3197/876, 3195/834, 433/711, and 4638/335, less approximately 1.049 acres conveyed to McDonald's Corporation and less approximately 0.358 acres to be conveyed as Northwest Twentieth Street.

> Style Code   97
> Area code: 45
> Tax number: 9228-13-002

Price—Listing price is $600,000.00. The property is free and clear, and the seller desires cash. The price per acre is $174,240.00 or $4.00 per square foot. Sale lease back is not available.

INSPECTION

This vacant property is 3.4+ acres, 150,000+ square feet, with 450 to 500 feet of frontage and irregular depth. The property is waterfront with the property line following river bank.

It is zoned for commercial land use and platted. No rezoning is required. A survey is available in the listing office. No improvements have been made.

FIGURE 7.16 *Sample field report* (Courtesy Vordermeier Company, Realtors; adaptation)

Minor clearing and/or grubbing, and fill will be required. The need for easements and restrictions are unknown at this time.

The property is accessible to Port Everglades waterport, Fort Lauderdale/Hollywood airport, and the main highways: I-95, Florida Turnpike, and Oakland Park Boulevard. No railroad access is available. The property has access to electricity, city water, and sewers.

ANALYSIS

The surrounding area is developing rapidly. New Lake Pompano Park adjoins the property at the north end, and a fast-food restaurant is being built immediately south of the subject property.

The land offers an excellent prospect for a retail or service business.

RECOMMENDATIONS

1.   Obtain the listing.

2.   List on Realtron Computer service

      Style code: 97 Commercial
      General Search codes: V2 Electricity
                              V3 Public Water
                              V4 Sewers or services
                              V5 Paved streets or sidewalks
                              V8 Major Road Frontage

3.   Verify financing at time of contract.

FIGURE 7.16   *continued*

MEMORANDUM

TO: Paul Austin, Superintendent, Ace Business Services, Inc.

FROM: Gloria Dunn, Field Claim Adjuster *G. D.*

DATE: March 26, 199X

SUBJECT: Fancy Fast Food Corporation - #43101-08459
Claimant Adele Clarke - Claim #172579

SUGGESTED RESERVE

Bodily injury - Adele Clarke - $10,000

FACTS

On 3/12/9X the claimant was a customer at the Fancy Fast Food premises located at 1688 South Lake Drive, Erie, Pennsylvania. The claimant was apparently bouncing on a chair at station 7 nearest the kitchen when the left, rear leg of the chair broke, collapsing the chair and causing the claimant to strike her chin on the edge of the table in the ensuing fall.

LEGAL VIOLATIONS

There are no known legal or code violations.

DIAGRAM

Enclosed is a diagram of the restaurant interior and station 7 showing the location of the table and chair at the time of the incident.

PHOTOGRAPHS

Enclosed is a photograph of the table and broken chair.

INSURED

The insured is Fancy Fast Food's licensee, 1688 South Ocean Boulevard, Miami, Florida. The manager's name is Raymond Krick. We have met with

FIGURE 7.17 *Sample field report*

Mr. Krick, and he has indicated that this is the first incident involving a collapsed chair.

The chairs and other furniture were purchased and installed in February, 198X, by Restaurant Suppliers, Inc. of Erie, Pennsylvania. The rest of the tables, banquettes, and chairs appear to be in good condition, and no defects are noted. His attached statement is self-explanatory.

BODILY INJURY - Adele Clarke

The claimant is ten (10) years old and lives with her parents, Mary and Jerry Clarke, at 7210 West Seventh Street, Johnstown, Pennsylvania.

<u>Injuries</u>

The claimant received two damaged teeth that were pushed completely up into her gums. The claimant was transported to Erie General Hospital emergency room where she was treated and then referred to an oral surgeon. The claimant will be having oral surgery including a bone transplant to correct the damage. The claimant's oral surgeon is Dr. M. C. Popper located at 1400 South Belvedere Street, Erie, Pennsylvania. Since the claimant is represented by an attorney, we were not able to obtain a statement or medical authorization from the claimant's parents.

<u>Damages</u>

The claimant's damages are unknown at this time; however, we expect the medicals and specials to be several thousand dollars.

CLAIMANT ATTORNEY

The claimant is represented by Attorney Julie King located at 609 North Andrews Avenue, Johnstown, Pennsylvania. We have spoken to Ms King and she is very cooperative and has indicated to us that the claimant seeks medical coverage because the Clarkes do not have any medical or dental insurance.

Although Attorney King did not make a definite statement about liability, she insinuated that a liability claim may be forthcoming.

FIGURE 7.17   *continued*

WITNESSES

Enclosed is the statement of waitress Paula Kline, an employee of Fancy Fast Food, and it is self-explanatory.

The claimant's mother, Mary, was seated in the booth when the accident occurred, but since she is represented, we have not obtained her statement. There were no other witnesses to the occurrence.

RECOMMENDATION

At this time there appears to be a valid liability claim on behalf of Fancy Fast Food Corporation as well as claim to medical bills.

Once we have been able to obtain the medicals and specials from the claimant's attorney, I recommend we pay the medicals and attempt to obtain a Parent/Guardian Release for the amount of the medicals. Should a liability claim be pressed, I recommend we attempt compromise.

UNFINISHED ITEMS

1. Obtain medical and special costs

2. Determine if liability claim is forthcoming

3. Next report 4/30/9X

ENCLOSURES

1. F2-205 Form

2. Diagram

3. Photograph

4. Transcribed statement of Raymond Krick

5. Transcribed statement of Paula Kline

GD:jv

FIGURE 7.17 *continued*

EXERCISES

1. Use the following information to write an incident report in memorandum format. You are the front desk reservations employee reporting to the general manager. Use the appropriate format, organization, visuals, and graphics to make your report clear and readable.

Incident:	Water pipe in ceiling burst; water damage to office equipment, carpet, and draperies.
When:	12:40 P.M., Friday, April 18, 199X
Where:	General office, Holiday Hotel
Cause:	Unknown
Damage:	Smith Corona electric typewriter (serial No. 809–71–2654) soaked; requires cleaning and oiling. Acme calculator soaked and short-circuited; requires replacement. Carpet (20′ × 16′) needs replacement. Draperies (6′ × 16′) need replacement. No personal injuries.
Costs:	Typewriter reconditioning—$35.00 Calculator replacement—$80.00 Carpet replacement—$512.00 Drapery replacement—$300.00 Plumber—$500.00
Further results:	Estimated one-week delay in preparation of promotion mailout project.
Recommendations:	Hire temporary typist for five days: estimated cost—$250.00

2. Use the following information to write a progress report in letter format. Arrange the data in sequential order. Use headings. Decide whether to present information in phrases or sentences.

Position:	You are an Ace Company training specialist reporting to a writing consultant whose services have been contracted to conduct on-premises occupational writing instruction at your company.
Project:	Writing seminar to upgrade employee skills—March 5, 6, and 7, 199X
Data:	(follow directions from above):

   a. Consultant evaluation forms to be devised.

   b. Negotiating luncheon menus with James Watkins, cafeteria manager; all three dates.

   c. Twenty registrants from 15 departments confirmed.

   d. Writing samples from each registrant being solicited to forward to consultant for evaluation.

   e. Training Room C scheduled 9:00–5:00 P.M., March 5, 6, 7.

   f. Certificates of Completion to be typed.

   g. Seminar announcements sent to 54 departments, February 1.

   h. Xeroxing and binding of twenty sets of instructional materials in progress.

   i. Overhead projector to be ordered for March 6, 9:00–5:00.

   j. Wayne Salsbury to be notified to prepare introduction of Consultant for March 5.

   k. Memos to supervisors explaining cost center billing sent on February 15, 199X.

   l. Tables to be arranged in semicircle for registrants on March 5, 6, 7.

3. Use the following information to write a feasibility report in memorandum format. You are the Grounds Committee Chairperson reporting to the Golden Lakes Condominium Association. Rearrange the data into logical organization. Present the data in appropriate graphics. Based upon the information, draw logical recommendations in your conclusion.

Problem: Remodeling of Golden Lakes Condominium recreation building has resulted in grass damage in common areas.

Fact: Rainy season begins June 15.

Data: Luxury Landscape will require three days to resod at bid of $4839. Guarantee includes six inspections in four-month period with necessary sod replacement at no extra charge.

Landscaping Professionals will require two days to resod at a bid of $3984. Guarantee includes six inspections in six-month period with necessary sod replacement at no extra charge.

Green Company will require three days to resod at a bid of $3707. No guarantee offered.

K-Mart Professional Crew will require three days to resod at a bid of $4000. Guarantee includes six inspections in 12-month period with necessary sod replacement at no extra charge.

Criteria: Twenty-square-foot area needs resodding. Budget allows $4500 expenditure. Guarantee required.

WRITING OPTIONS

1. *Incident reports.* Write an incident report on a real or imaginary business/industrial accident for your "employer." Suitable subjects are damaged equipment, brief fire, broken merchandise, minor burns or sprains, collapsed shelving, broken windows or doors, and so forth. Write a concise description of the incident or accident. Next, write a sequential analysis of the cause. Follow this with a review of the results, and, finally, present your recommendations to prevent the incident from recurring. Include graphics of the location and cost breakdowns.

2. *Periodic or progress reports.* Select one option.

    a. In letter form write a periodic report on your monthly expenses to your parents or spouse. Include a circle graph or bar chart on the percentage and the actual dollar expense of each category. Include, or comment on the lack of, the following categories:

Housing	School Supplies
Utilities	Insurance
Food	Charge Accounts and/or Car Payments
Transportation	Leisure
Clothes	Miscellaneous

    Include other categories as they are appropriate to your expenses. Conclude with an appraisal of your expenses.

    b. In memo form write a progress report to your academic advisor showing your progress towards completing a degree or receiving a certificate or license. Begin with a statement of your overall goal and its requirements. Include tables of your courses, credits, grades, and grade point averages for courses completed, courses in progress, and courses remaining. Conclude with a discussion of your career plans.

    c. Write a progress report on a project in which you are involved either in school or on-the-job. Include an introduction and sections on completed work, current work, future work, and an appraisal of progress. Be alert to graphic possibilities.

3. *Feasibility reports.* Select one option.

    a. Write a feasibility report which analyzes a new purchase. State your purpose and the requirements. Then describe two or more probable alternatives (cars, office equipment, water beds, appliances, and so forth). Next explain a method for evaluating the products (survey, testing, research). Present your findings. Evaluate the data, and conclude with logical recommendations for purchasing one of the optional items.

b. Write a feasibility report which analyzes a procedure or problem in your place of employment. Identify the problem (the present means of advertising a product, scheduling personnel, awarding salary increases, providing in-service training, promoting personnel, handling tasks, or other similar procedures). State the standards which should be set to remedy the problem. Devise two solutions to the problem and analyze the merits and limitations of each. Interpret the feasible solutions to draw logical recommendations for implementing one or the other.

4. *Lab or Test Reports*. Select two simple products (ballpoint pens, glues, paints, stepladders, brooms, car waxes, toothbrushes, garlic presses, and so forth). With the purpose of determining which is the better product, devise a method or procedure to test each. Carry out your testing and then write a test report which states the object or purpose of the experiment, the explanation of the test method, a step-by-step analysis of the test and the results, and your conclusions and recommendations on which is the better product. The results section should offer the opportunity to present data in a table or performance curve.

5. *Field reports*. On your campus or at your place of employment select a location to conduct a field examination which will include conclusions and recommendations about the efficiency or safety of the location. Suggested fields to investigate are

On the Campus	*At Work*
parking lot layout	room furnishings
cafeteria food arrangements	office layout
classroom layout	restroom facilities
registration procedures	lounge or coffee room
recreational areas	locker space
library study carel layout	emergency exit doors/ stairwells
campus bookstore displays	storeroom arrangements
a piece of equipment	a piece of equipment
a small structure	security arrangements

Write a field report structured to include the purpose of your inspection, the methods for gathering data, the facts and results of your investigation, and the conclusions and/or recommendations which will make the chosen field more efficient or safer. Use appropriate headings.

CHAPTER 8

Longer Reports, Proposals

DUFFY

by Bruce Hammond

INTRODUCTION

Although the need for conciseness is always present, a lengthy report is occasionally necessary. Quarterly and annual reports, long-range planning programs, and proposals are a few typical long reports which most organizations produce. This chapter will cover the special features of longer reports and review the particulars for a proposal.

PRESENTING THE LONGER REPORT

In order to avoid "gray material"—pages of dull, gray type—a longer report is distinguished by special features to make the information contained in it more accessible. These features may include

- Title page
- Transmittal correspondence
- Table of contents
- List of illustrations
- Abstract
- Report body with topical headings
- Supplements

Title Page

Include an attractive and clarifying title page. This page should include

- A precise title
- The name, title, and company of the person(s) to whom the report is directed
- The name, title, and company of the writer(s)
- The date

A precise title, such as

PROPOSAL FOR PURCHASE AND INSTALLATION OF IONIZATION
AND PHOTOELECTRIC FIRE ALARM SYSTEMS
IN OCEANVIEW CONDOMINIUM UNITS

is more effective than a vague title, such as

PROPOSAL TO DECREASE FIRE HAZARDS

Figures 8.1 and 8.2 include title pages to longer reports.

Transmittal Correspondence

A letter or memorandum of transmittal accompanies most longer reports. The purpose of the transmittal correspondence is to convey the long report or proposal in a suitable explanatory manner. It is usually very brief, three or four short paragraphs. It contains

1. The title and purpose of the report.
2. A statement of when it was requested or why it is being submitted.
3. Comment on any problems encountered.
4. Acknowledgement of other people who assisted in assembling the report.

Do not include repetitions of the data in the actual report. Figures 8.1 and 8.2 illustrate typical transmittal correspondence.

Table of Contents

Your reader(s) will want to be able to refer to sections quickly. A table of contents not only helps the reader(s) to turn rapidly to a particular section of the report, but also gives an initial indication of the organization, content, and emphasis of the report. A table of contents should accompany every written report that exceeds eight or ten pages and may be helpful in some shorter reports. Title the page *Table of Contents*. All headings used in the report are included in the table, and the subordination of sections is indicated by indentation. The starting page of each section is included as shown in the sample proposals in Figures 8.1 and 8.2.

List of Illustrations

If graphics (tables and figures) are used throughout your report, include their table and figure numbers, titles, and page references on the same or separate page from the Table of Contents. Center the title *List of Illustrations*. List tables separately from figures. Figures 8.1 and 8.2 illustrate lists of illustrations.

Abstract

An abstract is a brief *informative* or *descriptive* summary of a longer report. It is written after you have completed the full report, but it is intended to be read first by your audience. Occasionally the abstract is placed in the transmittal correspondence, but modern usage calls for it to be presented on a separate page placed after the table of contents and list of illustrations.

The *descriptive abstract* only identifies the areas to be covered in the report. It serves as an extended statement of scope and is useful only for a very extensive report because it indicates the report's organization, but not its content.

An *informative abstract* summarizes the entire report allowing the reader an overview of the facts before proceeding to read all of the detail. An abstract is seldom longer than one page. It should never exceed 10 percent of the length of the entire report or it defeats its purpose.

Besides expecting an abstract to accompany a formal report, a busy executive often requests assistants to prepare abstracts of newspaper and periodical articles in order that the executive might have access to the content of pertinent reading material in brief form. He or she can then decide whether to read the entire report or article.

Librarians subscribe to abstracting journals which provide brief descriptive or informative abstracts of articles published in a number of journals in a specific field. These allow the reader to obtain an overview of content without lengthy reading. The reader can then reject or pursue the lengthy articles.

Many busy people are likely to review your formal report or proposal. Most will rely on the information in the abstract to make initial judgments. Because these readers may not possess the technical knowledge and language which your full report embraces, be careful to avoid technical terminology.

To write an informative abstract, follow these steps:

1. Read the entire report to grasp its full contents.
2. Estimate the number of words and plan an abstract which should seldom exceed 10 percent of the original length.
3. Write down or underline in a report copy the key facts, statistics, and points under each heading.
4. Do not include the statement of scope.
5. Omit or condense lengthy examples, tabulated material, and other supporting explanations.
7. Rewrite the information which you have culled from the report in original sentences.
8. Edit the abstract for completeness and accuracy.

On the opposite page is the text of a brief proposal. The key points that should be included in an abstract have been underlined.

The proposal consists of approximately 500 words. There are definitely other important factors besides those that are underlined, but to include them would entail too lengthy an abstract. The purpose of the abstract is to convey an overview of the concrete details of the longer proposal. The abstract should serve to inform the reader of your key content and specific conclusions. The following abstract for the proposal consists of 59 words.

> I propose we hire a part-time telephone receptionist. Presently the pricing clerk assumes the telephone duties at a company cost of $7,440 per year. A part-time operator will cost $5,256. The operator will handle calls and perform other light duties. The company will save $2,184 on the cost of telephone answering services, avoid fringe benefits, and realize more efficiency from the pricing clerk.

Notice that the abstract does not include how the present costs were derived nor how new costs were calculated. It merely presents the most important totals. Additional sample abstracts appear in Figures 8.1 and 8.2.

PROPOSAL TO HIRE PART-TIME
TELEPHONE RECEPTIONIST

INTRODUCTION

Purpose:

**Key
purpose**

   The purpose of this proposal to hire a part-time telephone receptionist
is to increase the work productivity of the present employees of Bruce Essex
Supply Company.

Scope:

   This report will document the problem, propose the hiring of the
telephone receptionist, detail the cost, duties, hours, and location, and review
the advantages.

PROBLEM

**Key
problem**

Presently, the pricing clerk is assigned telephone reception duties. This
situation is costly to the company because the pricing clerk is salaried in
excess of the demand for such duties, and these duties interrupt the normal
productivity of the pricing clerk. Further, due to the volume of phone calls,
the pricing clerk must both work overtime and leave incomplete work.

**Key
cost
factor**

The present system costs the company $7440.00 per year as shown in
Table 1:

TABLE 1   COMPANY COST FOR TELEPHONE RECEPTION

Time	Calls	Time per Call at 45 sec	Cost at $5.00 per hour ($)	Estimated Overtime (hr)	Overtime at $7.50 per hour ($)
Day	400	300 min	25.00	1	7.50
Week	2000	25 hr	125.00	4	30.00
Month	1000	100 hr	500.00	16	120.00
6 Mo	48000	600 hr	3000.00	96	720.00
Year	96000	1200 hr	6000.00	192	1440.00

Total Cost of Telephone Duties: $7440.00 per year

Even though the pricing clerk is paid overtime, she is frustrated, overworked, and operating inefficiently.

PROPOSAL

Therefore, I propose the hiring of one part-time telephone receptionist to work six hours a day, thirty hours per week.

Key cost factor

Cost:
Total annual wages will be $5,256.00 as shown in Table 2:

TABLE 2   COST FOR PART-TIME TELEPHONE RECEPTIONIST

Time	# of Hours	Cost at $3.65 per hour ($)
Day	6	21.90
Week	30	109.50
Month	120	438.00
6 Mo	720	2,628.00
Year	1,440	5,256.00

The $3.65 per hour wage is in compliance with the 1985 minimum wage law.

Hours:
Because the majority of phone calls are between 9:00 a.m. and 4:00 p.m., recommended hours for employment are from 9:30 a.m. to 3:30 p.m. The telephone receptionist would have the opportunity for one or two hours extra work at the same wage during sales if management feels it is necessary.

Key duties

Duties:
Duties of the telephone receptionist should include transferring calls to the proper departments, screening management's incoming calls, light filing, typing, and posting the mail toward the end of each day.

Location:
The telephone receptionist may be positioned at either of the two extra desks which are already equipped with office phones. The existing switchboard can be moved from the pricing clerk's desk to the selected desk.

Schedule:
I propose that the operator be hired by April 15, 199X

ADVANTAGES

This proposal has numerous advantages:

Key cost
factor

1. The company will save $1,194.00 on the cost of telephone answering services.

Persuasive
factor

2. Because the position will be part-time, the company will not have to offer fringe benefits, such as overtime pay, profit sharing, or insurance.

3. By allowing the pricing clerk to concentrate on her duties, the position will be more cost efficient.

CONCLUSION

My proposal, if adopted, should prove to be both economical and practical. I urge you to give it serious consideration.

Supplements

It may be helpful to attach various supplemental materials to your report. The body of the report may summarize complex financial projections or survey results, tabulate the capabilities of new equipment, or recommend qualified personnel to assume new responsibilities. Supporting materials, such as financial spreadsheets, equipment brochures, copies of survey instruments, personnel resumes, and even bibliographies may be attached as exhibits or appendixes and grouped in the back of the binder. Should you include supplemental materials, follow these guidelines:

- Number and title each supplement

    Examples: Exhibit 1   Interview Topic Outline
    Exhibit 2   Sample Policy Matrix

    Appendix A   Employee Safety Survey
    Appendix B   Resume on Donald C. French

- Refer to the exhibits or appendixes in the body of your text.

    Example: Although I have interpreted the survey data here, the survey instrument and numerical tabulations are in Appendix C.

- Include the exhibit or appendix titles in your Table of Contents

Figure 8.1 and 8.2 include supplemental materials following the Conclusions sections of the sample proposals. Note their numbers and titles, their listings in the appropriate Tables of Contents, and references to them in the text.

PROPOSALS

A proposal is an action-oriented report. While most reports include recommendations for ongoing accomplishments, a proposal suggests a future task and includes a complete plan of how to accomplish this task. That is, a proposal contains procedure or equipment analysis, cost analysis, the capabilities of existing facilities, information on involved personnel, and usually a timetable for accomplishing the work. A brief report may recommend that a new policy be devised. A proposal provides exactly what the policy must cover, a schedule for adoption, a procedure for implementing the policy, and the personnel who should be in charge. A proposal's purpose is to persuade the reader.

To be persuasive a proposal must emphasize the advantages to the organization. You need to convince the decision makers to take action. As you develop your data and organize your material, stress one or more of the following advantages that your proposal will effect:

- Money savings or increased profits in the short and/or long term
- More efficient time applications
- Improved employee and client safety and comfort
- Compliance with laws or ethics
- Enriched employee morale

Motivate responsible people into action by appealing to their sense of responsibility and, perhaps, even playing to their fear of failure as leaders.

Types of Proposals

Proposals are classified as *internal* and *external*, *solicited* and *unsolicited*. Government and industry often solicit external proposals from outside agencies to solve problems or to develop services prior to awarding contracts or grants. A county commission may advertise for competing firms to submit proposals to develop a county-wide transportation system. A national airline may solicit proposals to develop a larger and faster jet. The federal government solicits grant proposals for services in education, environment, energy, science, medicine, rural development, and other areas. A university may hire a consulting firm to develop a long-range expansion program. The agency which solicits external proposals spells out general requirements, cost ceilings, deadlines, and criteria for evaluation.

In business and industry the internal proposal, one written by a member of the organization, may be solicited or unsolicited. Management may appoint an individual or a committee to devise a program to change or improve some existing procedure or practice. A cafeteria manager may ask employees to submit proposals to increase sales in the fast-food line. An office manager may solicit proposals for policy and procedure to avoid charges of sexual harassment. Or any employee or group of employees may initiate an unsolicited proposal to management to purchase new equipment, improve working schedules, or alter procedures.

Writing a good unsolicited proposal for your employer is an excellent way not only to improve working conditions, but also to demonstrate your interest in and commitment to your company.

Organization and Format

A proposal explains an existing problem and proposes the concrete measures, procedures, or steps for rectification, along with an explanation of costs, equipment, personnel needs, and a time schedule. A proposal usually involves

- A clear statement of what is being proposed and why
- An explanation of the background or problem
- A presentation of the actual proposal, including methods, costs, personnel, and action schedules
- A discussion of the advantages and disadvantages
- The conclusions, recommendations, or an action schedule

All formal reports are more readable if they contain headings. The following topical headings should be considered for organizational purposes for a proposal although each actual proposal will suggest additional major and minor headings.

Traditional Format	*Streamlined Format*
Introduction	Subject
Purpose	Objective
Scope	Problem
Background	Proposal
Investigative procedure	Advantages
Findings	Disadvantages
Proposal	Action
Equipment	
Capabilities	
Costs	
Personnel	
Timetable	
Consequences	
Advantages	
Disadvantages	
Conclusion	

The streamlined format (SOPPADA) is usually used only for *brief* proposals.

Writing the Proposal

For purposes of instruction we will concentrate on an unsolicited proposal, the kind you may originate in an entry-level career position or devise for consideration at your college or university. It is important to remember your audience. You essentially are writing a persuasive report; therefore, you must justify your proposal by presenting compelling reasons for its adoption. Although you may address your proposal to your immediate supervisor, a proposal is often reviewed by superiors further up the chain of authority. Your explanations, data, and language must be clear to those people who may not have any familiarity with the situation to which you address yourself. You must be objective and diplomatic.

Introduction. The introduction usually includes a statement of *purpose* and comments on the *scope* of the report. State briefly exactly what you propose along with a general statement of why the proposal should be given serious consideration. The scope statement will orient your reader(s) to the material to follow. Examples are:

This report proposes the purchase of a table saw to increase production in our store fixture manufacturing plant and to increase profits. This proposal will document the problem, examine the capabilities of the proposed equipment, detail the costs, recommend the location, discuss the advantages, and present conclusions.

Purpose: This proposal, to purchase and install bicycle supports and gate locks in the ABC Elementary School bike compound, is designed to eliminate prevalent vandalism and to decrease personal injuries.

Scope: In this report an examination of the problem, a tabulation of survey results, the description of the proposed concrete bicycle supports and gate locks are presented, followed by the layout, costs, product availability, and conclusions.

Problem/Background. The Problem/Background section details the existing problem, such as high costs, inefficiency, dangers or abuses, or low morale among employees. The solution you intend to propose will probably cost money or involve personnel in new responsibilities, so you must spell out that a very real and perhaps costly problem presently does exist. If it is not obvious how you researched the problem, you may need to include an explanation of your investigation techniques. If appropriate, research the operational costs of the present system. Project these costs over a week, a month, a year, or other appropriate time frames. Present data in tabular form.

Your problem may be that hazards or inconveniences exist under the present system. Document accidents, work slowdowns, late production schedules, or other related evidence. If the problem is causing low morale, research the turnover rate of personnel or incidents of friction.

The **deductive** organization pattern is easier to read than the **inductive** (see Chapter 2). In a proposal to purchase a computer for two floral shops the problem was documented as follows:

Problem:

The testing problem is that bookkeeper transportation and telephone costs are excessively high. Because both of our floral shops maintain separate inventory control of customer account information, bookkeeper Mary Jacobs must frequently travel between the two shops and telephone for customer account information. In addition, this system requires twice the amount of time necessary to review the total daily sales. Table 1 shows the transportation and communication expenses of the bookkeeper under the present system:

Table 1   Current Bookkeeper Transportation and Telephone Expenses

Time Frame	Travel Time (hr)	Gas ($)	Telephone Time ($)	Cost @ $6.00 per hr wage
Day	1	5	1	6
Week	5	25	5	30
Month	20	100	20	120
6 Mo	120	600	120	720
Year	240	1200	240	1,440

TOTAL COST $2,640.00

The $2,640.00 wage and gas expenditure can be put to more productive use.

The emphasis here is on inefficient costs. The following is from a proposal to establish a regulating committee to end sex discrimination at a community college. The problem does not entail costs, but details concrete evidence of unethical discrimination:

Problem:

Some sex discrimination facts present themselves:

1. Of the 215 faculty members 79 or 36.7 percent are women, a percentage which is not reflected in either administrative positions or standing committee membership.

2. Of the 36 administrators only three (3) are women; of the ten (10) division chairpersons none are women; of the twelve (12) department heads only two (2) are women; of the twenty (20) area leaders only five (5) are women; of the total 78 positions only ten (10) or 12.8 percent are women.

3. Of the 207 faculty and administrators serving on standing committees only 52 or 25 percent are women. One committee has no women members.

4. Women have voiced concern that the inequitable number of women in administrative and standing committee positions is a "negative incentive" for innovative teaching, volunteer assignments, and request for advancement consideration.

5. Women students have voiced concern through the agency of the student government association that the college does not actively counsel and provide for women students to excell nor to set goals commensurate with the expanding opportunities for entry into the previously male-dominated professions.

Be thorough and exacting in your documentation of the problem. The information in this section will be referred to when you detail the consequences of adopting your proposal.

Proposal.   Present the solution to the problem by providing all of the particulars of your proposal. As already suggested you may wish to consider the following subheadings:

Equipment/Procedure
Capabilities
Costs
Personnel
Timetable

If the proposal involves the purchase of new equipment, describe it accurately and explain its function and capabilities. If the proposal involves a new procedure or policy, explain exactly how it will work. Under costs include initial purchase price, financing, installation, labor, and training costs. If new or transferred personnel are involved, include the qualifications for the position or the qualifications of the employee. Summarize duties and salaries. If you use the traditional format, include a timetable or work plan for making your proposal operable in this section. If you use the streamlined format, place your schedule of tasks to be accomplished in the final Action section. An effective proposal not only seeks action but also becomes the blueprint by which the action shall be performed. Because the actual Proposal section of your report is often lengthy, samples are not given here but may be reviewed in Figures 8.1 and 8.2.

Consequences.   This section may be divided into *Advantages* and *Disadvantages* or *Strengths* and *Limitations*. Here you refer to the details in your Problem section and explain how each problem will be solved or alleviated.

If your proposal costs money, show in graphics how implementation will save the company money over projected periods of time. Often a costly expenditure will ultimately save the company money over a few years due to increased efficiency or production. If you propose a new system, number and list all of the benefits of it. Employee morale is an important concern of management; if adoption of your proposal will improve employee morale, detail these benefits.

Do not ignore disadvantages (temporary work stoppage, layoffs of employees, limited capabilities, and so forth). Discuss these disadvantages or limitations in a positive manner.

Following are brief sections from proposals outlining Consequences. The first example is from a proposal to pave an American Legion Hall parking lot:

Consequences:

By paving the existing parking lot we will be able to accommodate 30 or more cars than the present 140. By eliminating the problems of dust and erosion, the physical appearance and value of the property will be enhanced. During the two weeks of construction Sunset City officials have agreed in writing to allow our 57 employees and approximately 100 daytime visitors to park in the Sunset City Hall west parking lot.

The second example is from a proposal to adopt new displacement and furlough rules for an airline pilots' association:

Advantages:

Adoption of the system-wide seniority rules in the pilot displacement and furlough process results in the following advantages:

- Senior pilots are able to displace at any base.
- The total number of displacements arising out of a curtailment situation is small, and the displacements are mostly confined to the base where the curtailment situation occurs. Thereafter, significantly fewer pilots are affected by curtailment.
- A maximum of two base moves exists for every pilot curtailed.
- Protection of captaincy is guaranteed for all but the junior captain at base. The junior captain has base protection.
- The indicated cost savings is 30 percent over the current operating agreement.

Disadvantages:

These benefits are achieved at the cost of limiting pilots' freedom of choice in the following manner:

- A pilot's displacement choices are limited.
- If a captain desires to revert to first officer status to displace in a particular equipment, he may not be able to do so.

Conclusions.   The body of your proposal has examined the problem and presented a blueprint for action. You have anticipated the questions and possible objections to your proposal and objectively, but persuasively, responded to them. Your Closing section is essentially an urge to action. In the traditional format summarize your proposal features and reemphasize the advantages in numbered statements. Close with a persuasive statement, such as

> I urge you to give serious consideration to this proposal and am available to discuss its particulars with you.

In the streamlined format, title your section *Action* and present your schedule, work plan, or timetable. Figures 8.1 and 8.2 illustrate the optional Closing sections for proposals.

Your signature, position, and date are appended to the final page in the right-hand corner of the paper:

Janet Gorky
_____
                                   Janet Gorky, Assembler   11/15/9X

PROPOSAL TO IMPROVE

EMPLOYEE WORK SCHEDULES

IN THE

CUSTOMER INQUIRY DEPARTMENT

Prepared for

Andrea Brooks

Assistant Vice-president

Operations Division

State Trust Charter Bank

Bigtown, New Hampshire

by

Monica Ferschke

Administrative Assistant

October 19, 199X

FIGURE 8.1   *Sample proposal with formal report features* (Courtesy of Monica Ferschke)

TABLE OF CONTENTS

LIST OF ILLUSTRATIONS

FIGURE 8.1   *continued*

MEMORANDUM

TO: Andrea Brooks, Assistant Vice-president

FROM: Monica Ferschke, Administrative Assistant $\mathcal{M.F.}$

DATE: October 19, 199X

SUBJECT: Proposal to Improve Employee Work Schedules

Enclosed is a proposal to improve the employee work hours in the Customer Inquiry Department. Implementation of this proposal will increase the department's productivity and efficiency, raise employee morale, and, ultimately, improve the level of service to customers.

I am grateful for the cooperation that the department employees gave me by completing the survey and providing thoughtful comments.

May we discuss this proposal when I return from vacation on Monday, October 26?

MF/mb

Enclosure

iii

FIGURE 8.1   *continued*

ABSTRACT

The schedule of employee work hours in the Customer Inquiry Department needs revision. Staff experiences difficulties in completing work by deadlines, customers wait while staff work on assignments, and morale is low because of long hours and stressful pressures. The low volume of calls on Fridays after 4:00 P.M. doesn't warrant that a full staff be on hand. I propose the creation of two alternating shifts:

Week A   Monday–Thursday   8:00 A.M. to 4:30 P.M.

        Friday   8:00 A.M. to 4:00 P.M.

Week B   Monday–Thursday   8:00 A.M. to 4:00 P.M.

        Friday   8:00 A.M. to 6:00 P.M.

An equal number of employees will work in each shift, but employees will not have to work for ten hours every Friday. Adoption of the proposal will improve the department's productivity, efficiency, morale, and customer service.

FIGURE 8.1 *continued*

PROPOSAL TO IMPROVE EMPLOYEE WORK SCHEDULES

IN THE CUSTOMER INQUIRY DEPARTMENT

INTRODUCTION

Purpose

This proposal to change employee work hours in the Customer Inquiry
Department will provide a schedule to raise the levels of productivity and
efficiency, to improve morale within the department, and to provide more
attentive customer service.

Scope

This report documents the department's current operations, presents
employee survey results, proposes a new work schedule, and reviews the
advantages to the bank and its customers.

BACKGROUND

Problem

Currently, employee work hours in the department are 8:00 A.M. to 4:00
P.M. Monday through Thursday and from 8:00 A.M. to 6:00 P.M. every Friday,
a 10-hour work day. Training sessions are often conducted between 8:00
A.M. and 9:00 A.M. Monday through Friday, making it difficult for staff to
complete paperwork and assignments by deadlines. To accomplish
assignments, certain staff members must stop accepting customer calls
before 4:00 P.M. to complete the work. This creates added pressures for
staff members still accepting calls, and customers must wait longer for
service due to a smaller available staff.
  Employees have voiced their concerns to their supervisor, Ms.
Annabelle Higgins, who, in turn, recognizes that her staff's productivity
and attention to detail decreases after 4:00 P.M. on Fridays.

1

FIGURE 8.1   *continued*

2

Procedure

Initially, I examined the volume of calls after 4:00 P.M. on Fridays during September this year because that month has proven to be the busiest over the past three years. Appendix A contains a tabulation of calls per hour. Additionally, I conducted a survey among the staff regarding a change of their current work hours and asking for their comments on subsequent benefits to their department and the bank if hours were changed. Appendix B contains the survey instrument and numerical tabulations.

Findings

A.   Volume of Calls

After examining the volume of calls after 4:00 P.M. on Fridays during September, I find that the volume does not warrant having a full staff available. The departmental average number of calls per employee per hour is 50 (based on the annual number of calls divided by the hours of operation and the number of employees). Table 1 shows the actual number of calls handled by staff on Fridays in September after 4:00 P.M. and the number of employees needed to handle those calls.

Table 1   Number of Employees Needed for Calls after 4:00 P.M.

September Fridays	Hours	Calls Taken (#)	Employees Needed (#)
1st Week	4:00-5:00	45	1
	5:00-6:00	21	1
2nd Week	4:00-5:00	42	1
	5:00-6:00	16	1
3rd Week	4:00-5:00	53	2
	5:00-6:00	25	1
4th Week	4:00-5:00	46	1
	5:00-6:00	37	1

As illustrated in Table 1, only two employees are actually needed from 4:00 P.M. to 6:00 P.M. to answer customer calls. Assignments and paperwork are, in most cases, expected to be completed prior to 4:00 P.M. on Fridays; therefore, to require all ten employees to work after 4:00 P.M. is inefficient.

FIGURE 8.1   *continued*

3

B. Employee Survey

All ten staff members in the Customer Inquiry Department responded to my survey requesting their opinions regarding the implementation of a new schedule and commenting on the benefits of the change. Of the ten employees who responded,

- 100 percent favor the new schedule,
- 60 percent think that the proposed change will improve morale within the department,
- 70 percent feel the change will allow them to finish their work by deadline, and
- 80 percent feel customer services will be improved.

Employee opinion, long working hours on Fridays, and inadequate employee scheduling lead me to conclude that a change should be made regarding the work hours within the department.

PROPOSAL

Therefore I submit the following proposal.

Schedule

Employees will alternate work week schedules; there will be five employees on each schedule.

Schedule A (5)	Monday–Thursday	8:00 A.M. to 4:30 P.M.
	Friday	8:00 A.M. to 4:00 P.M.
Schedule B (5)	Monday–Thursday	8:00 A.M. to 4:00 P.M.
	Friday	8:00 A.M. to 6:00 P.M.

The number of hours worked by any one employee in a week will not change, but the assignment of long and short hours on Fridays will alternate.

This schedule will ensure that a sufficient number of employees will be on station to answer calls during additional operating hours on Fridays. Duties involving mid-week deadlines could be assigned to employees working the late (4:30) shift, allowing the extra half hour after calls to complete paperwork and assignments.

FIGURE 8.1   *continued*

4

Date

I propose that this new schedule be implemented by November 1.

CONSEQUENCES

By implementing the proposed hours, these advantages should accrue:
- Employees on the 4:30 A.M. shift will be able to complete more work, and accuracy should improve as interruptions will be minimal.
- Employee morale should improve. Acceptance of this proposal will demonstrate that management values employee opinions and that employees offer sincere efforts to increase operations efficiency.
- Customer service will improve because the entire staff will be available to answer calls until 4:00 P.M.

CONCLUSION

I strongly urge you to implement this proposal so that the Customer Inquiry Department can become a more productive and efficient work unit of the bank. Although Ms. Annabelle Higgins will have the final responsibility for monitoring the schedule, I will be happy to assist her in posting the schedule and clarifying its points to the staff. Please let me know your decision.

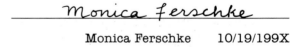

Monica Ferschke   10/19/199X

FIGURE 8.1   *continued*

APPENDIX A

CUSTOMER INQUIRY DEPARTMENT

CUSTOMER CALL LOG TABULATIONS

DATE	4–5 P.M. CALLS (#)	5–6 P.M. CALLS (#)
Friday 9/4	45	21
Friday 9/11	42	16
Friday 9/18	47	25
Friday 9/25	40	30

FIGURE 8.1   *continued*

APPENDIX B

SURVEY TABULATION

CUSTOMER INQUIRY DEPARTMENT

SCHEDULE SURVEY

This survey is being conducted to determine if you would be willing to work on a new rotating schedule. We would also like your comments on the benefits to the department which you foresee if such a schedule is adopted.

1.   Would you favor the following new hours?   <u> 10 </u> yes   <u> 0 </u> no

       Schedule A   Monday to Thursday   8:00–4:30

                      Friday   8:00–4:00

       Schedule B   Monday to Thursday   8:00–4:00

                      Friday   8:00–6:00

       (Alternate every other week)

2.   Would you like to suggest any other possible new schedule? (Please indicate in the white space.)

NONE

3.   If you answered "Yes" to Number 1, please comment on the foreseeable benefits.

"Better customer service Monday–Thursday"	10 mentions
"Free up unnecessary personnel on Fridays"	3 mentions
"Improve morale"	10 mentions
"Time to catch up on paperwork from 4:00 to 4:30"	5 mentions
"More flexibility for employees"	1 mention
"Should stimulate closer attention to detail"	3 mentions

FIGURE 8.1   *continued*

PROPOSAL TO DEVELOP
A REIMBURSABLE EXPENSE POLICY
AND
MONITORING AND CONTROL SYSTEM

Prepared for
Mr. Duane P. Morton
President
Ace Electronics Company, Inc.
Fresno, California

by

Charles E. Smith
Senior Partner
Smith Business Consultants
San Francisco, California

February 24, 199X

FIGURE 8.2   *Sample traditional proposal with formal report features*
(Courtesy of Charles E. Smith; adaptation)

SMITH BUSINESS CONSULTANTS
1000 Plaza Court
San Francisco, California

February 24, 199X

Mr. Duane P. Morton, President
Ace Electronics Company, Inc.
2120 West Broward Boulevard
Fresno, California   93710

Dear Mr. Morton:

We have completed the study which you authorized in November 199X concerning the control of reimbursable business expenses at Ace Electronics Company and are pleased to submit the enclosed proposal to make expense practices more equitable.

We appreciate the cooperation of your officers and other employees in conducting our study. All transcribed interviews and records research findings will be kept in confidence for six months should you need to review this material.

We thank you for this opportunity to be of assistance.

Very truly yours

Charles E. Smith

Charles E. Smith
Senior Partner

CES:jsv

Enclosure

ii

FIGURE 8.2 *continued*

TABLE OF CONTENTS

Page

FIGURE 8.2   *continued*

ABSTRACT

This report for Ace Electronics Company, Inc. proposes the development of a reimbursable expense policy along with a monitoring and control system to make expense practices more equitable, to allow for abuse detection, and to reduce costs.

Extensive interviews and expense records research reveal that expenses are excessive, existing policy is inadequate, and methods of approval and control are deficient. By implementing this proposal the approximate yearly $3.3 million reimbursable expenses may be reduced by as much as $1 million.

We propose the development of a written reimbursable expense policy which incorporates an expense matrix of all allowable expenses, categorizes employees, sets conditions and restrictions, and clearly states approval individuals. Further, we propose procedural regulations which establish periodic report periods and deadlines, entail new report forms, and institute a definite system of review and analysis. A work plan to carry out these proposals includes the appointment of a director, the establishment of committees, and a listing of chronological duties.

By implementing this proposal reimbursable expenses shall be reduced, and adoption may well lead to cost reduction sensitivity in other expense areas.

FIGURE 8.2 *continued*

PROPOSAL TO DEVELOP A REIMBURSABLE EXPENSE POLICY
AND MONITORING AND CONTROL SYSTEM

INTRODUCTION

Purpose
    This proposal to develop a reimbursable expense policy and monitoring
and control system is designed to make expense practices more equitable,
to establish a system which will detect and prevent abuses, and to reduce
costs.

Scope

    This report presents a description of our study, a review of our findings,
a dual proposal, the advantages of implementation, and the conclusions.

BACKGROUND

Procedure
    To determine the facts relating to reimbursable expenses we used a
sample basis. With the assistance of four senior executives, a sample of 25
of the approximately 100 executives at Ace was chosen. Personal interviews
were held with twenty of them, and extensive records research was
conducted for fifteen covering the second quarter of 199X, the period chosen
for the analysis.
    Our first step was to interview these officers, two financial managers,
and the personnel manager and to examine a sampling of expense reports.
From that work we prepared two documents: a list of discussion questions
for the interviews, and an outline of the records research requirement.
Appendixes A and B exhibit these documents and indicate the extensive
nature of the fact finding.
    The Smith consultants conducted the interviews, and an Ace team
directed by the assistant corporate controller conducted the records
research.

1

FIGURE 8.2 *continued*

2

Findings
A.   Scope of Expenses
Reimbursable business expenses represent a significant controllable cost at Ace. During the first nine months of 199X total expenses for officers and others was $2.5 million, an annual expense of over $3.3 million a year. For the officer group alone the figure was $1 million a year.

B.   Policies and Practices
Numerous examples of excessive expense practices and failure to control expenses are evident upon examination of the records and by admission of the officers in confidential interviews. We believe that reimbursable expenses at Ace could be reduced by $1 million a year without adversely affecting the business.

As a result of unclear or inadequate policy or poor communication, most interviewers displayed uncertainty about what was expected of them. During the interview officers were asked: "Can you identify the written expense policy/procedure as it relates to you?" Following are representative answers:
   "One might exist, but I'm not familiar with it."
   "There's only a memo on transportation."
   "There is no written policy."
   "Policies are not spelled out. I'm not familiar with any written policy. I do what I did for my former employer."
Further, existing written expense policies lack clarity.
   • A limited number of items that may be authorized are listed, but the conditions under which they are authorized are not always clear. For example, statements, such as "when time is a factor," "where necessary for company business," and "only to employees who hold the types of jobs that require such meetings," appear in the policies.
   • Some expenses require prior approval, but the approving individual is not always identified.
   • Some items of allowable expenses, such as home entertainment and telephone answering services, are not treated.

FIGURE 8.2   *continued*

3

- The frequency of reporting is not covered.
- A few items, such as social club memberships and access to the executive dining room, are inadequately treated. In some cases these are considered executive perquisites and in others reimbursable expenses.

C.   Approval and Control

Methods of approval and control are inadequate.

- Officers report they are not comfortable when questioning the expense practices of close associates, and rarely do so.
- Expense documentation and explanation are inadequate. Reporting forms fail to determine such things as class of air travel, cost of overnight accommodations per night, purposes of business meetings, the number of people entertained, and so forth.
- Budgetary control is difficult. Monthly reports do not show expenses by individuals, but by divisions.
- Expense reporting is often tardy. For the sample officers timeliness ran from prompt (2 to 3 days after the reported period) to late (6 months). Many officers reported weekly, others monthly, and some on less periodic schedule.
- The expense report is not a complete record of expenses. Some officers are reimbursed for expenses directly from petty cash, or the invoice for an expense item is paid directly by Ace and not shown on an expense report.

D.   Variations

The interviews and the records research reveal a wide range of variable practices.

- In the sample of the fifteen officers whose expense reports were analyzed, only 7 charged telephone expenses, 11 had social club expenses, 10 were reimbursed for gifts, and 5 incurred expenses for personal entertainment.
- Air travel practices further illustrate the variety that exists. During the analyzed quarter 3 of the officers made at least one flight, but 2 of them did not submit ticket receipts. Of the 11 other employees whose flights could be analyzed, 6 flew first class and

FIGURE 8.2   *continued*

4

only 2 paid the difference between first class and coach fare. Seven wives flew with their husbands at company expense, 2 of them first class.

- There is considerable variation in the cost of overnight room accommodations. The range is from $26.00 to $110.00 a night.
- The average per meal cost of business meetings range from $10 to $48. Business meetings were usually conducted at lunch.

The great variation in expense practice is the basis for our conclusion that substantial opportunities for cost reduction of at least $1 million a year exist.

<u>PROPOSAL</u>

To correct these deficiencies in the reimbursable/expense system, we propose

1. the development of a written reimbursable expense policy, and
2. the establishment of firm procedural regulations.

<u>Expense Policy</u>

Ace should prepare a written reimbursable expense policy that is clear with regard to each type of expense, that accommodates differences among employees, and that covers certain procedural requirements. To accomplish this

1. All personnel should be divided into categories. All employees should not be treated uniformly. Their expense spending requirements and privileges should be recognized in the policy. We recommend that the two categories be designated as follows:

   | Members of the Board | All Other |
   | Vice-presidents | Employees |

2. A policy matrix should be devised which lists all reimbursable expenses, employee category differences, restrictions and conditions, and approval authority. Appendix C illustrates a sample policy matrix.

FIGURE 8.2   *continued*

5

3. A clarifying policy should be written for wide distribution and inclusion in the Administrative Policy Manual. The policy should include guidelines and standards, procedures for advances, procedures for preparation, processing, and approval of the expense report, and specific guidelines and standards for each type of reimbursable expense in the matrix. Appendix D shows a sample administrative policy page.

Monitoring and Control
Procedural regulations should be established.
1. The report period should be monthly; deadline for submission should be one week thereafter.
2. Expense report forms should be revised to require documentation and explanation.
3. The Expense Report must be established as the sole vehicle for recording and reimbursing expenses.
4. Responsibilities of the reporting individual, the controller's department, and the approving individual should be developed into a definite system.
5. The role of the controller's department should be expanded. An editing function there should first evaluate the adequacy of the documentation and explanation, and the Expense Report should be returned to the reporting individual for correction if there are deficiencies. Next the report should be examined for conformance to policy, and any exception should be noted on a Buck Slip which, along with the Expense Report, should be forwarded to the approving individual.
The controller's department should prepare a summary analysis of each individual's expenses on a quarterly basis. Quarterly and cumulative expenses should be compared to budget.

FIGURE 8.2 *continued*

6

Work Plan
I.   Staffing
  A. Appoint the Vice-president of Finance as Project Director with
   responsibility for implementing all recommendations.
  B. Appoint a Corporate Expense Policy Committee to work with the
   Project Director.
  C. Assign a small staff to work with the Committee without
   interruption.
II. Expense Policy
  A. Establish the basis for assigning all personnel into the recom-
   mended two categories.
  B. Prepare an expense matrix and policy for each type of reimburs-
   able expense for each category of personnel.
  C. Submit the policy to officers for discussion and modification.
  D. Approve the policy.
  E. Disseminate the policy and conduct familiarization training.
III. Monitoring and Control
  A. Revise Expense Report format and create Daily Expense Diary,
   Buck Slip, and Quarterly Analysis.
  B. Establish the edit and analysis functions in each division
  C. Train expense report editors and analysts.
  D. Test the system and make adjustments.
  E. Commence live operation of the system.

ADVANTAGES

  By developing a written reimbursable expense policy and establishing
firm procedural regulations, the following advantages should accrue.
   1. Reimbursable expense practices should become more equitable
    over the broad organization due to clarification and control.
   2. A system for detection and prevention of abuses will be established.
   3. Superiors shall exercise more control of expenses.

FIGURE 8.2   *continued*

7

4. Quarterly analysis should encourage discipline and facilitate budget preparation.
5. Implementation should reduce costs.

CONCLUSION

An attractive scope for cost reduction exists and provides the basis for achieving improvements through implementing innovations in policy and control. In our opinion, the recommendations in this report are well worth implementing and, in addition, will lead to sensitivity towards cost reduction in other areas.

Charles E. Smith 2/24/9X

Charles E. Smith
Senior Partner

2/24/9X

CES:jsv

FIGURE 8.2 *continued*

APPENDIX A

REIMBURSABLE EXPENSES INTERVIEW TOPICS

1. Position held during second quarter, 199X
   a. Title
   b. Superior, subordinates
   c. Nature of position
   d. Approval authority for expense reports
2. Whose expense reports do you approve?
   a. Are summaries prepared?
   b. How do you control subordinates' expenses?
   c. Do you ever question their expenses? Details.
   d. Have you ever had a drive to reduce expenses? Explain.
3. Who approves your expense reports?
   a. Are summaries prepared?
   b. Are your expenses ever questioned? Details.
   c. Do you ever seek prior approval for expenses? Details.
   d. Do you have any prior understanding with regard to your expenses?
4. What is the budgetary control over your expenses?
   a. In what account in what cost center are your expenses accumulated?
   b. How do your expenses compare to budget?
5. Have you ever been told what the expense policy is as it relates to you? Details.
6. Can you identify the written expense policy/procedure as it relates to you? Details. What are the salient points?
7. Identify the forms that are used: expense reports, petty cash disbursements, report of outstanding advances, summaries.
8. What is the frequency of reporting and approval and what is your timeliness? Any difficulties?
9. What are the controlling policies/procedures with regard to advance accounts, and what are your practices?
10. List all of the categories of your reimbursable expenses.

8

FIGURE 8.2 *continued*

9

11. Do you incur reimbursable expenses that are not shown on your expense report? If so, where are they recorded?
12. What are the significant restrictions on your expense spending practices?
13. Do you ever misrepresent expense items? e.g. to combine minor items, to recover excessive charges?
14. What is the influence of your status on your expense practices? Is there discrimination by rank? Amplify?
15. How do you view the company attitude concerning expenses? Have there been any changes? How does it compare with other companies in which you have worked?

FIGURE 8.2 *continued*

APPENDIX B

RECORDS RESEARCH OUTLINE

I.   Sources of information
   A. Expense report
   B. Summary business expense report
   C. Petty cash disbursement form
   D. Report of outstanding advances
   E. Approval authority
   F. Quarterly Budget Report for appropriate cost center

II. Information required
   A. Controlling policy/procedure
   B. Approval authority
   C. Summary
   D. Type of form
   E. Completeness and deficiencies
   F. Date and total expenses for period
   G. Documentation check
   H. Assumptions

III. Quarterly Summary
   A. Transportation
   B. Hotel rooms
   C. Meals
   D. Business meetings
   E. Other

IV. Analysis
   A. Personnel category differences
   B. Direct payments
   C. Nature and amount of petty cash disbursements
   D. Timeliness
   E. Discrepancies
   F. Significance

10

FIGURE 8.2   *continued*

SAMPLE REIMBURSABLE EXPENSES POLICY MATRIX

Type of Expense	EMPLOYEE CATEGORY		Restrictions & Conditions	Approval Required
	President Vice-Pres or above	All Other Employees		
Airline and Railroad	First Class Reimbursable	a) Coach reimbursable b) First Class Restricted	Restrictions: a) Traveling in company of Pres., V-P, or above b) Duration of trip exceeds 7 hr c) Traveling with customer, etc	President Vice-Pres or above
Buses	Reimbursable	Reimbursable		
Rented Cars	Reimbursable	Reimbursable	Condition: a) Other forms of public transport cannot meet business requirements b) Standard size low-priced car	
Personal Cars	Reimbursable	Reimbursable	Condition: Must not be used on long trips when other transport is less expensive and obtainable	
Taxi Cabs	Reimbursable	Reimbursable	Condition: Other forms of public transport cannot meet business requirements	
Limousines and Company Cars	Restrictively Reimbursable	Restrictively Reimbursable	Restriction: a) Essential b) Mileage log maintained	President Vice-Pres or above
Air Charter	Reimbursable	Reimbursable	Restriction: Extreme emergency situation only	President Vice-Pres or above
Lodgings Single Rooms First Class Accommodations	Reimbursable	Reimbursable		
Suites	Restrictively Reimbursable	Restrictively Reimbursable	Restriction: Essential for the conduct of business	President Vice-Pres or above

11

FIGURE 8.2   *continued*

APPENDIX D

SAMPLE ADMINISTRATIVE POLICY PAGE

ACE Administrative Policy Manual

Section   Dist. List   Date Issued   Policy No.
  REIMBURSABLE BUSINESS EXPENSES 3   12/30/9X   RB-1
Subject   Page of
  Ace Reimbursable Business Expense Policy   3   39

III.   TYPES OF REIMBURSABLE BUSINESS EXPENSES
        For ease of reference, a matrix summarizing reimbursable expenses has been included in Section XI of this Policy.

    A. Transportation Expenses

        All requests for transportation should be submitted through the Transportation Department.

        Where use of the Transportation Department is impractical, an employee may arrange his own transportation.

        The restrictions and documentation required for transportation expenses are as follows:

        1. Airlines and Railroads - Coach type accommodations are to be used. All expenses in this category must be documented by a ticket stub when submitting the Ace Expense Report. When a ticket purchased by Ace is not used, it should be returned to the Controller's Department with the expense report for a refund. The amount of the unused ticket should be included on the expense report.

           When traveling to and from the airports and Ace, public transportation should be used wherever practical.

        2. Buses - The use of long-distance buses is permitted when they can reasonably meet the needs of the Company.

12

FIGURE 8.2 *continued*

APPENDIX D

3. <u>Rented Cars</u> - Use of rented cars should be limited to those situations where public transportation is not available or cannot meet business requirements. When the situation requires a rented car, short-term arrangements should be made by the individual. On rentals exceeding one month, arrangements should be made through the Ace Purchasing Department. On all rentals, a standard size, low-priced car should be used. In all cases <u>optional insurance should not be purchased</u> and where national car rental services are used, the discount should be obtained. When submitting this expense for reimbursement, a copy of the itemized invoice is required.

13

FIGURE 8.2 *continued*

EXERCISES

1. Locate, photocopy, and abstract an article from a professional journal in your field. Submit the copy of the article along with your abstract. Remember that your abstract should summarize the key *facts* and should not exceed 10 percent of the report length.

2. Write an abstract for the following brief proposal.

Subject:	Modification of the North Campus perimeter road and parking lot access road speed bumps.
Objective:	To alleviate complaints and to prevent further damage to student and visitors' automobiles.
Problem:	Since the installation of 80 speed bumps on the campus perimeter road and parking lot access roads in March 199X, over 100 students and other campus visitors have registered written complaints to the Security Department regarding damage to their automobiles. The height of the bumps is 8 in.; compact cars have only an 8-in. clearance. Further, 47 percent of the complaints are by drivers of large and intermediate automobiles. Reported damages include front end misalignments, rear end leakage, and muffler dents.

Inspection reveals that the bumps are excessively gouged and scraped. While some automobile damages may be due to excessive speed, a State Road Department inspector concurred, following his June 15, 199X visit, that the bumps are too high and too abrupt. Appendix A exhibits a copy of his letter.

Proposal:	Therefore, we propose that the 80 speed bumps be modified by grinding the peaks to a 6-in. height and sloping the sides with asphalt to a 35-degree slant. These modifications will eliminate the shock that automobiles are experiencing yet still deter speeding. Figure 1 shows a cross-section of the speed bumps before and after modification:

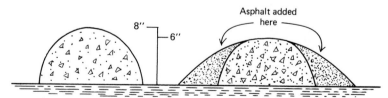

FIGURE 1   *Cross-section of a typical speed bump before and after modification*

Equipment:	Because the college does not own the equipment necessary for the modifications, the equipment must be rented. Necessary rental equipment includes

- One hand-held, gas-operated, heavy duty grinder with emery stone disc
- One gas-operated hot asphalt mixer
- One water-filled, hand-operated 500 pound roller

Labor: No special skills are needed to operate the equipment. Three Maintenance Department personnel can complete the modifications in an estimated 120 hours over two weeks.

Procedure: One man can grind the bumps at the rate of one and one-half hours per bump. Two men can mix and apply the asphalt in five six-hour shifts.

Cost: Modifications can be completed at an estimated $800.00 as shown in the following table:

Speed Bump Modification Cost Estimate

Item	Cost ($)	Time	Quantity	Total ($)
Grinder	55.00/wk	2 wk	—	110.00
Mixer	140.00/wk	1 wk	—	140.00
Roller	10.00/wk	1 wk	—	10.00
Asphalt Mix	2.00/55 lb bag	—	25	50.00
Pebbles	70.00/load	—	1	70.00
			TOTAL	800.00

Advantages:
1. Speed bumps will still deter speeding.
2. Damage to automobiles should decrease.
3. Project can be accomplished by existing staff.
4. Project can be accomplished prior to Term I traffic.

Action:
1. Approve proposal by July 15.
2. Arrange for rental equipment and supplies by August 1.
3. Modify speed bumps August 1–15 while the campus is closed to regular classes.

3. Title the proposal in Exercise 2 and compose a title page. You are the Supervisor of the Maintenance Department of your college presenting the proposal to the campus provost or dean.

4. Write a memo of transmittal. Include a brief abstract of the proposal. Acknowledge an individual or company for assistance in obtaining equipment and supply prices.

5. Devise a Table of Contents.

WRITING OPTIONS

Write a long proposal to solve a specific problem on your campus or at your workplace. Select a subject of sufficient complexity to warrant a proposal in longer report format, but do not tackle something beyond your scope. Chapter 10 discusses information access including library research, surveys, and subsidiary sources. Your proposal should require some research (a survey, interviews with authorities, journal articles, equipment brochure perusal, and related files). To clarify the problem, explain what procedures are being used now and how they are faulty. Document excessive costs, inefficient time use, damages, accidents, robberies, security problems, and so forth. Use survey results, interviews, and other research results to establish the severity of the problem. Present your actual proposal along with capabilities, costs, features, personnel, and a time schedule. Relate the points in your Consequence section to the points you made in the Background on Problem section, emphasizing how each problem will be solved or alleviated. After you complete your proposal draft, prepare all of the appropriate longer report features: title page, transmittal correspondence, table of contents and list of illustrations, abstracts, and supplements. Submit your proposal in an attractive folder. Suggested subjects are

Campus	*Work*
new equipment	new equipment
new system of registration	new uniforms
improved parking facilities	improved systems of duty
picnic or stone tables	roster
snack bars by classrooms	improved method of display-
additional computer lab time	ing wares
additional study carels	index for wage increases
new special interest club	improved lounge facilities
Saturday or 5:00 P.M. classes	improved working conditions
a women's center	new in-service training
a campus jogging path	program
student entertainment project	sports team program
free movie program	fire evacuation procedures
improved bomb scare	an advertising program
procedures	new staff orientation
other?	program
	grievance procedures
	dental insurance program
	other?

Neighborhood

condo security system
public lighting
additional sidewalks
improved recreational facilities
new stop sign or traffic light
one-way streets
rezoning
additional street signs
other?

NOTES

CHAPTER 9

Professional Papers

by Bruce Hammond

© 1983 Universal Press Syndicate. By permission.

INTRODUCTION

Many organizations will require that you prepare professional technical papers for information distribution within your organization and that you publish papers in journals of special interest in your field: electronics, engineering, health professions, psychology, teaching, and the like. Professional papers are journalistic articles about technical subjects. Written to inform, they are prepared by professionals or researchers and intended for other specialists who wish to keep abreast of current developments in their field.

Professional papers are published regularly in journals. You should seek out the journals which print papers in your field and read at least one or two of them regularly. Because the articles have been reviewed by an editorial board of specialists, you may rely on the authority of the material. Furthermore, the most recent findings in your field will be in the journals, not in your textbooks.

As a student you probably think that you won't be required to write such papers until much later in your career, but you will find that even entry-level positions require this type of writing. Actual publication in a journal will enhance your resume, and further publication will serve as a successful method of being noticed and promoted in your organization.

Types

Basically, there are three types of professional papers: the research experiment report, the review article, and the conference paper. The **research report** records the methods and materials, test results, and implications of new products, experiments, and procedures. The **review article** analyzes the published research on a specific topic, classifies the research, and evaluates the findings with suggestions for future applications. The **conference paper** presents the entire text of an oral presentation given by you at an organizational meeting, a professional seminar, or a full-blown conference. It allows the reader to review your presentation more carefully, and to circulate your research to others who missed your oral presentation. This chapter will concentrate on the actual writing strategies for both the professional and the student. Chapters 10 and 11 expand on information access and documentation techniques for the professional paper.

THE TECHNICAL RESEARCH REPORT

The professional technical writer must consider three strategies for successful publication:

- Selecting the intended journal.
- Writing the technical paper.
- Submitting the paper for publication.

Selecting the Journal

The first step is to review the journals in your field with an eye to selecting those which are most prestigious, most likely to publish your exact type of material, and aimed at your desired audience. By selecting the journal, you may then tailor your article to its requirements. Most journals publish statements of purpose which define the intended audience and comment on their editorial policy for selecting unsolicited articles. Figure 9.1 shows a typical editorial policy statement which spells out manuscript requirements.

Requirements for manuscripts may specify general length, margins, pagination, spacing, number of copies to submit, typing instructions, and methods for handling graphics. In addition, a clear policy will suggest the content organization of materials, the acceptable level of technical language, and expected prose style (paragraph length, passive or active voice, British or American English). A close review of published articles will also help you to ascertain the acceptable style.

The journal's editorial policy will also clarify which documentation techniques to use, how to title, and whether or not to use topical headings.

INSTRUCTIONS TO AUTHORS

Manuscripts: Reports of original research and special review articles that have been submitted solely to the Journal are considered for publication. Manuscripts devoted to the description of a procedure or an apparatus, to improvement of a procedure or apparatus, to nonexperimental research, or to case reports are not acceptable. Manuscripts should be written in clear, concise, and grammatically correct English. Those not adequately prepared will be returned to authors, since it is not possible for the editors to revise extensively or to rewrite manuscripts. Contributors who are unfamiliar with English usage are encouraged to seek the help of colleagues in preparing manuscripts for submission. Only those papers that meet high standards of scientific quality will be accepted for publication.

Submit manuscripts in triplicate (one original and two copies), double-spaced on 8½ x 11-inch bond paper.

After September 1, 1979, the submission fees of $45.00 for a standard paper and $25.00 for an Annotation will be discontinued. There will be no charge for papers that do not exceed five Journal pages (approximately 13 typewritten pages, including charts and photographs). A page charge of $100.00 will be assessed for each page over five.

All manuscripts should be submitted to Barnet M. Levy, Editor, The University of Texas Dental Branch, P.O. Box 20068, Houston, Texas 77025, U.S.A.

The editor reserves the right to edit manuscripts to ensure conciseness, clarity, and stylistic consistency. The corresponding author will receive page proofs for checking and reprint order information. Changes in page proofs should be minimal. Authors will be charged for excessive changes.

Length of Manuscripts: Manuscripts should not exceed five Journal pages or about 13 typewritten pages, *including* tables, charts, illustrations and references. Manuscripts requiring more than five Journal pages will incur a charge of $100.00 for each extra page.

Title Page: List a concise title, author(s), their professional address(es), and a short title for running heads. Include footnotes acknowledging sources of support on this page.

Synopsis: The second page should be a synopsis of 75 words or less.

Key Terms: A list of five or six terms descriptive of the subject matter should be supplied on the synopsis sheet for use in indexing and abstract services.

Text: Follow this standard form: Sections should be labeled Introduction, Materials and methods, Results, Discussion, and Conclusions. Proprietary names and sources of all commercial products must be given in footnotes; the text should contain only generic names. Follow the Council of Biology Editors Style Manual, 4th ed, 1978.

References: Type double-spaced on a separate sheet. Follow the Journal style, keeping the references to the text in numerical (not alphabetical) order. Limit references to those specifically referred to in the text. Lengthy reviews of the literature are not appropriate. Examples of the Journal form for bibliography are:

1. JONES, B. D.; BANNA, C. S.; and CISCO, F. O.: Experimental Induction of Bone, *J Dent Res* 58:22-24, 1959.
2. BINNER, B. A. and JONES, R. M.: **Book on Dental Materials,** 5th ed. Philadelphia: W.D. Leabiger Co., 1944, p. 359.

Illustrations: Submit in triplicate. Photographs should be unmounted black and white glossy prints of good quality. On the back of each, lightly pencil the author's name, the figure number, and indication of the top edge. Unmounted glossy black and white prints of diagrams, charts, graphs, and drawings are preferred. Lettering should be large enough to be read after the drawings are reduced to column or page width. All legends should be grouped on a separate sheet in the numerical order referred to in the text.

Tables: Type each table on a separate sheet. Tables should be titled and numbered consecutively. Do not use vertical rules. Footnotes should be brief. If the above format is not followed, the manuscript will be returned to the author for correction prior to review by the referees.

Brief Communications and Annotations: Brief communications reporting experimental data of immediate importance to scientists will be considered for accelerated publication after the usual review and acceptance. Standards for acceptance of brief communications are rigorous. The paper, including tables, illustrations and references, must not exceed three printed pages (about seven and a half typewritten sheets).

Annotations are limited to one printed page of 650 words. If illustrations or tables are included, the text must be correspondingly shorter. If the annotation exceeds the required length, processing will be delayed while it is cut by the author. Insert references within the text following the style used in current issues of the *Journal*.

Letters to the Editor: The editor invites concise letters commenting on papers published in recent issues. Those letters selected for publication will first be referred to the author, whose response may also be published. The editor reserves the right to reject any letter or to make appropriate editorial changes.

Rejected manuscripts should not be resubmitted to the Journal. All manuscripts will be quality-rated by at least two referees. Manuscripts with low ratings will not be accepted.

FIGURE 9.1 *Typical editorial policy statement* (From *Journal of Dental Research*)

The published statement may direct you to include an abstract (see Chapter 8), reference lists, your credentials in a formal or informal resume, institutional affiliations, or other support materials.

You may at this point wish to query those journals which seem most promising. In this brief letter you should ask if the journal is interested in your intended paper by clarifying the specific subject, emphasizing the importance of your article, explaining the approach you have used to develop the paper (lab findings, research), and summarizing the particulars (length, graphics, and the like). You should also include your credentials, organization, and phone number.

Writing the Report

The professional technical paper usually includes the following:

- A precise title
- Definition of the problem
- Review of the literature
- Methods and materials for the new findings
- Results clarification
- Conclusions and implications

Title.   Often a journal will require both a short title and a longer title such as "Environmental Stress Testing: Improving the Quality and Reliability of Testing Components."

Problem.   Define the problem and/or state the purpose of the technical report. Point out deficiencies in a product or procedure which currently exist. Next, review the literature to provide a context for your new discussion and to lend authority by indicating that you have command of the subject.

Methods.   Next, explain the methods and materials which you have used in your research. Decide whether to discuss your methods in the passive voice ("Next, the leg bone was connected to the thigh bone"), in the active voice ("The leg bone connects to the thigh bone") or in the instructional mode ("Connect the leg bone to the thigh bone").

Results.   Discuss the exact results of the investigation. The Methods section and Results section are the major components of your article.

Implications.   Finally, draw valid conclusions and suggest implications for future use of the product or procedure. These closing strategies are like the conclusions and recommendations of other reports.

If you have documented the paper, include a reference list of sources in the style required by the particular journal. Figure 9.2 shows a professional technical article from a journal.

MATERIALS SCIENCE

Microscopic Study of Smooth Silver-plated Retention Pins in Amalgam

Y. GALINDO,* K. McLACHLAN,** and Z. KASLOFF***

*Université Laval, Ecole de Médecine Dentaire, Ste-Foy, Québec, Canada G1K 7P4; **University of Manitoba, Faculty of Civil Engineering, Winnipeg, Manitoba, Canada R3T 2N2; and ***University of Colorado, School of Dentistry, Denver, Colorado 80262

A silver-plating technique was developed in an effort to produce good mechanical bonding characteristics between stainless steel pins and amalgam. Metallographic microscope and scanning electron microscope (SEM) studies were made to assess the presence, or otherwise, of such a bond between (a) the silver layer plating and the surface of the stainless steel pins, and (b) and silver plating and the amalgam. Unplated stainless steel and sterling silver pins were used as a control and as a comparison, respectively. A "rubbing" technique of condensation was devised to closely adapt amalgam to the pins. It is concluded that there is strong evidence for the existence of a good bond between the plated pins and amalgam. The mechanical performance of the bond is discussed elsewhere.[1]

J Dent Res 59(2):124-128, February 1980

Introduction.

Metallic pins are used in dentistry to retain large amalgam restorations and to oppose tilting forces when the restoration is subjected to occlusal loads. The inability of these pins to bond with amalgam contributes to the formation of high stress concentrations around the top of the pin.[2,3] Fracture of the amalgam is likely to ensue.

Previous investigations[2] have shown that stress concentrations around smooth pins possessing bonding properties with amalgam are significantly less than is the case with non-bonded pins. Likewise, such pins increase the retention of the restoration[3] and markedly reduce the occurrence of fracture and crack propagation.[4,5] The reduction of strength, due to the inclusion of pins in amalgam specimens, has been shown to be much less when bonded, rather than unbonded pins are used.[2,4,6,7,8]

Received for publication November 29, 1978
Accepted for publication February 29, 1979
This study was supported in part by the Medical Research Council of Canada, Grant MA-4065.
*Present address: Canadore College, Health Sciences, P.O. Box 5001, North Bay, Ontario, Canada P1A3X9

124

This evidence led to the investigation and development of smooth pins likely to provide a metallurgical bond with amalgam, and be clinically acceptable in all other respects. A microscopic evaluation was selected for establishing the goodness of the pin-amalgam metallurgical adaptation which, in turn, would indicate the likely quality of any bond.

Materials and methods.

Smooth, silver-plated, stainless steel pins were the primary subject of this study. They were compared with sterling silver and unplated stainless steel pins. Sterling silver pins were used only as a mode for comparison, since it has been shown that they adapt well and form a metallurgical bond with amalgam.[1,4,5,7,8] Unplated stainless steel smooth pins were also included as a control, because it is well known that they do not form a bond with amalgam.

Silver-plated stainless steel pins were made with a core of 18-8 stainless steel orthodontic wire. In order to achieve the plating, the passive layer which forms on stainless steel was first eliminated by pickling the previously cleaned wire in an acid chloride solution. To prevent the passive layer from forming again, a very thin, microscopically non-detectable flash of nickel was applied by a plating process. This process consisted of immediately transferring the wire to an acid nickel-chloride solution at room temperature, and using a nickel anode for the electroplating procedure. Once the passive layer had thus been eliminated, and its formation avoided by the nickel flash, successful electroplating of silver onto the surface was readily performed. In this case, an electrolytic, low concentration, silver-cyanide plating solution was used with a stainless steel strip anode. This was followed by the final plating process, involving a highly con-

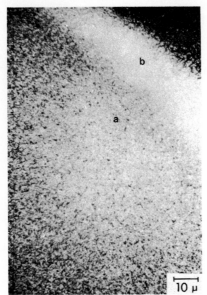

Fig. 1 – Nickel-plated stainless steel wire (X-ray microscope, scanning for nickel, 1250 X). (a) nickel contained in stainless steel wire (white dots), (b) nickel contained in layer of nickel plate.

centrated silver plating solution and a pure silver anode. In this manner, the good bonding characteristics expected from pure silver and amalgam could be combined with the desirable physical properties of stainless steel as a pin material.[3] This plating method is the one used for certain airplane sections, and was adapted for pins in dentistry.*

Because the thickness of the nickel flash was too minute to be observed directly, three separate stainless steel specimens were made. Each of these specimens was subjected to the nickel plating procedure for a period ten times as long as that used in preparing pins for the silver plating process. Under these conditions, the thickness of the nickel layer could be measured. Thus, an indirect measure of the thickness of nickel under the silver plating of the experimental pins could be obtained.

The method of making sterling silver pins is now described. Pin patterns were first made from the blue inlay wax and then cast

*Bristol Aerospace, Winnipeg, Manitoba, Canada

in sterling silver, using standard methods. Sterling silver pins, as cast, yielded properties which were poor in strength and in modulus of elasticity. These properties were greatly improved by heat-treating the pins at 650°F for one hour.[3,9]

Amalgam specimens containing each type of pin were prepared and all specimens were constructed in the same way. The mold utilized was similar to that used for dental amalgam specimens, described in the American Dental Association Specification No. 1. During the course of the investigation, a technique for achieving good adaptation of the amalgam to the pin was developed. It consisted of thoroughly rubbing the first portion of the freshly mixed amalgam around the pin with a plastic instrument. This procedure assured a reaction between the whole surface of the pin and the amalgam, thus eliminating voids around the pin. All specimens were between 24 hours and five days old when viewed microscopically.

The three special nickel-plated stainless steel pin specimens were mounted to be analyzed under X-ray microprobe. Four specimens of each type of pin used in this research were mounted on bakelite bases for metallographic microscope examination, and similar ones were mounted on stubs with a conductive silver com-

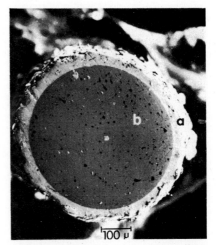

Fig. 2 – Silver-plated stainless steel wire (SEM, 170 X) (a) silver plate, (b) stainless steel wire. Transversal section.

FIGURE 9.2 *continued*

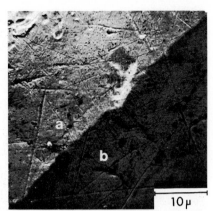

Fig. 3 – Silver-plated stainless steel wire (SEM 3000 X), (a) silver-plate layer, (b) stainless steel wire. Transversal section.

pound** for scanning electron microscope (SEM) study. All specimens within each group presented similar, reproducible characteristics. Therefore, only microphotographs of typical specimens of each type were made.

Results.

Results obtained from the pin-amalgam specimens used as controls confirmed two expected and well known facts: a total lack of bond between stainless steel and amalgam, and a very good adaptation of amalgam to sterling silver. The latter strongly implies the presence of a bond, and is consistent with findings of other researchers mentioned earlier. It was, therefore, judged unnecessary to present, in this paper, micrographs of these specimens.

An illustration of the nickel coating on a stainless steel pin is shown in Figure 1. This picture was obtained with an electron probe scan for nickel on one of the stainless steel specimens that was subjected to ten times the normal nickel-plating period. From this it can be seen that complete continuity between the nickel in the pin and that of the plated layer exists.

Silver-plated stainless steel wire specimens as seen under SEM are presented in Figures 2 and 3. The results of this examination were consistent and confirmed that the

**Silver Dag - Acheson Colloids Canada Ltd., Brantford, Ontario, Canada.

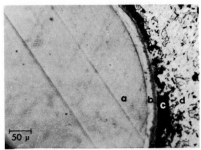

Fig. 4 – Silver-plated stainless steel pin in amalgam. Conventional method of amalgam condensation (metallographic microscope, 350 X). (a) stainless steel pin, (b) silver-plate layer, (c) void, (d) amalgam. Transversal section.

plated layer of silver adapts very well to the stainless steel.

The effectiveness of the "rubbing" technique prior to condensation is confirmed in Figures 4 and 5, which are views under the metallographic microscope. A continuous, intimate adaptation of the amalgam to the pin and an absence of voids at the interface is evident. Similar results were obtained with the sterling-silver pin and were consistent with all specimens of both types used in this experiment.

Pin-amalgam specimens were likewise viewed under SEM. Figures 6 and 7 illustrate the close adaptation of the amalgam to the surface of the silver plating, so that a definite boundary between them is not readily discerned. In order to confirm the above results, a longitudinal pin-amalgam section, seen under a metallographic microscope, is shown in Figure 8.

Discussion.

In establishing the quality of any bond for the stated purposes, mechanical tests will be the final arbiter. However, microscopic study of the interface regions was necessary to confirm that metallurgical conditions existed, and that satisfactory adaptation had been achieved.

From the indirect evidence of the X-ray microscope (Fig. 1), the thickness of the nickel flash upon which the silver plating was performed was about one micrometer. The same evidence also shows that the nickel contained in the stainless steel and that from the nickel-plated flash are

FIGURE 9.2 *continued*

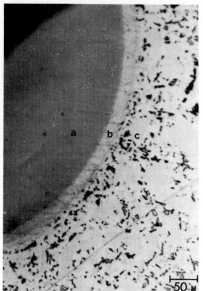

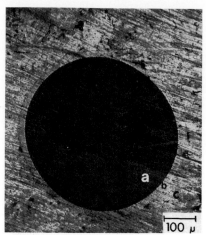

Fig. 5 – Silver-plated stainless steel pin in amalgam. Rubbing method of amalgam condensation (metallographic microscope, 305 X). (a) stainless steel pin, (b) silver-plate layer, (c) amalgam. Transversal section.

Fig. 6 – Silver-plated stainless steel pin in amalgam (SEM, 175 X). (a) stainless steel pin, (b) silver-plate layer, (c) amalgam. Transversal section.

continuous and, in all probability, chemically bonded.

Microscopic examinations (including SEM) of the layer of silver-plating on stainless steel (Figs. 2 and 3, typical) showed extremely good adaptation with no voids, therefore, strongly suggesting the presence of a good mechanical bond. Because silver is known to bond with amalgam, it was expected that the silver-plating would act as a "soldering" agent between stainless steel and amalgam. Micrographic evidence (Figs. 4 to 8) confirmed this expectation, particularly when compared with that from sterling silver pins in amalgam. It is, then, reasonable to suggest that good mechanical bonding between stainless steel and amalgam can be achieved through the plating method presented here.

When amalgam is condensed without using the "rubbing" technique, large voids are readily seen at both the silver-plated and sterling silver pin and amalgam interface. On the other hand, when rubbing is used, close adaptation is obtained, and only the small and expected voids of the amalgam

mass can be detected at the surface of the pin.

Conclusions.

Specimens utilized in this study confirmed the bonding potential between smooth pins and amalgam under the conditions of this research. The plating technique

Fig. 7 – Silver-plated stainless steel pin in amalgam (SEM, 1050 X). (a) stainless steel pin, (b) silver-plate layer, (c) amalgam. Transversal section.

FIGURE 9.2 *continued*

128 GALINDO ET AL. *J Dent Res February 1980*

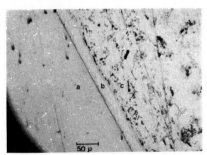

Fig. 8 — Silver-plated stainless steel pin in amalgam (metallographic microscope, 350 X). (a) stainless steel pin, (b) silver-plate layer, (c) amalgam. Longitudinal section.

used produced evidence of the strong possibility of a bond being present between silver and stainless steel. The technique of rubbing amalgam on the pin during condensation proved beneficial in achieving an excellent adaptation between the surface of the pin and amalgam. This technique is also useful in keeping stress concentration influences around the pin to a minimum, when retaining an amalgam restoration. The results of mechanical tests are needed to confirm the clinical usefulness of these conclusions.

Acknowledgments.

The authors are indebted to Mr. G. Freedman and Mr. Gordon Richardson from Bristol Aerospace, Winnipeg, Manitoba, for their guidance regarding the plating technique. Special thanks to Mr. B. Bergman for his help in constructing the special devices used in this research. We wish to acknowledge Dr. Peter Williams from the School of Dentistry and Dr. J. R. Cahoon from the Faculty of Engineering of the University of Manitoba for their advice.

REFERENCES

1. GALINDO, Y.; McLACHLAN, K.: and KASLOFF, Z.: Mechanical Tests of Smooth Silver-plated Retention Pins in Amalgam, *J Dent Res,* (in press).
2. DHURU, V.: A Photoelastic Study of Stress Concentration Produced by Retention Pins in an Amalgam Restoration, MSc Thesis, University of Manitoba, 1972.
3. GALINDO, Y.: The Development and Testing of Retention Pins which Metallurgically Bond with Dental Amalgam, MSc Thesis, University of Manitoba, 1973.
4. MOFFA, J. P.; GOING, R. R.; and GETTLEMAN, L.: Silver Pins: Their Influence on the Strength and Adaptation of Amalgam, *J Prosth Dent* 28:491-499, 1972.
5. LUGASSY, A. A.; LAUTENSCHLAGER, E.P.; and HARCOURT, J. K.: Crack Propagation in Dental Amalgam, *Aust Dent J* 16:302-306, 1971.
6. CECCONI, B. T. and ASGAR, K.: Pins in Amalgam: A Study of Reinforcement, *J Prosth Dent* 26:159-169, 1971.
7. DUPERON, D. F.: The Effect of Selected Pin Retention Materials on Certain Properties of Dental Silver Amalgam, MSc Thesis, University of Manitoba, 1970.
8. PETERSON, E. A. and FREEDMAN, G.: Laminate Reinforced Dental Amalgam, *J Dent Res* 51:70-87, 1972.
9. METALS HANDBOOK COMMITTEE: **Metals Handbook**, American Society for Metals, 6th ed., 1960.

FIGURE 9.2 *continued*

Submitting the Report for Publication

Mail your article with a cover letter, two copies, and a self-addressed, stamped envelope (SASE) or loose postage so that the editors will acknowledge receipt of your manuscript.

Pack the cover letter and manuscript between cardboard covers and mail it in a padded envelope (jiffy bag) to protect the contents. Don't despair if your article isn't accepted—less than 5 percent are. Instead, use the suggested revision notes (if included) as free advice and keep trying.

THE STUDENT REVIEW ARTICLE

Overall Writing Strategies

As a student you probably aren't involved in new technical products and materials on which you can report. Nevertheless, you can research the latest findings within your field and develop a journalistic article of value. This process will require a review of general expository writing skills that will help you to write clearly. These skills include

1. Selecting and limiting the subject
2. Formulating the thesis
3. Brainstorming the methods of development
4. Preparing the working outline
5. Writing suitable introductions and closings

Of course, you will want to prepare rough drafts and edit your work as discussed in Chapter 2, The Writing Process. Further, if you research printed material, you will need to locate authoritative sources, take notes with an eye toward avoiding plagiarism, and document your material. (See Chapters 10 and 11 on Information Access and Documentation.)

Selecting and Limiting the Subject

In the professional world the selection of a subject is usually yours, but a supervisor or professor may assign you a research report topic such as "New Findings of the Influence of Temperature on Viruses," "The Practicality of Laser Surgery on Heart Patients," or "The Impact of Microchips on Credit Cards." If the subject selection is entirely yours, consider the following three principles:

1. Select a subject which can be thoroughly investigated within the confines of your length limitations. "Computers" is too vast a subject and fails

to suggest a particular focus. But subjects such as "The Effectiveness of a New Computer Password System" or "Procedure to Develop an Electronic Component for Vocal Software" are both more narrow and focused.

2. Select a subject on which you either are an authority or are able to access a wide variety of published research material. "Cures for Acquired Immune Deficiency Syndrome (AIDS)" will not be productive because research is sketchy and inconclusive. "Procedure for a Magnetic Circuit Test on Transformer Performance" may be too specialized for you and your audience. "Methods to Reduce Pollution in Lake Aral (The Soviet Union)" is too far removed for you to obtain published, up-to-date material.

3. Select a subject which will allow you to formulate a judgment. A study on "The Smartcard Debit System" will yield plentiful material, but a study on "The Smartcard Debit System versus Traditional Credit Cards" will yield information on which you can formulate an informed comparative judgment.

Formulating the Thesis

The next strategy is to develop a preliminary thesis, a statement which focuses the purpose of your paper. This statement of the central idea to be developed in your paper will help you to organize facts, limit your note-taking, and eliminate needless research.

Consider what you know about your limited subject. You probably already have some opinions or new information or you would not have selected the subject in the first place. State in one sentence (or two if necessary) an opinion, conclusion, generalization, or prediction about your subject. For instance, if you have narrowed your subject to "The Effectiveness of Computer Access Control Systems," you may tentatively state, "Computer access control systems are improving." If you are an engineer who has been working on an improved system, your thesis may state, "A fail-safe method is now available to eliminate computer viruses."

Often the thesis of a technical paper refutes the benefits of a present system and points out new findings. Such theses frequently contain the words *however*, *instead*, *nevertheless*, *consequently*, and so forth.

Examples   For the past thirty years Medic Alert neck tags or bracelets have provided instant medical history; however, laser optic technology can now produce revolutionary medical data-memory cards containing up to 800 pages of information.

The consumer no longer has to withdraw money from a wallet or suffer through a time-consuming check approval process; instead, she can pay a retailer directly out of her checking account via an electronic fund transfer with the Smartcard.

While you are taking notes and extending your research, you should revise or refine your thesis. After you have assembled all of your data, reduce the thesis to one sentence to unite your findings. You may wish to add an organization clue to the structure of your paper. For instance, your final thesis may read, "Despite advances, computer access control systems demand constant upgrading due to the increasing amounts of sensitive computerized data, the expansion of networking systems, and the growing number of sophisticated, computer-competent criminals." This thesis not only contains an overall inference on the need for constant improvement, but also provides a clue to the sections of the report: the problems of data proliferation, networking, and unethical programmers.

Brainstorming the Methods of Development

There are several major strategies for approaching the organization of material. These include *narration* (telling of events), *description* (recounting in precise detail), and *exposition* (explaining certain points). The professional paper usually requires expository strategies although it may contain elements of the other strategies. Moreover, there are six methods of developing expository material which may be used singularly, but are more likely to be used in combination. They are

- Definition
- Classification and division
- Exemplification
- Comparison/contrast
- Cause/effect
- Process explanation (analysis or instructions)

Chapters 13 through 16 examine in detail strategies for definition, process analysis, instructions, and description of mechanisms. The student writer should study these strategies to produce effective professional/ technical papers. Ask yourself these questions:

1. Which terms will I need to define?
2. How will I classify (place into major sections) and divide (separate into subsections) my material?
3. What specific examples will support my thesis?
4. What comparisons (likenesses) and contrasts (differences) will help to explain my material?
5. Are cause-and-effect factors an essential part of my evidence?
6. Will I need to describe, instruct, or analyze a process in my paper?

Search for material (see Chapters 10 and 11 for information accessing and documentation techniques) that will support the pertinent strategies listed above. Then organize the strategies into a logical presentation.

Preparing the Working Outline

Develop a preliminary or working outline of your materials. Consider the writing strategies which you have brainstormed. Your first draft may be sketchy, but it will serve as a guideline to your note-taking. Without an outline you are likely to take notes on materials irrelevant to your purpose or overlook an area which should be explored.

You should not be totally bound by your working outline. As you think over your subject and take notes, you will want to expand, rearrange, discard, and subordinate your outline topics. Your final research report should include a final outline.

Format

Select a traditional or decimal outline format:

```
I.  A.
        1.                        1.0
        2.                            1.1
    B.                                    1.1.1.
        1.                                1.1.2.
        2.
                                      1.2
            a.                            1.2.1.
            b.                            1.2.2.
                (1)           2.0
                (2)               2.1
                    (a)               2.1.1.
                    (b)               2.1.2.
```

Although the Roman-numeraled, traditional outline allows for five levels of subordination, you will seldom find it necessary to use subheads beyond two subordinates. The decimal outline format is popular for technical presentations.

Topic Outline

Although each entry in an outline may be a sentence, a topic outline is not only easier to develop in the preliminary stage but also more common in the final draft. Major topics name the divisions of your paper. Next, subtopics are subordinated and indented under each major topic, and subsequent developmental topics are subordinated beneath each subtopic.

Partial Preliminary Outline

1.0 Introduction (thesis)
    1.1 Computer definition
    1.2 Access control definition
        1.2.1 Access control examples
        1.2.2 Access control processes
2.0 Causes of computer security violations
    2.1 Cause 1
    2.2 Cause 2
    2.3 Cause 3
3.0 Effects of computer security violations
    3.1 Effect 1
    3.2 Effect 2
    3.3 Effect 3
4.0 Examples of computer crimes
    4.1 Industrial crimes
        4.1.1 Company A
        4.1.2 Company B . . . (etc.)

Keep working on your outline as you take notes.

Partial Final Outline

2.0 Causes of computer security violations
    2.1 Faulty access control devices
        2.1.1 Telephone networking
        2.1.2 Passwords
    2.2 Excessive computerized information
        2.2.1 Pentagon's 8000 computers
        2.2.2 Rand Corporation statistics
    2.3 Number of trained computer specialists
        2.3.1 Number of military contractor clearances
        2.3.2 Number of U.S.-trained computer operators
    2.4 Amateur experimenters
        2.4.1 Milwaukee amateur club incident
        2.4.2 Soviets in Applied Systems Analysis group

Figure 9.3 shows a complete outline for a student review article.

OUTLINE

Thesis: Tomography, the innovative creation of a combination of scientific minds of our generation, is used to help cardiologists analyze the heart, to aid brain surgeons in the detection of cerebral disorders, to assist geologists in the study of earth's composition, and to permit aerospace technicians to inspect the MX missiles for malfunctions.

I. Introduction
II. Background
   A. Definition
   B. Origin
III. Cardiological applications
   A. Heart
      1. Disorders
      2. Normalities
   B. Cardiovascular system
      1. Arteries
      2. Veins
IV. Cerebral applications
   A. Brain scans
      1. Normal children
      2. Impaired children
   B. Oxygen /glucose loss
      1. Causes
      2. Effects
V. Geological applications
   A. Earth's core
   B. Earth's surface
VI. Aerospace applications
   A. Study of MX missiles
      1. Disorders
      2. Remedies
   B. Approval of MX missiles

FIGURE 9.3 *Sample student review article outline*

Writing Introductions and Closings

Consider your introduction and closing to the article. The introduction of the truly professional article is serious and forthright. If you have a particular broad-interest journal in mind, you may want to write a catchier introduction. The major purpose of the introduction is to state your thesis, but you may consider including

- A reader-attention device
- A context in which to consider your ideas
- Definition of key terms
- The thesis itself
- Organization clues

Useful strategies for engaging introductions include a direct quotation of a well-expressed statement, a startling fact or statement about your subject, a rhetorical question, a related anecdote, and the like. Here are some sample introductions for articles on point-of-sale transaction systems:

1. One of life's great excuses—"The check is in the mail"—may be headed for extinction. Financial institutions and retailers want to stop handling cash and checks so they are switching to cheaper, faster electronic point-of-sale (POS) transactions. Point-of-sale is the electronic transfer of money from a consumer's bank account to a merchant's bank account with the use of a plastic card and merchant computer terminals. The new system is creating a gradual revolution in the way people buy things and deal with their banks.

2. "In our opinion it is impossible to exist in the record industry without some sort of computerized point-of-sale system," says Irving Heisler, president of Montreal-based Discus Music World. Discus operates more than 100 units across Canada. The major advantages of the point-of-sale system lie in being able to serve customers better while at the same time lowering operating costs by making both inventory management and labor scheduling more efficient.

3. A shopper in a Dublin, California, Lucky Store wants to pay cash for her purchases. She no longer has to suffer a time-consuming check approval process. Instead, by using a debit card, in just seven seconds she can pay the retailer directly out of her checking account with an electronic funds transaction. This point-of-sale system effectively speeds the sale, reduces paperwork, and costs less than traditional credit card transactions.

Your closing section, which follows your conclusions and further implications of your subject, should be brief. Here you may draw a stronger conclusion, summarize your material, emphasize just one aspect of it, climax with a fact, or urge your reader to action. Some examples follow:

1. Besides use by individual consumers, point-of-sale systems should speed up corporate and even international financial transactions.
2. The POS system enables management to reduce losses by thousands of dollars. Ace Business Supplies increased its sales by 20 percent in the first year of use. You can't ask for more than that.
3. Quicker consumer service and lower operating costs should convince merchants to use the POS system.

Think ahead, too, to the type of graphics you will want to seek out or devise. With these writing and illustrating strategies in mind, you are ready to write your expository article.

Writing the Rough Draft

Using your outline as a structural guide and your note cards (Chapter 10) as the content guide, write a rough draft of your research report. Follow these guidelines:

1. Type or write your draft leaving space between each line in order to expand or revise your draft.
2. Write your introduction. Be sure your limited subject and final thesis are clearly stated. A clue to the overall organization of the paper is needed if it is not indicated by your thesis. Clearly define your key terms before beginning to present your evidence which supports your thesis.
3. Write the body paragraphs. Each should begin with a topic sentence, a sentence which clarifies the topic of the paragraph and states your opinion or generalization about it. Each paragraph must have unity (address itself to the same subtopics of your overall subject), coherence (logical progression of evidence), and transitions (words and phrases which connect the evidence, such as *for instance*, *in the first place*, *furthermore*, *finally*).
4. When paraphrasing opinions and conclusions or directly quoting any source material, be sure to include the author's name in the text. Check the five safeguards against a plagiarism charge (p. 263) to ensure that all of your evidence is documented.
5. Insert your internal reference notes in parentheses as you write and circle each in order not to overlook one when you prepare your final draft.
6. Write your conclusion. This may be one or several paragraphs which summarize your findings, present solutions, or recommend a particular action.
7. Edit all mechanics (spelling and punctuation) and style considerations (sentence construction, grammar, and usage).

Figure 9.4 reproduces a student review article on a new medicine. The article is documented in this case with the Modern Language Association (MLA) style explained in Chapter 11.

MEXILETINE HYDROCHLORIDE: AN INVESTIGATION

IN ANTIARRHYTHMIC TREATMENT

Submitted to

Professor Ima Smart

Technical Writing 2210

Submitted by

W. Jeanne Early

October 28, 199X

FIGURE 9.4   *Sample student review article* (By permission)

OUTLINE

Thesis: Mexitil is a promising new oral antiarrhythmic which is proving effective with few adverse effects and minimal drug interaction problems.

  I. Introduction

 II. Mechanism of action

     A. Lidocaine comparison

     B. Action potential

     C. Atrial, nodal, and ventricular fibers

III. Pharmacokinetics

     A. Absorption

     B. Half-life

     C. Excretion

IV. Dosage

     A. Campbell

     B. Heger and others

     C. Woolsey

  V. Adverse effects

     A. Cardiological

     B. Neurological

     C. Gastrointestinal

VI. Drug Interactions

     A. Antacids, cimetidine

     B. Analgesic narcotics

     C. Phenobarbital, dilantin, rifampin

     D. Cigarette smoking

ii

FIGURE 9.4 *continued*

MEXILETINE HYDROCHLORIDE: AN INVESTIGATION IN

ANTIARRHYTHMIC TREATMENT

Mexiletine hydrochloride (Mexitil–Boehringer Ingelheim) was recently approved by the U.S. Food and Drug Administration (USFDA) for treatment of ventricular arrhythmias as an oral agent in the practice of cardiology. Mexitil has been approved for use in countries other than the United States since 1969. Mexitil was used first as an anticonvulsant (Campbell 29). But after other anticonvulsants were found to have antiarrhythmic effects, Mexitil was also tested in laboratory animals and found to have an effect against ventricular arrhythmias (Woolsey 1058). Mexitil is a promising new oral antiarrhythmic which is proving effective with few adverse effects and minimal drug interaction problems.

Mexitil is similar to another common antiarrythmic. Mexiletine and lidocaine have close structural similarities which are shown in Figure 1:

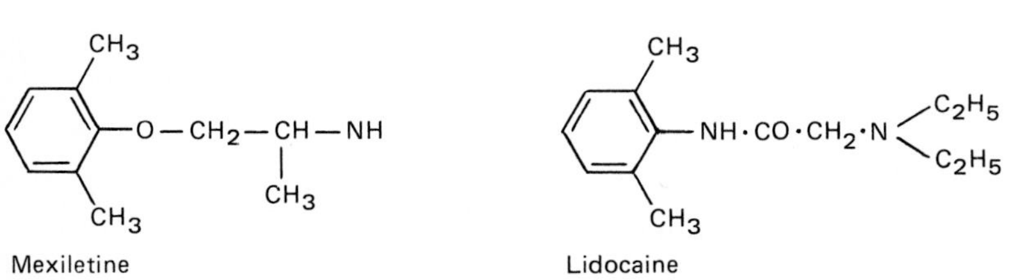

Mexiletine   Lidocaine

Figure 1   Structures of Mexiletine and Lidocaine From Campbell (29)

1

FIGURE 9.4   *continued*

2

Campbell states, "Mexitil . . . is a primary amine," and its chemical structure

much resembles lidocaine (29), but Mexitil is significantly smaller. This

may allow greater movement in and out of sodium channels which is

essential in effecting the action potential (Woolsey 1059). Mexitil decreases

the rate of depolarization and decreases the refractory period of Purkinje

fibers (cardiac electrical cells). Thus, the action potential duration is

shortened (1058). Campbell also states that the electrophysiologic effect

is to slow the maximal rate of the action potential. In human studies there

was no consistent effect on the sinus node or atrium unless there was

preexisting disease (30). Woolsey also notes that one study showed Mexitil

to have little effect on atrial arrhythmias (1060). Mexitil's main area of

activity is on ventricular arrhythmias. Mexitil's action is rate dependent

indicating better action for fast ventricular tachycardias (1059).

Mexitil is absorbed well in the gastrointestinal tract, but most of the

absorption is in the upper small intestine (Campbell 29). It has a great

absorption nearing 100 percent (Johansson and others 1100). Campbell's

study showed that the peak plasma level is usually in 1.5 hours, and the

elimination half-life can be 8–15 hours (29). Woolsey states, "Agents that

induce drug-metabolizing enzymes in the liver, such as rifampin and

phenytoin, decrease the elimination half-life of mexiletine" (1062). The

FIGURE 9.4   *continued*

3

liver is the main organ of metabolism although there is some renal excretion (Campbell 29). According to Johansson and his associates, the liver metabolism is mainly by oxidation and reduction and can be influenced by exposure to substances that can stimulate enzyme production in the liver (1100).

The recommended dosage of Mexitil varies little among different sources. Campbell recommends starting with a single loading dose of 400–600 mg to achieve a therapeutic level quickly (30). Then Campbell and Heger agree on 450–1200 mg in three equivalent divided doses every eight hours (Cf. Campbell 30, Heger 628). Woolsey believes therapeutic concentration can be achieved with 10–14 mg/kg/day in divided doses (1063). Studies continue.

Adverse effects to Mexitil that have caused discontinuation of the treatment have been infrequent. But ventricular arrhythmias have occurred in clinical trials requiring the discontinuation of Mexitil (Heger and others 629). Adverse cardiac effects on the sinus node, the A-V node, and cardiac contractility are uncommon with Mexitil (Campbell 32). Neurologic and gastrointestinal effects are the most frequent limiting effects of Mexitil. Heger reports, "The most common adverse reactions to mexiletine were nausea, vomiting, tremors, and dizziness" (629). Gastrointestinal side

FIGURE 9.4   *continued*

4

effects were diminished with smaller doses given more frequently and within

a few weeks disappeared (Johansson and others 1100–01).

Several different drugs affect different actions of Mexitil. Antacids,

cimetidine, and narcotics can delay absorption of Mexitil (Campbell 33).

Woolsey points out that use of narcotic analgesics, especially taken during

an acute myocardial infarction, can delay or impair Mexitil absorption

and should be closely monitored (1062). Other drugs which decrease the

half-life of Mexitil by inducing liver enzymes are phenobarbital, dilantin,

and rifampin (Campbell 33). Also, cigarette smoking decreases plasma

levels of Mexitil (Johansson and others 1100).

Mexiletine appears to be effective for the treatment of symptomatic

ventricular arrythmias. Lidocaine is usually given intravenously, and

procainamide and quinidine have undesirable side effects (1099). Therefore,

Mexitil is a much needed drug which should be used as a second-line

treatment of ventricular arrhythmias.

FIGURE 9.4   *continued*

WORKS CITED

Campbell, Ronald M.D.   "Mexiletine."   The New England Journal of
    Medicine, 316 (1987): 29–34.

Heger, James, M.D., and others.   "Mexiletine Therapy in 15 Patients with
    Drug-Resistant Ventricular Tachycardia."   The American Journal
    of Cardiology, 45 (1980): 627–32.

Johansson, Bengt, M.D., and others.   "Long-term Clinical Experience with
    Mexiletine."   American Heart Journal, 107 (1984):   1099–1102.

Woolsey, R. L., M.D.   "Pharmacology, Electrophysiology, and
    Pharmacokinetics of Mexiletine."   American Heart Journal, 107
    (1984):   1058–65.

FIGURE 9.4 *continued*

EXERCISES

1. Compile a list of at least five journals in your field.

2. Obtain editorial policy statements of three journals in your field.

3. Using the information in The Technical Research Report section of this chapter, write a one-page evaluation of the style, clarity, and organization of a published article of your choice. Include a copy of the article with your evaluation.

4. Rewrite the following broad thesis statement to indicate a more limited focus and purpose.

    a. Microchips have revolutionized the electronic industry.

    b. Many new medicines are decreasing the risk of secondary coronaries in heart-diseased patients.

    c. Macroengineering will improve continental travel in the future.

    d. Fusion power will replace fission power.

    e. The twenty-first century will usher in changes in the job market.

    f. Fire fighting techniques are improving.

    g. Family relationships are changing.

    h. Computers are an aid to education.

    i. Desalinization systems will provide more usable water.

    j. Sun Belt cities are expanding rapidly.

5. Revise the following brief outline from a traditional, sentence format to a decimal, topic outline.

    Thesis: Striking changes in transportation modes are predicted for the next century.

    I. Cars will still be the primary means of getting around.

        A. Cars will be totally electronic.

            1. Voice commands will turn the car on and off, select radio channels, and activate the interior ventilation system.

            2. All vehicles will be equipped with a radio-telephone.

            3. Electronics will control fuel use.

        B. Design will be streamlined.

            1. Future cars will be low-slung, with sharply raked windshields.

            2. Undercarriages and wheel wells will be enclosed.

            3. Windows will be flush with the body.

            4. Grilles and outside ornament will disappear.

    C. Fuel consumption will improve.

        1. Fuel mileage will improve to 75 to 100 mpg by 2010.

        2. Engines will be smaller and constructed of molded ceramics to decrease weight.

        3. Electronic fuel injection and transmission will maintain engines at near constant speed.

        4. More cars will be fueled by methanol fuel made from coal.

        5. Eventually cars will run on hydrogen and be able to travel on both water and land.

 II. Rapid-transit systems will ease congestion in cities and metropolitan areas.

    A. Urban rail systems will expand between cities.

    B. Double-deck, multisectional buses will carry as many as 150 people on separate busways.

        1. Sleeper seats, videograms, and meals will be standard.

        2. Fare collection will be simplified by electronically coded cards and single monthly bills.

    C. Moving sidewalk belts will glide along elevated guideways at speeds of 10 to 15 mph.

    D. Rail travel will improve.

        1. "Bullet" passenger trains will travel between major urban areas at 160 mph.

        2. Magnetic-levitation trains which can travel at more than 250 mph are being tested in Japan.

III. Future generations will witness new ventures in the sky.

    A. By the year 2000 jetliners will carry as many as 1000 people.

    B. One-passenger flying machines are being tested at Lockheed.

WRITING OPTIONS

1. Research and write a review article on a breakthrough discovery in your field. Investigate who made it, how it was made, how it works, what benefits it offers, what problems it poses, and what future applications are possible. Present a three-step topic outline, if your professor assigns one for inclusion. Use the documentation techniques assigned by your professor. At minimum include a list of references.

2. *Research and write a professional review article on some aspect of the twentieth century. Delineate a problem, discuss what advances*

are being made, explain a new process or product, discuss its results, draw conclusions, and point out future implications of the innovation. Following is a list of broad subjects which can be narrowed to focused topics:

the American family	role of the Far East
education	transportation
health care	fuels
medicine	travel modes
crime	satellites
life expectancy	electronic marvels
food production	genetic engineering
minerals and materials	weather modification
pollution	architecture
the shape of cities	home appliances
computer capabilities	population
the economy	space exploration
merchandising	new occupations
other?	

Follow your professor's advice on titling, outlines, and documentation techniques.

NOTES

CHAPTER 10

Accessing Information

by Drake Young

Reprinted with special permission of King Features Syndicate, Inc.

INTRODUCTION

Research is the process of investigating and discovering facts. Research may consist of testing, polls, questionnnaires, interviews, letters of inquiry, observation, and the like, or it may consist of investigating the works of other researchers who have published in general books, encyclopedias, abstracts, specialized dictionaries, handbooks, manuals, almanacs, pamphlets, and so on. A research report gives formal credit (documentation) to the sources used or quoted; that is, parenthetical references to the works cited are included within the text, and a list of "Works Cited" is included at the end.

Strategies for accessing and researching material are used along with the writing strategies for a professional paper discussed in Chapter 9 (selecting and limiting the subject, formulating and polishing the thesis, brainstorming the methods of development, writing introductions and closings, and writing drafts and final papers). Accessing/researching the source material consists of three more strategies:

1. Researching print and electronic sources
2. Taking notes
3. Preparing surveys and questionnaires

If the paper requires formal documentation, refer to Chapter 11, Documenting Reports, to review Bibliography Styles and Referencing the Sources (bibliography formats and in-text parenthetical references).

249

RESEARCHING MATERIALS

Objectives

In researching the source material you must accomplish three objectives:

1. **Skim reading of the material.** Skim read the material as you locate it in order to become familiar with the data on your subject. Look over the table of contents and index. Read the preface and introduction which may present an overview of the book's contents. Check the appendix and glossary for supplemental materials and definitions. Search for bibliographies that suggest more related sources for you to investigate.
2. **Refinement of your thesis.** Refine and amplify your thesis as you learn more about your subject.
3. **Preparation of bibliography cards.** Prepare a bibliography card for each source which contains information in support of your thesis so that you can quickly relocate the material for note-taking after your overview of materials.

Library

Familiarize yourself with your school, company, or public library. Locate the card catalogue, the reference work stacks, the indexes to periodical literature, the government publication indexes, the vertical file, the microfilm readers, and the photocopying equipment. Determine if the library catalogues its collection of books by the Dewey Decimal System or the Library of Congress System.

Dewey Decimal System.   The Dewey Decimal System divides all books and journals and arranges them on the shelves by the following general subject categories:

000–099	General Works
100–199	Philosophy
200–299	Religion
300–399	Social Sciences
400–499	Language
500–599	Pure Sciences
600–699	Technology (Applied Sciences)
700–799	Fine Arts
800–899	Literature
900–999	History

Each of these general categories is, in turn, divided into ten smaller categories. For example the Technology (Applied Science) classification (600–699) is divided into the following:

600–609   Technology
610–619   Medical Sciences
620–629   Engineering
630–639   Agriculture
640–649   Home Economics
650–659   Business and Business Methods
660–669   Chemical and Related Technologies
670–679   Manufacturing (metal, textile, paper, etc.)
680–689   Miscellaneous Manufactures (hardware, furniture, etc.)
690–699   Building Construction

Library of Congress System.   The Library of Congress System arranges the books on the shelves by classifying the books by 21 letters to designate the following major subject categories:

A   General Works
B   Philosophy and Religion
C   History and Auxiliary Sciences
D   Universal History and Topography
E/F   American History
G   Geography, Anthropology, Folklore, etc.
H   Social Sciences
J   Political Science
K   Law
L   Education
M   Music
N   Fine Arts
P   Language and Literature
Q   Science
R   Medicine
S   Agriculture
T   Technology
U   Military Service
V   Naval Services
Z   Library Science and Bibliography

Each of these classes is subclassed by a combination of letters for subtopics. For example, T (Technology) contains 16 subclasses:

TA   General engineering, including general civil engineering
TC   Hydraulic engineering
TD   Sanitary and municipal engineering
TE   Highway engineering
TF   Railroad engineering
TG   Bridge engineering
TH   Building construction
TJ   Mechanical engineering
TK   Electrical engineering, Nuclear engineering
TL   Motor vehicles, Aeronautics, Astronautics
TN   Mining engineering, Mineral industries, Metallurgy
TP   Chemical technology
TR   Photography
TS   Manufactures
TT   Handicrafts, Arts and crafts
TX   Home economics

A number notation is also assigned to each book.

Card Catalogue.   Begin your research by searching the card catalogue for reference and general books on your subject. The catalogue
will contain three separate alphabetized cards for every book, filmstrip,
phonograph album, and tape in the library. A separate card is filed under
the author's name, title of the work, and subject heading. Thus, a book
by Donn B. Parker titled *Fighting Computer Crime* will be catalogued
under *P* for *Parker, Donn B.*, under *F* for *Fighting Computer Crime*,
and under *C* for *Computer Crimes—Prevention*. Figure 10.1 shows a typical author card with explanations of the data.

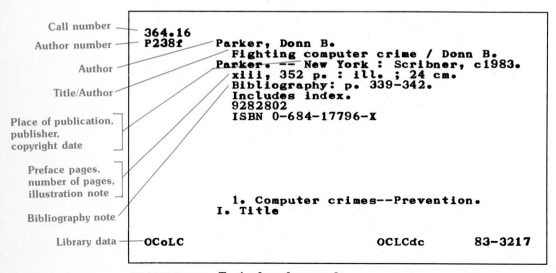

FIGURE 10.1   *Typical author card*

```
                    Fighting computer crime
  364.16
  P238f        Parker, Donn B.
                 Fighting computer crime / Donn B.
              Parker. -- New York : Scribner, c1983.
                 xiii, 352 p. : ill. ; 24 cm.
                 Bibliography: p. 339-342.
                 Includes index.
                 9282802
                 ISBN 0-684-17796-X




                 1. Computer crimes--Prevention.
              I. Title

  OCoLC                                OCLCdc        83-3217
```

FIGURE 10.2   *Typical title card*

Figure 10.2 is the title card for the same book.

If you do now know the authors or titles of books on your subject, you may locate books by looking up *subject headings*. The subject heading "Computers" will be further divided into subcategories, such as "Computer Crimes—Prevention" and "Computers—Access Control." Figure 10.3 shows the subject card for the same book.

```
                 COMPUTER CRIMES--PREVENTION.
  364.16
  P238f        Parker, Donn B.
                 Fighting computer crime / Donn B.
              Parker. -- New York : Scribner, c1983.
                 xiii, 352 p. : ill. ; 24 cm.
                 Bibliography: p. 339-342.
                 Includes index.
                 9282802
                 ISBN 0-684-17796-X




                 1. Computer crimes--Prevention.
              I. Title

  OCoLC                                OCLCdc        83-3217
```

FIGURE 10.3   *Typical subject card*

Reference Books

Reference books—general encyclopedias, technical encyclopedias, almanacs, handbooks, dictionaries, histories, and biographies—are listed in the card catalogue. These are good sources to skim read first because the material is general and often contains bibliographies which will lead you to more specific sources. There are reference books for every discipline. Following is a partial list of technical reference books:

Encyclopedias

Encyclopedia Americana
Encyclopaedia Britannica
Collier's Encyclopedia
Encyclopedia of Careers and Vocational Guidance
Encyclopedia of Computer Science
Encyclopedia of Food Technology and Food Service Series
Encyclopedia of Management
Encyclopedia of Marine Resources
Encyclopedia of Materials Handling
Encyclopedia of Modern Architecture
Encyclopedia and Dictionary of Medicine, Nursing, and Allied Health
Encyclopedia of Photography
Encyclopedia of Textiles
Encyclopedia of Urban Planning
McGraw-Hill Encyclopedia of Energy
McGraw-Hill Encyclopedia of Environmental Science
McGraw-Hill Encyclopedia of Food, Agriculture, and Nutrition

Dictionaries

Funk & Wagnalls New Standard Dictionary of the English Language
Oxford English Dictionary
Random House Dictionary of the English Language
Webster's Third New International Dictionary of the English Language
Webster's New World Dictionary, Third College Edition
American Heritage Dictionary
Random House College Dictionary
Webster's New Collegiate Dictionary
Dictionary of Architecture and Construction
Dictionary of Business and Finance
Dictionary of Nutrition and Food Technology
Dictionary of Practical Law
Duncan's Dictionary for Nurses

Funk & Wagnalls Dictionary of Data Processing Terms
McGraw-Hill Dictionary of Scientific and Technical Terms
Paramedical Dictionary
Stedman's Medical Dictionary

Handbooks, Manuals, and Almanacs

Book of Facts
Building Construction Handbook
CRC Handbook of Marine Sciences
Fire Protection Handbook
Nurse's Almanac
U.S. Government Manual
The World Almanac

Indexes to Essays Within Books

Following your search of general and reference books on your subject, you may want to refer to one or more indexes of essays on your subject which are published within books of collected essays. Your search of the card catalogue subject cards may not turn up these essays unless the entire collection of essays is on one subject.

The *Essay and General Literature Index* catalogues essays by author and subject. It directs you to material within books and collections of a biographical and/or critical nature. Figure 10.4 shows a section of a page from the *Essay and General Literature Index*.

At the back of each index volume is a "List of Books Indexed" which contains an alphabetized list by author of the books in which the essays appear. The call numbers of those books held by the library are often penciled in by librarians. If the call number is not penciled in, you may locate the book by checking to see if it is listed in the card catalogue.

Other indexes to books and collections are the *Bibliographic Index* and the *Biography Index*: *A Quarterly Index to Biographic Material in Books and Magazines*.

Abstracts

A library abstract is an index which, in addition to listing author's names, publishers, titles, and publication data, includes a brief summary of the content and scope of the book, article, or pamphlet. By skim reading the summaries, you can determine if the work is relevant to your subject. Do not take notes from an abstract; always cite material from the original work. Some technical abstracts include:

ESSAY AND GENERAL LITERATURE INDEX, 1975-1979   311

Composition (Music)—*Continued*
Sessions, R. Problems and issues facing the composer today. *In* Sessions, R. Roger Sessions on music p71-87
Sessions, R. Song and pattern in music today. *In* Sessions, R. Roger Sessions on music p53-70
Composition (Photography)
Borcoman, J. W. Notes on the early use of combination printing. *In* One hundred years of photographic history p15-18
Composition (Rhetoric) See Rhetoric
Compostela, Spain. See Santiago de Compostela, Spain
Comprehension
Bauman, Z. Consensus and truth. *In* Bauman, Z. Hermeneutics and social science p225-46
Bauman, Z. The rise of hermeneutics. *In* Bauman, Z. Hermeneutics and social science p23-47
Bauman, Z. Understanding as expansion of the form of life. *In* Bauman, Z. Hermeneutics and social science p194-224
Bauman, Z. Understanding as the work of history: Karl Mannheim. *In* Bauman, Z. Hermeneutics and social science p89-110
Bauman, Z. Understanding as the work of history: Karl Marx. *In* Bauman, Z. Hermeneutics and social science p48-68
Bauman, Z. Understanding as the work of history: Max Weber. *In* Bauman, Z. Hermeneutics and social science p69-88
Bauman, Z. Understanding as the work of life: From Schutz to ethnomethodology. *In* Bauman, Z. Hermeneutics and social science p172-93

Compulsory non-military service. See Service, Compulsory non-military
Computer composition. See Computer music
Computer music
Bamberger, J. In search of a tune. *In* Perkins, D. and Leondar, B. eds. The arts and cognition p284-319
Computer reliabilty. See Computers—Reliability
Computer translating. See Machine translating
Computers
Le Roy Ladurie, E. The historian and the computer. *In* Le Roy Ladurie, E. The territory of the historian p3-6
See also Electronic data processing

  Reliability
Thomas, L. To err is human. *In* Thomas, L. The medusa and the snail p36-40
Computers and civilization
Lowi, T. J. The information revolution, politics, and the prospects for an open society. *In* Galnoor, I. ed. Government secrecy in democracies p40-61
Computers in literature
Rhodes, C. H. Tyranny by computer: automated data processing and oppressive government in science fiction. *In* Clareson, T. D. ed. Many futures, many worlds p66-93
Computing machines. See Calculating-machines
Comstock, W. Richard
On seeing with the eye of the native European. *In* Seeing with a native eye p58-78

— Subject head
— Author, article
— Book author
— Book title
— Page of essay
— See also note
— Subhead
— Second entry

FIGURE 10.4   *Sample Essay and General Literature Index page section*
(Copyright 1975, 1976, 1978, 1979 and 1980 by the H. W. Wilson Company.
Materials reproduced by permission of the publisher.)

Abstract on Criminology and Penology
Air Pollution Abstracts
Biological Abstracts
Criminal Justice Abstracts
Current Index to Journals in Education
Index to Publications of the United States Congress
Nursing Research
Oceanic Abstracts
Solar Energy Update

Figure 10.5 shows a section from the *Current Index to Journals in Education*.

EJ 335 570 CG 530 221
Counseling Center Hiring Preferences. Corazzini, John G.; And Others *Journal of Counseling Psychology;* v33 n1 p78-80 Jan 1986 (Reprint: UMI)
Descriptors: Counselors; *Employment Patterns; Employment Opportunities; *Guidance Centers; *Counselor Selection; *Student Personnel Services
Explored counseling center change by examining current hiring preferences of counseling center directors. In the first study, 130 counseling center directors rated a clinical or counseling vita for agency fit, likelihood of being licensed, and general competence. In the second study, position advertisements were classified as clinical, counseling, or either. Results of both studies are given. (Author/ABB)

EJ 335 571 CG 530 222
Comparison of Thought-Listing Rating Methods. Tarico, Valerie S.; And Others *Journal of Counseling Psychology;* v33 n1 p81-83 Jan 1986 (Reprint: UMI)
Descriptors: Comparative Analysis; *Self Evaluation (Individuals); Testing; Cognitive Processes; *Cognitive Measurement; *Rating Scales; Interrater Reliability; *Predictive Validity; *Anxiety
Compared three methods of rating thoughts: self-rating by subjects, rating by experts with thoughts presented randomly, and rating by experts with thoughts presented in context among 107 students who listed their thoughts prior to giving a speech. Results indicated all three methods were equal in predictions of speech anxiety and performance. (Author/ABB)

EJ 335 576 CG 530 227
Measuring Work and Support Network Satisfaction. Maynard, Marianne *Journal of Employment Counseling;* v23 n1 p9-19 Mar 1986 (Reprint: UMI)
Descriptors: *Social Support Groups; *Social Networks; *Job Satisfaction; *Measures (Individuals); Test Construction; *Test Reliability; High Risk Persons
Identifiers: *Work and Support Network Satisfaction Scale
The development and pilot testing of a Work and Support Network Satisfaction Scale (WSNS) for early detection and intervention of troubled and dissatisfied workers is described. The results suggest the scale has potential use in detecting at-risk workers. (Author)

EJ 335 577 CG 530 228
Social Interpersonal Skills of Handicapped and Nonhandicapped Adults at Work. Lignugaris/Kraft, Benjamin; And Others *Journal of Employment Counseling;* v23 n1 p20-30 Mar 1986 (Reprint: UMI)
Descriptors: *Adults; *Disabilities; *Interpersonal Competence; *Work Environment; Success
Identifiers: *Social Interaction
The pattern and content of social interactions of successful disabled and nondisabled employees were observed in two employment settings. Data suggest that both groups were active social interactants who frequently worked cooperatively, yet interacted relatively infrequently with their supervisors. Implications for future research are discussed. (Author)

Access number
Clearing house number
Article title
Author
Journal title
Publication data
Descriptors, Identifiers
Descriptive note

FIGURE 10.5 *Sample page section of Current Index to Journals in Education July–Dec. 1986 (172)*

Indexes to Periodical Literature

In addition to books, libraries also subscribe to and hold periodical literature: magazines, journals, and newspapers. The articles in these various periodical indexes are listed by subject, author, and sometimes titles (books and films). Scan the library's periodical holdings list to determine which magazines, journals, and newspapers are bought by your library. Some of the materials will be microfilm copies of the periodicals. Periodical literature can not generally be checked out of a library, so be prepared to photocopy those articles from which you want to take notes.

Magazines and Journals

The Readers' Guide to Periodical Literature
Social Sciences Index (formerly the *International Index* and the *Social Sciences and Humanities Index*)
Accountant's Index
Applied Science and Technology Index
Biological and Agricultural Index
Business Periodicals Index
Criminal Justice Periodical Index

Cumulative Index to Nursing and Allied Health Literature
Education Index
Energy Index
Environmental Index
Hospital Literature Index
Index to U.S. Government Periodicals
Index to Legal Periodicals
Index Medicus
International Nursing Index
Microcomputer Index

The *Readers' Guide to Periodical Literature* is the most comprehensive. It indexes articles from over 150 popular magazines and journals and is published every few weeks, helping you to locate very recent articles. Figure 10.6 shows a section of a page from *The Readers' Guide*.

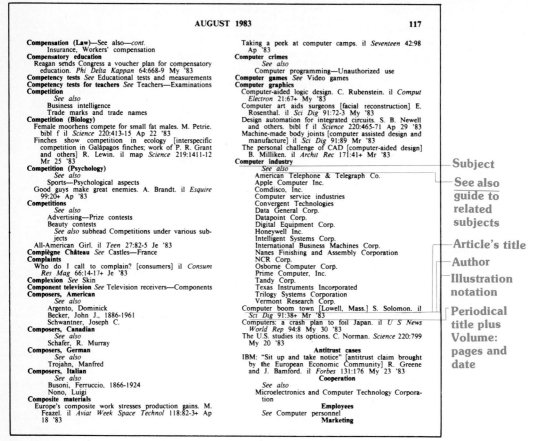

AUGUST 1983   **117**

Compensation (Law)—See also—*cont.*
  Insurance, Workers' compensation
Compensatory education
  Reagan sends Congress a voucher plan for compensatory education. *Phi Delta Kappan* 64:668-9 My '83
Competency tests *See* Educational tests and measurements
Competency tests for teachers *See* Teachers—Examinations
Competition
  See also
  Business intelligence
  Trade marks and trade names
Competition (Biology)
  Female moorhens compete for small fat males. M. Petrie. bibl f il *Science* 220:413-15 Ap 22 '83
  Finches show competition in ecology [interspecific competition in Galápagos finches; work of P. R. Grant and others] R. Lewin. il map *Science* 219:1411-12 Mr 25 '83
Competition (Psychology)
  See also
  Sports—Psychological aspects
  Good guys make great enemies. A. Brandt. il *Esquire* 99:20+ Ap '83
Competitions
  See also
  Advertising—Prize contests
  Beauty contests
    See also subhead Competitions under various subjects
  All-American Girl. il *Teen* 27:82-5 Je '83
Compiègne Château *See* Castles—France
Complaints
  Who do I call to complain? [consumers] il *Consum Res Mag* 66:14-17+ Je '83
Complexion *See* Skin
Component television *See* Television receivers—Components
Composers, American
  See also
  Argento, Dominick
  Becker, John J., 1886-1961
  Schwantner, Joseph C.
Composers, Canadian
  See also
  Schafer, R. Murray
Composers, German
  See also
  Trojahn, Manfred
Composers, Italian
  See also
  Busoni, Ferruccio. 1866-1924
  Nono, Luigi
Composite materials
  Europe's composite work stresses production gains. M. Feazel. il *Aviat Week Space Technol* 118:82-3+ Ap 18 '83

Taking a peek at computer camps. il *Seventeen* 42:98 Ap '83
Computer crimes
  See also
  Computer programming—Unauthorized use
Computer games *See* Video games
Computer graphics
  Computer-aided logic design. C. Rubenstein. il *Comput Electron* 21:67+ My '83
  Computer art aids surgeons [facial reconstruction] E. Rosenthal. il *Sci Dig* 91:72-3 My '83
  Design automation for integrated circuits. S. B. Newell and others. bibl f il *Science* 220:465-71 Ap 29 '83
  Machine-made body joints [computer assisted design and manufacture] il *Sci Dig* 91:89 Mr '83
  The personal challenge of CAD [computer-aided design] B. Milliken. il *Archit Rec* 171:41+ Mr '83
Computer industry
  See also
  American Telephone & Telegraph Co.
  Apple Computer Inc.
  Comdisco, Inc.
  Computer service industries
  Convergent Technologies
  Data General Corp.
  Datapoint Corp.
  Digital Equipment Corp.
  Honeywell Inc.
  Intelligent Systems Corp.
  International Business Machines Corp.
  Nanes Finishing and Assembly Corporation
  NCR Corp.
  Osborne Computer Corp.
  Prime Computer, Inc.
  Tandy Corp.
  Texas Instruments Incorporated
  Trilogy Systems Corporation
  Vermont Research Corp.
  Computer boom town [Lowell, Mass.] S. Solomon. il *Sci Dig* 91:38+ Mr '83
  Computers: a crash plan to foil Japan. il *U S News World Rep* 94:8 My 30 '83
  The U.S. studies its options. C. Norman. *Science* 220:799 My 20 '83
        Antitrust cases
  IBM: "Sit up and take notice" [antitrust claim brought by the European Economic Community] R. Greene and J. Bamford. il *Forbes* 131:176 My 23 '83
        Cooperation
  See also
  Microelectronics and Computer Technology Corporation
        Employees
  See Computer personnel
        Marketing

—Subject
—See also guide to related subjects
—Article's title
—Author
—Illustration notation
—Periodical title plus Volume: pages and date

FIGURE 10.6   *Sample Readers' Guide page section* (Copyright 1983 by the H. W. Wilson Company and reproduced by permission of the publisher.)

All of the specialized subject indexes are similar to *The Readers' Guide*.

Several indexes to the articles printed in newspapers are generally available in libraries.

Newspapers

The New York Times Index

Newspaper Index (Washington Post, The Chicago-Tribune, New Orleans Times-Picayune, and *The Los Angeles Times)*

Wall Street Journal Index

In addition, every newspaper indexes its own publication. These indexes are available at a newspaper office section, "the morgue." Companies also index their newsletters. Both newspaper offices and companies will assist you with their indexes.

The New York Times Index is the most comprehensive of the large indexes. It indexes stories and articles which have appeared in the *Times* since 1851 by subject and author. The index also summarizes articles and occasionally reprints photographs, maps, and other illustrations which accompanied the original article. Figure 10.7 shows a section of a page of *The New York Times Index*:

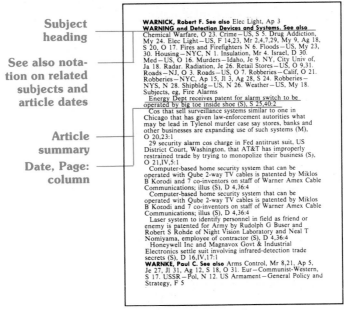

Subject heading

See also notation on related subjects and article dates

Article summary

Date, Page: column

WARNICK, Robert F. See also Elec Light, Ap 3
WARNING and Detection Devices and Systems. See also
Chemical Warfare, O 23. Crime—US, S 5. Drug Addiction, My 24. Elec Light—US, F 14,23, Mr 2,4,7,29, My 9, Ag 18, S 20, O 17. Fires and Firefighters N 6. Floods—US, My 23, 30. Housing—NYC, N 1. Insulation, Mr 4. Israel, D 30. Med—US, O 16. Murders—Idaho, Je 9. NY, City Univ of, Ja 18. Radar. Radiation, Je 26. Retail Stores—US, O 9,31. Roads—NJ, O 3. Roads—US, O 7. Robberies—Calif, O 21. Robberies—NYC, Ap 15, Jl 3, Ag 28, S 24. Robberies—NYS, N 28. Shipbldg—US, N 26. Weather—US, My 18. Subjects, eg, Fire Alarms
  Energy Dept receives patent for alarm switch to be operated by big toe inside shoe (S), S 25,40:2
  Cos that sell surveillance systems similar to one in Chicago that has given law-enforcement autorities what may be lead in Tylenol murder case say stores, banks and other businesses are expanding use of such systems (M), O 20,23:1
  29 security alarm cos charge in Fed antitrust suit, US District Court, Washington, that AT&T has improperly restrained trade by trying to monopolize their business (S), O 21,IV,5:1
  Computer-based home security system that can be operated with Qube 2-way TV cables is patented by Miklos B Korodi and 7 co-inventors on staff of Warner Amex Cable Communications; illus (S), D 4,36:4
  Computer-based home security system that can be operated with Qube 2-way TV cables is patented by Miklos B Korodi and 7 co-inventors on staff of Warner Amex Cable Communications; illus (S), D 4,36:4
  Laser system to identify personnel in field as friend or enemy is patented for Army by Rudolph G Buser and Robert S Rohde of Night Vision Laboratory and Neal T Nomiyama, employee of contractor (S), D 4,36:4
  Honeywell Inc and Magnavox Govt & Industrial Electronics settle suit involving infrared-detection trade secrets (S), D 16,IV,17:1
WARNKE, Paul C. See also Arms Control, Mr 8,21, Ap 5, Je 27, Jl 31, Ag 12, S 18, O 31. Eur—Communist-Western, S 17. USSR—Pol, N 12. US Armament—General Policy and Strategy, F 5

FIGURE 10.7. *Sample New York Times Index page section*

(Copyright © 1983 by The New York Times Company. Reprinted by permission.)

Vertical File

Most libraries maintain a vertical file by subject of pamphlets, booklets, bulletins, and clippings on timely subjects. Ask the reference librarian to assist you in locating the file and the material contained within it.

Electronic Media

During your research period, be alert to television and radio programs on your subject. Many programs are extremely authoritative and will contain hard data and discussions which will provide you with further information. Check your library or learning resource files to find films, filmstrips, slide programs, and videotapes on your subject.

Any number of computer data banks exist which file information on specific subjects. Consult your library to determine which on-line computer services are available. These services, such as BRS, DIALOG, and Mead, access a wide variety of subjects, usually providing bibliography listings under subject headings called *descriptors*.

Taking Notes

Keeping your thesis in mind at all times and using your working outline as a guide, you now begin to record the notes from each of your sources. Notes are written on 3 by 5-in. or 4 by 6-in. index cards. Use a consistent system to record your information:

1. Enter only one item of information on each card so that you can shuffle and rearrange the cards during all stages of research.
2. Write on only one side of each card. A note continued on the back may be overlooked. If an item of information is too lengthy for one card, use two or more and staple them together.
3. Record the source at the top left of the card. This may be an abbreviated form of the bibliography card, such as the author's last name, the book or article title, or both.
4. Write the note in the center of the card. This may be a summary, a paraphrase, or a quotation. Not all of your notes will be jotted down in complete sentences; some may contain statistics, definitions, phrases, or other fragmentary information to be rewritten carefully in the report draft.
5. Record the exact page number(s) of the source from which you took the note.
6. Label the card in the upper right-hand corner with a word or two which indicates the topic of the note. The topic notation may correspond with an entry in your outline. Figure 10.8 shows a sample note card.

FIGURE 10.8 *Sample note card*

Summary and Paraphrase Notes

Most of your notes will consist of summaries or paraphrases, that is, condensations or restatements of the source material in your own words. Following is an excerpt as it appears in the original source material. Notice that the note (Figure 10.9) both summarizes the information and restates the message in the note taker's own language.

Original

For workers one of the most fearful aspects of the computer is its capacity of controlling machinery to perform tasks that were formerly done by human labor. The unemployment that results is called *technological unemployment*. Employees who are eliminated by automation are generally unskilled and semiskilled workers who find difficulty in seeking new employment. Because of the growing use of computerized checkouts in supermarkets, the Retail Clerks Union fears a loss of 25 to 30% of supermarket jobs. Perhaps many of these fears are unjustified. The telephone companies now employ more persons than they did before the use of computerized switching services.

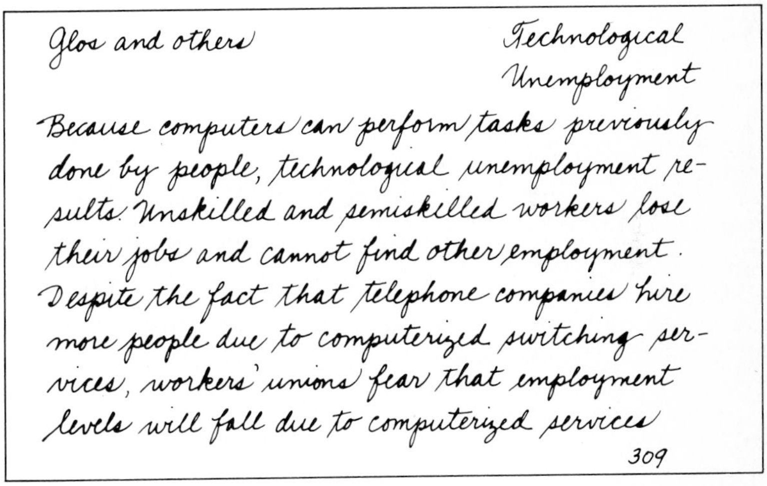

Glos and others — Technological Unemployment

Because computers can perform tasks previously done by people, technological unemployment results. Unskilled and semiskilled workers lose their jobs and cannot find other employment. Despite the fact that telephone companies hire more people due to computerized switching services, workers' unions fear that employment levels will fall due to computerized services

309

FIGURE 10.9 ***Summary and paraphrased note***

Direct Quotation

Occasionally, you will want to quote the exact words of an author. Usually no more than 10 percent of the text should consist of direct quotation. Take notes of direct quotation only if the material conveys a highly original idea, opinion, or conclusion of the author which, if paraphrased, would lose its striking effect or distort the meaning.

Following is an original excerpt plus two sample notecards (Figures 10.10 and 10.11), one employing full sentence quotation and the other employing partial sentence quotation. Note the use of the ellipsis (. . .) to indicate omitted words and the brackets ([   ]) to indicate slight additions by the note taker.

Original

Because of the sea of dangers, past practice has been to isolate sensitive computers. That strategy proved itself this summer at the Los Alamos National Laboratory in New Mexico when young raiders from Milwaukee succeeded only in cracking an unclassified computer. There is no evidence that they actually obtained classified information or gained access to the top-secret computers, which remain unconnected to networks.

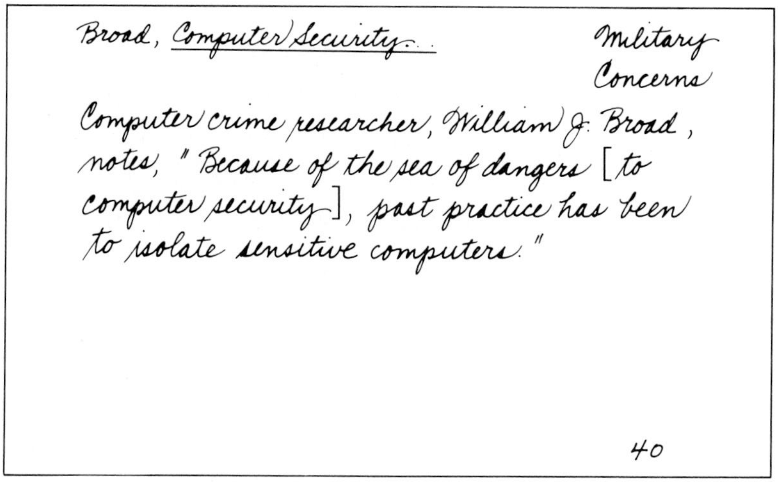

Broad, Computer Security   *Military Concerns*

Computer crime researcher, William J. Broad, notes, "Because of the sea of dangers [to computer security], past practice has been to isolate sensitive computers."

40

FIGURE 10.10   *Full sentence quotation note*

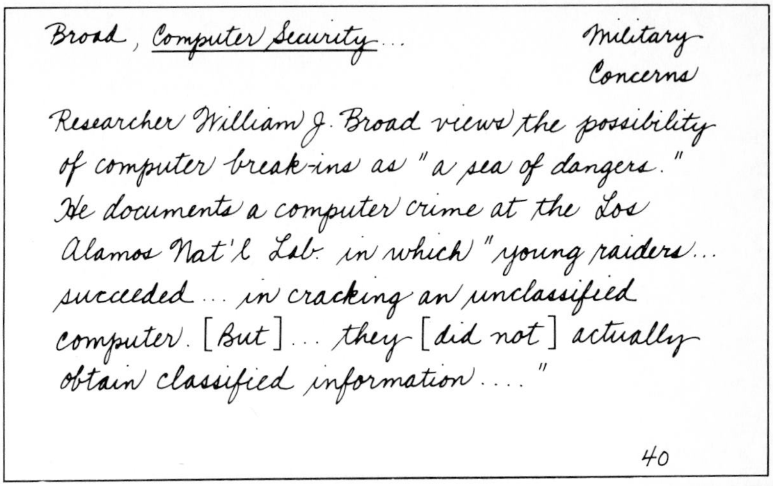

Broad, Computer Security...

Military Concerns

Researcher William J. Broad views the possibility of computer break-ins as "a sea of dangers." He documents a computer crime at the Los Alamos Nat'l Lab. in which "young raiders... succeeded... in cracking an unclassified computer. [But]... they [did not] actually obtain classified information...."

40

FIGURE 10.11 *Partial quotation note*

Plagiarism

Notes must be recorded carefully to avoid plagiarism. The word *plagiarism* derives from the Latin word *plagiarus* which means "kidnapper." In effect, plagiarism in writing is kidnapping the words (apt phrases or entire sentences) and ideas (the organization of material, another's argument, or a line of thinking) and presenting them as if they were your own original phrasing and thinking. Published words, ideas, and conclusions of an author are protected by law; therefore, use of the material must be acknowledged whenever you use them in your own work. Failure to provide acknowledgment may result in a failed paper, failure in the course, or expulsion from school. To avoid plagiarism, follow five rules:

1. Introduce all borrowed material by stating in the text the name of the authority from whom it was taken.
2. Enclose the exact words within quotation marks.
3. If you summarize or paraphrase material, make sure that the information is written in your own style and language.
4. Provide a parenthetical reference note for each borrowed item.
5. Provide a "works cited" entry for every source which is referenced in your text.

Following is an original excerpt followed by three note cards. The first two (Figures 10.12 and 10.13) are unacceptable plagiarisms, while the last (Figure 10.14) is an acceptable note.

Original

The explosive development of the computer has created change both inside and outside an organization. Inside the organization the computer has altered work assignments and provided management with new tools for decision making. Outside the organization the computer is greatly changing our way of life and will continue to exert a force for change. Some of the social concerns related to the computer are: generation of unnecessary information, organizational changes, fear of technological unemployment, invasion of privacy, security of data, and depersonalization.

FIGURE 10.12   *Plagiarized note*

FIGURE 10.13   *Less obvious, but plagiarized note*

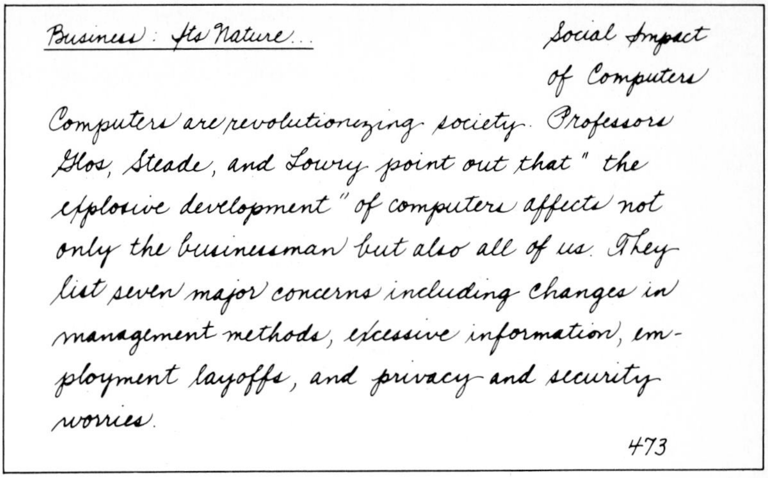

Business : Its Nature ...   Social Impact
                                                               of Computers

Computers are revolutionizing society. Professors
Glos, Steade, and Lowry point out that " the
explosive development " of computers affects not
only the businessman but also all of us. They
list seven major concerns including changes in
management methods, excessive information, employment layoffs, and privacy and security
worries.

                                                                      473

FIGURE 10.14 *Acceptable note*

In the acceptable note (1) the information is summarized, (2) the language is the note taker's, (3) the authors' phrase is quoted, and (4) the source is acknowledged in the text. In addition, a parenthetical reference to the source and a complete "Works Cited" entry will appear in the final draft of the report.

Ellipses and Brackets

Perhaps you noticed that some of the note cards which contain direct quotations include the ellipsis (three spaced periods) and brackets ([ ]). Although you cannot change a direct quotation, you can omit a phrase or even several sentences. You may also add a word or brief phrase to clarify a passage so that less of the original must be quoted. Great care must be taken, however, so as not to distort the meaning and intent of the original passage.

The ellipsis is usually used within a passage, but it may be needed at the beginning or end if introductory or closing words are omitted. To facilitate blending just a brief quoted phrase or partial sentence into your own paper, you may omit opening and closing ellipses as long as the meaning is not distorted. Some examples follow:

Casson likens the early small question mark to "a bedraggled telephone doodle."

(No ellipsis is used because the quote is a brief phrase.)

Howard stressed, "The technical writer . . . must master punctuation." (Ellipsis is used to indicate that the words *as well as the professional writer* have been omitted.)

Not only did Samuel Johnson standardize spelling and punctuation, he also ". . . ran the world's greatest library, put out a definitive edition of Homer's *Iliad* and *Odyssey*, and even found time to write a book about courtesans," points out Lionel Casson.

(The ellipsis is used at the beginning of the quote to indicate that the words *Not only did he earn himself the right to be called the father of punctuation* have been omitted.)

Casson explained, "The Cooper Union show had a big section devoted to the whys and wherefores of leaving out punctuation marks. . . ."

(A period follows the ellipsis to indicate that words from the end of the sentence were omitted.)

Occasionally, words of clarification are needed within a quoted passage which has been taken out of its original context. You may add a brief clarifying word or phrase by using square brackets. If your typewriter is not equipped with brackets, allow space to draw them in neatly. Do not use curved parentheses

Mr. Mills stated, "They [personal computers] have revolutionized the business."

(The bracketed words *personal computers* have been included to clarify the pronoun reference.)

Display Quotations

If you need to include a quotation of more than four typed lines, use a display format. Set it off from your text by beginning a new line, indenting each line of it ten spaces from the left margin, typing it double-spaced, and omitting the quotation marks. The introductory sentence to a display quote explains its purpose and is usually followed by a colon although sometimes your text may require a different punctuation mark or none at all. Do not indent the first line of the display quotation if you are quoting only one paragraph or only part of a paragraph. If you quote two or more paragraphs, indent the first line of each paragraph an additional three spaces.

Dan Rather, a prominent newscaster, works hard to avoid peculiarities of his Texan accent:

> I worked on my own for a while trying to say *e* as in "ten" correctly. Texans, including me, tend to say *tin*. I also tried to stop dropping *g*'s. It never seemed to be a problem except sometimes when I was tired (still the case I fear), I tended to say *nothin'* instead of "nothing."

Use the ellipsis, brackets, and display quotes sparingly.

SURVEYS AND QUESTIONNAIRES

Surveys and questionnaires are often used to gather data to guide the writer and to back up conclusions. Essentially questionnaires serve three purposes. They

- Gather opinions of many people
- Determine solutions to problems
- Substantiate predetermined positions

Care must be taken in selecting the test group, motivating a response, constructing the questions, and compiling the results. The survey sheet itself is referred to as the **survey instrument** or the **questionnaire.**

Data compiled from the survey may be presented within the report in tables, bar charts, circle charts, line graphs, and the like (see Figure 10.16). In a proposal, for instance, some of the data may be used under the Problem heading to demonstrate the extent and complexity of the problem. Other data may back up your position in the Proposal section and/or offer other solutions that have come to light as a result of the survey. Finally, data can determine advantages and disadvantages of a proposal in the Consequences section. A copy of the survey instrument or questionnaire should be included along with the final tabulations as supplementary material.

Advantages

The advantages of written surveys are:

1. Carefully formatted questions which require only a check-mark in a box speed up the survey response process.
2. A large sample of data may be collected in a short time.
3. Even distribution (employee mailboxes, targeted mailings) ensures that all relevant people are actually contacted within a given time frame.
4. Printing and distribution are less costly and more efficient than person-to-person inquiries and interviews.
5. Written responses are usually less biased than those garnered by personal interviews.
6. The data can easily be tabulated by counting or computer keypunching.
7. The data is on hand to point out other problems and the trends for future study.

Disadvantages

A survey is not always advantageous. Certain disadvantages or drawbacks may occur through the use of written surveys or questionnaires. They are

1. A *low* response rate (under 90 percent of those both affected by the study and actually surveyed) will result in unreliable data.
2. A *slow* response rate slows up your findings.
3. Certain members of your group may not respond to written surveys because they are uninformed, disinterested, careless, lazy, prejudiced, or offended.
4. A certain number of your group may not respond accurately due to inability to read or to understand the precise meaning of your terms.
5. Some people may be reluctant to respond to questions regarding personal data or to offer opinions for fear of repercussions.

Test Group

Selecting the size of the test group and determining the number of responses to assure validity are problems for the true statistician. For purposes of accessing information for your reports, try to survey all of the people who will probably be affected by your proposal for change, such as all of the employees in an office or department, all of the users of an inadequate parking lot, all of the residents of your apartment or condominium complex, or all of the neighbors touched by a city project. Remember, you need a 90 percent response rate of those affected and surveyed for validity. Consider whether you wish to collect numbers or percentages, or both, as well as comments, suggestions, and the like.

Familiarize yourself with your survey group. Are they knowledgeable about your subject? Are you looking for new data, substantiation of a position, or opinions and suggestions to determine direction? What prejudices might influence answers (age, sex, race, organization rank, religion, politics, length of involvement, and so forth)? Should your tone be formal or folksy?

Motivating Responses

You need a clearly defined goal first. What are you trying to determine? Do your own research of the problems and develop possible solutions before developing your survey. Consider the following motivating factors.

Time.   Do not begin to write your proposal or other type of report until you have your survey results. Consider a schedule for devising, typing, printing, distributing, collecting, and tabulating your data. Distribute forms at a peak time, not when people are on vacation or occupied with IRS returns, Christmas, and the like. Sometimes distribution at a large meeting of the affected people will guarantee a quick, high return on the spot. Preference and opinion questions do not require research on the part of the respondents. Urge your group to return the form(s) to you quickly by hand, by mailing a preaddressed envelope, or by collecting the forms at a designated spot at a set date and time.

Sponsorship. Make it clear that you are seeking the information under the auspices of an institution, organization, professor, manager, or the like. Gathering data for a college professional and technical writing course project should lend prestige to your inquiry.

Cover Sheet. A cover letter, memo, information sheet, or simply an explanatory paragraph above the survey questions may accompany the survey instrument stating the purpose, nature of the report, and how the data will be analyzed. This is a logical place to state the sponsorship of the survey. Emphasize the importance of the survey and offer to share results of the study if that is feasible. Above all, stress that you need a return as soon as possible.

Anonymity. Allow for anonymity by guaranteeing confidentiality. Do not ask for names on the forms, particularly if the material covers touchy subjects such as opinions about supervisors or administrators, work schedules, and raises. Ensure anonymity also for questionnaires about highly personal feelings on such issues as abortion, capital punishment, personal habits, and so on.

Format

The overall appearance and arrangement of the instrument should motivate responses. Follow these suggestions:

1. Select a good quality, possibly colored, paper which suggests care in preparation.
2. Title the survey carefully to clarify the content.
3. Keep your questions as brief as possible.
4. Provide tick boxes for responses and printed lines for comments.
5. Do not crowd your questions. Allow for plenty of white space.
6. Use language carefully. Such words as *should, might,* and *could* often "lead" answers. Do not ask offensive or very personal questions if possible. (Avoid: *Should employees be blood-tested for AIDS?* [ ] yes [ ] no)
7. Ask for only one piece of information per question. (Avoid: *Do you favor a personnel reorganization of your department or would you be interested in a new position?* [ ] yes [ ] no)
8. Ask for comments, opinions, or other alternatives when it is appropriate to do so. Type in lines rather than just leaving white space for the answers.

Types of Questions

There are six conventional types of questions. Each has its own advantages and disadvantages in tabulation.

1. **Dual alternatives.** This is the easiest type of data to tabulate in that there are only two choices: yes or no, positive or negative, true or false, and so on. Take care to ensure that there really are only two possible answers to your question.

   Sample: Have you eaten purchased cookies in the past month:

   [   ] yes   [   ] no

2. **Multiple Choice questions.** This type also produces easy-to-tabulate data in that you provide a number of alternatives to indicate a fact, preference, or opinion. Your survey may ask for a single tick or multiple ticks.

   Sample: Check the **one** cookie brand you most prefer.

   [   ] Hydrox   [   ] Fig Newtons
   [   ] Oreo   [   ] Pepperidge Farm
   [   ] Duncan Hines   [   ] Almost Home

   or

   Check **all** of the cookie brands you purchase on a regular basis.

   [   ] Hydrox   [   ] Fig Newtons
   [   ] Oreo   [   ] Pepperidge Farm
   [   ] Duncan Hines   [   ] Almost Home

3. **Rank Ordering.** This format provides respondents with a series of items to rank according to preference, frequency of use, or other criteria. Tabulating this data is easy. However, distortion may occur if the mean (the average) differs from the mode (the most frequently occurring response). The items must be significantly different to make rank choices.

   Sample: Rank (1 highest to 6 lowest) the following cookie brands in order of your preference.

   _____ Hydrox
   _____ Oreo
   _____ Duncan Hines
   _____ Fig Newtons
   _____ Pepperidge Farm
   _____ Almost Home

4. **Continuum Scales.** This format is similar to rank ordering in that it provides a method for respondents to express opinions by rank ordering numerically or verbally on a continuum. Scales are most valid if they have an *even* number of choices (usually 4–6). If a scale has a middle choice, respondents choose it a disproportionately large percentage of the time.

Sample: Mark the response which best indicates the frequency of your cookie purchases per grocery trip.

[ ] always   [ ] often   [ ] seldom   [ ] never

5. **Completions.** This format asks respondents to provide facts and/or opinions in either fill-in or open-ended responses. Questions on age, frequency, or amount are easier to tabulate than are questions which allow for open-ended responses.

Samples: (Fill-in type) I usually buy _____ cookie
products a month.   number

or

Completion type. The quality which most determines my cookie product choice is

_____

6. **Essays.** This format asks respondents to express fully opinions or facts. The results may be difficult to tabulate and arrange into groupings. Such questions are more effective if they urge a focus on certain criteria.

Sample: Suggest criteria which would motivate you to purchase Fig Newtons more frequently. Consider butter content, sugar content, thickness, consistency, and amount of filling.

_____

_____

_____

_____

Figure 10.15 is a sample survey to determine popularity of a brand cookie, who buys it, and how the product should be improved. It asks for respondent classification data and employs a variety of types of questions.

PRODUCT PREFERENCE SURVEY

————————— Classification —————————

(multiple choice)

1. Please indicate your age bracket.

    [   ] 16–20 [   ] 21–30 [   ] 31–40 [   ] 41 or over

(dual alternative)

2. Are you   [   ] male [   ] female?

(multiple choice)

3. What is your primary occupation?
    [   ] student   [   ] housewife
    [   ] professional manager   [   ] farmer
    [   ] operative/laborer   [   ] retired
    [   ] foreman/craftsman   [   ] not employed
    [   ] clerical/sales

(completion)

4. Fill in the blank with a number. I generally shop for groceries
    ——— times a month.

————————— Cookie Questions —————————

(dual alternative)

1. I am the primary cookie shopper in my household.
    [   ] yes [   ] no

(continuum)

2. In the span of a year I purchase cookie products
    [   ] often [   ] frequently [   ] seldom [   ] never

(multiple choice)

3. Check all of the brands of cookies which you purchase on a
    regular (once or more a month) basis.
    [   ] Hydrox   [   ] Fig Newtons
    [   ] Oreo   [   ] Pepperidge Farm
    [   ] Duncan Hines   [   ] Almost Home

FIGURE 10.15 *Sample Survey/Questionnaire*—*continues on page 273*

(rank order)

4. Rank your order of preference (1–6) for each brand.
   [   ] Hydrox   [   ] Fig Newtons
   [   ] Oreo   [   ] Pepperidge Farm
   [   ] Duncan Hines   [   ] Almost Home

(completion)

5. Fill in the number. I usually buy ____ cookie products a month.

(multiple choice)

6. Which factor most determines your cookie brand choice?
   [   ] packaging   [   ] overall taste
   [   ] calorie content   [   ] cost
   [   ] additives (nuts,   [   ] consistency (chewy,
        raisins, fillings)   crisp, crunchy)

(essay)

7. Please comment on improvements which would motivate you
   to purchase Fig Newtons more often.

   _____

   _____

   _____

   _____

FIGURE 10.15 *Sample Survey/Questionnaire* continued

Figure 10.16 suggests ways that such data may be incorporated into the text of your report.

Personal testing, interviews, letters of inquiry, and direct observation may also provide you with material for a carefully researched paper.

Figure 10.17 shows the text of a paper which contrasts hospital and hospice care for dying patients. Note cards, a list of the sources, and the survey instrument are also included. The sample gives clear evidence of the variety of sources researched, the note taking which was involved in the paper's development, and the incorporation of some survey material. Although the internal referencing and other documentation techniques have not yet been covered, they are discussed in Chapter 11.

Female respondents indicate a lower incidence of cookie purchases than do males. Figure 1 shows the frequency of cookie purchases by sex:

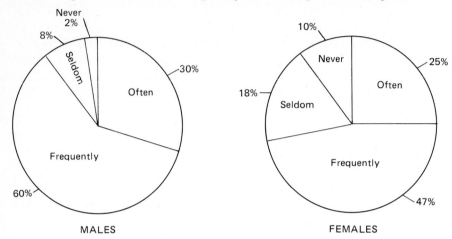

Figure 1   Frequency of cookie purchases per month by sex

Seventy-two percent of female respondents purchase cookies often or frequently; whereas, a full 90 percent of male respondents purchase cookies often or frequently. The mean number of cookie sales per month is two for all occupational categories except for students who indicate a mean number of six purchases per month. Table 1 shows the number of purchases a month by occupational categories:

Table 1   Mean number of purchases per month—600 respondents

Category	Number of purchases
Professional/manager	4
Operative/laborer	2
Foreman/craftsman	2

FIGURE 10.16   *Samples of data incorporation into text using graphics*

Clerical/sales	2
Housewives	3
Farmers	1
Retirees	2
Not employed	0
Students	6

The 600 respondents indicate that taste is the major factor in determining cookie brand selection. Figure 2 shows the percent of respondents who indicate other determining factors:

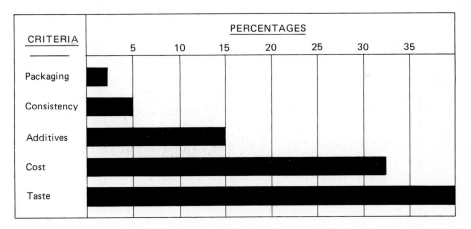

Figure 2   Determining purchase factors—600 respondents

As is indicated, a full third of the respondents indicated that cost is the major factor. Packaging has the least influence on cookie purchasing.

FIGURE 10.16   *continued*

Venci 1

Cathy Venci

Professor M. Minnassian

English Comp. 2210–09

December 12, 1989

HOSPICE VERSUS HOSPITAL:

AN EXAMINATION OF CONTRASTING APPROACHES

TO PATIENT CARE

Medicine and health care have made enormous life-saving

advancements in this age of technology. Such procedures as organ

transplants and laser surgery are now used routinely. Due to

scientific research, many diseases that once were life threatening

no longer pose a serious threat to our health. However, despite

scientific advancements, there comes a point when technology

reaches its limits. This is when the health-care professional must

face the reality of the terminally ill patient. This patient has very

special needs that go beyond medical treatment. The hospice

movement is meeting the needs of these dying patients. Mosley's

Medical Dictionary defines hospice as "a program offering

continuous supportive care to dying people; enabling them to live

FIGURE 10.17   *Sample researched paper with survey content* (Courtesy of student Cathy Venci)

Venci 2

out the final days of their lives comfortably and as fully as possible" (518). The hospice concept of care differs from the traditional hospital in the approach to the treatment of the patient and his family, the role of the health-care professional, and the development for care in the future.

A brief history of hospice care will further define the philosophy behind the modern hospice care movement. In the Middle Ages, the hospice was a place of refuge for the traveler. The religious sects that operated the hospice offered food and shelter to the poor. In the middle 1800s these shelters developed into retreats for people who were dying from incurable diseases such as tuberculosis (Encyclopedia Americana 436). According to Hamilton and Reid, the advancement of hospice care came in 1867 when Cicely Saunders opened St. Christopher's Hospice in London. Hamilton and Reid state that St. Christopher's Hospice was formed with the purpose of helping the terminally ill patient to remain comfortable and relatively free from pain without any artificial means to prolong dying (58–60). These same principles are the foundation of the hospice concept in America today.

The hospice program has taken a different approach to the treatment of the patient. Although the hospital and hospice are

FIGURE 10.17 *continued*

Venci   3

both committed to medical needs of the patient, the hospital

emphasis is on the victim of acute illness. The goals of the

hospital, according to Michael Hamilton and Helen Reid, authors of

A Hospice Handbook, are to diagnose and cure disease through

modern technology (131). Another hospice expert, Kenneth P.

Cohen, states that since technology is the main source of treatment,

it is used to the extent of prolonging life, even when there is no

known cure. He adds that life support systems and aggressive

treatment are normal procedures in the hospital setting (79–80).

Health reporter Jane Toot notes that some of the treatment of the

terminal patient includes

- intravenous fluids

- forced feedings

- nasogastric tubes, and

- laboratory examinations (671).

Cohen says that the most important treatment the dying

patient needs is pain control therapy. According to Cohen, hospital

procedure has a fixed routine of medication every four hours or so.

The patient may be experiencing serious pain before relief is

given (92).

     According to Toot, the hospital is not equipped to deal with

FIGURE 10.17   *continued*

Venci   4

the dying patient's family. She states that the patient is often in an acute-care ward which has very strict visiting regulations. This tends to create a sense of isolation for both the patient and the family. Toot notes that the family is often confused over the treatment of the patient. She states this confusion is due to the hospital excluding the family in making decisions concerning the treatment of the patient (671).

The hospice is developed to accommodate the terminally ill patient. The emphasis is on caring for the patient's symptoms and not curing his disease (Toot 667). Hamilton and Reid refer to the hospice as "a place for dying" (48). According to Hamilton, there are no life support systems in the hospice program. He states that there are no last-minute life saving attempts (135). Toot notes the major treatment of the patient is pain control. She states that pain-killing drugs, such as morphine, are given to keep the patient free from pain. Other forms of treatment, according to Toot, consist of:

massage   for relaxation

heat therapy   for circulation, and

exercise   for flexibliity (666)

FIGURE 10.17   *continued*

Venci 5

Family participation is encouraged by hospice staff. Toot points

out that the patient goes home frequently to spend time with the

family. She further notes that the hospice gives the patient

access to

- unlimited visiting hours for family,

- personal belongings and pets,

- around-the-clock medical care, and

- counseling and spiritual guidance.

This daily care is for the purpose of emphasizing the quality of life

at all times (671). The whole hospice program can be summarized

in one statement: "Dying patients are human beings. These people

have real needs and cares that need to be attended to" (Corr and

Corr 12).

A survey (see attached instrument with numbered tabulations)

of 100 hospice patients in Moore County reveals the value patients

place on hospice services. Figure 1 shows the number one ratings

of four services by percent:

FIGURE 10.17   *continued*

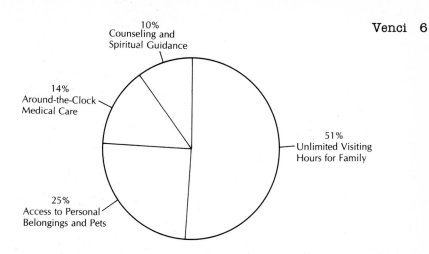

Figure 1   Number one ratings for four hospice services

In addition, 41 percent selected access to belongings and pets as the second highest value. Thirty percent rated around-the-clock medical care as third highest, and 50 percent rated counseling and spiritual guidance as last. Clearly being in their own homes with family, belongings, and pets nearby is the premier desire of terminally ill patients.

Another area of contrast between hospice and hospital care concerns the role of the health-care professional. Cohen notes that the hospital staff is increasingly involved in the challenge of technical care and diagnosis. He states,

> hospital staff do not necessarily ignore the dying patient,
> but they give priority to patients for whom they can
> provide life-saving measures. This is not unreasonable,

FIGURE 10.17   *continued*

considering their training and emphasis on curative

functions rather than caring functions needed by the

dying (79).

Table 1 shows the contrast of involvement in hospital and hospice

staff members:

Table 1   Contrast between staff members in hospice and hospital

Hospital staff	Hospice staff

Hierarchy system of care
   physician
   nurses
   aides
	Team approach to
	   sharing responsibility

Rotation of wards and
   shifts by staff members
	Daily care of same
	   patient

Little communication
   concerning patient cases
	Daily discussions and
	   meetings concerning
	   patient cases

Few volunteers on staff	Many volunteers on staff

Based on Toot (667–671)

The cost of hospital and hospice care differs. The hospital trend

will continue to focus on technology and research. Due to the high

cost of these components, the cost of hospital care will continue to

increase. Peter Mudd states that bed space in a hospital is now

$240.00 and upward per day. He also notes that this same bed

space in the hospice is $34.00 per day (Hastings Center Report

11–14). This difference in medical expenses will be one of the

FIGURE 10.17   *continued*

Venci 8

major factors in the future of hospice growth. A <u>New York Times</u> reporter points out that another factor in growth is the age of the population. With the shift in population, there will be a greater number of people who will need the kind of care hospice programs offer (Freidland sec. 11: 6). She also states that two-thirds of the hospice patients are over sixty-five years of age (sec 11: 1). In the past the majority of funding came from donations by individuals, civic groups, and church organizations (Boundy 6). Freidland comments that Medicare is now paying some of the expenses. She notes that ten years ago there were only 100 hospice programs in the United States. There are now over 1000 groups, and Freidland states that with the help of Medicare funding there will be even greater numbers (1).

In conclusion, hospitals are doing an excellent job in providing a cure for the victim of acute illness and accident. The hospital should continue to do everything possible to advance research and technology to meet the needs of the patient who has a chance to return to society. On the other hand, with the increase of the age of our population, it is apparent there will be a greater need for the care and counseling that hospice programs provide to those in their final days of living.

FIGURE 10.17 *continued*

Venci   9

HOSPICE SERVICES SURVEY

The purpose of this survey is to determine the value you place on benefits received through hospice care. Results will be included in a brief paper examining hospital versus hospice care.

1. Please rate the following benefits of hospice care in your opinion. (Place a 1 before the service you deem most valuable, a 2 before the second most valuable service, a 3 before the third most valuable service, and a 4 before the least valuable.)

_____ a. unlimited visiting hours for family

_____ b. access to belongings and pets

_____ c. around-the-clock medical care

_____ d. counseling and spiritual guidance

FIGURE 10.17   *continued*

Venci   10

Results

Most valuable selections:

    51 selected a

    14 selected b

    26 selected c

    10 selected d

Second most valuable:

    22 selected a

    41 selected b

    10 selected c

    27 selected d

Third most valuable:

    17 selected a

    30 selected b

    30 selected c

    23 selected d

Fourth most valuable:

    10 selected a

    15 selected b

    50 selected c

    25 selected d

FIGURE 10.17 *continued*

Venci   11

WORKS CITED

Boundy, Donna.   "Growth of Hospice Programs is Cited."   The New York

Times 20 May 1984, sec. 22: 6.

Cohen, Kenneth P.   Hospice: Prescription for Terminal Care.

Germantown, Md: Aspen Publications, 1979.

Corr, Charles, and Donna Corr.   Hospice Care Principles and

Practices.   New York: Springer Publishing Company, 1983.

Freidland, Sandra.   "Hospice Benefit Off to Slow Start."   The New York

Times 11 Nov. 1984, sec. 11: 1+.

Hamilton, Michael, and Helen Reid.   A Hospice Handbook.   Grand

Rapids: William B. Eerdmans Publishing, 1980.

"Hospice Care."   Encyclopedia Americana. 1983 ed.

Mosley's Medical Dictionary, 1983 ed.

Mudd, Peter.   "High Ideals and Hard Cases."   Hastings Center

Report   April 1982: 11–14.

Toot, Jane.   "Physical Therapy and Hospice."   Physical Therapy Journal

64 (1984): 665–670.

Venci, Cathy.   Survey on value of hospice services.   Moore County, 1987.

FIGURE 10.17   *continued*

EXERCISES

1. Locate the magazine and journal indexes in your library. Select an index appropriate to your field (*Applied Science and Technology Index, Business Periodicals Index, Criminal Justice Periodical Index, Hospital Literature Index, Microcomputer Index, Education Index, General Science Index*, and so forth) and look up a general subject, such as nutrition, fire science, radiology, capital punishment, electronics, dentistry, hotel administration, landscape design, tourism, cardiology, dental hygiene, pollution, aviation, and so on. List five subclassifications which could be researched for development of a brief (500 words) paper. Consider if the material is recent, not too technical, and available in sufficient amount.

2. Read the following excerpt from an article on the environment:

UTILITIES

Antidote for A Smokestack

Question: What do 52 million trees in Guatemala have to do with one coal-burning power plant in Uncasville, Conn.? Answer: they form a healthy environmental equation. That is the hope of Virginia-based Applied Energy Services, a builder and operator of power plants in Texas, Pennsylvania and California. Like any other coal-fired generator, the 180-megawatt plant now under construction in Uncasville will spew carbon dioxide, the chief culprit in the globe-warming greenhouse effect. But acting on a recommendation from the World Resources Institute, a Washington environmental-policy research center, AES has voluntarily donated $2 million in seed money to a CARE project in Guatemala designed to stave off the climatic crisis by replanting depleted forests.

The AES donation, along with help from the Peace Corps and the Guatemalan forestry service, will help an estimated 40,000 local farmers plant some 52 million seedlings that eventually will absorb a quantity of CO_2 roughly equal to the amount generated at Uncasville over the 40-year life-span of the facility. Says AES chief Roger Sant, "Given the scientific consensus on the seriousness of the greenhouse problem, we decided it was time to stop talking and act." ∎

a. Write a summary note of the entire excerpt.

b. Write a paraphrase note of the sentence: "Like any other coal-fired generator, the 180-megawatt plant now under construction in Uncasville will spew carbon dioxide, the chief culprit in the globe-warming greenhouse effect."

    c. Write a note containing a logical *partial* quotation from the sentence: "But acting on a recommendation from the World Resources Institute, a Washington environmental-policy research center, AES has voluntarily donated $2 million in seed money to a CARE project in Guatamala designed to stave off the climatic crisis by replanting depleted forests."

3. Devise a survey to determine facts about on-campus or at-work parking facilities. Determine number and hours of day lot(s) are used, and problems encountered (no spaces, puddles, distance, accidents with doors, vandalism, muggings, etc.). Suggest options to improve the facilities and determine group ratings of the options. Leave space for additional comments. Use a variety of question types.

WRITING OPTIONS

1. Use the data that you compile (or make up) for the above survey and write a very brief paper which analyzes the data. Present your findings in at least two graphics to back up your written text.

2. Select a subject from Exercise 1. Obtain the source material from at least three sources. Place the usable information on note cards, and using the note cards ONLY write a brief (300-word) report. Use the information in Chapter 9 for organization (subject selection, thesis, writing strategies, outline, introductions and closings). If your professor asks you to document the paper, use the methods discussed in Chapter 11.

NOTES

CHAPTER 11

Documenting Reports

GOOSEMYER   by Parker & Wilder

© Field Enterprises, Inc., 1982. By permission.

INTRODUCTION

Your professional papers (Chapter 9) and researched reports (Chapter 10) may often require formal credits (documentation) for the sources used or quoted. That is, parenthetical references to the works cited are included within the text, and a list of references written in one of the very specific formats is included at the end. There are a variety of documentation styles endorsed by different disciplines, such as

- The Modern Language Association (MLA) style for language and literature
- The American Psychological Association (APA) style for the social sciences, biological and earth sciences, education, linguistics, and business
- The number system for the applied sciences (chemistry, computer science, math, and physics)
- The traditional footnote systems for papers in fine arts, history, philosophy, and religion

Moreover, every scholarly journal has its own style requirements, and there is no academic field in which procedures are completely uniform. The new MLA style is the most popular for most undergraduate assignments. Familiarity with this system will allow you to make the changes from it to other styles when it becomes necessary.

The documentation strategies are

1. Compiling a working bibliography on cards,
2. Preparing the list of Works Cited (or References),
3. Providing the in-text parenthetical documentation, and
4. Presenting the paper in a formal format.

BIBLIOGRAPHY STYLES

New MLA Style for "Works Cited"

The Modern Language Association style is the most widely used system for documentation format. Recently, MLA developed a new, official style to simplify documentation procedures. Because a considerable amount of your research is bound to involve works documented according to the former system, you will want to familiarize yourself with the former MLA style as well as the new style. The former style is described on pages 311–13.

The following is a guide to the new MLA style for a "Works Cited" listing. Figure 11.1 shows a typical bibliography card for a book with one author.

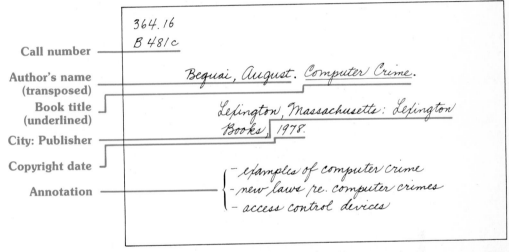

Call number

Author's name
(transposed)

Book title
(underlined)

City: Publisher

Copyright date

Annotation

FIGURE 11.1   *Typical bibliography card for a book with one author*

BOOKS

1. **Book with one author (Figure 11.1)**

2. **Book with two authors**

   Hemphill, Charles F., and Robert D. Hemphill. Security Safeguards for the Computer. New York: Amocon, 1979.

3. **Book with three authors**

   Hsiao, David K., Douglas S. Kerr, and Stuart E. Madnick. Computer Security. New York: Academic Press, 1979.

   or

   Hsiao, David K., and others. Computer Security. New York: Academic Press, 1979.

4. *Edited book*

> Shank, Roger C. Computer Models of Thought and Language. Ed. by Roger C. Shank and Kenneth Mark Colby. San Francisco: W. H. Freeman, 1973.

5. *Book with corporate authorship*

> Management Information Corporation. Computer Privacy. Cherry Hill, N.J.: Management Information Corporation, 1982.

6. *Essay in an edited collection*

> Le Roy, Ladurie Emmanuel. "The Historian and the Computer." Territory of the Historian. Ed. by Ladurie E. Le Roy. Chicago: University of Chicago Press, 1979. 16–36.

7. *Translated book*

> Cardoza, Juan. Access Control of Computers. Trans. by Alan Jameson. New York: New American Library, 1981.

8. *Work of several editions or volumes*

> Parker, Donn B. Crime by Computer. 2nd ed. New York: Scribners, 1976.

> Anderson, Martin. Computer Networks. 2 vols. Englewood Cliffs, N.J.: Prentice-Hall, Inc., 1981.

ENCYCLOPEDIAS, YEARBOOKS, DICTIONARIES

9. *General encyclopedia article*

> Smythe, Charles John. "Computers." Encyclopaedia Britannica. 1983 ed.

10. *Specialized encyclopedia article*

> Parker, D. B. "Crime and Computer Security." Encyclopedia of Computer Science. Ed. by Anthony Ralston and Charles E. Meeks. New York: Mason/Charter Publishers, Inc., 1976.

11. *Statistical abstract*

> "Computer Services." Statistical Abstract of the United States, 82 (1979): 72.

12. *Yearbook*

> "Another Wire-transfer Theft." Facts On File, 1979, 239.

PERIODICALS

13. *Unsigned weekly magazine title*

> "Locking the Electronic File Cabinet." Business Week 18 Oct. 1982: 123–124.

14. *Signed weekly magazine*

Taflich, P. "Opening the Trapdoor Knapsack." Time 25 Oct. 1982: 88.

15. *Monthly magazine*

Lord, K. M. "Fingerprint Scanner: Security System With a Personal Touch." Popular Mechanics Oct. 1982: 128.

16. *Journal with continuous pagination*

Kolata, G. "Students Discover Computer Threat." Science 2115 (1982): 1216–17.

17. *Signed newspaper article*

O'Neill, Robert. "Computer-based Home Security Systems Sales Soar." New York Times 15 Dec. 1983, sec. 2: 7.

18. *Unsigned newspaper article*

"Computer Security Concerns U.S. Military." Fort Lauderdale News/ Sun-Sentinel 25 Sept. 1983, sec. B: 4.

MISCELLANEOUS SOURCES

19. *Bulletin*

Brown, Earl. "Computer Laboratory Security Measures." Gainesville, Fla. 1984. (Bulletin of the University of Florida, No. 72.)

20. *Public document*

U.S. Congress. House Committee on Interstate and Foreign Commerce. Federal Cigarette Labeling and Advertising Act. House Report 449 to accompany H.R. 3014, 89th Congress, 1st Session. 1965.

21. *Pamphlet*

Radio Shack, A Division of Tandy Corporation. TRS-80 Model II Micro-Computer System. U.S.A. 1981. (Pamphlet of Radio Shack, A Division of Tandy Corporation.)

22. *Letter*

Larsen, Robert H. Information in a letter to the author. R. H. Larsen and Associates, Fort Lauderdale, Fla., 11 Mar. 1984.

23. *Interview*

Lessin, Arlen, President of Smart Card International, New York. Personal interview on microchip security. 12 Apr. 1984.

24. *Photocopied source*

Baird, Jane. "Access Control Systems." Pompano Beach, Fla., 14 Mar. 1975. (Photocopied.)

25. *Public address or lecture*

> Davis, Ralph. "The Value of Grading by Computers." Gainesville, Fla., 12 May 1981. (Address presented at the University of Florida Staff and Program Development Seminar.)

26. *Telecast or radio broadcast*

> "Should We Get On With Computer Literacy?" The Firing Line. Washington, D.C.: PBS-TV, 16 Oct. 1983.

27. *Tables or illustrations*

> Buckley, Charles L. Accounting system flowchart. Introduction to Accounting. New York: Oxford University Press, 1980.

28. *Computer software*

> PFS: Professional Write. Computer software. Software Publishing Corporation, 1987.

29. *Computer service material*

> Schomer, Howard. "South Africa: Beyond Fair Employment." Harvard Business Review May–June 1983: 145+. DIALOG file 122, item 119425–833160.

30. *Films, slides, filmstrip, videocassettes*

> Marathon Man. Dir. John Schlesinger. United Artists, 1979.

> Marijuana: The Addiction Question. Slide program. Developed by Project Cork, Dartmouth Medical School, Milner-Fenwick, 1982. 55 slides.

> Kafka's Life. Sound filmstrip. Educational Products, 1989. 100 fr., 15 min.

> The Story of English: "The Mother Tongue." Videocassette. Dir. Robert MacNeil. PBS Video, 1986. 56 min.

Final Format

When you type your final research report, include an alphabetized list of all of the works actually used in your study. This list should include only those works from which you quoted or paraphrased material. Title your list "Works Cited." A sample is shown in Figure 11.2.

The eighth entry indicates a second work by the above-named author (Wright, John). Three hyphens are used to highlight the fact that the entry is alphabetized by the titles of Wright's works.

Works Cited

"Architects."   Encyclopedia of Careers and Vocational Guidance.   6th

ed.   Ed. by William E. Hopke.   Chicago: I. G. Ferguson Publishing

Company, 1984.

Daley, Thelma T., and others, eds.   4: Construction.   2nd ed.   Encino,

California: Glencoe Press, 1984.   (Pamphlet.)

Ducat, Walter.   A Guide to Professional Careers.   New York: Julian

Messner, 1970.

McReynolds, C. M.   "So You Want To Be An Architect."   Progressive

Architecture June 1984: 55.

Szerdi, John, President of Szerdi and Associates.   Fort Lauderdale, Florida.

24 Oct. 1985.

U. S. Department of Labor.   Occupational Outlook Handbook.

Washington, D.C.: U. S. Government Printing Office, April 1984.

Wright, John W.   The American Almanac of Jobs and Salaries.   New

York: Avon Books, 1982.

———.   "Careers in Architecture."   Architectural Record May 1988: 200–

206.

FIGURE 11.2   *Sample MLA Works Cited page*

Author/Year Style

If you are writing a paper or report in the field of biological science, physical science, mathematics, or psychology, consult your instructor to determine the preferred style. Documentation styles in these fields are very different from the conventional Humanities style. Furthermore, modifications exist from field to field, and to complicate things further, every scholarly journal has its own style requirements which may deviate from the general rules of the Author/Year style. In the *Author/Year system* you generally

- Capitalize only the first word of book and article titles or
- Omit the periodical article title entirely
- Abbreviate the title of a periodical
- Omit the underline of a periodical title
- Underline the periodical volume number

The following bibliography entries illustrate a typical book and periodical entry for several scientific fields:

Biology

Lewin, R. A. 1982. Symbiosis and parasitism; definitions and evaluations. Bio Science. 32: 254.

Mader, Sylvia S. 1976. Inquiry into life. W. C. Brown Co., Dubuque, Iowa, 740 p.

Chemistry

J. M. Widom, "Chemistry, an Introduction to General, Organic, and Biological Chemistry." W. H. Freeman, San Francisco, 1981.

R. Seeber and S. Stefani, Anal. Chem., 53, 1011–1016 (1981).

Geology

Thomas, W. L. Jr. (ed.) 1956. Man's role in changing the face of the earth: Chicago, University of Chicago Press, 437 p.

Brocker, W. S. 1970. Man's oxygen reserves. Science, v. 168, p. 1537–1538.

Mathematics

D. G. Crowdis, Precalculus mathematics, Glencoe Press, Beverly Hills, Calif., 1976.

S. MacLane, Mathematical models: a sketch for the philosophy of mathematics, Amer. Math. M. 88 (1981), 462–472.

Physics

L. A. Marschall, Am. J. Phys. <u>49</u>, 557–561 (1981).

S. Gasiorowicz, <u>The Structure of Matter: a Survey of Modern Physics</u> (Addison-Wesley Publishing Company, Reading, Massachusetts, 1979).

Psychology

Bugelski, B. R., and Graziano, A. M. <u>Handbook of practical psychology.</u> Englewood Cliffs, N.J.: Prentice-Hall, Inc., 1980.

Szucho, J. J., and Kleinmuntz, B. Statistical versus clinical lie detection. <u>American Psychologist,</u> 1982, <u>36</u>, 488–96.

Alphabetize your "List of References" at the end of your paper.

Number Style

The bibliography format of the *Number System* is similar to the Author/ Year system. However, in the compiled "List of References," each entry is numbered. The list may be alphabetized and numbered consecutively, or the list may forego an alphabetical listing and entries may be numbered and listed as they are referred to chronologically in the text. The following is an example:

1. Z. M. Sahakian and A. Angell, "Resonant High Voltage Transformer," <u>Proceedings of the Power Electronics Show & Conference,</u> Boxborough, MA, April 27–29, 1987, pp. 60–70.

2. R. F. Powell, <u>Testing Active and Passive Electronic Components,</u> Marcel Dekker, Inc., New York, 1987.

REFERENCING THE SOURCES

When you actually write your paper, you must reference the sources within your text. By indicating in parentheses the author, title, or page number of your research material, you enable your reader to connect these internal references to the works cited or reference list at the end of your paper.

As you write your first draft from your note cards, immediately include the parenthetical reference at the end of direct quotations, paraphrased materials, or summaries. The references should be as brief and as few as necessary to indicate where you found each borrowed item.

New MLA Reference Style

Page references for cited sources must be included in parentheses in the text with the author's last name, possibly a short title of the work (or both) added as necessary.

The following is a guide to the MLA style:

1. *Reference identification when the author's name is mentioned in the text.*

   E. M. Johnson suggests that the increase in computer networking poses the greatest security problem (101).

   or

   E. M. Johnson suggests that the increase in computer networking poses the greatest security problem (Newsweek 10).

2. *Reference identification when the author's name is not mentioned in the text.*

   The notion is put forth in Computer Security that computer passwords pose another problem (Lloyd 720).

3. *Reference identification when neither the author nor the work is mentioned in the text.*

   Because the data may be raided by unscrupulous individuals, computers may not be the cure-all for streamlining manufacturing procedures (Foster, Computers Today 19–20).

   or just

   Because the data may be raided by unscrupulous individuals, computers may not be the cure-all for streamlining manufacturing procedures (Foster 19–20).

4. *Reference identification when two works by the same author are listed in "Words Cited."*

   One authority argues that technology can overcome computer security problems (Lanshe, "Beating the Risk" 78).

5. *Reference identification when part of a larger work or specific volume is indicated.*

   (Computers 2: 214–15).

6. *Reference identification in the middle of a sentence.*

   Following several data thefts from Ace Electronics (Laird, Computer Crime 142), the industry moved toward . . .

   or

   Others, like Noosinow and Austin (408–12), hold an opposite point of view.

7. *Reference identification when the text makes it clear that consecutive sentences are from the same source.*

H. Charles Howard suggests that the military is experiencing "gargantuan problems" due to computer viruses. He stresses the necessity for heavy penalties for hacks and professionals who build these bugs into software (36–40).

8. *Reference identification when the text includes a quotation of someone other than the source author(s).*

French points out, "The problem of implanted viruses into hardware looms large" (qtd. in Marley 78).

9. *Reference identification when the text includes a display quote.*

Rick Dyer, engineer and businessman, promotes Halycon:

Halycon is not a game. Halycon is about total involvement. These [home video programs] are adventures. You start to forget it's not real. You make the choices and the decisions. [Halycon] is mind-stimulating, not wrist-stimulating like video games. (Chicago Tribune D17)

10. *Reference identification for figures (after title).*

Figure 14 Schematic symbol for a resistor. From Kline (89).

11. *Reference identification for tables (below the material).*

Table 2   Computer Systems Comparisons

Brand	Customer accounts	Cost ($)
Apple	1,000	5,000
TRS-80	1,000	4,000
Altos	12,000	20,000

Source: Consumer Reports (97)

Content Notes

Content footnotes—or, more usually, endnotes—may be used for definitions, explanations, acknowledgments, or amplifications of the text. Because such notes are distracting to readers, you should consider carefully whether the comments should be integrated into the text. Use only those notes that strengthen the discussion.

If you include content notes, type raised Arabic numeral superscripts at the points in the text that refer to the notes. Type the notes on a separate page(s) following the last page of the text. Title the page "Notes." Type content notes in the following form:

[1] Briefly, the Keynesian theory states that a modern capitalistic society is naturally unstable because of a built-in lag in total demand.

The first line of a note is indented and is preceded by the raised superscript number that corresponds to the text reference.

A content note may also include a reference citation:

[2] In addition, Keynesian theory has influenced other economic policies, notably the Full Employment and Balanced Growth Act (Rust, *Business in Society* 700).

Complete documentation of a content note source reference must be included in your "Words Cited" list.

Author/Year Style

In the Author/Year system the documentation consists of an alphabetized "List of References" (pp. 296–97) and internal reference notes in parentheses. Although this system is similar to MLA style, page references are excluded.

Guidelines for the Author/year system follow:

1. If your text does not include the author's name, insert both the author's name and date within parentheses.
2. If your text includes the author's name, insert the publication date only within parentheses.
3. For a source with two authors, employ both names.
4. For three authors, name them all in the first instance, but thereafter use the first author's name and *et al.*
5. For four or more authors, employ the first author's name plus *et al.*
6. Use small letters (a, b, c) to identify two or more works published in the same year by the same author. (The "List of References" must include the letter after the publication year.)
7. Specify additional information (volume number, two works by the same author on the same subject published in different years, and pages) if necessary.

Following are sample internal notes in a text:

Author in text; year only	Argyle contends that women are more receptive than men to nonverbal encoding and decoding (1967). In a study using all male subjects, it was found that men who were good at displaying their emotions nonverbally
Two authors	tended to be poor at understanding other nonverbal expressions (Lanzetta and Kleck, 1970). Women are more able to interpret the nonverbal messages
Three works, one which is by four or more authors	of other people (Argyle, 1967; Buch et al., 1972a; Faltico, 1969). For instance, smiling can release aggressive tension or soften the impact of hostile words
Two works by same author in same year	(Mehrabian, 1971a). The meaning of a smile depends very much upon the context in which it is used since it has so many possible meanings (Mehrabian, 1971b). Mothers' smiles have little relationship to the verbal messages
Three authors; third volume of work	they give their children (Bugenthal, Love, and Gianetto, 1971, III).

Number System

Using the numbered "List of References" required for the Number system, insert the appropriate number within your text in parentheses. The following variations occur:

1. If the sentence construction names the author, insert the number immediately after the authority's name within parentheses.

Example

J. S. L. Gilmore (1) gives an exactly analogous circular definition. Simpson (2) also emphasizes the subjective element in species classifications.

2. If the sentence construction does not require the authority's name, either
   a. insert both author and number within parentheses:

Example

But everyone (Gilmore, 1; Huxley, 3; Simpson, 2) agrees that the empirical material places large constraints upon the systematist's inclinations.

    b. insert both author and number within parentheses and enclose
the number within brackets:

Example

There is remarkable agreement among competent workers, at least in the
fairly well-worked animal groups. One first examines the material, and
then one exercises "flair" (Huxley [3]).

or

    c. insert the number only, enclosing it within parentheses or brack-
ets.

Example

It is known [1] that every ontogeny is a developmental history that begins
either with the fusion of two cells or with the cleavage of an unfertilized
female gamete.

PREPARING THE FINAL DRAFT

Usually the fully documented report is presented with specific items
(optional title page, outline, text, and the like) and organized and fastened
together in a binder or held with a paper clip. Your professor or supervisor
may have specific instructions, but in general the following guidelines
should suffice:

    1. Paper. Use only white, twenty-pound, 8½-by 11-in. paper. Do not submit
erasable paper or onion skin. Type the paper with a black ribbon and
clean type unless your instructor accepts handwritten work. Use only
one side.

    2. Layout. Except for page numbers, leave one-inch margins at the top
and bottom and on both sides of the text. Some word processing software
systems have preset, standard margins which are acceptable. Indent
the first word of a paragraph five spaces from the left margin. Indent
display quotations ten spaces from the left margin. Double space throughout the text including the title, display quotations, and the bibliography
list. Skip every other line in a handwritten paper.

    3. Title. A research paper does not need a title page, but often an instructor
will require one. If one is required, type a descriptive title, your name,
name of the course or organization, the name and title of the person to
whom the report is submitted, and the date. (See the sample on page
238.) Instead of a separate title page you may type your name, instructor's
name, the course number, and the date on separate, double-spaced lines
beginning 1 in. from the top of the page and flush with the left margin.
Do not underline your title, nor put it in quotation marks, nor type it
in all capital letters. These guidelines differ from the older, traditional
MLA style.

James O'Neill

Professor K. Mason

Composition 1101-12

May 5, 199X

The Technical Writing Consultant:

An Examination of a Career

4. **Outline.** If your professor requests an outline, include a separate page for a correctly punctuated, capitalized, and grammatically parallel outline. Title the page with the word *Outline* and number the pages with lower-case Roman numerals. Sometimes the professor will request you to write your thesis at the beginning of the outline.

5. **Page numbers.** Number all of the rest of the pages consecutively throughout the manuscript in the upper right-hand corner, ½ in. from the top. From page 2 on, type your last name before the page number, as a precaution in case of misplaced pages. Do not punctuate a page number by adding a period, a hyphen, or any other mark or symbol (such as the abbreviation "p").

6. **Internal reference notes.** Add the appropriate author, work, and page references in parentheses within the text.

7. **Explanation notes.** Consecutively numbered content notes may be placed at the bottom of the appropriate page but preferably are placed on a separate page(s) entitled "Notes" or "Endnotes" following the text, but before the "Works Cited" list.

8. **Bibliography lists.** Use a separate page titled "Works Cited" to list alphabetically the sources used in the preparation of the manuscript.

Figure 11.3 shows a student research paper which demonstrates the above guidelines using MLA documentation techniques. Following the sample paper the older MLA style of documentation (bibliography and footnotes) is covered.

Shawn Sabga

Professor J. VanAlstyne

English Comp. 2210-04

May 1, 1988

The Phenomenal Facsimile Machine

Librarian Joan Rutledge helped a student locate a

bibliography in a book in another library of a multi-campus

university. In the past, Rutledge would have to telex a request to

the other library to send the book to the first campus. But now

she can request the other campus to send a copy of the

bibliography immediately by the use of a facsimile machine. This

process will save the student hours, if not days, in her research

activities. The facsimile machine transmits documents

electronically. All one needs are a telephone line and two parties

with machines. Faxing popularity is growing to auspicious heights

due to evolution of its capabilities, the simplicity of the

transmission process, innovative features, and the practical cost.

1

FIGURE 11.3   *Sample paper documented in MLA style*
(Courtesy of student Shawn Sabga)

Sabga 2

Most people think that the facsimile machine (the fax) is a
modern invention. Actually its origin dates to 1926, when it was
invented by Radio Corporation of America (Costigan 2). The first
facsimile transmission was sent through radio waves in 1937 (6).
Even though the military used these early crude devices to
transmit maps, orders, and weather charts (McCarroll 38), the
machine did not gain public recognition until much later. In the
early 1970s fax machines were used regularly by newspaper
companies to transmit thousands of photos daily (Costigan 12).
But the fax did not become commercially successful until the
1980s when Japanese companies developed better machines by
replacing mechanical parts with sophisticated computer circuitry
(McCarroll 38). This upgrade cut transmission time for a single
page from six minutes to ten seconds, and also dramatically
improved the quality of copy that was transmitted ("The Fax
Revolution" 14).

The transmission process, though very complex, is now
greatly improved. On the older fax machines, the process
consisted of converting visual details of a document to analogous

FIGURE 11.3   *continued*

Sabga 3

electric current, conditioning the current for transmission by wire

or radio waves to a receiver, and restoring it to its original form

at the receiver. These older fax systems used electromechanical

scanning techniques to convert visual tonal variations for

transmission to a receiver. The machines then recorded

transmission by using transducers that came in contact with the

electromechanical scanners (Costigan 47–56). But modern fax

machines send electronic copies of documents over ordinary

telephone lines to a fax machine on the opposite end. These

modern fax machines are equipped with innovative computer

circuitry, and when contact is made, an electronic scanner is

activated. As the scanner moves across the page, it converts the

text, charts, and pictures into electrical pulses that are carried

over the telephone line. On the receiving end the process is

reversed (McCarroll 38). The user does not have to worry about

the difficulty of the procedures. The human part of the process is

incredibly simple. First, the sender feeds the copy through the

paper feeder; then in a matter of seconds a copy of the document

reaches the receiving fax to be printed exactly as it was sent. The

receiving person does not have to be present when the document

FIGURE 11.3   *continued*

Sabga 4

arrives because the document will feed automatically on the

receiving fax (39). This, of course, makes it perfect for

transmitting vital data to a time zone out of sync with one's own.

Financial centers in New York, London, and the Far East fax

material before and after business hours ("The Fax Revolution"

14).

Another reason for the sudden boost in popularity is the

innovative features of the modern fax machines. Engineer Robert

Johns points out that a standard top-of-the line fax comes with a

photocopy machine, an answering machine, a telephone and the

fax system. Once considered too bulky and costly to be practical,

Johns reports that fax machines have shrunk to half the size of

personal computers. This transformation in size has been taken to

the limit. Mitsubishi Electric has introduced a fax unit that fits

under a car dashboard and connects to the cellular car phone

(McCarroll 38). Already New York-based Medbar Enterprises Inc.

is selling a Japanese-made model targeted for executives on the

go. It is battery operated and can be used from a plane or train

as long as a telephone line is available (Gelfond 59).

FIGURE 11.3 *continued*

Sabga 5

The fax has not only shrunk in size but also in price. In 1971 fax transceivers sold for as much as $10,000 and up (McCarroll 38). Later in the 1970s prices dropped to $3,000 to $5,000 ("The Fax Revolution" 16). In the 1980s faxes the size of a portable typewriter entered the market for as low as $1,500 to $2,000. The 1990s will see machines available from $500 to $800 (16). If these prices do not attract the buyer's eye, there is still one more cost factor to consider: the amount of money that could be saved when using a fax. Federal Express charges about $15.00 to deliver a one-page letter overnight. The same letter can be faxed in a matter of seconds for less than fifty cents. To telex a document, a keyboard operator must retype it on a computer terminal before sending it to its destination. This process can require more than an hour and cost about $5.00 for fifty words (McCarroll 38). Mark Winther, an electronics analyst at Manhattan-based LINK Resources, says, "The growth of fax is coming out of the hides of Federal Express and Western Union. Fax poses a serious threat to overnight mail, and it could make telex obsolete" (qtd. in Costigan 227). As a result of the cost

FIGURE 11.3   *continued*

Sabga 6

analysis, sales have soared from some 200,000 units sold in 1986

to over 700,000 units in 1988. By the mid-1990s sales should hit

one million (McCarroll 38 and "The Fax Revolution" 14).

The fax offers a host of benefits:

It eliminates the need for a typist to send something, as

you do when you telex. There are no anxieties about

typing errors—especially worrisome if you're sending

critical financial numbers. You can maintain some

degree of confidentiality if the document goes directly

from you to a protected receiver. In contrast to

electronic mail, you don't have to be computer literate

to send or receive ("The Fax Revolution" 16).

Fascination with communicating by fax is international. "It's

the electronic boom," declares John A Widlicka, who is in charge

of marketing fax machines in the United States for Sharp

Electronics Corporation (qtd. in Gelfond 59).

FIGURE 11.3 *continued*

Sabga 7

Works Cited

Costigan, Daniel. FAX: The Principles and Practice of Facsimile

Communication. Philadelphia: Chilton Books, 1971.

"Fax Revolution, The." Travel & Leisure Oct. 1988: 14–16.

Gelfond, Susan. "Will There Be a FAX in Every Foyer?"

PC Magazine 23 June 1987: 59.

Johns, Robert, Engineer with Canon Products, Chicago. Personal

interview on facsimile machines. 1 Dec. 1989.

McCarroll, Thomas. "Just the FAX, Ma'am." Time 31 Aug. 1987:

38.

FIGURE 11.3   *continued*

Former MLA Bibliography Style

The former MLA system requires a list of consulted references entitled "Bibliography," "Selected Bibliography," or "Words Cited." The titles "Bibliography" and "Selected Bibliography" indicate that the list includes background sources which are not actually referenced in the text. The former style of listing references differs from the new style in only a few ways. Entries for general books and reference works are the same. Magazine, journal, and newspaper entries differ as follows:

1. *Magazine article (p. and pp. used for page references).*

    "Locking the Electronic File Cabinet."   Business Week, 19 Oct. 1982, p. 124.

2. *Journal with continuous pagination (comma rather than colon used after date).*

    Kolata, G.   "Students Discover Computer Threat."   Science, 2115 (1982), 1216.

3. *Newspaper (p. and pp. plus column reference used).*

    O'Neill, Robert.   "Computer-based Home Security Systems Sales Soar."   New York Times, 15 Dec. 1983, p. 6, col. 1.

Former MLA Footnote Style

Under the former MLA system source references are inserted as footnotes or endnotes rather than as in-text, parenthetical notes. Raised Arabic superscripts are used in the text to indicate a source reference. The references are then typed either at the bottom of the appropriate page (footnotes) or on a separate page following the last page of the text. The notes are numbered sequentially throughout.

Under the MLA System a footnote or endnote for a book differs from a bibliographic entry in six ways:

1. *Book with one author*

    Bibliography entry:

    Bequai, August, Computer Crime.   Lexington, Massachusetts: Lexington Books, 1978.

    Footnote entry:

    [1] August Bequai, Computer Crime (Lexington, Massachusetts: Lexington Books, 1978), p. 50.

First, the footnote entry is indented; second, the appropriate raised superscript number is included; third, the author's name is not transposed; fourth, the punctuation tends toward commas rather than toward periods; fifth, the publication data is within parentheses; and sixth, a specific page reference is included.

The following is a guide to the former MLA system of footnoting:

2. *Book with two authors*

[2] Charles F. Hemphill and Robert D. Hemphill, Security Safeguards for the Computer (New York: Amocon, 1979), p. 72.

3. *Book with three authors*

[3] David K. Hsiao, Douglas S. Kerr, and Stuart E. Madnick, Computer Security (New York: Academic Press, 1979), pp. 201–202.

or

[3] David K. Hsiao and others, Computer Security (New York: Academic Press, 1979), pp. 201–202.

4. *Edited book*

[4] Roger C. Shank, Computer Models of Thought and Language, ed. Roger C. Shank and Kenneth Mark Dolby (San Francisco: W. H. Freeman, 1973), p. 528.

5. *Essay in an edited collection*

[5] Emmanuel LeRoy Ladurie, "The Historian and the Computer," in Territory of the Historian, ed. Emmanuel LeRoy Ladurie (Chicago: University of Chicago Press, 1979). p. 303.

6. *Work in several editions or volumes*

[6] Donn B. Parker, Crime By Computer, 2nd ed. (New York: Scribners, 1976), p. ix.

[7] Martin Anderson, Computer Networks, 2 vols. (Englewood Cliffs, N.J.: Prentice-Hall, Inc., 1981).

or

[8] Martin Anderson, Computer Networks (Englewood Cliffs, New Jersey: Prentice-Hall, Inc., 1981), II, 81.

(Notice that footnote 7 indicates the reference is to the works as a whole; therefore, no page number is included. Footnote 8 indicates that the reference is to material in the second volume, the Roman numeral, on page 81.)

7. *Encyclopedia*

[9] John Charles Smith, "Computers," Encyclopaedia Britannica, 1983.

8. *Statistical abstract*

[10] "Computer Services," Statistical Abstract of the United States, 82 (1979), 72.

9. *Yearbook*

[11] "Another Wire-transfer Theft," Facts on File, 1974, p. 239.

10. *Magazines*

[12] "Locking the Electronic File Cabinet," Business Week, 18 Oct. 1982, p. 124.

11. *Journal with continuous pagination*

[13] G. Kolata, "Students Discover Computer Threat," Science, 2115 (1982), 1216.

12. *Newspaper article*

[14] Robert O'Neill, "Computer-based Home Security Systems Sales Soar," New York Times, 15 Dec. 1983, p. 6, col. 1.

13. *Bulletin*

[15] Earl Brown, "Computer Laboratory Security Measures," Gainesville, Fla., 1984, p. 3.

14. *Pamphlet*

[16] National Center for Research in Vocational Education. Preparing for High Technology: Strategies for Change, Pamphlet No. 230 (Columbus, Ohio: Ohio State University, n.d.), p. 7.

15. *Letter*

[17] Information in letter to the author from Robert H. Larsen, President of R. H. Larsen and Associates of Fort Lauderdale, Fla., 11 Mar. 1984.

16. *Interview*

[18] Personal interview on microchip security with Arlen Lessin, President of Smart Card International of New York, 12 April 1984.

17. *Table or illustration*

[19] Charles L. Buckley, Accounting system flowchart, Introduction to Accounting (New York: Oxford University Press, 1980), p. 237.

Former MLA Subsequent Reference Style

Once the full reference data for a source **(a primary citation)** has been provided, a shortened form for all subsequent references to the same source **(a subsequent citation)** is employed. A subsequent citation usually consists of the author's last name and reference. If no author is listed, the citation includes the article title or abbreviated article title and the page. If the author is named in the text, the note contains only the book or article title and the page reference. If more than one work by the same author is cited, the note contains the author's name, title of the work, and the page. If two entries by different authors with the same last name are used, the note includes the author's given name initial, the last name, and the page. Note the following sequence of primary and subsequent footnotes:

[1] August Bequai, Computer Crime (Lexington, Massachusetts: Lexington Books, 1978), p. 50.

[2] Bequai, p. 201.

[3] August Bequai, Computer Security (New York: Scribners, 1980), p. 28.

[4] Bequai, Computer Security p. 30.

[5] Marion Bequai, "Access Control Security," Time, 13 March 1981, p. 102.

[6] M. Bequai, p. 308.

[7] "Locking the Electronic File Cabinet," Business Week, 18 Oct. 1982, p. 124.

[8] Locking the Electronic . . . ," p. 127.

Some published works use the Latin abbreviations *Ibid.* (in the same place), *op. cit.* (in the work cited), and *loc. cit.* (in the place cited) for subsequent citations.

Figure 11.4 shows an endnote reference listing for the sample student research report as it would appear with a documented paper employing the former MLA style.

Title is
capitalized

ENDNOTES

Note
identification

[1]Webster's Seventh New Collegiate Dictionary. 1980 ed.

[2]Thomas E. Pearsall and Donald H. Cunningham, How To Write for the
World of Work (New York: Holt, Rinehart and Winston, 1982), p. 1.

[3]"Communications," Encyclopaedia Britannica, 1983 ed.

[4]Judith S. VanAlstyne, an interview on the subject of technical writing
consultation in her office, Broward Community College, Fort Lauderdale,
Fla., 12 Mar. 1983.

Second
reference
to source

[5]Pearsall and Cunningham, p. 1.

[6]VanAlstyne.

[7]Emerson Clarke and Vernon Root, A Definitive Study of Your Future in
Technical and Science Writing (New York: Rinehart Rosen Press, Inc.,
1972), p. 32.

[8]Thermo Serv Company, a division of Dart and Kraft, Anoka, Minn.

n.d. means
no date

(a leaflet accompanying the product, n.d.).

[9]"The Editorial Department," Publishers' Weekly, 10 July 1981, p. 18.

Titled page
is numbered
at bottom

12

FIGURE 11.4 *Sample former MLA style endnotes*

13

[10]J. R. Gould and Wayne A. Losano, Opportunities in Technical Writing Today (Louisville: V.G.M. Publishing, 1976), p. 29.

[11]Thomas E. Pearsall, "Building a Technical Communications Program," ADE Bulletin, Spring 1982, p. 17.

[12]Pearsall, p. 17.

[13]VanAlstyne.

[14]P.J. Schemehaur, ed. Writer's Market, 1983 (Cincinnati, Ohio: Writer's Digest Books, 1983), p. 855.

[15]Schemehaur, p. 855.

[16]United States Department of Commerce, The Statistical Abstract of the United States (Washington, D.C.: U.S. Government Printing Office, 1983), p. 236.

[17]William Yeoman, "The Future of Technical Writing," in Jobs 1982–1983 (New York: G. P. Putnam's Sons, 1982), p. 236.

[18]VanAlstyne.

[19]Clarke and Root, p. 17.

FIGURE 11.4   *continued*

EXERCISES

1. What is missing on the following bibliography card?

> Zalud, Data Manag.   Advantages
>   Conflict of Int.
> In the law office a computer
> system can check on client history
> to avoid conflict of interest which
> can occur by accepting a new client
> who was connected with a former
> adversary.

2. Rewrite the following information in the new MLA style for a "Works Cited" listing.

   a. An article in Journal of Technical Writing and Communication by Earl E. McDowell, L. David Schuelke, and Chew Wah Chung, entitled "Evaluation of a Bachelor's Program in Technical Communication," on pages 1951–2000 of volume 10 in 1980.

   b. Technical Writing: Structure, Standards, and Style, by Robert W. Bly and Gary Blake, published in 1982 by McGraw-Hill Book Company in New York.

   c. A U. S. News and World Report article, "When Job Training Will Be a Lifelong Process," on pages 25–26 of the May 9, 1988, issue.

   d. An Encyclopaedia Britannica article, "Technical Communications," published in 1982, written by E. Charles Lloyd.

   e. "Computer Industry Demands Writers" by David Hall, in the New York Times, page 4, section 7, December 2, 1987.

3. Rewrite the following information in the Author/Year style for a "References" list for an article in the psychology discipline.

   a. An article, "Recognition and Retrieval Processes in Free Recall," published in the 1972, vol. 79 edition of Psychological Review, written by J. R. Anderson and G. H. Bower on pages 97–123.

   b. An Appleton-Century-Crofts publication in New York of a book, Macromolecules and Behavior, by John Gaito in 1966.

   c. An article, "On Turning Psychology Over to the Unwashed," by G. A. Miller in the December 1969 edition of Psychology Today on pages 53–54.

4. Rewrite the following information in the Number system for the "List of References" list of an article on computer science.

   a. A book, <u>The Design and Analysis of Computer Algorithms</u>, written by A. V. Aho, J. E. Hopcroft, and J. D. Ullman, published by Addison-Wesley in Reading, Massachusetts, in 1974.

   b. An article by R. C. Holt in <u>Computer Survey</u> volume 4, on pages 179–96, in September 1972.

WRITING OPTIONS

1. Write a documented report on careers in your field. Include a background review, optional opportunities, education requirements, salaries, details of the work performance activities, locations, numbers in the field, and prospects for the future. Use the new MLA documentation style for crediting sources and preparing the final manuscript.

2. Write a documented paper on a *breakthrough discovery*. Use the appropriate format for the field (new MLA for language and literature; Author/Year for social science, biological and earth sciences, education, linguistics, and business; Number system for applied science, such as chemistry, computer science, math, and physics; or the traditional footnote system for the fine arts, history, philosophy, and religion. Sample subjects are

new heart medicine	Omega-3 fish oil
new food source	suction lipectomy
fiber optics	minoxidyl
new surgical glues	vocal computers
hormone studies	laser surgeries
new fuels	tomography
robotics	AIDS care
new weapons	contact lenses
radial keratotomy	new cancer cures
arthroscopic knee surgery	cloning
Magnetic Resonance Imaging	education
crime	life expectancy
the shape of cities	transportation
satellites	electronic marvels
weather modification	building materials

other?

PART 3

The Technical Strategies

CHAPTER 12

Preparing Manuals

by Bruce Hammond

INTRODUCTION

Manuals are written guides or reference materials which are used for training, assembling mechanisms, operating machinery or equipment, servicing products, or repairing products. Typically a manual includes

- Precise definitions
- Descriptions of mechanisms
- Step-by-step instructions
- Analyses of processes

In a large company professional or technical writers may prepare manuals for the operation and repair of products or equipment. In smaller companies the preparation, editing, and component-parts review may fall to all competent writers. Those employees who use in-house manuals for training, procedures, and assembling are continually encouraged to review and improve the component parts. This chapter will consider the operation manual because it is the most common. Chapters 13, 14, 15, and 16 will consider the writing tasks of definition, description, instruction, and process analysis.

AUDIENCE

A major consideration for manual writing is audience. The language and technical detail must fit the intended user. Frequently the user of a product manual is a novice or layperson; thus, he or she has a need for definitions, mechanism description, operating instructions, and an analysis of possible problems in a product's operation. Although the product may be a highly complex mechanism, the manual information must be simple, clear, and accurate. Writers of such operation manuals often aim their writing at the comprehension level of an eighth-grade student. Technical terms, abbreviations, symbols, and mathematical procedures are simplified or avoided. If the audience is a group of skilled technicians, the language, of course, may be more technical; however, the writer must be alert to provide definitions, explanations of theory, and graphic reinforcement.

The following two examples illustrate language differences in manuals intended for two different audiences. The first example shows the introductory information from an operation manual for a personal pager. The intended audience is the layman purchaser:

Introduction

Congratulations! You are now using the world's first microprocessor-controlled 900MHz pager. Motorola's advanced technology offers unique features and benefits which provide the ultimate in performance and reliability.

The Dimension 1000 pager is a versatile unit that is designed to provide reliable communications for a variety of applications. To get the full benefit from the pager, please read these operating instructions carefully.

Coding Data Label

Dimension 1000 pagers come in several model configurations equipped with a variety of options which affect the operation of your pager. To determine how your pager operates, refer to the coding-data label located under the belt clip. The pager is capable of one, two, or three calls, depending upon how it was ordered from the factory. The coding-data label indicates the number and type of calls (Figure 2). Tone-only calls are indicated by a "T," and voice calls are indicated by a "V." If a particular call is not present, that area will be blank.[1]

The next example contains the introductory material from an instruction manual for servicing a walkie-talkie radio. The intended audience is skilled service technicians:

Introduction

The MX 300-T "Handi-Talkie" radio described in this manual is the most advanced two-way radio available. Hybrid modular construction is used throughout, reflecting the latest achievements in microelectronic technology. The plug-in modules provide greater flexibility, greater reliability, and easier maintenance.

Each radio contains plug-in hybrid modules. These modules contain over 90% of the electronics—providing faster service and less down-time.

[1] Motorola, Inc., *Motorola Dimension 1000 Binary GSC Pager* (Fort Lauderdale, Florida: Motorola, Inc., Paging Products Division, 1982), a manual.

Guide pins are provided on the modules to assist replacement and prevent incorrect insertion. Instead of complex wiring harnesses, printed flexible circuits are used in the radio. These durable, thin plastic films eliminate broken, pinched, or frayed wires—with a neat, easy-to service interior.[2]

The first example is written with a "you" perspective. The language is general and nonspecific. The second example is less personal and contains such technical terms as *hybrid modular construction*, *plug-in hybrid modules*, *down-time*, and *flexible circuits*, terms familiar to technicians.

MANUAL PREPARATION

Let us consider the writer's procedural steps for the preparation of an operation manual for a highly technical product.

Step 1—Determining Audience.   The writer must determine if the audience consists of laypersons or skilled technicians. The audience will have a bearing not only on the language, but also on the complexity of the graphics, the extent and scope of the data, and the manual size and format. If the intended manual user is a layperson, the writer must consult the marketing department to determine who will buy the product, what language is appropriate, and what detail is essential.

Step 2—Consulting the Engineering Department.   Engineers of various specialties must be consulted to determine how the product works, what instructions and warnings must be stressed, and how much detail should be included for different audiences. Considerably more detail, graphics, schematics, and diagrams will be included in manuals for technicians than in those for laypersons.

Step 3—Deciding on Manual Production.   Once the audience and the intent of the manual is established, the writer must make initial decisions on the content and appearance of the manual. She must prepare a rough draft of the content, deciding on headings and numbering systems and on whether or not to use a title page, table of contents, and so forth. Bearing in mind the four common writing components of manuals (definition, description, instructions, and process analysis), the writer must decide on the emphasis and amount of each to include.

He must decide if the manual shall be a folded pamphlet which can be inserted into the product packaging or if it will be a booklet with bound pages. He must decide on the paper quality, type of print, color usage, and number of manuals.

[2] Motorola, Inc., *Motorola MX300-T Five Channel "Handi-Talkie" Portable Radio* (Fort Lauderdale, Florida: Motorola, Inc., Portable Products Division, 1982), a manual.

Step 4—Preparing the Graphics. Although graphic consideration goes hand-in-hand with Step 3, it is important enough to warrant separate discussion. While actual photographs may be used to depict the overall product, drawings are used more extensively in manuals because they can emphasize parts and relationships by the judicious use of exploded, cutaway, and schematic sketches. Lists of items or features should be incorporated into tables. The writer usually devises rough sketches of the desired graphics even though professional graphic artists will prepare the actual art work.

Step 5—Reviewing the Copy. Once the copy is prepared, the competent writer reviews the manual carefully with marketing and engineering personnel. Editing the work is essential for a successful manual.

Step 6—Producing the Manual. Finally, the copy is given to typesetters who prepare camera-ready copy, print it, and bind or fold the manuals.

Figure 12.1 shows an operation manual for a Motorola Dimension 1000 Binary SC Pager. The original manual was printed as a $2\frac{5}{8}$ in. by $3\frac{5}{8}$ in., twelve-panel, folded booklet designed to fit the packaging of the pager.

To familiarize you with a typical product operation manual, the complete Motorola pager manual is included in Figure 12.2, along with explanatory comments.

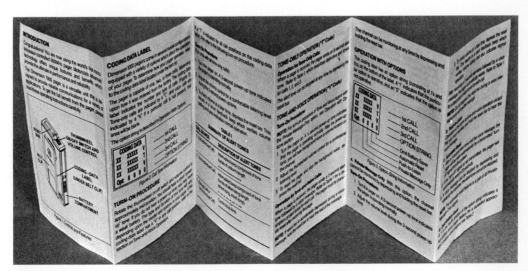

FIGURE 12.1 *Folded operation manual for personal pager*
(Courtesy of Motorola Inc., Fort Lauderdale, Florida)

Company name & trademark plus name of product

 MOTOROLA DIMENSION 1000
Binary GSC Pager

Actual photograph provides graphic *description* of product.

Title states purpose of manual.

Operating Instructions
68P81025C65-O

FIGURE 12.2   *Operation manual for a Motorola Dimension 1000 Binary GSC pager* (Courtesy of Motorola, Inc., Fort Lauderdale, Florida)

INTRODUCTION

Congratulations! You are now using the world's first microprocessor-controlled 900MHz pager. Motorola's advanced technology offers unique features and benefits which provide the ultimate in performance and reliability.

The Dimension 1000 pager is a versatile unit that is designed to provide reliable communications for a variety of applications. To get the full benefit from the pager, please read these operating instructions carefully.

The "you" identifies audience.

Brief mechanism *definition* is followed by manual purpose.

Drawing of overall mechanism labels parts to familiarize audience with controls and features.

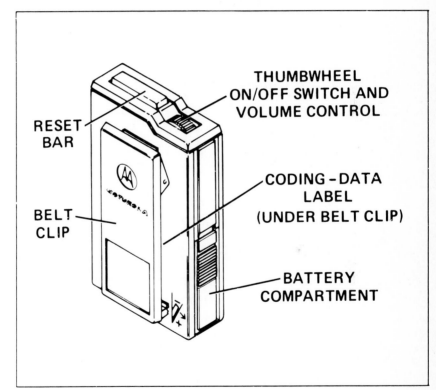

Figure 1. Controls and Features

FIGURE 12.2 *continued*

CODING DATA LABEL

Dimension 1000 pagers come in several model configurations equipped with a variety of options which affect the operation of your pager. To determine how your pager operates, refer to the coding-data label located under the belt clip.

The pager is capable of one, two, or three calls, depending upon how it was ordered from the factory. The coding-data label indicates the number and type of calls (Figure 2). Tone-only calls are indicated by a "T," and voice calls are indicated by a "V." If a particular call is not present, that area will be blank.

The option string is described in Operation With Options.

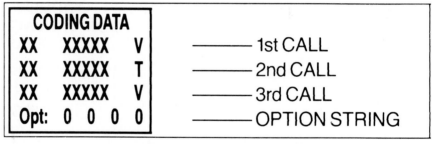

Figure 2. Call Type Information

TURN-ON PROCEDURE

Rotate the thumbwheel on/off switch and volume control to approximately mid-position. You should hear a short "power-up" tone. If you do not hear a power-up tone, you may have a weak battery. The type and duration of this tone will vary, depending upon the model and options in your pager. If the coding-data label has a "V" in any call position, refer to the section on Tone-and-Voice Operation.

FIGURE 12.2   *continued*

If a "T" is indicated for all call positions on the coding-data label, then refer to the following turn-on procedure:

Turn-On Procedure
(For units with all tone-only calls):

Instructions emphasize action (*turn, adjust, depress*).

1. Turn the pager on. A 3-second power-up tone indicates the pager is operating normally.

2. Adjust the volume control for a comfortable listening level during the 3-second power-up tone.

3. To check volume at a later time, depress the reset bar. This results in a short feedback beep which verifies volume setting and also indicates normal operation.

TABLE 1
SUMMARY OF ALERT TONES

Alert Tones are summarized in a formal table for easy reference.

CALL SOURCE:	DESCRIPTION OF ALERT TONES
1 (1st Individual Call)	Interrupted beep composed of tone bursts of uniform length.
2 (2nd Individual Call)	Interrupted beep composed of tone bursts of alternating length (short-long, short-long).
3 (Group Call or 3rd Individual Call)	Continuous tone.

FIGURE 12.2 *continued*

TONE-ONLY OPERATION ("T" Code)

Operation for Tone-Only Calls:

When a page is received, the pager emits an 8-second alert tone. Refer to Table 1, which describes distinctive alert tones for calls 1, 2, and 3.

The alert tone can be stopped at any time by depressing the reset bar.

TONE-AND-VOICE OPERATION ("V" Code)

Turn-On Procedure:

NOTE: For turn-on procedure of Tone and Voice pagers with the Private-Message-Only option, see Operation with Options section.

1. Turn the pager on. A ¼ second power-up tone indicates that the pager is operating normally. After the power-up tone, you will hear background noise or communication on the channel.

2. Adjust the thumbwheel volume control for a comfortable listening level.

3. To reset the pager and stop the background noise, depress the reset bar.

Operation for Tone-and-Voice Calls:

When a page is received, the pager emits a 2-second alert tone followed by a voice message. Refer to Table 1 for a description of alert tones for each call. The pager must be manually reset after receiving the page.

NOTE: If reset bar is accidentally depressed during a voice message, hold the reset bar to hear the rest of the message.

FIGURE 12.2   *continued*

Sidebar annotations (left margin):

Section provides brief *analysis* of operation.

The word *note* is used for emphasis.

Numerical *instructions* use action verbs (*turn, adjust, depress*).

Paragraph provides brief *analysis* of operation.

The word *Note* is used for emphasis.

The channel can be monitoring at any time by depressing and holding the reset bar.

OPERATION WITH OPTIONS

The coding label has an option string (consisting of 1's and 0's) on the bottom of the label. A "1" indicates that the particular option is operative, and an "0" indicates that the option is not operative.

Graphic blow-up is more effective than an actual photograph.

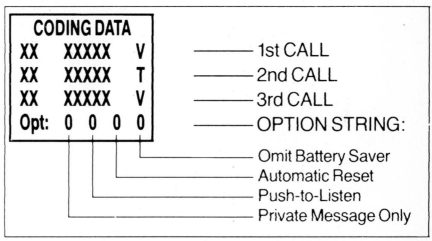

CODING DATA

XX	XXXXX	V	————	1st CALL
XX	XXXXX	T	————	2nd CALL
XX	XXXXX	V	————	3rd CALL
Opt:	0 0 0 0		————	OPTION STRING:

———— Omit Battery Saver
———— Automatic Reset
———— Push-to-Listen
———— Private Message Only

Figure 3. Option-String Information

a. Private-Message-Only With this option, the channel cannot be monitored by depressing and holding the reset bar.

Turn-On Procedure:

Instructions are continued.

1. Turn the pager on. A 3-second power-up tone indicates the pager is operating normally.

2. Adjust the volume level during the 3-second power-up tone.

FIGURE 12.2 *continued*

Instructions
are continued
with use of
note to
provide
emphasis.

3. To check volume at a later time, depress the reset bar. This results in a short feedback beep which verifies volume setting and also indicates normal operation.

After receiving a 2-second alert-tone followed by a voice message, the pager automatically resets. Refer to Table 1 for a description of alert tones for each call.

NOTE: Do not depress the reset bar during a voice message or you will lose the message.

b. Push-to-Listen

Operation is the same as tone-and-voice operation *except* that you must depress and hold the reset bar to hear the voice message.

c. Automatic-Reset

1. After a 2-second alert tone and the voice message, the pager will be reset automatically by a transmitted "turn-off" signal from the system.

2. If the "turn-off" signal is not transmitted, the pager will automatically reset in 20 seconds.

3. A voice message can be stopped by depressing and releasing the reset bar; the alert tone cannot be stopped.

NOTE: The automatic-reset feature is a part of all Private-Message-Only pagers.

d. Omit-Battery-Saver

Brief analysis
is provided.

A "1" in the fourth position of the option string indicates a non-battery-saver pager. Battery life is increased appreciably in battery-saver pagers; see Table 2.

FIGURE 12.2 *continued*

e. Fixed Alert (not indicated in option string)
The alert tone is always at maximum volume, but the voice-message volume can be adjusted.

BATTERY INFORMATION
LOW-BATTERY ALERT

Whenever the pager is reset, the battery voltage is monitored. If the battery level is low, a special alternating high-low alert tone will sound. If the low-battery alert sounds, replace the mercury battery or recharge the nickel-cadmium battery. Battery life remaining after a low-battery alert is approximately three hours for nickel-cadmium batteries and eight hours for mercury batteries.

Battery Life: Battery life will vary depending upon the system. The following figures are given as a general indication of expected battery life.

TABLE 2
BATTERY LIFE (Approximate)

BATTERY TYPE	BATTERY-SAVER	NON-BATTERY-SAVER
Mercury	200-220 Hours	64-70 Hours
Nickel-Cadmium	66-73 Hours	20-22 Hours

Battery Installation or Replacement:

1. Locate the battery compartment on the side (closest to volume-control thumbwheel) as shown in Figure 4(a).
2. **Slide the ribbed latch down** so that the red indicator is visible.

FIGURE 12.2 *continued*

Battery information analysis precedes instructions for battery changing.

Graphic table provides easy reference data.

Instructions stress action verbs and employ boldface print for emphasis.

Numbered
instructions
continue.

3. Pull open the battery-compartment door (hinged at the bottom) as shown in Figure 4(b). Remove the old battery.
4. Place the positive end of the new battery into the compartment (see polarity marking on the housing shown in Figure 4(b). Push the battery down until it makes contact with the + battery contact.
5. Close the battery-compartment door and slide the ribbed latch up until the red indicator no longer appears.
6. If the battery is an approved rechargeable nickel-cadmium type, charge the battery in the pager as described in the Battery Charging paragraph.

Blow-up
drawings
assist the
written
instructions.

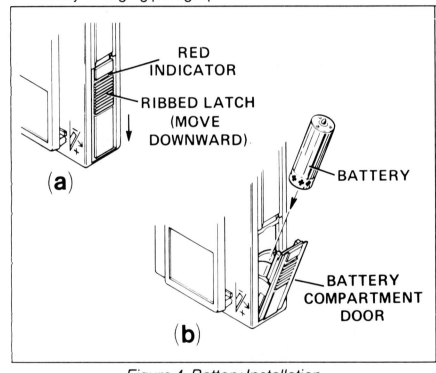

Figure 4. Battery Installation

FIGURE 12.2   *continued*

Battery Types:

Explanation actually provides instructions.

Either disposable mercury or rechargeable nickel-cadmium batteries are available.

Mercury Battery Model: 1.4V N-Size, Motorola NLN6199A

Nickel-Cadmium Model: 1.3V N-Size rechargeable, Motorola Type NLN6965A

> Pager performance
> and battery life cannot be guaranteed if
> other types of batteries are used.

Battery Charging:

Brief analysis is followed by numbered instructions.

(Approved Motorola nickel-cadmium battery only)

The Motorola charger (either single or multiple-unit models) charges a pager and a spare N-cell size nickel-cadmium battery simultaneously.

1. Operate the charger from the correct line voltage as indicated on the charger.

2. Insert the pager in the charger with pager power (thumbwheel switch) set to off. For best results, charge the pager at least 12 hours (overnight).

3. A separate nickel-cadmium battery may be charged also by inserting the battery in the auxiliary charging compartment. Observe the correct battery polarity orientation.

The word note provides emphasis.

NOTE: The charger is designed to prevent accidental charging of mercury batteries.

FIGURE 12.2   *continued*

BATTERY CHARGERS:

These Motorola single and multiple-unit chargers are available for recharging nickel-cadmium batteries.

*Informal
table is
instructional.*

NLN4508B   Single-Unit Charger, 117VAC

NLN4509B   Single-Unit Charger, 230VAC

NLN4510B   Multiple-Unit Master Charger
(5 receptacles), 117VAC

NLN4511B   Multiple-Unit Auxiliary Charger
(6 receptacles); three units can
be powered from multiple-unit
master (NLN4510B)

FIGURE 12.2   *continued*

Repair and
maintenance
note provides
instructions.

REPAIR AND MAINTENANCE

The Dimension 1000 pager, properly handled, will provide years of service. However, should it require repair, Motorola's National Service Organization, staffed with specially trained technicians, offers strategically located repair and maintenance facilities. Consult your Motorola sales representative for service locations in your area.

Copyright
information
is standard.

COMPUTER SOFTWARE COPYRIGHTS

The Motorola products described in this manual may include copyrighted Motorola computer programs stored in semiconductor memories or other mediums. Laws in the United States and foreign countries preserve for Motorola certain exclusive rights for copyrighted computer programs, including the exclusive right to copy or reproduce in any form the copyrighted computer program. Accordingly, any copyrighted Motorola computer programs contained in the Motorola products described in this manual may not be copied or reproduced in any manner without the express written permission of Motorola, Inc. Furthermore, the purchase of Motorola products shall not be deemed to grant either directly or indirectly or by implication, estoppel, or otherwise, any license under the copyrights, patents or patent applications of Motorola, except for the normal non-exclusive, royalty free license to use that arises by operation of law in the sale of a product.

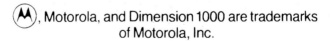, Motorola, and Dimension 1000 are trademarks
of Motorola, Inc.

© 1982 by Motorola, Inc., Paging Products Division
8000 W. Sunrise Blvd., Ft. Lauderdale, FL 33322
Printed in U.S.A. 8/82

FIGURE 12.2   *continued*

EXERCISE

1. Collect three or four operation manuals for such products as a digital
    clock with alarm, a telephone answerer, a camera, a walkie-talkie,
    an electric coffee maker, or an electric can opener. Identify in the
    margins which type of writing is stressed in each section: definition,
    description of the mechanism, instructions, or analysis.

WRITING OPTION

1. Select the best manual (see Exercise) and write a brief report on
    its effectiveness. Comment on its overall format (size, type of paper,
    layout, headings, color, boldface print, numbering system), its lan-
    guage, its graphics, the definitions, the descriptions of the mechanism,
    the instructions, the analysis of operating procedures or problems.
    Use headings in your own report. Attach the manual or photocopied
    pages.

NOTES

CHAPTER 13

Defining Terms

INTRODUCTION

A writer must always be alert to the need for a definition of a term or phrase in all reports. A definition is a statement of the meaning of a word or word group or a sign or a symbol. The need for precise definitions is so crucial that sometimes a separate section of a report or manual is devoted to lists of terms and their meanings.

Every field of endeavor has its own vocabulary. Allied health students must master precise definitions of specific diseases, disorders, procedures, and other medical terminology. Electronics study demands an understanding of *capacitance, resistance, frequency,* and other related terms. In recent years anyone who has shopped for a home computer has been suddenly introduced to a mind-boggling new vocabulary including *byte, floppy disk, computer friendly,* and *CP/M,* to name only a few terms. In fact, the computer age has ushered in many new terms, including *cyberphrenetic,* or one who is excessively excited and fanatical about the study of computers.

AUDIENCE

Audience determines the need for and the extent of definitions. Writers of informal or formal reports must define all terms which may be unfamiliar to the audience, words which may have more than one meaning, or those which are used in a special or stipulative manner.

Consider the simple word *tongue,* which has at least nine distinct meanings to different audiences. To a biologist, a tongue is a fleshy, movable portion of the floor of the mouth of most vertebrates that bears sensory end organs and small glands and which functions in taking and swallowing food, and in man as a speech organ. To a geographer, however, a tongue is a long, narrow strip of land projecting into a body of water. To a cobbler, a tongue is a flap under the lacing or buckle of a shoe at the throat of the vamp. To a linguist, a tongue is the spoken language, manner or quality of utterance, or the intention of a speaker. To a belt maker, a tongue is a movable pin in a buckle. To a carpenter, a tongue is the rib or one edge of a board that fits into a corresponding groove in an edge of another board to make a joint flush. Yet, to a bell manufacturer, a tongue is a metal ball suspended inside a bell so as to strike against the side as the bell is swung. And finally, to some religious groups, tongue is the charismatic (divinely inspired) gift of ecstatic speech. The parenthetical definition of *charismatic* underscores the need for definitions as an essential to meaningful communication.

Definitions may be integrated into a report, may constitute a major portion of a report, or may be the entire report. An instruction manual may include an introductory list of terms to be used within the instructions. A policy handbook may introduce each chapter with relevant definitions. Sometimes an appendix of terms must accompany a report.

METHODS

The extent to which a term should be defined depends not only on the audience but also on the complexity of the term itself. Terms may be defined by

- Parenthetical expression
- Brief phrase
- Formal sentences
- Extended paragraphs

Parenthetical Definition

The simplest way to define a term is to include a synonym in parentheses directly after the term:

The top half of a drainage map drawing is the plan (aerial view); the bottom half is the profile (horizontal view).

The ring top (round, spoked, carrying handle) of the fire extinguisher corroded.

Definition by Brief Phrase

Sometimes a defining phrase will clarify your term:

If the body temperature is abnormal, that is above or below a range of 97.6°F to 99°F, further diagnostic procedures should follow.

Formal Sentence Definition

A specific pattern exists for precise definition of terms. The pattern consists of three parts: the name of the term, the class of the term, and the characteristics of the term which distinguish it from all other members of its class. Some examples follow:

Term	*Class*	*Distinguishing Characteristics*
Arbitration	is a process	by which both parties to a labor dispute agree to submit the dispute to a third party for binding decision.
Sediment	is matter	which settles to the bottom of a liquid.
Assets	are items owned	such as cash, receivables, inventories, equipment, land, and buildings.
Paranoia	is a personality disorder	in which a person feels persecuted or has ambitions of grandeur.
Arson	is a criminal act	of purposely setting fire to a building or property so as to collect insurance.
A patent	is an inventor's exclusive right	which is granted by the federal government, to own, use, make, sell, or dispose of an invention for a certain number of years.
Down-time	is a period	during which a computer system is inoperable due to power failure or hardware breakdown.

Sometimes a formal definition requires more than one sentence in order to read smoothly:

A rifle is a firearm which has spiral grooves inside its barrel to impart a rotary motion to its projectile. It is designed to be fired from the shoulder and requires two hands for accurate operation.

These definitions concentrate on just one meaning of the term. The term *rifle* is also a verb, *to rifle*, which is "to cut grooves, or to ransack, rob, or pillage, or to search and rob."

To be useful a definition should not contain terms which are more technical or confusing than the term itself. Consider which of these two definitions is more useful to a layperson:

Dysgraphia is a transduction disorder which results from visual motor integration disturbance.

Dysgraphia is a writing disorder which results from a difficulty in writing what one sees.

The first definition might well convey meaning to a group of learning disability specialists, but the second is more helpful to an undergraduate student.

The definition writer must avoid certain definition fallacies (misleading errors). For instance, when naming the term's class, one must be careful not to be too broad. To write "A rifle (term) is an object (class)" is too broad. "A rifle (term) is a firearm (class)" is more precise. Conversely, to classify a term too narrowly as in "A chair is a four-legged seat . . ." restricts the possibility that a chair may have a single pedestal for a base, or have five or more legs arranged in a circle.

It is also important to avoid using any form of the term in the second and third parts of the definition; to do so takes your reader in a circle. Consider this statement: "A radical is a person having radical views concerning social order and systems." Does it define *radical*? Other examples of circular definition are

Comatose is the state of being in a coma.

Fertilization is the process of fertilizing.

A surveyor is one who surveys.

Finally, one must avoid the terms *when* and *where* in formal definition. To write "A crypt is where one is buried" fails to classify the term as a subterranean chamber or to distinguish it from a mausoleum or a cemetery, other places where people are buried. To write "Osmosis is when fluid passes through a membrane" fails to point out that osmosis is a digestive process.

In summary, when devising formal definitions *do not* (1) use needlessly technical language, (2) employ classifications which are too broad, (3) employ classifications or list characteristics which are too narrow, (4) use any form of the term itself in the class or characteristics citation, or (5) use the terms *where* or *when* in place of a classification.

EXTENDED DEFINITION

If your intent is to define a term so that your audience has a thorough understanding of it, you may need to extend your formal definition. You may want to include physical description, examples, synonyms, comparisons or contrasts, analogies, explanations of the origin of the item, an etymology (origin) of the term itself, discussions of cause and effect, or analysis of the involved process. Such a definition is called an *extended definition*.

The extended definition may be a few sentences, a paragraph, several pages, or an entire lengthy report.

Should you decide that an extended definition is necessary, a number of strategies are at hand to add to your formal definition. Select as many of the methods as are necessary to clarify completely the meaning of your term. There is no formula for the number or order of the methods to be employed.

Description

Following your formal definition, which distinguishes the item from other members of its class, it may be wise to describe the physical parts of the item, if, indeed, the term names an object. The following example begins with a formal definition and includes a brief physical description:

> An otoscope is a hand-held, diagnostic instrument which is used for examining the external canal of the ear and the ear drum. Composed of plastic, aluminum, and glass, it consists of three main parts: a dry-cell battery barrel assembly, a lens assembly, and a speculum (reflector).

To further describe its parts, subparts, dimensions, weight, and method of use would entail other specific writing strategies which are covered in Chapter 14. A graphic illustration incorporated into the text would help to clarify the term. Figure 13.1 shows the main parts of an otoscope.

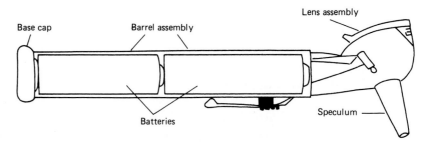

FIGURE 13.1   *The main parts of an otoscope*

Examples

A second approach to extended definitions is to provide examples. These may be brief or longer themselves. Two samples follow:

> A parasite is a plant or animal which lives on or within another organism, from which it derives sustenance or protection without making compensation. Some parasites are tapeworms, sheep ticks, lice, and scabies.

A market is a state of trade which is determined by prices, supply, and demand. In salesmanship the term *market* may refer to a trade or commerce in a specific service or commodity, such as the housing market, the stock market, or the designer jean market. Investors in a market study it carefully before investing. In the stock market, a potential investor studies the stock market exchange, current rates of stocks, and current prices of stocks to determine if the "market" is going up or down and to determine whether an investment would be profitable at a particular time.

Synonym

A third expansion of the basic definition is to list synonyms for the term. When readers are familiar with the synonym, they can better understand the definition. Here are some examples of synonym extension:

> A law is a rule of conduct which is established and enforced by the authority, legislation, or custom of a given community or other group. *Rule, regulation, precept, statute,* and *ordinance* are all synonyms for the word *law*.
>
> A motive is an inner impulse or reason that causes a person to do something or to act in a certan way. The terms *intent, incentive,* and *inducement* are sometimes used synonymously with *motive*.

One must be careful to remember that no two words are ever exactly synonymous. Meanings may overlap, but a careful examination of the differences is what conveys precise meaning.

Contrast/Negation

A fourth writing strategy for extended definitions is to contrast or to negate the term from those terms or items in the same class with which it may be confused. For example:

> In criminal investigation *motive* and *intent* are not truly synonymous. A man who provides a lethal drug to a terminally ill patient has the "motive" to alleviate suffering. Still his "intent" is to kill, making him criminally liable for the death.
>
> A stalactite is an elongate deposit of carbonate of lime which hangs from the roof or sides of a cave. It is not a stalagmite, which is a cone-shaped deposit of carbonate of lime which extends vertically from the floor of a cave.

We often understand better what a thing is by knowing what it is not.

Comparison

Conversely, we can better understand what some terms denote if we can examine similarities to things more familiar. Two comparisons for extending definitions follow:

> A stalactite resembles an icicle in that both are hanging, cone-shaped deposits formed by dripping water. In the case of the stalactite the water evaporates leaving the lime deposit; in the case of an icicle the dripping water freezes.

> Resistance, the opposition to the passage of electrical current which converts electric energy into heat, may be compared to friction between any two objects. When a sulfur-coated matchstick is rubbed against an abrasive surface, the friction creates a spark which ignites the sulfur and produces heat.

Analogy

The extended comparison of two otherwise dissimilar things is an analogy. Although a computer and a weather thermometer are basically different, the following analogy helps us to understand an analog computer:

> An analog computer is an electronic machine which translates measurements, such as temperature, pressure, angular position, or voltage into related mechanical or electrical quantities. The operating principle of an analog computer may be compared to that of an ordinary weather thermometer. As the weather becomes cooler or warmer, the mercury in the glass tube rises or falls. The expansion and contraction of the mercury has a relationship to the conditions of the weather. The thermometer provides a continuous measurement that corresponds to the climatic temperature. The analog computer makes continuous scientific computations, solves equations, and controls manufacturing processes.[1]

Origin

Examining the source of an item helps us to grasp the meaning of the word. The following passage briefly explains the source, the mining, and the metallurgy of tin:

---

[1] Raymond E. Glos and others, *Business: Its Nature and Environment*, 9th ed. (Cincinnati, Ohio: South-Western Publishing Company, 1980), p. 457.

The earliest known tin is found in bronze (a copper-tin alloy) items found at Ur, dated about 3500 B.C. Tin is an element which occurs in cassiterite deposits. The ore is recovered by both opencut and underground mining. The smelting processes include roasting and leaching in acid to remove all of the impurities. The crude tin is resmelted and then refined by further heat treatments of two steps: liquation or sweating, and boiling or poling. Finally, the pure tin is cast in the form of 100-lb ingots in cast iron molds.

Etymology

Examining the origin of a term, its etymology, also helps to convey meaning. Both standard and specialized dictionaries provide etymologies of almost all words in modern English usage; the following are some:

The term *cyclone* is derived from the Greek word *kykloma* which means "wheel" or "coil."

The term *gerrymander*, the practice of dividing a voting area in such a way as to give unfair advantage to one political party, is derived from Elbridge *Gerry*, the governor of Massachusetts in 1812 when the method was employed, plus the word *salamander* which describes the shape of the redistricted Essex County.

Cause/Effect

To understand completely some terms, an examination of causes and effects is useful. The following example describes the causes and effects of a tornado to amplify the formal sentence definition:

A tornado is a storm characterized by a violently rotating funnel cloud which has a narrow bottom tending to reach to the earth. The cloud may rotate clockwise or counterclockwise at approximately 100–150 mph. The funnel cloud results from the condensation of moisture through cooling by expansion and lifting of air in the vortex. The air outside of the funnel cloud is also part of the vortex, and near the ground this outer ring becomes visibly laden with dust and debris. Although a tornado takes only a minute or so to pass, it results in devastating destruction. Buildings may be entirely flattened, exploded to bits, or moved for hundreds of yards. Straws are known to be driven through posts. The roar of a tornado can be heard as far as 25 miles away.

Process Analysis

A final strategy of expanded definition is to analyze the process in which the item is involved:

> A skeleton is the bony framework of any vertebrate animal. It gives the body shape, protects soft tissue and organs, and provides a system of levers, operated by muscle, that enables the body to move. Bones of a skeleton store inorganic sodium, calcium, and phosphorous and release them into the blood. The skeleton houses bone marrow, the blood-forming tissue. Bones are joined to adjacent bones by joints. The bones fit together and are held in place by bands of flexible tissue called *ligaments*.

> A pressure cooker is an airtight metal container which is used for quick food preparation by means of steam under pressure. When the lid of the pot is secured by means of a rubber gasket and the container is placed on a heat source, fast-flying molecules of steam constantly bump against each other and the inside surface of the container. The combined blows from all molecules exert heat and pressure, "cooking" the food in approximately one-third of the time required by conventional cooking methods.

Process analysis may be extended into a separate writing strategy and is discussed thoroughly in Chapter 16.

Figures 13.2 and 13.3 contain two sample extended definitions. Each begins with a formal sentence definition and utilizes several extended-definition writing strategies. Brief graphics enhance the definitions. The writing strategies are noted in the left margin. Both samples are intended for a lay audience. More detailed and complex definitions would be necessary for a law textbook on patents or for a medical textbook on cancers. Be prepared to critique the samples in class.

A DEFINITION OF LEUKEMIA

Formal Definition

Leukemia is a progressive, malignant disease of the blood-forming tissues which is characterized by an abnormal and persistent increase in the number of leukocytes (white blood cells) and the amount of bone marrow

Etymology

with enlargement of the spleen and lymph glands. The term leukemia is derived from the Greek words leukes, which means "white," and haima,

Synonym

which means "blood." Leukemia is also called blood cancer. Historically, leukemia is a relatively new disease with no reference in biblical or Roman

Origin

writings. It was first described in 1845. There are two main varieties of

Examples

leukemia: myelogenous and lymphatic, and a number of less common forms. Figures 1 and 2 show normal and cancerous cells:

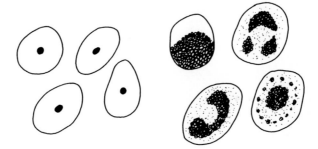

Descriptive Graphics

Figure 1   Normal cells   *Figure 2   Cancerous cells*

Causes

The cause of leukemia is not known although it is known that exposure to radiation is a clear factor. Other causes may include genetic, chemical, viral,

FIGURE 13.2   *Sample extended definition*

Effects

and hormonal factors. Usually the first symptoms of leukemia are weakness, increased fatigue, and anemia or hemorrhages. In the acute form symptoms may be severe, the progress rapid, and fever present. In the chronic form early symptoms may be overlooked until enlargement of the spleen or lymph glands is detected. The white blood cell count may increase to 100 times the normal amount, or it may be lower than normal. Ill-formed leukocytes appear in the blood. Although the disease may be treated or the patient can experience spontaneous remission, leukemia is usually fatal.

FIGURE 13.2   *continued*

A DEFINITION OF VOLCANO

Formal definition

A volcano is a hill or mountain which is formed by lava, ashflows, or ejected rock fragments that come from a central

Etymology

vent. The word *volcano* derives from the name of the little island in the Mediterranean Sea called Vulcano. Many centuries ago, the people of this island believed that this lava and ash came from the forge of Vulcan, god of fire and metalworking. In

Cause

actuality, the lava flows from a magma chamber close to the earth's surface. This chamber is formed from rock which melted due to increased temperature or reduced pressure. This second

Analogy

cause, reduced pressure, might best be compared to a pressure cooker. While its lid is on, pressure is maintained, and the food is slowly being cooked. However, when the lid is removed, the pressure drops rapidly, and steam rises violently into the atmosphere. If the pressure underneath the earth remains constant, rock will stay in its motionless, solid state, but if the pressure drops, rock will quickly melt and rise toward the earth's

Description

surface. There are three major types of volcanoes. First, the shield volcano has a gently sloping cone because it is formed from solidified lava flows. The slopes are usually between 2 degrees

FIGURE 13.3 *Sample extended definition*
(Courtesy of student Debra Fuhrhop)

and 10 degrees. Second, the cinder cone consists of ejected rock fragments, called pyroclasts, such as dust, ash, cinders, and bombs. Since many of the fragments land near the central vent, a peak usually forms. Slopes are generally 30 degrees for this type. Third, the composite volcano is formed by alternating layers of pyroclasts and solidified lava flows. Because of its construction, it erodes at a slower rate than the other two types of volcanoes and has a steep slope. Figures 1–3 show a shield, cinder cone and composite volcano:

Figure 1 Shield Volcano

Figure 2 Cinder Cone

Figure 3 Composite Volcano

Examples   Some examples of composite volcanoes are Mount Rainier and Mount St. Helens in Washington State, Mount Hood in Oregon, Mount Cotopaxi in Ecuador, and Mount Fuji in Japan.

FIGURE 13.3   *continued*

EXERCISES

1. What is wrong with these formal definitions? Rewrite each by providing a precise class and distinguishing characteristics. Consult dictionaries and specialized encyclopedias.

   a. A latent image is a prephotographic image on a film which cannot be seen.

   b. Cramming is when a student attempts to learn most of the contents of a course in a day or two.

   c. Asthma is a condition of continuous or paroxysmal labored breathing which is accompanied by wheezing, a sense of constriction in the chest, and often attacks of coughing or gasping.

   d. Celluloid is a substance which is thin and inflammable, used for photographic films.

   e. A bond is when two things, such as concrete and steel, are adhered.

   f. A potentiometer is a device used as a resistor.

   g. An azimuth is a 45 degree angle measured clockwise from any reference meridian.

   h. A journal is a diary in which the analysis of each of the daily financial transactions of a business are recorded as they occur.

   i. A binary cell is a cell in a computer's memory which is restricted to storing binary numbers.

   j. Anxiety is when you are paralyzed with fright and do not know what you are afraid of.

2. In the following extended definition identify each writing strategy by writing the methods in the space provided after each sentence.

   A cyclone is a storm that may range from 50 to 900 miles in diameter and that is characterized by winds of 90 to 130 mph blowing in a circle—counterclockwise in the northern hemisphere and clockwise in the southern hemisphere—around a calm center of low atmospheric pressure while the storm itself moves from 20 to 30 miles per hour. _____ _____ Cyclones may be called whirlwinds, hurricanes, and typhoons. _____ The term *hurricane*, however, is properly applied only to a cyclone of large extent and suggests the presence of rain, thunder, and lightning. The term *typhoon* refers to tropical cyclones in the region of the Phillipine Islands or the China Sea. _____ _____ A tornado is not a cyclone. Although a tornado consists of whirling winds, it is characterized by a funnel-shaped cloud which is far smaller in diameter than a cyclone and by winds far exceeding the velocity of winds in a cyclone. _____ The term *cyclone* is derived from the Greek word *kykloma* which means "wheel" or "coil."
   _____

3. Add a parenthetical definition for each word in italics.

   a. The culture was studied *in vitro*.

   b. She painted and *pickled* the pine chest.

   c. An *implosion* occurred during the experiment.

   d. She drew a *cycloid* on the working drawings.

   e. The *loess* improved the fertility of the soil.

4. Write one-sentence **formal** definitions for five of the following terms. Check your first effort to edit for fallacies (too broad, too narrow, circularity, too technical, use of *when* or *where*).

flextime	veto	recession (economics)
marl	kinetics	chiaroscuro
credit card	teakettle	Teflon
Kaplan turbine	marinade	perforation
lift (aviation)	telephone	graffiti
spectrum	nuclear power	plutocracy
steroid	carcinoma	

WRITING OPTIONS

1. Select five related terms from your professional field. For this report try to avoid terms which name mechanisms. Title your assignment by stipulating the field of the terms: e.g., "Terms Used in Radiation Technology," "Terms Used in Electronics." Develop formal sentence definitions for each of the terms. Each definition must state the term, classify the term, and cite the distinguishing characteristics which differentiate your term from all others in its class. Avoid the fallacies. Following are some suggested terms in specialized fields:

Word Processing	*Computers*
menu	byte
wordwrap	hashing
block move	live screen
global search	modem
dedicated function	virus

Fashion	*Electronics*
godet	electron
grommet	resistance
stonewashed	frequency
peplum	capacitance
double-faced linen	Ohm's law

Criminal Justice	Allied Health
larceny	emphysema
felony	atherosclerosis
manslaughter	angina
assault	escemia
battery	vasodilation

Fire Science	Psychology
arson	anxiety
pyromaniac	psychosis
flammable	neurosis
purple K	schizophrenia
cartridge	manic depressive syndrome

Marketing	General Business
a good	sole proprietorship
convenience good	partnership
shopping good	limited partnership
specialty good	corporation
unsought good	conglomerate

Surveying	Architecture
azimuth	fascia
stadia	cantilever
transverse	soffit
hub	strut
transit	beam

Political Science	Astronomy
democracy	nova
communism	black hole
socialism	albedo
oligarchy	transit
monarchy	solar eclipse

Incorporate graphics into this definition report wherever they are appropriate.

2. Select a broad term (one naming a field of study or a concept) from your professional field. Write an expanded definition of the term which is suitable for first-year students in the field. Begin with a formal sentence definition and then expand it by employing at least five extended definition writing strategies. Employ graphics if possible. Use parenthetical or phrase definitions for unusual terms within your extended definition. In the margin jot down the writing strategies which you have employed. Approximately 250 words.

Describing Mechanisms

DUFFY   by Bruce Hammond

INTRODUCTION

Written descriptions of the tools, appliances, apparatus, and machines which we purchase or operate are necessary for us to understand thoroughly their function. We may call any object which has functional parts a mechanism. We are considering, then, not only a simple pocket knife or rachet wrench, but also a tape recorder, a camera, a stethoscope, a lawn mower, an automobile, and even body organs.

Writers must describe mechanisms to spur sales, to explain assembly, to instruct on operating and procedures, to explain functions, or to analyze strengths and weaknesses. Such descriptions may appear in textbooks, owner and service manuals (see Chapter 12), merchandise catalogues, specialized encyclopedias, specification catalogues, and do-it-yourself trade books.

Except for sales promotion materials which may involve some subjective writing, descriptions of mechanisms are characterized by objectivity, specificity, and thoroughness. A well-written description should enable a reader to understand the mechanism and the function of its parts. Further, the description should enable the reader to judge the efficiency, reliability, and practicality of the mechanism.

AUDIENCE

The purpose of the description and the audience for whom it is written will dictate the length and the amount of technical detail to be included. A *general* description, written for an encyclopedia or a general how-things-work book will emphasize the overall appearance of the mechanism and its parts and explain its purpose, function, and operation. A *specific* description written for an owner's manual or service manual will emphasize not only an overall description of the mechanism and its parts but also will include a detailed description of each part, subpart, or assembly of parts. In addition, a description of a specific mechanism will discuss its strengths, limitations, optional equipment, and/or similar models to allow the reader to judge the usefulness of the particular brand or model.

ORGANIZATION

Whether your description is general or specific, logical organization will aid your reader. An outline should be developed and followed carefully. There are three major sections to a general description of a mechanism:

1.0 General description, or the mechanism as a whole

2.0 Functional description, or the main parts

3.0 Concluding discussion, or assessment

An outline could be much more detailed. The components of a specific description of a mechanism could be outlined, for example, in the following manner:

1.0 The mechanism as a whole (introduction)
    1.1 Intended audience
    1.2 Formal definition and/or statement of purpose or function
    1.3 Overall description (with graphics)
    1.4 Theory (if applicable)
    1.5 Operation (if applicable, with procedural graphics)
        1.5.1 Who (qualifications)
        1.5.2 When
        1.5.3 Where
        1.5.4 How
    1.6 List of main parts (with labeled graphic)
2.0 The main parts (body)
    2.1 Description of first part
        2.1.1 Definition and/or purpose statement
        2.1.2 List of subparts (if an assembly)
        2.1.3 Shape, dimensions, weight (with graphic)
        2.1.4 Material and finish
        2.1.5 Relationship to other parts and method of attachment
    2.2 Description of second part . . . (etc.)
3.0 Concluding discussion/assessment (closing)
    3.1 Advantages
    3.2 Disadvantages
    3.3 Optional uses and equipment
    3.4 Other models (with graphics)
    3.5 Cost
    3.6 Availability

This outline is only a guide. The purpose of your description and the intended audience will suggest the amount of detail needed for each report. If you are going to give an oral description of a mechanism, check the evaluation sheet in Figure 17.4.

PREFATORY MATERIAL

Titles

A brief, clear, limiting title is the first writing strategy. A specific description will include the brand and model designation in the title.

Examples

Description of a Turbine Bypass Valve

Description of a Japanese K-D Socket Wrench

Description of a Universal Pressure Cooker, Model 4S

Intended Audience

An introductory statement of the intended audience and the purpose of the description may be included.

Examples

This description of a tubine bypass valve is intended for engineering students interested in the general construction, operation, and function of such valves.

This description of an Ace bit brace is intended for a junior high shop class instructional manual.

This description of a K & E pencil-lead holder is intended for a descriptive catalogue of architectural, designer, and drafting supplies.

Definition/Purpose

As the outline indicates, it is logical to include a formal definition and/ or statement of the purpose and function of the mechanism.

Examples

The pressure cooker is an airtight, metal container which is used to cook food by steam pressure at temperatures up to 250°F.

The K-D socket wrench is a hand tool designed to hold and turn fasteners, such as bolts, nuts, headed screws, and pipe lugs.

It is often helpful to compare the mechanism to something similar which is likely to be more familiar to the reader.

Examples

The pressure cooker resembles an ordinary "dutch oven" pot or a large, covered saucepan.

The heart is like a pump in that both draw in liquid and then cause it to be forced away.

Overall Description

Next the physical characteristics of the mechanism are examined. Include a description of the mechanism's shape and/or dimensions, the weight, the materials from which it is constructed, the color, and the finish. Graphic illustration of the mechanism will help the reader to visualize the mechanism.

Example

The K-D socket wrench is made of variable grades of steel. The handle is etched to provide a firm grip. The wrench shaft is $6\frac{1}{2}$ inches long, and the head is 2 inches deep. It weighs 13 ounces. Figure 1 shows the K-D wrench and its overall dimensions:

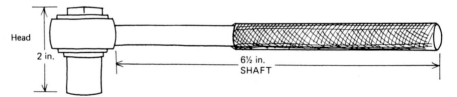

FIGURE 1   *The Japanese K-D socket wrench*

Theory

If knowledge of theory is essential, it should be included in the introductory or prefatory material.

Examples

The functioning principle of an ordinary mercury thermometer is based on the property of thermal expansion possessed by many substances; that is, they expand when heated and contract when cooled.

The microwave oven cooks food by producing heat directly in the food. As microwaves enter the food, they cause the moisture or liquid in the food to vibrate, and the resulting friction causes the food to heat.

Operator/Process

If the mechanism requires an operator, the qualification or specialty of the operator should be named. If helpful, clarify when and where the process is performed. Next, the process of the mechanism in action should be explained. An explanation of process should not be confused with instructions which give commands. In explaining the mechanism's process, use third-person subjects and present-tense verbs, in either the active or passive voice.

Examples

Cooks or chefs who wish to extract fresh garlic juice without pulp and skin use the garlic press. The cook (*third person*) places (*present tense, active voice*) the bulb of garlic inside the hollow wedge section of the strainer next to the plate of the press. He (*third person*) squeezes (*present tense, active voice*) the handles together, flattening the garlic and forcing the juice through the small holes of the strainer.

The stethoscope is designed to be used by doctors, nurses, and trained paraprofessionals to convey sounds in the chest or other parts of the body to the ear of the examiner. The earpieces (*third person*) are placed (*present tense, passive voice*) in the examiner's ears. The bell (*third person*) is held (*present tense, passive voice*) against the area of the body to be examined. The sounds (*third person*) are amplified (*present tense, passive voice*) through the tubing by the diaphragm assembly.

A graphic drawing may help the reader to visualize the mechanism in action.

List of Parts

Finally, the main parts of the mechanism are listed. The sequence should have organizational logic. You may list the parts spatially (from outside to inside or top to bottom), functionally (the order in which the parts work), or chronologically (the order in which the parts are put together).

If a part is complex—that is, it contains a number of subparts, such as nut, bolts, springs, pins, and so forth—the part may be called an assembly. Use the following sentence pattern:

Sentence pattern   The _____ consists of _____ main parts: the _____, the _____, the _____, and the _____.

Spatial example   The K & E lead holder consists of five main parts: the casing, the push knob, the spring, the tube, and the jaws.

Functional example	The camera consists of six main parts: the housing assembly, the film feed assembly, the lens, the shutter, the distance setting, and the viewfinder.
Chronological example	The Schwinn 3-speed bicycle consists of six main parts: the frame and rear wheel assembly, the front wheel assembly, the handlebar assembly, the gear-cable assembly, the brake assembly, and the seat assembly.

THE MAIN PARTS

This section, possibly the lengthiest part of your report, should define and describe each part or assembly in detail. However, a general description of a mechanism will not require as much detail as will a specific description.

Definition/Purpose

Each part requires a formal definition or statement of its purpose. Use one of the following sentence patterns to introduce each part or assembly:

Sentence patterns	First, the _____ is designed to _____.
	The _____, the first main part, supports _____.
	The first functional part, the _____, connects _____.
Examples	First, the etched handle is designed to provide a firm grip.
	The base, the first main part, supports all of the other parts.
	The first functional part, the pedestal, connects the base to the hole punch.

If a main part is an assembly, its subparts should be named.

Sentence pattern	The _____ assembly consists of the following subparts: the _____, the _____, and the _____.
Example	The direction assembly consists of the following subparts: the tension spring, the pin, and the knob.

Description

Next, the shape, dimensions, and weight of the part are described. If the material and finish of a part differ from the overall description, each should be described. The strategy should be to explain how each part is related to the other parts and how each is attached to the overall mechanism. If the part is an assembly, each subpart should be described in the order listed.

A graphic illustration of each part or assembly may be appropriate. Such graphics may include exploded drawings, sections, or schematics.

Example

The container, the first main part, is designed to hold and to measure the food to be chopped. It is a round, glass bowl which is $4\frac{1}{2}$ inches high and $3\frac{1}{2}$ inches in diameter. The container is etched in 2-ounce gradients, and it has a capacity of 12 ounces ($1\frac{1}{2}$ cups). The top rim is threaded to receive the lid. (Figure 2)

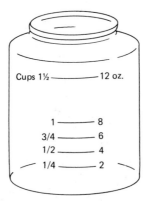

FIGURE 2 *Food chopper container*

The plunger assembly, the second main part, consists of the following subparts: shaft, knob cap, shaft housing, shaft housing cap, spring, and blades. When the plunger assembly is depressed, the blades rotate and chop the food in the container.

The shaft is a solid piece of pot metal $8\frac{1}{2}$ inches long and $\frac{3}{16}$ inches in diameter. It is slightly spatulate at the end where the blades are welded to it. Two stopper tabs protrude $2\frac{1}{2}$ inches from the blade end to secure the shaft in position.

A bulb-shaped, wooden knob cap is pressed securely to the top end. The cap is $\frac{3}{8}$ inches long and $\frac{1}{2}$ inch wide.

The shaft housing is a hollow tube $3\frac{1}{8}$ inches long and $\frac{1}{8}$ inch in diameter. The housing fits over the shaft and contains the spring. A threaded shaft housing cap secures the spring into position.

The steel spring coils around the shaft inside of the housing. The spring is 3 inches long.

The two blades, the final subparts of the plunger assembly, are razor-sharp steel. Each is $2\frac{1}{2}$ inches long and $\frac{1}{2}$ inch high. They are bent at a 45° angle and welded to the spatulate end of the shaft.

Figure 3 shows the plunger assembly parts:

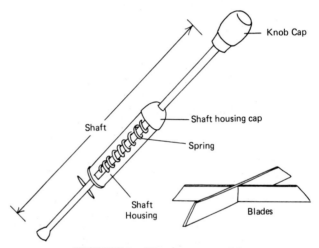

FIGURE 3   *Plunger assembly*

A complete description of a manual food chopper would include description of the other main parts: the lid and the chopping pad.

GRAPHICS

Descriptions of mechanisms should use ample graphics. Consider an overall drawing with the main parts and dimensions labeled. A sketch of the mechanism in action also will help your reader to envision its use. As you describe each main part or assembly, picture just that portion of the mechanism. Sometimes this will entail exploded or cutaway views. Figure 14.1 shows some typical mechanism drawings. Figure 14.2 contains a list of terms used in mechanism descriptions; use the list to name configurations, materials, shapes, finishes, and methods for attachment of parts of your mechanism.

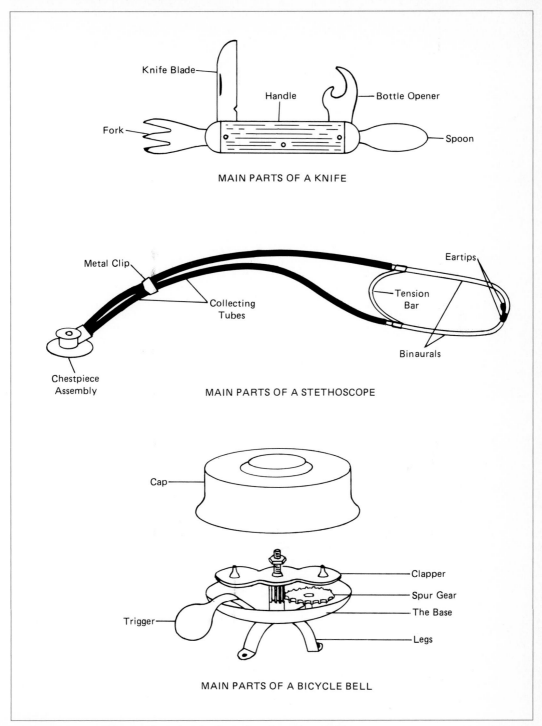

MAIN PARTS OF A KNIFE

MAIN PARTS OF A STETHOSCOPE

MAIN PARTS OF A BICYCLE BELL

FIGURE 14.1 *Typical drawings of mechanisms (overall)*

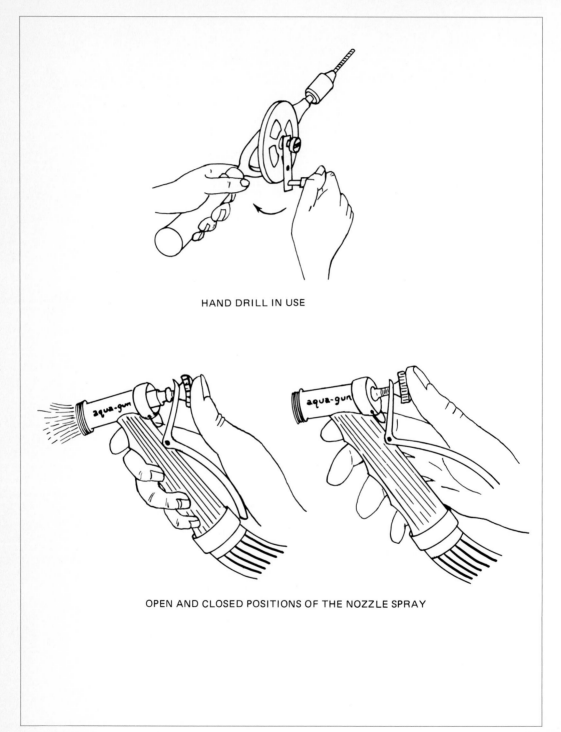

HAND DRILL IN USE

OPEN AND CLOSED POSITIONS OF THE NOZZLE SPRAY

FIGURE 14.1 *continued (**process graphics**)*

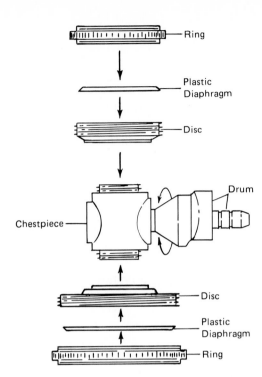

EXPLODED VIEW OF STETHOSCOPE CHESTPIECE ASSEMBLY

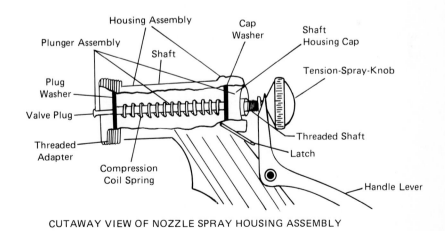

CUTAWAY VIEW OF NOZZLE SPRAY HOUSING ASSEMBLY

FIGURE 14.1   *continued* (***exploded and cutaway views***)

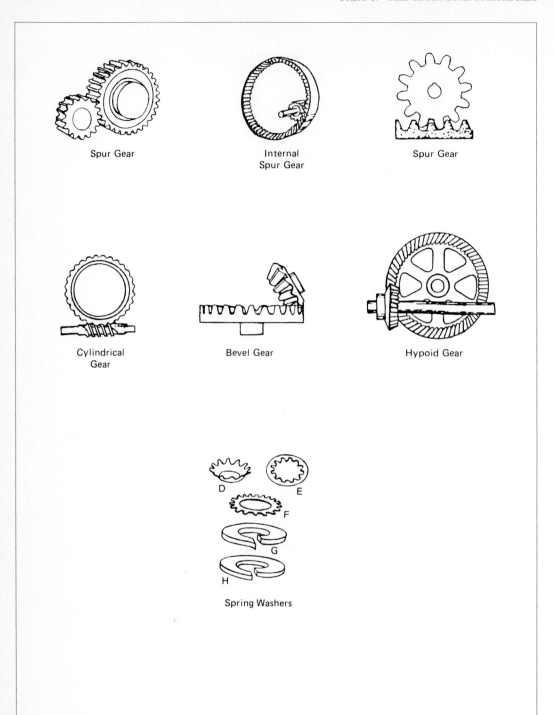

FIGURE 14.1   *continued (**gears and washers**)*

TERMS USED IN MECHANISM DESCRIPTIONS

arc	face	nut	teeth
arm	fin	slotted	threads
assembly	fitting	square	tip
	flange	wing	toe plate
ball	frame		tray
bar	funnel	O-ring	trigger
barrel			tube
bearing	gauge	pad	
bevels	gear	pin	wand
blade	gradients	plate	washer
bolt	groove	plug	webbing
bore	guide	plunger	wedge
bow		pocket clip	
brace	handle	point	yoke plate
bracket	hinge		
buckle	hook	ratchet	
bushing	housing	reservoir	*Materials*
	hub	ribbing	aluminum
calibrations		ring	copper
cap	jacket	rivet	non-corroding
casing			metal
channel	key	screw	plastic
clamp		metal	pot metal
clip	latch	recess	steel
coil	leg	wood	anodized
collar	leg ring	shell	drop-forged
cone	lever	sleeve	galvanized
cotter pin	lip	slot	stainless
		socket	
diaphragm	marking	spline	
disk	matting	spool	
dowel	mouth	spring	
		stem	
extension arm	nib	stopper	
eye bolt	nozzle	switch	

FIGURE 14.2 *Some terms used in mechanism descriptions*

Finishes	Shapes	Attachment methods
brushed	circular	coiled
buffed	concave	compressed
etched	conical	crimped
glazed	convex	flange/slot attachment
lacquered	cylindrical	
lustrous	flared	glued
matte (dull)	grooved	riveted
stain	hexagonal	screwed
semi-gloss	hollow	soldered
	octagonal	welded
	rectangular	
	solid	
	square	
	tapered	
	triangular	
	u-shaped	

FIGURE 14.2   *continued*

CONCLUDING DISCUSSION/ASSESSMENT

The concluding discussion assesses the efficiency, reliability, and practicality of the mechanism. This assessment may include an examination of the mechanism's advantages and disadvantages, its limitations, its optional uses, the comparison of one model to another model, and the cost and availability.

Example

The Bostich B8 desk stapler is compact and lightweight, making it easy to store and to transport. The finish is scratch resistant and rust proof. It can be used as a tacker as well as a paper stapler.

No more than 20 pages of copy can be stapled at one time. The Bostich Standard stapler is recommended for larger volume.

The recommended retail price is $8.95. A box of 5000 staples is approximately $3.00. The Bostich Standard stapler is sold for $16.75. The Bostich staplers are available in most office supply stores.

Figures 14.3 and 14.4 show sample mechanism descriptions. Figure 14.3 is a general description while Figure 14.4 is a specific mechanism description employing far more detail. Be prepared to critique the samples in class.

A STOP VALVE

**Definition
and purpose**

    A screw-down stop valve is a tap which is used to control the flow of liquids and gases. A water faucet is a stop valve.

**Operation of
parts**

    A stem or screw spindle is surmounted by a handwheel. The water flows through an opening whose edge forms the valve seat. The stem has a disc which is usually provided with a replaceable sealing washer to make the actual contact with the seat and thus stop the flow of water.

**Parts named
in text**

    To open the tap, the disc is raised by rotating the handwheel in a counter-clockwise direction so that the stem is screwed out of the valve body. Clockwise rotation brings the valve disc into contact with the seat and thus closes the tap. Figures 1 and 2 show the screw-down stop valve in the closed and open positions.

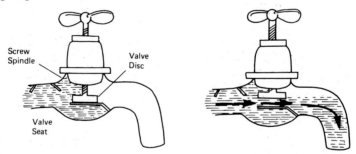

Figure 1   Closed   **Figure 2   Open**

**Concluding
discussion**

    Other types of taps are plug cocks and sluice valves. The screw-down stop valve allows for more accurate control of the rate of flow of the fluid

FIGURE 14.3   *General description of a mechanism*

than does the plug cock. Sluice valves, which have stuffing boxes to prevent

leakage, are used to control the flow in water mains, pipelines, and so forth.

Screw-down stop valves are readily available from plumbing supply houses.

FIGURE 14.3   *continued*

DESCRIPTION OF THE VENOJECT BLOOD COLLECTION SYSTEM

Intended audience

This description of the Venoject Blood Collection System, which is used for obtaining blood specimens for laboratory tests, is intended for medical laboratory students.

General Description

Definition and purpose

The Venoject Blood Collection System obtains blood specimens for laboratory tests. It is designed to obtain multiple blood sample tubes from a patient with only one puncture site required.

Overall description

Assembled, the steel, glass, and plastic parts measure approximately 6 inches long depending upon the length of the selected tube. Figure 1 shows the assembled system:

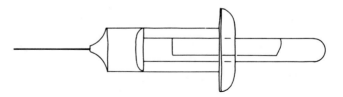

Figure 1   The Venoject Blood Collection System

Theory

The system operates on the principle of a vacuum in the collecting tube. First, the stopper on the top of the tube is punctured by the needle, allowing

Process

the blood sample to flow into the tube and stop when the tube is full. Second,

FIGURE 14.4   *Specific description of a mechanism* (Courtesy of student Joanne Fata)

when the full tube is removed, the needle stops the blood flow until another tube is punctured by the needle. This procedure can be repeated for each tube needed for specific blood tests with no discomfort to the patient. Figure 2 shows the Venoject System in a venipuncture procedure:

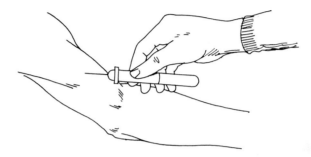

Figure 2   Venoject System in venipuncture procedure

List of parts

The Venoject System consists of three main parts: the double-pointed needle assembly, the adapter, and the blood-collecting tube.

Functional Description

Purpose of first part

The first main part, the needle assembly, functions in two ways: it pierces the skin at the site, and it closes off the blood flow when a collecting tube is not attached. The needle assembly consists of three subparts: the

Description

needle, the connector, and the cover. The 2.4-inch sterile needle is hollow steel. A 2.1-inch plastic connector fits securely over the needle at the halfway point. It has threads that screw into the holder and an extended tube to

FIGURE 14.4   *continued*

protect the end of the needle which is inserted into the collecting tube. A

plastic cover protects the needle until it is to be used. Figure 3 illustrates

the needle and plastic cover:

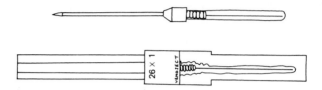

Figure 3   *Venoject double-pointed needle with plastic cover*

**Purpose of
second part**

Description

The second functional part, the adapter holder, connects the needle and

the collecting tube. The 2.8-inch, plastic, cylindrical holder has a diameter

of ¾ inch. One end is threaded to receive the needle; the other end is open

to receive the collecting tube. Figure 4 shows the holder:

Figure 4   *Venoject System holder*

FIGURE 14.4   *continued*

Purpose of
third part

Description

The third part, the collecting tube, is designed as a vacuum to collect the blood. It consists of three subparts: the tube, a rubber stopper, and a label tape. Hollow, glass tubes are available in 3-inch, 3½-inch, and 4-inch lengths; the two shorter tubes have a ¼-inch diameter while the 4-inch tube has a ½-inch diameter. A color-coded rubber stopper is inserted into or over the open end of the tube. The color of the stopper indicates whether the tube contains an anti-coagulant which is necessary for certain blood tests. The collecting tubes in general use are not sterile; sterile tubes are available when needed for bacterial determinations. A plastic label to record the patient's name and date is taped onto every tube. Figure 5 shows three collecting tubes with rubber stoppers and labels in place:

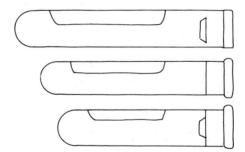

Figure 5 Venoject collecting tubes

Concluding Discussion

Assessment

The Venoject Collecting System is an efficient apparatus for collecting

FIGURE 14.4 *continued*

blood for any number of laboratory tests. It allows the technician to obtain

multiple samples while preserving the patient's vein. Because it is a

disposable system, bacteria and hepatitis can not be transmitted from one

patient to another. It is available at medical supply houses.

FIGURE 14.4   *continued*

EXERCISES

1. Reorganize these sentences into a logical description.

    a. The air pump consists of three main parts: barrel assembly, the plunger assembly, and the hose.

    b. It is compact, lightweight, and portable.

    c. The hand-operated air pump is designed for inflating bicycle tires and sporting goods, such as basketballs, footballs, rubber rafts, and so on.

    d. It has a 60 psi (pounds per square inch) rating.

    e. The rustproof, steel construction will ensure many years of useful service.

    f. The brass, octagonal barrel cap allows access to the pump mechanism diaphragm. It is threaded to attach to the housing and has a $\frac{1}{4}$-in. hole in its center to slide over the shaft. A $\frac{1}{8}$-in. hole in the side of the cap allows air to enter the housing.

    g. The barrel assembly consists of three subparts: the housing, a barrel cap, and a toe plate.

    h. The operator clamps the hose nozzle onto the filler stem of a tire to be inflated, stands on the toe plate, and pumps the plunger up and down to inflate the tire with air. If the item to be inflated is a sporting good, the supplied filler needle is inserted into the nozzle clamp.

    i. The housing is a hollow, $4\frac{1}{2}$-in. by 17-in. steel barrel. The top end is threaded to receive the barrel cap.

    j. The 18-in., fabric-covered, rubber hose screws into the barrel housing 1 in. above the base with an air-tight brass fitting.

    k. A 6-in., wood handle threads onto the top of the rod.

    l. Welded to the bottom of the barrel housing is a $4\frac{1}{2}$-in.-long toe plate base on which the operator stands during the operation of the pump's plunger mechanism.

    m. The plunger assembly consists of three subparts: a rod, a handle, and a diaphragm.

    n. The locking clamp nozzle is inserted into the hose end and is secured with a $\frac{1}{8}$-in. metal band. A thumb chuck allows quick release for regular and high-pressure use.

    o. The rod is a $\frac{1}{4}$-in. by $16\frac{1}{2}$-in., threaded steel shaft.

    p. The plunger assembly fits into the housing and is secured by the barrel cap.

    q. The pump is $16\frac{1}{2}$ in. high and is constructed of steel with rubber hosing and brass fittings.

    r. A diaphragm, a leather washer, is secured to the lower end of the rod by two $\frac{1}{4}$-in. nuts.

2. Rewrite the following portion of a mechanism description to eliminate the instructional commands. Use third-person subjects, present-tense verbs in the active or passive voice.

> The operation of a socket wrench is simple. First, select the proper socket size for a specific fastener. Second, lock the socket into place on the driving lug. Third, fit the socket end of the wrench over the fastener. Fourth, set the direction control to the right or left by moving the fastener counterclockwise. Fifth, move the handle in a right to left or left to right motion to twist the fastener. Simultaneously, place your free hand over the wrench and fastener to secure the wrench to the fastener.

3. Correct the mechanics of these sentences by adding hyphens and commas.

    a. The frame is nine and one half centimeters long.

    b. The six in. long handle connects to the barrel with two 12 mm long copper rivets.

    c. The top portion has a centered 25 centimeter circular cutout.

    d. Figure 9 illustrates a spring loaded L shaped latch.

    e. The base is bolted to the cylinder by two in. diameter bolts.

WRITING OPTIONS

1. Write a *general* description of one of the following mechanisms or a mechanism used in your field of study. Do not concentrate on a particular brand. Select a non-electric mechanism which consists of four or five main parts with subassemblies for at least three of the parts. Use graphics whenever possible.

a. deadbolt lock	h. hand drill	o. drawing compass
b. skateboard	i. eggbeater	p. pencil sharpener
c. paper punch	j. folding lawn chair	q. manual can opener
d. Rolodex file	k. toggle switch	r. kerosene lamp
e. tape cassette	l. stethoscope	s. sink trap
f. technical pen	m. butane hair curler	t. lawn sprinkler
g. bicycle seat	n. garlic press	

2. Select a mechanism from the above list or one used in your field and write a *specific* description of it; that is, describe a specific model or brand, such as a Honda Accord automobile jack, a Staedtler/Mars drafting compass, or a Flint eggbeater. Refer to the sample outline in this chapter. Do not stint on details, and use graphics whenever possible.

3. Select a "mechanism" from the following list and write a description of it. Refer to the sample outline in this chapter. Again, use copious detail and graphics for a complete description.

a. flatworm	e. human tongue	h. goldfish
b. human ear	f. human eye	i. amoeba
c. human knee	g. human heart	j. housefly's eye
d. microwave oven		

CHAPTER 15

Giving Instructions

by Bruce Hammond

After studying this chapter, you should be able to

1. Define *instructions*.
2. Appreciate the need for instructions in all enterprises.
3. Accurately title and provide prefatory material for a specific set of instructions.
4. Select appropriate formats for simple and complex instructions.
5. Critique a set of instructions for logical (sequential) organization and for completeness.
6. Critique a set of instructions for appropriate language.
7. Write a simple set of instructions embodying the appropriate writing strategies and graphics.
8. Write a complex set of instructions embodying the appropriate writing strategies and graphics.

INTRODUCTION

The ability to write clear, precise instructions in all career fields is crucial. Instructions are step-by-step commands which relay to the user how to locate something; how to make, assemble, maintain, or repair an item; or how to perform a task. In your professional training you have been bombarded with instructions on how to set up accounting ledgers, how to inspect a landscape project, how to administer cardiopulmonary resuscitation, how to construct a printed circuit board, how to approach a suspected felon's automobile, or how to perform other specific tasks in your particular field. In addition, you have probably mastered instructions on how to operate the mechanisms and machines used in your career.

From the first day of your employment you will rely on both oral and written instructions to learn what must be done and how to perform your tasks in the most efficient manner. Responsible employees are assigned to devise new instructions or to revise those on hand. These include how to fill out various forms, how to operate machines, how to expedite sales and services, and how to perform the myriad of processes particular to each profession.

In order to advance to supervisory and administrative positions, you, too, will need to be able to devise specific, accurate instructions for all phases of activity under your supervision.

In product-oriented businesses and industries, professional technical writers combine the writing strategies of definition, descriptions of mechanisms, instructions, and sometimes analysis of a process to produce comprehensive owner and service manuals (see Chapter 12). Such writers call upon the expertise of all other employees to perfect these essential documents.

AUDIENCE

The language of instructions must be slanted toward the intended audience. Usually, the user of written instructions is a novice (a beginner); therefore, the language should be very simple and nontechnical. Even in instructions for highly technical procedures, care should be taken to define all terms which are not in general usage. Graphics are key to effective instructions. Simple procedural drawings, illustrations of the mechanisms or printed forms to be employed, or even photographs of step-by-step actions will guide the user to perform the procedure correctly.

ORGANIZATION

Titles

The first strategy in writing effective instructions is to provide a precise, specific, and limiting title. "How to Inject Lidocaine into a Finger to Produce Numbness" is far more informative than "How to Perform a Digital Block." "Instructions for Removing a Faulty Transistor from a Printed Circuit Board" is more precise and limiting than "How to Repair a Circuit Board." Your title should indicate to the reader exactly what your instructions cover.

Instructions seldom read as a continuous narrative, but are numbered to separate each command. In simple instructions an Arabic numbering system (1, 2, 3, 4 and so on) is usually appropriate. Complex instructions may involve main steps divided into substeps. Preliminary outlining with attention to logical groupings will reveal the main steps and their parts. Several numbering systems may be considered: a variety of decimal systems or a digit-dash-digit system. The most reliable are shown on the following page.

Decimal System A		*Decimal System B*	
0.0	Preliminary section	0.0	Preliminary section
1.0	Section	1.0	Section
1.1	Component	1.01	Component
1.1.1	Subpart	1.02	Component
1.1.2	Subpart	1.021	Subpart
1.2	Component	1.022	Subpart
1.2.1	Subpart	2.0	Section
1.2.2	Subpart	2.01	Component
2.0	Section		

Digit-Dash-Digit System

0–1   Section
1–1   Section
    1–2   Component
        1–3   Subpart
        1–4   Subpart
    1–5   Component
2–1   Section

The digit-dash-digit system relies, in part, on indentation to divide the components and subparts under the sections. The decimal numbering systems may also use indentation to aid the eye. These numbering systems are more reliable than the traditional Roman numeral outlining system which combines Roman numerals, letters, and Arabic numerals.

Prefatory Material

Because instructions emphasize *what* to do but not *why*, it is helpful to include preliminary statements, such as naming the intended operator, stating the behavioral or instructional objective, defining key terms, or stressing the importance of the procedure. These may be included in the "O" preliminary sections of your format. Some sample prefatory materials follow:

0.0   These instructions are to be used by field service personnel to install a repaired DA-1203 antenna. Alignment of the DA-1203 to the aircraft's horizontal position gyro is necessary for proper operation of stabilized weather radar.

0–1   These instructions are intended for an allied health student learning minor surgical techniques. If followed properly, the student can anesthetize (that is, cause loss of pain and temperature sensation in) a finger. Anesthesia is necessary prior to finger surgery or before manipulation of broken finger bones. The anesthetizing of a finger or toe is termed a <u>digital block</u>.

Cautions, Warnings, Notes

The next strategy is to display preliminary warnings, cautions, or notes which apply to the entire procedure. Because such notations are not part of the instructions proper, it is advisable to capitalize, box, or underline such notices. Two examples follow:

CAUTION: DO NOT take an oral temperature if the patient

1. has difficulty in breathing,

2. is coughing,

3. is too weak to hold the thermometer in his or her mouth,

4. has a very dry mouth,

5. is mentally unbalanced or delirious,

6. has a nose or mouth injury,

7. is an infant or child who is not old enough to hold the thermometer in place, or

8. has had something hot or cold in the mouth within the last ten minutes.

Warning: Resist ink solvent and etching solution will cause skin damage. Always use rubber gloves when handling these substances. In case of accidental contact, wash the skin thoroughly with cold water.

Throughout your set of instructions there may be such cautions, warnings, or notes which apply to only one step. These should be placed before the step and should stand out from the actual instructional steps by the use of visuals.

Sequencing

Each of the actual steps or commands must be in chronological order. In the following excerpt from instructions on soldering a circuit board connection, Step 9 is obviously out of place; the joint would have to be secured prior to the actual soldering:

6. Preheat the joint to melt the solder.

7. Apply the solder to the joint.

8. Place the soldering iron tip against the solder and the joint for 2 or 3 seconds.

9. Secure the joint with a vise to avoid motion.

The writer of instructions is usually quite knowledgeable about the procedure, but the user is not. Therefore, not only is careful chronological order essential but also the inclusion of all steps is a must for effective operation. It is just as important to instruct users to turn on a word processing computer CRT as to instruct them on how to perform a global search of a text.

Language

Instructions demand precision, clarity, parallel construction, simplicity, and thoroughness. Each step usually begins with a command word, that is an active-voice verb stated in the imperative mood, such as *switch*, *disconnect*, *lift*, *depress*.

Incorrect	The following tools *should be collected*.
Correct	*Collect* the following tools.
Incorrect	*You cut* out the premarked damaged section.
Correct	*Cut* out the premarked damaged section.

Further, the command verbs should be precise.

Vague	Remove the bolt.
Precise	Unscrew the bolt by rotating the wrench in a counterclockwise motion.
Vague	Turn on the typewriter.
Precise	Depress the ON/OFF key to the ON position.

Occasionally you must precede the action command with explanatory words, such as

While depressing the RECORD button with your left forefinger, push . . .

Using a straightedge, outline the damaged portion . . .

Similarly, avoid all other vague terms.

Vague   Check the patch to ensure that a good bond has been obtained.

Precise   Pack the edges of the patch with stiff spackling compound to eliminate wobbling.

Vague   Allow the glue to dry adequately.

Precise   Allow the glue to dry for six hours.

Vague   Screw the woodscrews only partially into the anchors.

Precise   Place a stack of three nickels (approximately $\frac{7}{32}$ in.) against the mounting surface next to one of the screw locations and turn the woodscrew in until the head touches the coins.

In a set of simple instructions which are not numbered, words, such as *first*, *second*, *next*, *following*, and so forth, mark time and sequence.

Short sentences are easier to understand and to execute than are wordy commands.

Wordy   Insert the mounting post of the breaker arm into the recess in the cylinder so that the groove in the mounting post fits the notch in the recess of the cylinder.

Short   Fit the mounting post groove into the notch of the cylinder's recess.

Component parts of your instructions should be expressed in parallel (identical) grammatical form.

Nonparallel   1.0 Remove the damaged wall board.
    2.0 Prepare the patch.
    3.0 The patch should be spackled and painted.

Parallel   1.0 Cut out the damaged wall board.
    2.0 Fit a wall-board patch into the hole.
    3.0 Spackle and paint the patch.

In your effort to eliminate wordiness, do not eliminate articles (*a*, *an*, or *the*) or use pronouns (*it*, *them*, *that*). Instead of writing "Push them through circuit board holes" write "Push leads A and B through the circuit board holes."

Tools, Materials, Apparatus

A command to collect or assemble the necessary tools, materials, or apparatus is logically Step 1 of most instructional sets. A list that is vague will cause frustration for the operator if he or she only realizes halfway through the task that extra tools or materials to get the job done are needed. A precise list follows which accompanies a set of instructions on how to replace the points and condenser of a Briggs and Stratton #234 $3\frac{1}{2}$ horsepower lawnmower engine:

1.0   Collect the following tools and materials:

1.1 $\frac{1}{4}$ in. nutdrive

1.2 $\frac{3}{8}$ in. wrench

1.3 $\frac{7}{16}$ in. wrench

1.4   flywheel holder

1.5   starter clutch wrench

1.6   Briggs and Stratton #562 flywheel puller

1.7   screwdriver

1.8   .020 in. gap tool

1.9   Briggs and Stratton #25 points and condenser with depressor tool and breaker arm spring

1.10   flywheel key

1.11   five or six large rags

List such obvious items as old newspapers, running water, pencils, and paper. Do not assume that the user of your instructions has any familiarity with the task that you have probably performed many times. If you are planning an oral presentation, refer to the checklist in Chapter 17 (Figure 17.5).

Figures 15.1 and 15.2 show sample sets of instructions. Figure 15.1 uses a simple Arabic numbering system and graphics. Figure 15.2, because it involves main and substeps, illustrates a complex numbering system. Be prepared to critique each set in class.

HOW TO ASSEMBLE A HANDLEBAR AND STEM
WITH A LOCKING WEDGE ON A BICYCLE

To prevent any instructions or parts from being discarded, keep the carton until the handlebar is completely assembled. Keep all instructions on assembly for future reference.

NOTE: Torque (the measurement which indicates how much a nut or bolt must be tightened) is measured in foot pounds with a torque wrench.

1. Collect the following tools:

    adjustable wrench

    torque wrench

2. Slide the expander bolt washer onto the expander bolt.

3. Insert the bolt with washer into the top of the stem.

4. Slide the wedge onto the protruding bottom of the expander bolt as shown.

5. Unscrew counterclockwise the clamp nut, washer, and the

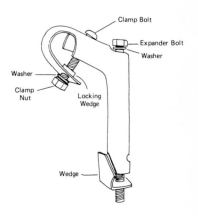

FIGURE 15.1 *Sample simple instructions*

locking wedge and remove the part from the stem.

6. Fit the stem over the small curved area of the handlebar and slide the stem to the center of the handlebar as shown.

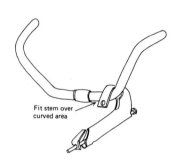

Fit stem over curved area

7. Assemble the clamp bolt, locking wedge, washer, and the clamp nut to the stem as shown and tighten loosely.

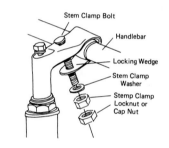

Stem Clamp Bolt
Handlebar
Locking Wedge
Stem Clamp Washer
Stemp Clamp Locknut or Cap Nut

8. Push the stem into the fork tube at least 2½ in. as shown on the side of the stem.

9. Align the straight part of the handlebar at a right angle (90 degrees) to the front wheel as shown.

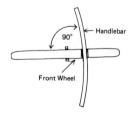

Handlebar
90°
Front Wheel

10. Using a torque wrench, tighten the expander bolt to a torque of 18 foot pounds.

FIGURE 15.1 *continued*

CAUTION: APPLY THE CORRECT TORQUE TO THE EXPANDER BOLT

OR THE FORK TUBE OF THE BICYCLE CAN BE DAMAGED

CAUSING A PROBLEM WITH THE STEERING.

11. Making sure the stem is at the

center of the handlebar, use a

torque wrench to tighten the

clamp nut to a torque of 23 foot

pounds.

FIGURE 15.1   *continued*

INSTRUCTIONS FOR TAKING AN ORAL
TEMPERATURE WITH AN ELECTRO:THERM

0.0   These instructions are intended for a medical assistant who is working in a doctor's office. If followed properly, the assistant will obtain an accurate temperature reading in less time than if one used a mercury type thermometer.

> CAUTION: <u>DO NOT</u> take an oral temperature with the electro:therm if the patient
> 1. has a mouth injury,
> 2. is an infant or young child who is not old enough to hold his lips closed when told to do so, or
> 3. has had something hot or cold in the mouth in the last five minutes.

1.0   Collect the following apparatus and place on the counter:
    1.1   an electro:therm thermometer
    1.2   a box of sterile plastic covers that are made to be used with the electro:therm
    1.3   a box of clean tissues
2.0   Familiarize yourself with the electro:therm by studying the parts as diagrammed in Figure 1:

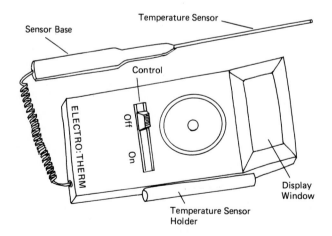

Figure 1.   *Parts of an Electro:therm*

FIGURE 15.2   *Sample instructions with complex numbering system*

3.0   Prepare the electro:therm for operation.

    3.1   Remove the temperature sensor from the control base by pulling the temperature sensor back towards the cord with your left thumb and first finger.

    3.2   With your right hand, pick up one sterile plastic cover by its paper wrapping.

> WARNING: Your hands should NOT come in contact with the sterile plastic covering.

    3.3   Insert the temperature sensor into the sterile plastic cover until the plastic cover is completely engaged over the narrow sensor rod.

    3.4   Gently pull off the paper wrapping leaving the sterile plastic cover on the temperature sensor.

Figure 2 shows what the temperature sensor looks like with the plastic in place:

Figure 2.   Temperature sensor with plastic cover in place.

    3.5   Switch the base of the temperature sensor to your right thumb and first finger.

    3.6   Pick up the control base with your left hand.

    3.7   With your left thumb, turn the control base to the ON position.

    3.8   Observe the electro:therm's flashing numbers in the display window.

> NOTE: The numbers are flashed every second and give the temperature in degrees to the nearest tenth of a degree, as illustrated:
>
> | 99.5 | | 99.8 | | 99.8 | | 99.8 |

FIGURE 15.2   *continued*

4.0   Take temperature reading.

> CAUTION: Unlike the mercury thermometer, the temperature
>   sensor should be held continually in the patient's
>   mouth while taking the temperature.
>   DO NOT remove the sensor from the patient's
>   mouth until the same degree displays at least two
>   times in a row. The electro:therm is so sensitive
>   that a patient taking a breath can lower the
>   reading.

   4.1   Insert the sterile, plastic-covered temperature sensor into the
      patient's mouth making sure it is under the tongue.

   4.2   Instruct the patient to keep lips closed tightly and not to talk.

   4.3   Leave the temperature sensor in the patient's mouth for one
      minute.

   4.4   After the minute has lapsed, observe the temperature as displayed
      on the control base.

   4.5   When the same numbers have flashed for two times, remove the
      temperature sensor from the patient's mouth.

5.0   Deactivate the electro:therm.

   5.1   Turn the control base switch to the OFF position with your left
      thumb.

   5.2   Place the control base on the counter.

   5.3   Switch the base of the temperature sensor to your left thumb and
      first finger.

   5.4   With a tissue in your right hand, pull the used plastic cover off
      of the temperature sensor and discard the tissue and the plastic
      cover.

   5.5   Slide the temperature sensor back into its holder on the side of
      the contrl base.

6.0   Record the patient's temperature on the chart.

FIGURE 15.2   *continued*

EXERCISES

1. Most of you have recorded a cassette tape and are familiar with the recording steps. Edit and rewrite the following instructions. Look for errors in organization, sequence, and completeness. Remember that notes, warnings, and cautions should be separated from the actual steps.

INSTRUCTIONS FOR RECORDING CASSETTE TAPES ON A STEREO SYSTEM

1. Press the PAUSE key.
2. Turn the selector to the program source: AM STEREO, FM STEREO, PHONO, OR AUXILIARY.
3. Press the STOP/EJECT key to open the tape door.
4. Simultaneously press the PLAY and RECORD keys.
5. Adjust the Record Level Controls so that the left and right VU meters will read −3 to 0.
6. VU meters show the recording and relative playback level of each channel. During recording, the meter pointer should move as high as possible, but not past the 0 db mark for best sound.
7. When ready to record, press the PAUSE key again to start the tape movement.
8. When one side is recorded, the tape will automatically stop.
9. Press the STOP/EJECT key again to open the door to remove the tape.
10. To stop recording, press the STOP/EJECT key once.

2. Edit the following set of instructions for language problems. Look for verbs which are not expressed in the imperative mood, active voice. Also look for vague verbs and other terms, too lengthy sentences, nonparallel constructions, eliminated articles, and questionable pronoun references.

INSTRUCTIONS FOR THE HOLGER-NEILSON (BACK PRESSURE-ARM LIFT) METHOD OF MANUAL ARTIFICIAL RESPIRATION

1–1 Positioning the victim
    1–2 Check the victim's mouth for foreign matter and wipe it out quickly.
    1–3 WARNING: CHECK it for obstructions every 30 seconds.
    1–4 Place the victim face down, bend elbows, and hands are upon the other.
    1–5 The victim's head should be turned slightly to one side with head extended and chin jutting out.

2–1 Administering the respiration
    2–2 Kneel at his head.
    2–3 You place your hands on the flat of victim's back.
    2–4 Rock forward until your arms are vertical to his back.
    2–5 The weight of the upper part of your body should now be forced down to exert a steady, even pressure downward upon your hands which are already placed on the back of the victim.
    2–6 Slide your arms to the arms of the victim just above elbows and draw the arms upward and toward you.
    2–7 NOTE: Enough lift to feel resistance and tension in his shoulders should be applied.
    2–8 The victim's arm must be lowered to the ground.
    2–9 Repeat this cycle twelve times a minute.

WRITING OPTIONS

1. Write a *simple* set of instructions of only twelve to fifteen steps using an Arabic numbering system. Select one of the following subjects or use a subject from your career field. Use graphics whenever possible.

   a. How to carve a turkey

   b. How to tune a violin

   c. How to build a campfire

   d. How to prune a bush

   e. How to care for poinsettias

   f. How to hem an unlined skirt

   g. How to make a back-up disc on a computer

   h. How to take an oral temperature

   i. How to make a thin blood smear

   j. How to set an alarm on a digital clock

   k. How to hit a golf ball (particular club)

   l. How to make a magazine rack

   m. How to wax a car

   n. How to take a blood sample

   o. How to operate an electric drill

   p. How to load film into a particular camera

   q. How to rescreen a door

   r. How to iron a long-sleeved blouse

2. Write a *complex* set of instructions which involves main steps and substeps. Select a digit-dash-digit or a decimal numbering system. Select a subject from the following list or use a subject from your career field. Use graphics whenever possible.

   a. How to move a block of type from one file to another file on a computer

   b. How to make a printed circuit board

   c. How to perform a preflight aircraft check

   d. How to install a smoke detector

   e. How to administer glucose intravenously

   f. How to operate a scuba regulator

   g. How to decorate a living room

   h. How to install vertical blinds (or floor tile, acoustical tile, and so on)

   i. How to edit an hour-long videotape for a 15-minute program

   j. How to design a magazine advertisement

   k. How to perform an engineering procedure

   l. How to operate a complex mechanism

   m. How to perform any procedure in your field which requires an operator to perform the task

3. Write a detailed set of instructions to a hypothetical substitute who must perform your job any given day next week.

NOTES

CHAPTER 16

Analyzing a Process

DUFFY   by Bruce Hammond

INTRODUCTION

Process analysis is a method of explaining how something occurred, how something is done, or how something is organized by separating the process into its parts to find out their nature, proportion, function, and relationship.

A process analysis may contain elements similar to instructions or mechanism descriptions but should not be confused with either. Instructions emphasize *what to do*, and mechanism descriptions emphasize *how something is put together*; neither often explains *why*. An effective analysis of a process emphasizes *what, where, when, how, to what degree, to what extent, under what conditions*, and, most important of all, *why*. The reader of an analysis must be able to judge the reliability, practicality, and efficiency of the process. The reader should be able to estimate the difficulty of the process, the problems likely to occur, and successful solutions to these problems.

Types of Analysis

An informational process analysis informs the reader about a particular process for the purpose of increasing his or her general knowledge. There are three basic types of process analysis:

1. The historical analysis explains how and why an idea or event occurred, or an institution originated.
2. The scientific, mechanical, or natural analysis explains how such processes occur or should occur.
3. The organizational analysis explains the steps, pitfalls, and methods of efficiently performing a human process.

Historical analysis explores such subjects as how the microcomputer was developed or how American teachers unionized. Subjects appropriate to scientific, mechanical, or natural analysis include how chemotherapy cures cancer, how sound waves are transmitted, or how the eye sees. Organizational analysis examines subjects such as how a plant is propogated or how a manager motivates a staff of workers.

AUDIENCE

The reader of any given process analysis is usually a novice; therefore, the language should not be highly technical. The writer should provide ample background material, define all terms, and use simple language. Remember that the reader wants to judge the process. Graphics, such as a flow chart or pictograph of the steps, drawings, or schematics of the process steps, and charts or tables of costs and time are helpful.

Language

Directions are written in the imperative mood to give a series of commands: *put*, *spread*, *you apply*, and so on. Process analyses are written in the indicative mood to explain steps: the technician *applies*, the worker *spreads*, the layer of resin *is smoothed*. These indicative mood verbs may be active or passive voice.

Avoid the words *you* and *your* in a process analysis.

Incorrect	All banks recommend when *you* receive *your* monthly bank statement that *you* reconcile *your* records immediately.
Correct	All banks recommend that their depositors reconcile their records as soon as they receive their monthly bank statements.

or

All banks recommend checking the monthly statements immediately to rectify personal records.

ORGANIZATION

A process analysis essentially consists of three parts: prefatory material, an analysis of the steps, and concluding discussion. This organization is similar to that used in a description of a mechanism (see Chapter 14). The following presents a typical process analysis.

1.0 Prefatory material (introduction)
   1.1 Intended audience
   1.2 Definition/purpose
   1.3 Background and theory
   1.4 Who, when, where
   1.5 Special considerations
   1.6 Tools, materials, supplies, apparatus, (if applicable with graphics)
   1.7 List of chronological steps (or graphic flow chart)
2.0 Analysis of the steps (body)
   2.1 First main step (with appropriate graphics)
      2.1.1 Definition and/or purpose
      2.1.2 Theory (if applicable only to the specific step)
      2.1.3 Special considerations (if applicable only to the specific step)
      2.1.4 Substeps (if applicable)
      2.1.5 Analysis of the step
   2.2 Second main step . . . (etc.)
3.0 Concluding discussion/assessment (closing)
   3.1 Results evaluation
   3.2 Time and costs (if applicable)
   3.3 Advantages
   3.4 Disadvantages
   3.5 Effectiveness
   3.6 Importance
   3.7 Relationship to larger process

A process analysis is usually written in a narrative format although it may employ outline, decimal numbering, or digit-dash-digit techniques (see Chapter 15). The writing strategies of process analysis may be interspersed with instructions and descriptions of mechanisms in an operator's or service manual (see the sample in Chapter 12). See Chapter 17 for a rating sheet and checklist for an oral analysis of a process (Figure 17.6).

PREFATORY MATERIAL

Titles

The title should be precise, descriptive, and limiting. Avoid a "how-to" title which implies that instructions, rather than an analysis, are to follow.

Examples

The Process of Taking Blood Pressure with a Sphygmomanometer

Preparing an Income Statement for a Small Business

How a Congressional Bill Becomes a Law

Audience Statement

You must consider the purpose and audience of your process analysis. Your audience will determine the extent of your analysis and the degree of technicality in it. State exactly what the purpose is and for whom the analysis is intended.

Examples

The process analysis of taking a patient's blood pressure is designed for a beginning nursing student with no prior experience.

This analysis of fire code inspection procedures, for fire chiefs, firefighters, and firefighter trainees, is designed to simplify and to regularize practices.

Definition/Purpose

A formal definition of the process or a clear statement of the purpose of the process is necessary before an analysis of the parts. The prefatory material may include definitions of other key terms to be used within the body of the report to avoid later interruption.

Example

Blood pressure is the force exerted by the blood against the walls of the blood vessels. It is created by the pumping action of the heart. The greatest pressure, known as *systolic pressure*, occurs during the contraction of the heart. The lowest pressure, known as *diastolic pressure*, occurs during the relaxation or rest period of the heart. The purpose of taking a patient's blood pressure is to relate it to other health factors, to determine if the patient is healthy, or to determine the cause of illness.

Background/Theory

It may be necessary to explain the historical or scientific background, theory, or principle of a process. Such discussion also belongs in the prefatory material.

Example

A brief understanding of the conditions under which blood circulates in the body is necessary. Blood passes from the heart throughout the body by way of a system of vessels that eventually return the blood to the heart. This journey is so rapid that a single drop of blood usually requires less than one minute to move from the heart through the body and back to the heart.

A single tube leading from the heart divides into smaller and smaller vessels, the arteries. The smallest arteries branch into capillaries, the most minute blood vessels. Through the thin walls of the capillaries, the blood supplies the body with oxygen from the lungs and collects the waste products of the body for subsequent removal by the kidneys and other excretory channels.

Beyond the capillaries, the branching process is reversed. The capillaries join to make slightly larger tubes, which next unite to form larger vessels, the veins. Eventually the blood is returned to the heart by two large veins. Therefore, pressure is greatest in the arteries and least in the veins.

One records blood pressure as a fraction, such as 120/80 mm Hg (the chemical symbol for mercury). The normal blood pressure for a healthy, resting adult ranges from 100 to 140 mm Hg systolic and from 60 to 90 mm Hg diastolic.

Who/When/Where

If your analysis involves an operator, the qualifications of the operator should be specified in the prefatory material. When and where the process is performed should also be explained.

Example

Nurses, doctors, medical assistants, and other paraprofessionals trained in the use of a sphygmomanometer determine blood pressure in the daily routine of patient care for diagnostic purposes. Because blood pressure will vary at different times of the day and because readings are usually taken for the purpose of comparison with previous readings, readings should be taken at the same time every day. Generally, only a doctor is qualified to evaluate blood pressure readings in relation to a patient's sickness or health. The readings are taken in a doctor's office, a hospital, at the scene of medical rescue operations, or in other clinical settings.

Special Considerations

Special conditions, requirements, preparations, and precautions which pertain to the entire process, and not just to one step, should be indicated in the prefatory material.

Example

It should be noted that many factors influence blood pressure. A patient should be asked if any of the following factors could be influencing his blood pressure at the time of the reading:

1. Increasing blood pressure factors
   a. eating
   b. stimulants
   c. exercise
   d. emotional stress

2. Decreasing blood pressure factors
   a. rest
   b. fasting
   c. depression

Other factors which should be considered are pain, climate variation, tobacco, bladder distension, hemorrhage (blood loss), blood viscosity (thickness), and the elasticity of the arteries.

Tools/Materials/Supplies/Apparatus

A precise, detailed list of all tools, materials, supplies, and apparatus used in the performance of the process should be provided. It may be necessary to write a brief description of an unusual mechanism used in the process (see Chapter 14).

Example

The following supplies are used to take an accurate blood pressure reading:

1. Stethoscope, an instrument used to magnify the sounds of arterial pulse.

2. Sphygmomanometer, a three-part instrument consisting of a mercury pressure gauge, an arm band with an inflatable rubber bladder, and a pressure bulb to control the flow of air going through connecting tubes in and out of the bladder.

3. Alcohol to clean the earpieces of the stethoscope.

4. Cotton balls to apply the alcohol.

List of Chronological Steps

After dividing the process into its main steps, each based on completion of a stage of work or action, the steps should be listed in chronological sequence: first, second, third, and so on. Use the following form or a flow chart.

Pattern   The process consists of _____ main steps; first, _____ing the _____; second, _____ing the _____; third, _____ing the _____; and finally, _____ing the _____.

Example   The process of taking a blood pressure reading consists of nine main steps: first, preparing the patient; second, assembling the sphygmomanometer; third, attaching the arm cuff to the patient; fourth, placing the stethoscope over the brachial artery; fifth, closing the pressure control valve; sixth, inflating the cuff; seventh, opening the control valve; eighth, taking the reading; and ninth, removing the apparatus.

ANALYSIS OF THE STEPS

The body of the process analysis thoroughly examines and analyzes each step. Your emphasis here should be to explain why the process is performed in a particular manner. Analyze what would happen if the process were not performed in the correct manner.

Definition/Purpose

Identify each step and write a formal definition and/or a statement of purpose of the step.

Example

The fourth step, placing the stethoscope over the brachial artery, is done so that the clinician can hear the rhythmical, thumping sounds of the blood. The brachial artery is the large artery of the arm at the inner crease of the elbow.

Theory

If a particular step is based on a theory, explain how the theory applies to the step.

Example

The brachial artery is used because it is near the heart, large enough for specific recognition, and near the surface of the skin.

Special Conditions

Describe in detail any special considerations, requirements, apparatus, preparations, and precautions which apply to this step only.

Example

In most patients, the brachial artery is found quite simply. If there is any difficulty in locating it, the opposite arm may be more yielding. An injured arm or one that contains an intravenous injection should not be used.

Substeps

If a main step contains substeps, list them chronologically prior to explaining each.

Example

The third step, attaching the arm cuff to the patient, consists of three substeps: checking the cuff bladder, positioning the cuff, and attaching the cuff to the arm.

Analysis of Steps

Finally, explain each step and its substeps with attention to the reasons each is performed in a specific manner.

Example

The cuff bladder should not contain any air at the time of positioning the cuff. If it does, a secure fit will not be affected. The armband is wound around the arm above the elbow at a level with the heart allowing room beneath it for the stethoscope bell. The band is fastened by means of the hooks, snaps, or Velcro material provided for this purpose. If no means of fastening are provided, the end of the band may be tucked securely under the top of the band. If the band is wound too tightly, it will bind the arm, create extra pressure, and cause discomfort to the patient. If the band is wound too loosely, the sounds will be deadened by the cushion of air required to tighten the band sufficiently to compress the brachial artery.

Each main chronological step should be analyzed by the same writing strategies.

CONCLUDING DISCUSSION/ASSESSMENT

One or more of the following factors should be discussed in the conclusion:

- Time and cost
- Advantages
- Disadvantages
- Effectiveness
- Importance
- Relationship to a larger process

Some of these points may already have been covered in the introduction. Keep in mind that your reader is seeking to assess the efficiency of the process.

The following concluding discussion explains time and cost, advantages, importance, and relationship to the process.

Example

Taking a blood pressure reading requires only a few minutes. Because such readings are routine in regular medical check-ups and patient care, the cost is included in the consultation fee. Many health associations provide free blood pressure readings to the public in such places as shopping centers, libraries, and schools.

A blood pressure reading is the one sure method of detecting hypertension, the silent killer. Early detection can prevent strokes, coronaries, and kidney failures.

It is important to have an ongoing record of readings so that variations can be detected. By itself, a reading will not tell the doctor what is wrong, but along with other diagnostic procedures, it will help to determine a patient's condition.

Figure 16.1 shows another organizational process analysis. Be prepared to critique the sample in class.

STOPPING THE FELONY SUSPECT'S VEHICLE

Audience

This analysis is designed for police academy trainees with no prior police experiences.

Purpose/Definition

The purpose of this analysis is to familiarize police academy students with the correct, efficient, and safe way to stop a felony suspect in a vehicle. A felony is any crime, defined by law, for which the culprit could receive imprisonment in a penitentiary or the death sentence.

Background

During a tour of duty a police officer may observe thousands of vehicles. He may observe a license number of a wanted or stolen vehicle, or he may recognize a wanted criminal inside a vehicle. In any such encounter, the police officer must immediately distinguish between proper procedures and carelessness. At times, officers have failed to make full use of the advantages which proper procedures offer. Fear of being called "overcautious" of or "crying wolf" have led some officers to disregard the responsibility of self protection.

Precaution

Before stopping a suspected felon in a vehicle, the officer should ascertain that a supporting or back-up officer will be available for assistance.

Who/When/Where

This process could be performed by any police officer in any city, county, or state when a felony suspect is spotted in a vehicle.

Tools

The officer requires a patrol car, a two-way radio, and a service pistol.

Steps

Stopping a felony suspect in a vehicle consists of five main steps:

FIGURE 16.1 *Sample process analysis* (Courtesy of student Madalyn McGown)

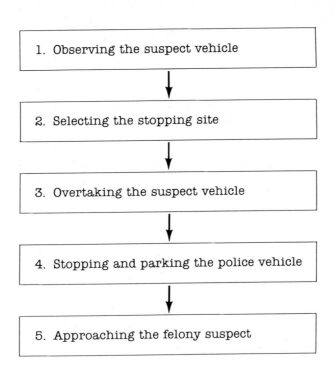

Analysis of Steps

The first step, observing the suspect's vehicle, requires the officer to notify the radio dispatcher at once. The officer gives the following information:

1. identification of the police unit,
2. location of the contact,
3. description of the vehicle and license number,
4. description and number of occupants, and
5. direction of travel and name of the last cross street passed.

The last cross street is broadcast at intervals to aid the dispatcher in predicting the suspect's course of travel, thereby hastening the arrival of supporting police units. The officer writes the license number, description of the car, and the number of occupants on a memo pad inside the police car. This is necessary in case the dispatcher did not receive all of the officer's radio transmission. The suspect's vehicle is trailed until the supporting

FIGURE 16.1   *continued*

units are close. The officer should be alert for sudden stops, turns, or other evasive action on the part of the suspect's vehicle.

The second step, selecting a stopping site, requires the officer to select a location with which he is familiar. Familiar surroundings will be to the officer's advantage as he will be able to direct additional assistance to the location more quickly. The officer will also be in a better position to make an apprehension if the suspect attempts to flee. Stopping near alley entrances, openings between buildings, vacant lots, and other easy escape should be avoided. At night, a well-lighted area will enable the officer to observe whether or not the suspect is disposing of any evidence or a weapon.

In the third step, overtaking the suspect's vehicle, the officer maintains constant vigilance to guard against any evasive action on the part of the suspect. At this time, the officer operates the siren and vehicle emergency lights. The police car is driven directly to the rear of the suspect's vehicle. Overtaking the suspect's vehicle is illustrated in Figure 1:

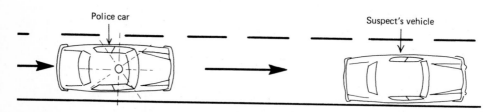

Figure 1   Overtaking the suspect's vehicle

The distance between the two vehicles will vary with the speed. Usually a distance of one car length for every ten miles per hour provides a safety zone for the officer. The officer should constantly consider the safety of other motorists and pedestrians in overtaking and stopping the suspect's vehicle. The suspect's vehicle should be stopped as far as possible to the right side of the roadway or off of the roadway altogether.

In the fourth step, stopping and parking the police car, the officer notifies the dispatcher of the location of the stop. The officer should park his vehicle about 10 feet behind the suspect's vehicle with the front of the police vehicle pointing toward the center of the street. The police vehicle should be on a 45° angle to the suspect's vehicle. The police vehicle position is illustrated in Figure 2:

FIGURE 16.1   *continued*

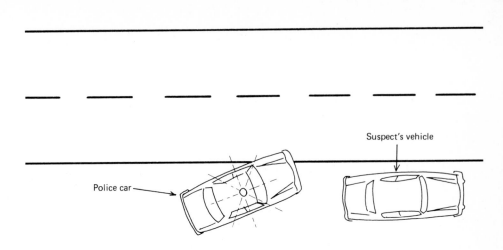

Figure 2 Parking position of stopped vehicles

The police vehicle emergency lights are left on so that other motorists will be warned of danger and the supporting police units will be able to find the officer quickly.

In the fifth and final step, approaching the suspect, the officer making the stop should take complete command of the situation. He should get out of the police vehicle and with gun drawn proceed to the left front fender of the police vehicle. Using the body and engine of the vehicle as protection, the officer identifies himself in a loud, clear voice: "Police officer! You are under arrest! Turn off your motor and drop the keys on the ground." The officer may order the suspect to place both of his hands out the driver's window or to place his palms against the inside of the windshield. The officer should stay by his police vehicle until a supporting or back-up officer arrives. The back-up officer should park his police vehicle to the rear and a little to the right of the first police car. The back-up officer should proceed to a position off the right rear of the suspect's vehicle with his gun drawn. The position of the police vehicles and officers are illustrated in Figure 3:

FIGURE 16.1 *continued*

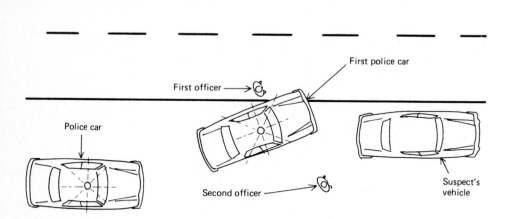

Figure 3   Position of vehicles and officers

The suspect should be made aware of the second officer's presence by the first officer to reduce the possibility of sudden attack from the suspect. The suspect is ordered out of his vehicle by the first officer. The first officer then orders the suspect to assume a search position.

Conclusion

Searching a suspect is another process and is not discussed here. No two felony stops are identical in nature. The unpredictable actions of the felony suspect make the officer rely on his training and judgment in each case. By following the steps in this process, the danger to the officer is minimized.

FIGURE 16.1   *continued*

EXERCISES

1. Classify the following process analysis subjects as historical (H); scientific, mechanical, or natural (S); or organizational (O).
    a. How earthquakes occur
    b. Changing a tire on a hill
    c. How the liver functions
    d. Planning a trip to Disney World
    e. The planning of a new mall
    f. How AIDS is treated medically
    g. How Hawaii became a state
    h. How intravenous fluids are administered

2. The following excerpt is from a process analysis of developing black and white film. Rewrite it to eliminate commands and the pronouns *you* and *your*. Use third person subjects and indicative mood verbs in the active or passive voice.

    In the first step, loading the film into the roll, you attach the film to the developing reel. Place the end of the film into the notch in the reel. Wind the entire roll onto your reel. Next, you place the reel into the developing tank. Snap the top securely into place. You may now turn on your lights.

WRITING OPTIONS

1. Write a *scientific* or *historical* process analysis on one of the following subjects. Use appropriate language and graphics.
    a. How women won the vote
    b. How the Honda Accord has been modified
    c. How the Appalachian Mountains evolved
    d. How dot matrix printers have been improved in the past five years
    e. How abortions became legal
    f. How Russia initiated *glasnost*
    g. How astronauts are trained
    h. How gum disease develops
    i. How a television image is transmitted
    j. How the lungs function
    k. How soap is manufactured
    l. How osmosis occurs

    m. How the telephone works

    n. How sound waves are transmitted

    o. How the president is elected

    p. How a compact disc is made

    q. How a fire extinguisher works

    r. How plants propagate

    s. How icicles form

    t. How rust forms

    u. How salmon procreate

2. Write an *organizational* process analysis employing appropriate language and graphics. You may select a subject from the following list or analyze a process performed in your particular field of study.

    a. Making clay tiles

    b. Tuning the motor of a particular car

    c. Recording a tape from a record

    d. Manufacturing tar

    e. Taking X-rays of the hand

    f. Preparing a porcelain filling for a tooth

    g. Blowing glass

    h. Applying vinyl (or ceramic or acoustical) tile

    i. Judging a debate

    j. Selecting an automobile

    k. Maintaining a fresh water fish aquarium

    l. Taking fingerprints

    m. Keeping records for income tax purposes

    n. Performing a preflight check

    o. Writing an airline toll ticket

    p. Apprehending a shoplifter

    q. Taking an EKG

    r. Removing sutures

    s. Checking a circuit board for mistakes

    t. Obtaining a credit card

    u. Interviewing a job candidate

    v. Planning a campus election

    w. Applying for a transfer to a university

PART 4

Oral Strategies

Verbal Communications

© 1982 Universal Press Syndicate. By permission.

INTRODUCTION

Effective oral communications are important in the work setting. Every organization requires its employees to develop speaking skills. To gain employment you must be able to speak persuasively about your own potential as well as express yourself knowledgeably about the organization which has granted you an interview. Secondly, once you are employed, you will be expected to demonstrate careful interpersonal communication skills in a variety of tasks ranging from telephone transactions and group decision-making discussions to formal speech presentations. You should even be aware of the nonverbal communications you will send and receive.

INTERVIEWS

Chapter 6 covers the writing strategies of the resume and cover letter necessary to obtain an interview. Speaking skills are equally important once the interview has been granted.

Preparation

There are many things you can do to prepare yourself for an interview:

1. Determine if the interview is a **screening interview** or a **line interview.** In a screening interview, numerous applicants are invited to speak with a number of interviewers, perhaps a search committee as well as the officers and directors of an organization. The objective is to narrow the pool of candidates for more intensive, follow-up interviews. In the line interview, only a few select applicants will be intensively interviewed by fewer personnel. The screening interview will be more informal than the line interview, yet in both situations what you say and how you say it will be assessed carefully.

2. Learn about the organization and the job. Speak to present employees, professors, and professionals who have contact with the organization. Know what services or products the company offers. Review its annual report if possible. Find out as much as you can about employment policies, potential layoffs or transfers, opportunities for advancement, union relations, competitive situations, and on-the-job training opportunities. Ask for a job description in advance to determine exactly what skills are required for the position.

3. Review your resume. Prepare brief, oral answers to the questions which are likely to be asked and prepare your own questions. This chapter will provide lists of potential questions.

At the Interview

Getting Started.   Although the interviewer has set the time, place, and type of interview and will control the line of questioning, you, the interviewee, have power to control certain factors which will put you at ease in order to present yourself at your best. You have alternatives, such as suggesting alternate times for the interview, asking for clarification of questions, taking your time in responding, refusing to answer personal questions which are not relevant, and asking questions of your own.

Body Movement.   Upon entering, pay attention to your posture and bearing. Shake hands firmly. If you are a woman, offer your hand first, for many males are still uncertain if it is proper etiquette to initiate a handshake with a woman. A handshake establishes confidence and warmth.

Sit comfortably without slouching or appearing too stiff. Keep both feet on the floor, and lean slightly forward occasionally to project poise and interest. Control your nervousness by avoiding any fidgeting or fiddling with pens, hair, papers, purses, briefcases, and the like. Do not drum your fingers or tap your feet.

Personal Space.   Establish a distance between you and your interviewer which is close enough to convey warmth and sincerity yet far enough to convey a degree of formality. Avoid sitting side-by-side. Do not violate the interviewer's space by sitting too close, moving behind the desk, touching beyond the initial handshake, or touching objects on the desk.

Eye Contact.   Look directly at your interviewer. Eye contact suggests confidence, honesty, and interest. Watching the other person will reveal how that person is reacting to your answers. You can expand, modify, or cut short your responses. Control your own facial expressions. Look alert and be responsive to the discussion. Try to judge the impression you are making during all stages of the interview.

Voice.   The acoustics of the room, the distance from the interviewer, and your own anxiety should be noted in order to modulate your voice to create a friendly, yet assertive, impression. If you talk too loudly or too high pitched, you will be offensive and boorish. If you talk too softly, you will appear "wishy-washy" or uninterested.

Accept or ask for water or coffee if your voice becomes raspy. A few sips will relax your vocal cords.

Questioning Skills

Your resume and application will have presented basic information about you, but both your interviewer and you will ask questions. The interviewer will expect you to summarize your qualifications. In addition, the employer wants to learn about your potential, your expectations, your attitude toward the organization, and your personality and character. By thinking about the following questions which you may be asked, you can prepare oral responses which are complete and confident.

Interviewer's Questions

1. Can you tell me about yourself? Expand on your resume? (Give a summary of your employment, educational, and personal background.)
2. Why do you believe you are qualified for this position? (Stress skills.)
3. Why did you select us in your job search? (Demonstrate that you have done your homework about the organization.)
4. What are your long-term career goals? What do you want to achieve in five years? Ten years? (Demonstrate that you have goals and expectations which are realistic.)
5. What are your strongest (weakest) personal qualities? (Name two or three each; negatives can be balanced against positives or recognized with a goal for improvement.)
6. How do you handle stress? How would you handle conflict between yourself and a subordinate (supervisor, peer)? (Summarize how you cope with personal stress, such as physical exercise, reading a book, gardening, and the like. Be prepared to answer how you approach problems.)

7. What have been your most satisfying and most disappointing school or work experiences? (Recite your accomplishments and stress how you overcame disappointments.)

8. What are your attitudes toward unions (absenteeism, punctuality, geographical transfers, shift work, weekend assignments, travel)? (Know in advance what the organization expects.)

9. Do you have any home or personal problems which may bear on your performance? (Be honest while stressing how such situations are being modified.)

10. What salary do you have in mind? Would you accept x amount? (Be prepared to give a minimum or a range, emphasizing need and goals. Accept or ask for clarification about work hours, promotions, and raise potential.)

Throughout the interview you should feel free to ask questions yourself. Seek clarification of any vague questions asked of you. Let your own line of questioning reflect that you are interested and serious about the organization. Decide which of these typical questions you want answered.

Interviewee's Questions

1. What are the organization's long- and short-term plans? Is the organization expanding or shrinking?

2. What is the potential for advancement in this position?

3. How does your organization support employee advancement? Are there educational opportunities? Grants? Training programs? Performance reviews?

4. What is the leadership structure? Will I have any decision-making authority?

5. What are the organization's relations with the community? Consumers? Related organizations?

6. What are the grievance procedures? Layoff policies? Leave policies?

7. What are your hours of operation? How much travel is expected? Do employees normally work many hours of overtime?

8. Are there any benefit provisions? (Insurance, pension plans, stock options, cars or housing provided, travel per diem, employee discounts, and the like.)

9. How is the housing market in this area? What cultural, recreational, and social opportunities are available in this city? How would you rate public transportation, schools, municipal services?

10. What are the wages and salaries? Are increases based on performance or indexes? What are the means of advancement?

Ending the Interview

The interviewer will usually signal the end of the interview, but you should have some closing questions. Ask what further information you should supply, what follow-up steps will be appropriate, and how and when you will learn the outcome. Remember that your interviewer is a busy person with others to interview and additional tasks to perform. Do not dawdle, but thank the person for the time and interest provided to you and leave decisively.

TELEPHONE CONVERSATIONS

Once you have the job, you become a representative of the organization. Many transactions are conducted by telephone both within and without the company. Your telephone etiquette reflects not only your own oral skills but also the organization's image.

Certain basic strategies will help you to convey and to receive messages in a professional manner. Talking on the phone involves both talking and listening skills. Pay attention to the volume, tone, and clarity of your voice. Do not shout or whisper. Your mouth should be about an inch or two from the speaker. Your tone should be warm and pleasant. Enunciate clearly; avoid slurring of "Hullo," "Whajasay?" "Yeah," and the like. Avoid distracting background noises, such as another conversation, typewriters, radios, tapping, blowing, or chewing.

Be prepared to take notes. Have a notepad, pens, and pencils on hand near your telephone. Have on hand, too, any reports, letters, or other printed matter which may be references for your conversation. Nobody wants to wait while you put down the telephone to search for these things.

Placing a Call.   When placing a call, identify yourself by a courteous "Hello" and state your name and other identifying comments, such as "Hello, this is Judy Withrow, the training consultant with Writing Skills Management. I spoke to you last Friday about the possibility of conducting a seminar for your midlevel management people." After an acknowledgment, proceed to state the purpose of your call, such as "I'm calling to determine if you received the brochures I mailed to you and set a date for an interview." After transacting your business, specify what it is you want your listener to do: call you back in an hour or a week, mail you material, or confirm details in writing. If it is appropriate, thank the listener for the information, interest, or time.

Receiving a Call.   When receiving a call, say "Hello" courteously and identify yourself, your department, or your organization: "Hello, Tom Brown speaking," "Hello. Personnel Department, Miss Shipley speaking," or "Ace Company. This is Bob Martin, Sales Manager. May I help you?" End the conversation courteously, too. It may be appropriate to say, "Thank you for calling," "I'll send the materials to you in today's mail," or "I hope I've assisted you." Say "Goodbye" in response to the caller's closing, and hang up carefully. A receiver which is banged down or dropped on its cradle may unduly irritate the caller who has not yet hung up.

If you answer the telephone for someone else, be doubly courteous. Let the caller know that the right number has been reached: "Hello, Ms. Steven's office; this is Jerry Thomas, her assistant, speaking. May I help you?" Do not make lame excuses for another's absence, such as "She's busy right now" or "I don't know where she is." State that the individual is engaged, in conference, or out to lunch, and offer to take a message. Do whatever you can to have the call returned.

OTHER ORAL COMMUNICATIONS

As a professional worker you will be expected to take part in a variety of oral information situations. These may include group or panel discussions, information gathering interviews, and appraisals and reprimands.

Group Discussions

From time to time you will be part of a decision-making group—a committee, a department, or even a larger group. Large groups tend to operate through parliamentary procedure to reach decisions while small groups operate less formally. We are concerned here only with small task groups.

A number of factors affect group processes, such as the purpose for which the group exists, the personal goals of its members which may be in conflict with the overall purpose, the permanency of the group, the power and relationships of the members of the groups, and the methods used for deciding. The most effective group is one with a clear purpose which is understood and supported by all of its members. Further, the longer a group can work together the less it tends to be dominated by one or two people. And, finally, a group which knows its decision will be accepted by others will be more successful than a group that perceives an outside threat or overriding decision-maker.

Decisions are made in groups by *majority rule*, *compromise*, or *consensus*. Majority rule, a decision by a vote, is common but tends to polarize the two camps making the losers less committed or even antagonistic to the decision. In a compromise decision, both sides give up a little in order to gain a little. Collective bargaining uses compromise decision-making methods. Compromise is effective if members of the group have to answer to larger constituencies. The constituencies can feel they won something and were not total losers, yet since nobody is 100 percent pleased with the decision, members may not work very hard to implement the decision. In consensus decisions all members agree on the decision. It is the most difficult way to decide but the most effective because all members are satisfied, which will lead to better productivity and commitment to implementation of the decision.

In order for a group to reach consensus decisions, all members should participate in clarifying a goal and establishing procedure. Establishing an agenda will facilitate consensus. If you are the initial leader of the group, you may exert a positive influence. Let each member talk freely about the goal and suggest procedures for the group to follow. Next, encourage or participate in a group discussion to determine the status and causes of the problem or situation. If appropriate, an effective group will then set criteria for evaluating solutions or decisions. Brainstorming solutions is a creative way to consider all possible solutions. In the brainstorming strategy all members offer as many different solutions as possible with no interrupting criticism or evaluation. These suggestions should be listed on a chalkboard or flip chart. Next, the solutions are weighed against the criteria to determine which is best in terms of effectiveness, cost, simplicity, possible implementation, and acceptability to the group. Finally, the group should decide how to implement the solution, delegating and accepting responsibility.

Information Gathering

You may often find yourself acting as an interviewer to obtain information from your co-workers, superiors, and people in other organizations. Do not waste time. Determine in advance exactly what you need to know, and organize and jot down topics which need to be covered. Be prepared to take notes.

In the actual interview clarify your overall purpose for the inquiry. Ask clear questions. Keep each question brief so as to elicit specific responses. Give the person plenty of time to answer. Be courteous and express your appreciation for the assistance. Finally, offer to share the results of your information gathering.

Appraisals and Reprimands

You will probably meet with your supervisor from time to time to assess your job performance. As you move up the career ladder, it may become your responsibility to appraise the performance of your subordinates. Giving and receiving reprimands are also inevitable transactions in any organization. Both appraisals and reprimands tend toward emotional communication, so strategies should be aimed toward objectivity.

A performance appraisal interview should be scheduled in advance so that both sides can prepare. The interview should be limited to a specific time period—fifteen to thirty minutes—to avoid repetitious harangues. Ideally, both parties should prepare separate written assessments of the performance. With these exchanged in advance, the parties may enter the actual interview prepared to concentrate on task-related factors rather than personalities. Explanations for poor performance may be offered, but the discussion should center on goals and methods for improvement.

In the reprimand situation, objectivity is also the key. One should offer written policies or procedural manuals which spell out the expected activity to substantiate that a violation occurred. The supervisor should attempt to determine if the violation was due to lack of information or was willful. Clear communication is essential. The supervisor needs to ask questions, use feedback, and be sensitive to the feelings of and possible penalty to the violator. The violator must be honest and concerned. Questions about recourse, appeals, and corrective actions are appropriate.

NONVERBAL MESSAGES

Oral communications involve more than the words being spoken. Our senses of sight, hearing, touch, and smell are also receiving messages which can color our perceptions of the spoken word. These perceptions are called *nonverbal messages*. A number of the message carriers have already been mentioned—posture and position, voice modulation, eye contact, handshaking, background noise, and the like. For effective communications you should be alert both to the nonverbal messages you send and those you receive. Ideally, nonverbal messages will be consistent with verbal messages, but such consistency is often violated.

Overt Actions.   Actions often do speak louder than words. Obvious actions, such as jabbing with a finger, pacing back and forth, waving papers around, and pounding on desks quite obviously signal aggression and anger. But subtle body actions, such as slouching, staring at the ceiling, standing with crossed arms, and the like, convey messages, too. Slouching conveys boredom; staring at a ceiling conveys disinterest; and crossed arms convey coldness or aggression. Open arm and body positions convey trust, warmth, and sincerity.

Covert Actions.   Some actions, such as blushes, tight jaws, smiles, and the like, reveal how a person is feeling. Who has not been confused by the person with furrowed brow and a tight-mouthed smile asserting, "No, I'm not mad at you"? Be alert to these signals in interpersonal communications, and learn to control your own covert actions in order to convey consistent verbal and nonverbal messages.

Eye Contact.   Eyes are the primary conveyers of nonverbal messages. Direct eye contact conveys interest and receptivity while reduced eye contact may convey concentration or deceit. Between communicators eye contact regulates interactions and monitors the verbal messages. Use your eyes to your advantage.

Appearance.   Physical appearances also convey messages although often inaccurately. We tend to stereotype persons according to three basic body types: athletic, frail, or obese. We expect the athletic person to be strong, mature, or self-reliant while we expect the frail person to be indecisive, bookish, or pessimistic. Examine your personal tendency to stereotype people by their body type and actively rethink the validity of these prejudices. Be aware of how your own body type influences the perceptions of others. Changeable factors in appearance— length of hair, mustaches, eyeglasses, uniforms, jewelry, cosmetics, hem lengths, and so on—convey impressions too. We attribute skills, personality traits, and abilities based on how people look.

Space.   Space is also an important nonverbal message carrier. The arrangement of office furniture or conference facilities can enhance or detract from open communications. Also individuals have a sense of territory; to encroach on another's space is perceived as a threat or an aggression. Even the distance that we set between ourselves and those with whom we are communicating conveys messages. Arabs and Latins tend to communicate at much closer distances than do North Americans or the British. Sensitivity to space arrangements will aid you in communicating the messages you intend.

ORAL REPORTS

You will be called upon in your career to make any number of informal or formal oral reports. These may be reports at meetings of your peers and supervisors, presentations at training seminars, speeches at conventions or before civic groups, or presentations to explain proposals and other projects. Oral reports are classified as:

- Impromptu speeches
- Memorized speeches
- Manuscript speeches
- Extemporaneous speeches

The impromptu speech is an off-the-cuff presentation likely to occur at a meeting where either you are asked about a project or you decide to present your views on an agenda item. A memorized speech may be appropriate for material which must be communicated many times, but it is difficult to avoid sounding wooden and mechanical in memorized speeches. A manuscript speech, one which is read, may be appropriate to convey very technical or detailed information but calls for exacting practice to avoid a monotone delivery and lack of eye contact. The extemporaneous report is the most widely used and effective oral presentation.

EXTEMPORANEOUS REPORTS

The extemporaneous report requires careful audience analysis, clear purpose, logical organization, supportive visual materials, sufficient rehearsal, and skillful delivery.

Audience

Previous chapters have stressed that an analysis of your audience is essential for effective written reports. The public speaker must also consider the audience who will listen to the oral report. Besides thinking about how much the audience already knows about your subject, what level of technical language is appropriate, and your relationship to the group, you should seek to discover in advance the average age of the group, political persuasions, religious or ethnic affiliations, rural or urban interest, and sex. Knowledge of these factors will help you to infer how the listeners will receive your information. These factors should indicate the degree of formality appropriate to your talk.

It is equally important to continue analyzing your audience during your speech through feedback. You can gauge your audience's reactions to your speech by noting facial expressions, postures, applause, and the like. The alert speaker will make adjustments in delivery based on this feedback.

Purpose

It is important to have a clear purpose in mind: to entertain, to persuade, or to inform. We are not concerned here with the entertaining speech, but as a professional many of your reports will persuade or inform your audiences.

Persuasion. The persuasive speech attempts to bring about overt action or to change beliefs and attitudes. Examples of overt actions are the purchase of products, the election of officers, the adoption of policies, or the alterations of procedures. A persuasive speech may also change workers' attitudes toward minority and women workers, encourage pride in organizational membership, and so forth.

Three strategies will help you to deliver an effective persuasive speech. First, consider *credibility*. Arrange to give your speech in a setting which is comfortable for the audience. Arrange, also, to be introduced by a person who is well-liked by the group and who will stress your qualifications to speak on the subject. Second, establish *identification* with the group by the way you dress and act or by actually expressing similarities in ideas, beliefs, or experiences. State your goals in an honest, friendly, and assertive manner emphasizing the rewards (anything that meets the needs and desire of the group) that your listeners will receive if they are persuaded. Finally, be prepared to present not only your evidence for your conclusions but also the *reasons* for believing the evidence is relevant to the conclusions.

Information.   The informative speech is the most common among professionals. Such reports may be patterned along the same lines as written reports, such as progress reports, instructions, analyses of processes, descriptions of mechanisms, and so forth. Do not lose sight that your primary goal is to impart information.

Organization of Report

Your evidence or data must be logically organized. A listener is not a reader. A listener cannot back up to review information or skip ahead to the conclusion. Organize your report with the listener in mind.

If your purpose is to persuade, you may consider the problem-solution organizational approach or the advantages-disadvantages approach. Figure 17.1 illustrates the overall organization of these approaches.

If your purpose is to inform, you will organize along the lines of the type of report which you are presenting orally. Figure 17.2 illustrates an overall organization approach to your speech.

Outlining.   Next prepare an outline of your actual speech and gather your information. Other chapters in this book review outlines and organization for specific types of reports.

Notecards.   Third, using your outline, prepare 3 by 5-in. or larger notecards of the main topics of your speech. Underline key points in red, and indicate by asterisks where you plan to use your visual materials. Use only one side of the notecards, and do not overload a card.

PROBLEM-SOLUTION APPROACH

I. Approach
    A. Gain attention and goodwill.
    B. Develop credibility, if necessary.
    C. Orient receiver to subject and purpose.

II. Body
    A. Develop problem.
        1. Explain symptoms or results (problem description).
        2. Explain size and/or significance.
        3. Explain cause.
    B. Develop solution.
        1. Explain solution.
        2. Explain how solution eliminates problem.

III. Conclusion
    A. Appeal for action or desire belief.
    B. Allow for discussion.

ADVANTAGES-DISADVANTAGES APPROACH

I. Introduction
    A. Gain attention and goodwill.
    B. Develop credibility, if necessary.
    C. Orient receiver to subject and purpose.

II. Body
    A. Explain disadvantages of present situation.
    B. Explain advantages of new idea, proposal, policy, or situation.
    C. Explain that advantages cannot be obtained without proposed
        changes.

III. Conclusion
    A. Appeal for action.
    B. Allow for discussion.

FIGURE 17.1 *Persuasive oral report approaches*

INFORMATIVE SPEECH APPROACH

I.   Introduction
    A.   Gain attention and goodwill.
    B.   Orient receiver to subject and purpose.

II.   Body
    A.   Present data in logical organization.
    B.   Repeat key terms and provide verbal transitions between parts.
    C.   Employ visual aids.

III.   Closing
    A.   Summarize.
    B.   Emphasize.
    C.   Allow for questions and/or discussion.

FIGURE 17.2   *Informative oral report approach*

Visual Material

Prepare visuals to clarify and emphasize your information. Visual materials may include chalkboard or flip-chart notes and drawings; posters of tables, charts, drawings, and the like; handout sheets; exhibits of models, equipment, or brochures; dramatizations and demonstrations; and/or projections of slides, filmstrips, or transparencies.

The size of the room or auditorium, the kind of people in your audience, the available monies, the available equipment (chalkboards, projectors, tables, and so forth), and the nature of your speech are all factors for consideration in planning visual material.

Chapter 3 discusses the value and conventions of graphics in written reports. Those same principles govern visual materials for oral reports.

Posters and Transparencies. Two simple graphic materials to construct are posters and transparencies. Posters do not require special equipment. They may be mounted on a wall, blackboard, or tripod near your podium for reference during your speech. Use a pointer to direct attention to visual detail. Be careful not to block the content with your body. Allow your audience to examine the supplements following the report.

Transparencies will require an overhead projector and a screen or blank wall. You may cover some information with paper and then expose the data as you are ready to discuss a point. You may add notations or color to transparencies during your speech without losing eye contact. In addition, your artwork can be photocopied for handouts to relieve your audience from copying complex graphics.

Effective Design. Effective visual materials are characterized by five factors:

- Simplicity
- Unity
- Emphasis
- Balance
- Legibility

1. **Simplicity.** Fewer elements are more pleasing to the eye than are a hodgepodge of detail. Bold, key detail has more impact than does complex art. If the material contains verbal data, limit it to fifteen to twenty words.
2. **Unity.** Unity may be achieved by overlapping elements, arrows, and a conformity of shapes and sizes on any one graphic. Do not lay out your drawings randomly.
3. **Emphasis.** Use color, bold sizes, and white space to achieve emphasis.

4. **Balance.** Balance may be formal or informal. Formal balance is achieved when an imaginary axis divides the design into two mirror halves horizontally or vertically. Informal balance is asymmetrical. It is more dynamic and more attention-getting.

5. **Legibility.** Wording on visual materials should be minimal. Sanserif or gothic letters are easier to read than script. Use capital letters for short titles and labels, but use a combination of upper- and lowercase letters for verbal content of six or more words. Base your letter size on the maximum anticipated viewing distance. The maximum viewing distance is generally accepted as being eight times the horizontal dimensions of the graphic. Thus, a 2-foot-wide poster has a maximum viewing distance of 16 feet, and a transparency projection on a 4-foot screen has a maximum viewing distance of 32 feet. Minimum letter sizes are 1-in. high on posters and $\frac{1}{4}$-in. high for transparencies. Thick letters are more legible than thin letters.

Rehearsal

Rehearse your speech a number of times before you actually give it. Practice before a mirror, and use a tape recorder. If possible, give your speech to a small group of friends. Ask them to assess your poise, eye contact, voice, gestures, and rate.

Your voice should be conversational, confident, and enthusiastic. Avoid a monotonous sound by varying the pitch, intensity, volume, rate, and quality of your voice.

Delivery

All of the preceding steps should prepare you for an effective delivery. How your audience perceives you and your information depends on skillful delivery.

General Appearance.   Dress appropriately. Approach the podium confidently and maintain good posture. Gesture naturally. Gestures may be larger in a large room than in a small room. Be animated and maintain eye contact. Do not be ramrod stiff nor clutch the podium. Do not jingle keys and the like or make distracting adjustments to your hair, glasses, or clothes.

Audience Interaction.   Pause before you begin your speech to gain the listeners' attention. Begin forcefully and engagingly. Keep tabs on your audience. Your listeners will be confirming or contradicting what you say through nonverbal messages. Allow for questions and discussion at the end of your report.

Notes and Visual Usage. Use your notes and visuals with ease. Place these items in comfortable positions. Do not fidget with your cards or pointers. Stand aside when referring to visual materials and maintain eye contact as you make your points about the materials.

Voice. Try for vocal variation. Let your voice exude warmth and sincerity. Pronounce your words clearly and distinctly. Do not vocalize "uh's," "um's," and other nervous sounds. Pause when appropriate.

ORAL RATING SHEETS

Figures 17.3 through 17.6 show speech rating blanks. Figure 17.3, a general speech rating blank, may be used to assess any extemporaneous speech. Figures 17.4, 17.5 and 17.6 may be used to assess an oral description of a mechanism, instructions, or an analysis of a process, respectively.

EXTEMPORANEOUS SPEECH
RATING SHEET

Speaker _____ Subject _____ Evaluator _____

ITEMS	COMMENTS	SCORE
ORGANIZATION: Clear arrangement of ideas? Introduction, body, conclusion? Pattern of development adapted to ideas and audience?		
LANGUAGE: Clear, accurate, varied, vivid? Appropriate standard of usage? In conversational mode?		
MATERIAL: Specific, valid, relevant, sufficient, interesting? Properly distributed? Adapted to audience? Personal credibility? Use of evidence?		
DELIVERY: Poised, at ease, communicative, direct? Eye contact? Aware of audience reaction to speech? Do gestures match voice and language?		
ANALYSIS: Approach to subject original, interesting? Central idea, purpose clear, divided into significant, interesting, subordinate ideas?		
VOICE: Pleasing, adequate, distracting? Varied or monotonous in pitch, intensity, volume, rate, quality? Expressive of logical emotional meanings?		

TOTAL _____

SCALE:

10	7	4	1
Superior	Average	Inadequate	Poor

FIGURE 17.3 *Extemporaneous speech rating sheet*

MECHANISM DESCRIPTION RATING SHEET

Speaker _____ Instructions _____ Evaluator _____

Did the speaker	Yes	Somewhat	No	Comment
1. Make necessary preparations before starting?	_____	_____	_____	_____
2. Define intended audience?	_____	_____	_____	_____
3. Name mechanism precisely?	_____	_____	_____	_____
4. Define and/or state purpose of mechanism?	_____	_____	_____	_____
5. Provide an overall description?	_____	_____	_____	_____
6. Discuss the operational theory?	_____	_____	_____	_____
7. State by whom, when, and where the mechanism is operated?	_____	_____	_____	_____
8. Provide a list of the main parts?	_____	_____	_____	_____
9. Describe the parts in the order listed?	_____	_____	_____	_____
10. Define and/or state purpose of each part?	_____	_____	_____	_____
11. List subparts of assemblies?	_____	_____	_____	_____
12. Describe each part adequately?	_____	_____	_____	_____
13. Avoid wordiness?	_____	_____	_____	_____
14. Assess the advantages and disadvantages?	_____	_____	_____	_____
15. Describe optional uses?	_____	_____	_____	_____
16. Compare the mechanism to other models?	_____	_____	_____	_____
17. Discuss the cost and availability of mechanism?	_____	_____	_____	_____
18. Avoid reading the presentation?	_____	_____	_____	_____
19. Use adequate, well-organized notecards?	_____	_____	_____	_____
20. Show evidence of rehearsal?	_____	_____	_____	_____
21. Maintain effective eye contact?	_____	_____	_____	_____
22. Speak clearly so all could hear?	_____	_____	_____	_____
23. Use appropriate graphics?	_____	_____	_____	_____
a. Number and title clearly?	_____	_____	_____	_____
b. Print legibly?	_____	_____	_____	_____

FIGURE 17.4 *Rating sheet for oral description of a mechanism*

Did the speaker   Yes   Somewhat   No   Comment

    c.   Keep graphics simple and un-
        cluttered? ____   ____   ____ _____

    d.   Lay out logically? ____   ____   ____ _____

    e.   Credit sources of graphics? ____   ____   ____ _____

24. Handle graphics with ease? ____   ____   ____ _____

25. Do you feel you can judge the reliability,
practicality, and efficiency of the
mechanism? ____   ____   ____ _____

SUGGESTED GRADE _____

FIGURE 17.4 *continued*

INSTRUCTIONS RATING SHEET

Speaker _____ Instructions for _____ Evaluator _____

Did the speaker	Yes	Somewhat	No	Comment
1. Make necessary preparations before starting?	_____	_____	_____	_____
2. Define intended audience?	_____	_____	_____	_____
3. Provide a specific, limiting title?	_____	_____	_____	_____
4. State the instructional or behavioral objective?	_____	_____	_____	_____
5. Stress the importance of the instructions?	_____	_____	_____	_____
6. Define key terms?	_____	_____	_____	_____
7. State preliminary warnings or cautions?	_____	_____	_____	_____
8. Divide the process into main steps?	_____	_____	_____	_____
9. Provide a precise list of tools, materials, etc.	_____	_____	_____	_____
10. Divide the main steps into substeps?	_____	_____	_____	_____
11. Provide warnings and notes for individual steps?	_____	_____	_____	_____
12. State each step as a command?	_____	_____	_____	_____
13. Avoid combining steps and substeps?	_____	_____	_____	_____
14. Express all steps in parallel, grammatical terms?	_____	_____	_____	_____
15. Avoid wordiness?	_____	_____	_____	_____
16. Avoid reading presentation?	_____	_____	_____	_____
17. Use adequate, well-organized notecards?	_____	_____	_____	_____
18. Show evidence of having rehearsed?	_____	_____	_____	_____
19. Maintain effective eye contact?	_____	_____	_____	_____
20. Use appropriate graphics?	_____	_____	_____	_____
a. Number and title clearly?	_____	_____	_____	_____
b. Print legibly?	_____	_____	_____	_____
c. Keep graphics simple and uncluttered?	_____	_____	_____	_____
d. Lay out logically?	_____	_____	_____	_____

FIGURE 17.5 *Rating sheet for oral instructions*

Did the speaker	Yes	Somewhat	No	Comment
e. Credit sources of graphics?	____	____	____	_____
21. Handle graphics with ease?	____	____	____	_____
22. Invite questions from the audience?	____	____	____	_____
23. Do you feel you could perform the set of instructions accurately and efficiently?	____	____	____	_____

SUGGESTED GRADE _____

FIGURE 17.5   *continued*

PROCESS ANALYSIS RATING SHEET

Speaker _____ Process _____ Evaluator _____

Did the speaker	Yes	Somewhat	No	Comment
1. Make necessary preparations before starting?	___	___	___	_____
2. Define intended audience?	___	___	___	_____
3. Name process precisely?	___	___	___	_____
4. Select a process primarily involving human action?	___	___	___	_____
5. Define or state purpose of process?	___	___	___	_____
6. Define or explain terms?	___	___	___	_____
7. Explain theory on which process is based?	___	___	___	_____
8. Indicate by whom, when, and where the process is performed?	___	___	___	_____
9. Indicate special conditions, requirements, preparations, precautions which apply to the entire process?	___	___	___	_____
10. Precisely list materials, tools, and apparatus?	___	___	___	_____
11. Divide process into five or six main stages?	___	___	___	_____
12. Arrange steps in numbered, chronological order?	___	___	___	_____
13. Provide a flow chart of main steps?	___	___	___	_____
14. Discuss steps in order listed?	___	___	___	_____
15. Define or state purpose of each main step?	___	___	___	_____
16. Divide main steps into substeps?	___	___	___	_____
17. Describe special conditions for each step?	___	___	___	_____
18. Explain theory which applies only to one step?	___	___	___	_____
19. Adequately analyze each main step with emphasis on why, to what degree, to what extent, etc.?	___	___	___	_____

FIGURE 17.6 *Rating sheet for oral analysis of a process*

Did the speaker	Yes	Somewhat	No	Comment
20. Avoid excessive detail?	___	___	___	_____
21. Evaluate effectiveness or process?	___	___	___	_____
22. Discuss advantages/disadvantages?	___	___	___	_____
23. Discuss importance of process?	___	___	___	_____
24. Evaluate results of process?	___	___	___	_____
25. Explain how process is part of larger process?	___	___	___	_____
26. Compare process to similar processes?	___	___	___	_____
27. Assess cost and time factors?	___	___	___	_____
28. Avoid reading presentation?	___	___	___	_____
29. Use adequate, well-organized notecards?	___	___	___	_____
30. Show evidence of rehearsal?	___	___	___	_____
31. Speak clearly so all could hear?	___	___	___	_____
32. Avoid shifting to instructions?	___	___	___	_____
33. Use appropriate graphics?	___	___	___	_____
a. Number and title clearly?	___	___	___	_____
b. Print legibly?	___	___	___	_____
c. Use color effectively?	___	___	___	_____
d. Keep graphics simple and uncluttered?	___	___	___	_____
e. Lay out logically?	___	___	___	_____
34. Handle graphics with ease?	___	___	___	_____
35. Invite questions from the audience?	___	___	___	_____
36. Do you feel you can judge the reliability, practicality, and efficiency of the process?	___	___	___	_____

SUGGESTED GRADE _____

FIGURE 17.6　*continued*

EXERCISES

1. Working in pairs, devise interview questions to use both as interviewer and interviewee for a specific type of position at an appropriate fictitious company. Role play in front of the class the interview situation. The class will assess your verbal and nonverbal communication skills.

2. Working in pairs, role play a business telephone transaction. Devise your own transaction or try the following situation. The caller has mailed a cover letter and resume to the director of personnel. The caller is trying to find out if the letter arrived and to arrange an interview next week. The callee, the director of personnel, is eager to arrange an interview. The class will assess the skills of both the caller and the callee.

3. Role play a group discussion among five or six classmates. The group is to reach a consensus on one of the following situations:

   a. A donor has offered $5000 for a scholarship in a professional field. The group is to decide how to implement the scholarship.

   b. A department in a business has $5000 budgeted for employee travel to professional conferences and seminars around the country for the fiscal year. There are ten members in the department; each member has two or three conferences he or she would like to attend. Expenses would range from $200 for short, in-county seminars to $2000 for week-long, out-of-state conferences. The group must decide on the criteria to spend the money. Following the discussion the class will assess the verbal and nonverbal skills of the participants.

4. Prepare a six- to ten-minute extemporaneous oral report with visual materials for one of the following situations:

   a. *A persuasive speech.* Choose a controversial subject (four-day work week, class registration procedures, bookstore policies, degree requirements in your field, and so on). Prior to your speech, pass out index cards to the class and ask each member to write opinions on this subject. Deliver your speech. Each classmate will evaluate your presentation by rating you according to the rating blank in Figure 17.3. Following the speech, ask your classmates to read their opinion cards and discuss how you have or have not changed their opinions.

   b. *An informative speech.* Refer to the chapters on instructions, descriptions of mechanisms, and analysis of a process. Select one of the report strategies; prepare and deliver an informative oral report. Each classmate will assess your presentation by filling out the appropriate rating blank in Figures 17.4, 17.5, or 17.6.

Conventions of Construction, Grammar, and Usage

INTRODUCTION

Effective communication depends not only on content and format but also on precise adherence to the conventions of sentence construction, grammar, and usage. This section will provide you with a brief handbook, exercises, and reference tables of professional and technical writing conventions.

The conventions that govern written English are not prescriptive rules. Rather, they are patterns developed by careful writers over decades and accepted by publishers, professional and technical writers, educators, and the public. Because English is a living language, these conventions alter over periods of time. For instance, it has long been conventional to use a comma before *and* in a written series of three or more items (i.e.: *He assembled the nuts, bolts, and rivets*). In recent years some publishers, businesses, and industries have agreed to omit the comma (i.e.: *He assembled the nuts, bolts and rivets*). Those who are concerned with language classify the conventions as *standard English* and *general English*. The majority of professional and technical writers adopt standard English conventions; therefore, this appendix covers the more formal conventions. Use these conventions to edit your texts and to troubleshoot your writing problems.

THE SENTENCE

Main Sentence Elements

A sentence is a group of words containing a subject and verb and expressing a complete thought. English sentences are arranged in many word order patterns which convey meaning. Lewis Carroll's nonsense sentence

> T'was brillig and the slithy toves did gyre and gimble in the wabe.

reveals patterns which make sense to English-speaking people. We recognize a subject and verb (*T'was*), the conjunctions (*and*), a helping verb (*did*), a preposition (*in*). Using the pattern we can develop any number of sentences:

> It was Monday, and the electronic technicians did assemble and test in the plant.
> It was noon, and the construction workers did toil and sweat in the sun.

There are five basic sentence patterns in English. Subjects, objects, and complements are nouns or pronouns. Verbs are words which express action (*jump*) or state of being (*is, seem*).

Pattern 1:   Subject + Verb

      S + V

Water boils.

Pattern 2:   Subject + Verb + Direct Object

      S   +   V   +   DO

Foremen supervise construction.

Pattern 3:   Subject + Linking Verb + Subjective Complement

      S + V + SC

Helium is a gas.

                 (A subjective complement renames the subject.)

Pattern 4:   Subject + Verb + Indirect Object + Direct Object

      S + V   + IO   + DO

The company gave Ms. Barnes a plaque.

              (An indirect object is the receiver of the direct object.)

Pattern 5:   Subject + Verb + Direct Object + Objective Complement

      S   +   V + DO + OC

The union elected him president.

              (An objective complement renames the direct object.)

There are actually many patterns beyond these basic five and many ways to invert or expand a sentence with single, one-word adjectives and adverbs or multi-word phrases and clauses. Consider that a Pattern 2 sentence

      S + V +   DO
      The man has a compass.

may be inverted to ask a question

      Has the man a compass?

or expanded to

               adjective clause
      The man <u>who shares my drafting cubicle</u> has

      adjective   **prepositional phrase**
      a <u>metric</u> compass <u>in his hand</u>.

Recognition of the basic elements allows you to construct sentences which make sense and to punctuate the elements according to the conventions.

Secondary Sentence Elements

Secondary sentence elements are typically used as modifiers; that is, they describe, limit, or make more exact the meaning of the main elements.

Adjectives and adverbs. Single words used as modifiers are related to the words they modify by word order. Adjectives modify nouns or pronouns and usually stand before the word modified.

ADJ   ADJ

He is a precise, concise writer.   (modifies <u>writer</u>)

Adjectives may stand after the modified noun or pronoun or follow a linking verb:

N   ADJ

The temperature made the metal brittle.   (modifies <u>metal</u>)

N   ADJ

The metal was brittle.   (modifies <u>metal</u>)

Adverbs, which modify verbs, adjectives, or other adverbs, are more varied in position. They usually stand close to the particular word or element modified.

ADV

He worked late.   (modifies the verb <u>worked</u>)

ADV

He worked quite late.   (modifies the adverb <u>late</u>)

ADV

He was rather late. (modifies the adjective <u>late</u>)

ADV

He had never been late. (modifies verb phrase <u>had been</u>)

ADV

Unfortunately, he was always late. (modifies whole sentence)

Edit your writing so that the modifiers are clearly related to the words or statements they modify.

Ambiguous:	The plasterers have finished the wall <u>almost</u>. (<u>Almost</u> seems to modify <u>wall</u>.
Clear:	The plasterers have <u>almost</u> finished the wall.
Ambiguous:	I <u>only</u> need a few seconds.
Clear:	I need <u>only</u> a few seconds.
Ambiguous:	The red brick doctor's office.
Clear:	The doctor's red, brick office.

Do not place an adverb within an infinitive phrase (<u>to read</u>, <u>to plan</u>, <u>to construct</u>).

Split infinitive:	We have to <u>further</u> plan the assembly.
Clear:	We have to plan <u>further</u> the assembly.

Exercise

Add adjectives or adverbs within each sentence. If more than one position is possible, explain what change of emphasis would result from shifting the modifier.

1. **Add <u>only</u>.**   Last week I ordered a computer package with a spelling checker.
2. **Add <u>definitely</u>.**   I am convinced that you are the one to complete the audit.
3. **Add <u>hardly</u>.**   Although I adjusted the lever, I could hear the bass resonate.
4. **Add <u>engineer's</u>.**   The well-worn report lay on the shelf.
5. **Add <u>carefully</u>.**   The committee has to read all of the reports.

Phrases as modifiers. A phrase is a group of related words without a subject or verb. It cannot stand alone. A phrase is connected to a sentence or to one of its elements by a preposition or a verbal.

Prepositional phrases. A prepositional phrase consists of a preposition (*in, at, by, from, under, at,* etc.) followed by a noun or pronoun plus, possibly, modifiers. It functions as an adjective or adverb, depending on what element it modifies.

He entered <u>from the door</u> (modifies the verb <u>entered</u>) <u>of my office</u> (modifies the noun <u>door</u>).

Verbal phrases. A verbal phrase consists of a participle, gerund, or infinitive (verb forms without full verb function) plus its object or complement and modifiers. A participial phrase functions as an adjective; a gerund phrase as a noun; and an infinitive phrase as either a noun, adjective, or adverb.

Participial phrase:	Circuit boards <u>containing any defects</u> should be scrapped. (modifies <u>boards</u>)
Gerund phrase:	<u>Drafting the blueprint</u> was the next task. (functions as noun subject)
Infinitive phrase:	<u>To conduct a market survey</u> (functions as noun subject) is the easiest way <u>to determine the cost.</u> (functions as adjective modifying <u>way.</u>)

Place modifying phrases next to the word modified. Participial and infinitive phrases will give you the most trouble.

Misrelated:	He distributed notebooks to the trainees <u>bound in plastic.</u> (The participial phrase seems to modify <u>trainees.</u>)
Revised:	He distributed notebooks <u>bound in plastic</u> to the trainees.
Misrelated:	The man who was lecturing <u>to emphasize a point</u> pounded the podium. (The infinitive phrase seems to modify <u>lecturing.</u>)
Revised:	The man who was lecturing pounded the podium <u>to emphasize a point.</u>
Dangling Participial Phrase:	<u>Looking up from my desk,</u> Jane gave me the report. (The phrase seems to modify <u>Jane.</u>)
Revised:	<u>Looking up from my desk,</u> I accepted the report from Jane.

Clauses. A clause is a group of words that contains a subject and verb plus modifiers. An **independent** (main) **clause** is a complete expression which could stand alone as a sentence. A **dependent** (subordinate) **clause** also has a subject and verb but functions as part of a sentence. It is related to the independent clause by a connecting word which shows its subordinate relationship either by a relative pronoun (*who, which, that,* etc.) or a subordinate conjunction (*because, although, since, if,* etc.).

Independent clauses:	<u>The water tastes brackish</u> because it is contaminated.
	<u>The laser beam penetrated the metal plate,</u> and <u>the plate glowed red.</u>

Dependent clauses:	If your engine is hot, add antifreeze.
	The drive belt which slipped shredded.
	After I attached the heat sink, the rectifier cooled.
	We will make a final test because a dry run was never completed.

Sentence Classification

Sentences may be classified according to the kind and number of clauses they contain as simple, compound, complex, or compound-complex.

Simple sentences. A simple sentence contains an independent clause and no dependent clauses. It may contain any number of modifiers or compound elements.

> The capsule exploded.
>
> The tiny, white, plastic capsule expanded and exploded due to the high temperature in the storage bin.

Compound sentences. Compound sentences contain two or more independent clauses and no subordinate clauses. They may be joined by coordinating conjunctions (*and, or, but,* etc.), semicolons, or conjunctive adverbs (*nevertheless, therefore, however,* etc.).

> A dot matrix printer is acceptable, but a daisy wheel printer produces easier-to-read copy.
>
> A Radio Shack computer is flexible; it allows you to print hard copy of graphics.
>
> A personal computer is expensive; nevertheless, it is a practical tool for the professional writer.

Complex sentences. A complex sentence contains one independent clause and one or more dependent clauses.

> Because it is raining, the slump test will be postponed.
>
> The engineer who originally specified seven pilings changed her mind when she considered the sand content of the soil.

Compound-complex sentences. A compound-complex sentence contains two or more independent clauses and one or more dependent clauses.

> Because the text is illustrated with tables and sample materials, it is an indispensable guide for technical writers, and it may be used by students and professional writers in business and industry.

Complex sentences are used more frequently than simple, compound, or compound-complex sentences in published writing today. Complex sentences allow for more variety than simple sentences and allow the writer to manipulate emphasis. Recognition of independent and dependent clauses is necessary also for adding conventional punctuation.

Exercise

1. Combine these simple sentences as directed.
   a. Combine into a compound sentence.
      A v-t voltmeter measures sine waves. An oscilloscope measures nonsinosuidal voltage.
   b. Combine into a complex sentence.
      Pressure-sensitive tapes serve the electrical industry well. They insulate all manner of equipment and last longer than other tapes.
   c. Combine into a compound-complex sentence.
      Magnetic memories can store more digital information on a par with optical disks. Optical disks can recreate visual images at a lower cost than magnetic memories. Optical disks can recreate visual images at a higher speed.
2. Rewrite these complex sentences to shift the emphasis as directed.
   a. Emphasize the idea that he disliked his car rather than the idea that it uses too much gas.
      He disliked the car because, as far as I could determine, it used too much gas.
   b. Emphasize the idea that soaking will separate the components rather than the idea that you can separate them in acids.
      If you like, you can separate the components by soaking them in acids.

BASIC SENTENCE ERRORS

Sentence Fragments

If a group of words is written as a sentence, but the group lacks a subject or a verb or cannot stand alone independently, it is called a sentence fragment. A fragment may be corrected by adding a subject or verb, joining it to another sentence, or rewriting the passage in which it occurs.

Fragment: The siphons, which were described earlier.

Revision: The siphons, which were described earlier, <u>must be</u> <u>ordered</u>. (verb added)

Fragment: The company continues to lose money. Although production has increased.

Revision: The company continues to lose money although production has increased. (joined to another sentence)

Fragment: Effective writing requires many skills. For example, a command of conventional grammar and the application of correct mechanics.

Revision: Effective writing requires many skills, such as a command of conventional grammar and the application of correct mechanics. (rewritten and combined into a sentence)

Exercise

Rewrite or combine these fragments into complete sentences.

1. Although we are trying to please the personnel of each department by presenting a variety of training programs.
2. The late arrivals having been named in this report along with the reasons for their tardiness.
3. The arrangements should be checked immediately. Registrants to be confirmed immediately.
4. Each month more than $1500 can be saved if the department buys a copy machine. No increase in quality if the machine is top quality.
5. I recommend we use copper. Not zinc.

Sentence Parallelism

Parallel structure involves writing related ideas in the same grammatical constructions. Adjectives should be parallel with other adjectives, verbs with verbs, phrases with phrases, and clauses with clauses.

Nonparallel: Tungsten steel alloys are <u>tough</u>, <u>ductile</u>, and <u>have</u> <u>strength</u>. (adjective, adjective, verb plus noun)

Parallel: Tungsten steel alloys are <u>tough</u>, <u>ductile</u>, and <u>strong</u>. (all adjectives)

Nonparallel: He must <u>learn</u> the language and <u>to be knowledgeable</u> about his computer. (verb and infinitive)

Parallel: He must <u>learn</u> the language and <u>become</u> knowledgeable about his computer. (both verbs)

Nonparallel: He will be hired <u>if he has the required training</u>, <u>if he
has three years experience</u>, and <u>by being recom-
mended by his former employer</u>. (dependent clause,
dependent clause, phrase)

Parallel: He will be hired if he has the required training, if he
has three years of experience, and if he is recom-
mended by his former employer. (all dependent
clauses)

Edit your writing to ensure that parallel ideas are expressed in parallel structures.

Exercise

Rewrite the nonparallel structures.

1. The computer is inexpensive, compact, and it is easy to use.
2. Before studying architecture, you should assess whether you have
   design ability and if you are exacting with numbers.
3. To write well one must be able to organize materials, have a flexible
   vocabulary, and one should know grammatical and mechanical conventions.
4. He was well liked and had training in management skills.
5. She attached the sphygmomanometer by positioning the patient,
   placing the cup above the elbow, and the clasp was secured.

Run-on and Comma-spliced Sentences

A run-on (also called a fused) sentence occurs when two or more independent clauses are written as one sentence without appropriate punctuation.
A run-on sentence may be corrected by separating the fused clauses with
a period or semicolon or by rewriting the sentence.

Run-on: Ace Company will revise its maternity policy men will
be eligible for child-rearing leave.

Correction: Ace Company will revise its maternity policy; men will
be eligible for child-rearing leave.

or

Ace Company will revise its maternity policy by allowing men to be eligible for child-rearing leave.

A comma-spliced sentence occurs when two or more independent clauses not joined by a coordinating conjunction or conjunctive adverb are written with only a comma between them.

Splice: Employees are entitled to eight sick days per year, they may be concurrent.

Correction: Employees are entitled to eight sick days per year; they may be concurrent.

or

Employees are entitled to eight sick days per year. They may be concurrent.

Splice: The restaurant requires a deposit for our annual dinner engagement, therefore, we must send a $50.00 check.

Correction: The restaurant requires a deposit for our annual dinner engagement; therefore, we must send a $50.00 check.

Using your understanding of clause structure, edit your writing to avoid run-on and comma-spliced sentences.

Exercise

Correct these run-on and comma-spliced sentences.

1. This guide is a product of months of research, compilation was done by Specialist Jim Smith.
2. Adult education opportunities are plentiful, moreover, all classes may be offered at our training facility.
3. After three straight days of bargaining, the talks broke down they will resume on Monday.
4. The union refused to consider benefit reductions but it did express willingness to negotiate increased work hours.
5. Mr. Larsen has participated in other civic activities in addition to his involvement in public schools he is a member and past officer of the Chamber of Commerce.

AGREEMENT

The most common grammar errors are subject-verb disagreements and pronoun-antecedent disagreements. For instance, if a subject is plural, then its verb must be plural as well, and if a pronoun antecedent is singular, then its pronoun must be singular as well.

Subject and Verb Agreement

Verbs change form from the singular to the plural. Consider:

Singular	*Plural*
I am	We are
He is	They are
She was	They were
He edits	They edit

A verb must agree with its subject in number. Generally, English-speaking people make these alterations automatically, but problems arise in a variety of structures.

In a sentence with compound subjects joined by *and* the verb is plural unless the subjects are considered a unit.

> The <u>technician</u> and <u>engineer</u> **are** consulting. (two persons)

> The <u>accountant</u> and <u>auditor</u> **reviews** my books monthly. (one person)

In a sentence with compound subjects joined by *or, nor, either . . . or, neither . . . nor* the verb usually agrees with the closest subject.

> The <u>diodes</u> or the <u>transistor</u> **is** faulty.

> Neither the <u>transistor</u> nor the <u>thermistors</u> **are** operating.

A singular subject followed by a phrase introduced by *as well as, together with, along with, in addition to* ordinarily takes a singular verb.

> The <u>president</u> as well as the vice-president **was held** responsible for the mismanagement.

Collective nouns (*committee, jury, crowd, team, herd,* etc.) usually take a singular verb.

> The <u>committee</u> **is meeting** Tuesday.

> The <u>jury</u> **is arguing** with the judge.

When a collective noun refers to members of the group individually, a plural verb is used.

> The <u>jury</u> **are arguing** among themselves.

Expressions signifying quantity or extent (*miles, years, quarts,* etc.) take singular verbs when the amount is considered as a unit.

> Ten dollars **is** too much to pay for a tablet.

> Six hours **is** too long to work without lunch.

A singular subject followed by a phrase or clause containing plural nouns is still singular.

> The highest number of diesel trucks **is** produced in Europe.

> The nurse who tends the heart patients **finds** them to be grateful.

When a sentence begins with *there is* or *there are,* the verb is determined by the subject which follows.

> There **are** an estimated 100 employees in this building.

> There **is** a conflicting opinion over capital punishment.

A verb agrees with its subject and not with its complement.

> Our chief trouble **was** (not were) malfunctions in the testing equipment.

Exercise

Select the appropriate verb to agree with its subject.

1. Three semesters (*is, are*) not enough to master French.
2. The bulk of our tax dollars (*go, goes*) to defense spending.
3. He is one of those people who (*is, are*) always willing to help.
4. The best benefit (*is, are*) the vacations.
5. Either the man or the woman (*assist, assists*) me with the payroll.

Pronoun Agreement

A pronoun is a word which takes the place of a noun, such as *he, who, itself, their, ourselves,* etc. (A complete list of pronouns is reviewed in Table A.1.)

> The technician checked **his** circuit boards.

The <u>woman</u> **who** trained me could assemble the parts **herself**.

A pronoun must agree in number with the word for which it stands, its antecedent.

Faulty: <u>Ace Company</u> is furloughing twenty of **their** employees.

Correct: <u>Ace Company</u> is furloughing twenty of **its** employees.

Faulty: Send the receipts to the <u>bookkeeping department</u>. **They** will issue the refunds.

Correct: Send the receipts to the <u>bookkeeping department</u>. **It** will issue the refunds.

Faulty: <u>Anyone</u> can take **their** accrued sick leave when necessary.

Correct: <u>Anyone</u> can take **his** (or **his or her**) accrued sick leave when necessary.

Table A-1   Pronouns

PERSONAL PRONOUNS:

	Subject	Object	Possessive
First person			
Singular	I	me	my, mine
Plural	we	us	our, ours
Second person			
Singular & plural	you	you	your, yours
Third person			
Singular			
masculine	he	him	his
feminine	she	her	her, hers
neuter	it	it	its
Plural	they	them	their, theirs
RELATIVE PRONOUNS:	who	whom	whose
	that	that	
	which	which	whose, of which
INTERROGATIVE PRONOUNS:	who	whom	whose
	which	which	whose, of which
	what	what	

REFLECTIVE AND INTENSIVE PRONOUNS:

myself, yourself, himself, herself, itself, oneself, ourselves, yourselves, themselves

DEMONSTRATIVE PRONOUNS: this, these, that, those

INDEFINITE PRONOUNS:

all	both	everything	nobody	several
another	each	few	none	some
any	each one	many	no one	somebody
anybody	either	most	nothing	someone
anyone	everybody	much	one	something
anything	everyone	neither	other	such

RECIPROCAL PRONOUNS: each other, one another

NUMERAL PRONOUNS: one, two, three . . . first, second, third . . .

When a pronoun's antecedent is a collective noun, the pronoun may be either singular or plural, depending on the meaning of the noun.

> The <u>committee</u> planned **its** next meeting. (the unit)

> The <u>committee</u> gave **their** reports. (the individual members)

Usually a singular pronoun is used to refer to nouns joined by *or* or *nor*.

> Neither <u>Jane</u> nor <u>Judy</u> did **her** share.

When the antecedent is a common-gender noun (*customer, manager, instructor, student, supervisor, employee,* etc.), the traditional practice has been to use *he* and *his* as in

> A <u>manager</u> routinely evaluates **his** employees.

However, writers who are sensitive to sexist elements of our language are more prone to use both *his* or *her* if the gender of the antecedent is not known.

> A <u>manager</u> routinely evaluates **his or her** employees.

If *his or her* must be repeated frequently, the cumbersome usage may be avoided by changing the singular antecedent to a plural construction.

> <u>Managers</u> routinely evaluate **their** employees.

Some indefinite pronouns (*some, all, none, any,* etc.) used as antecedents require singular or plural pronouns, depending on the meaning of the statement.

Everyone, everybody, anyone, anybody, someone, no one, and *nobody* are always singular.

> Everyone must turn in **his or her** timesheet.

> Somebody erased **his or her** floppy disk.

All, any, some, or *most* are either singular or plural, depending on the meaning of the statement.

> All of the employees received **their** payroll deduction forms. (All refers to employees and is plural; all is the antecedent of their.)

> All of the manuscript has been typed, but **it** has not been proofread. (All refers to manuscript and is singular; all is the antecedent of it.)

In standard English usage *none* is usually singular unless the meaning is clearly plural.

> **Standard:**   None of the men finished **his** work.
> **General:**   None of the men finished **their** work.
>
> **Clearly plural:**   None of the new computers **are** as large as their predecessors. (The sentence clearly refers to all new computers.)

When a pronoun is used, it must have a clearly identified antecedent.

> **Ambiguous:**   The CRT fell on the keyboard and broke **it**. (It could refer to CRT or keyboard.)
> **Clear:**   The CRT broke when **it** fell on the keyboard.
>
> **Ambiguous:**   The consultants recommended a new method of shipping parts. This is the company's best alternative for the future. (It is not clear if this refers to method or to the implied word recommendation.)
> **Clear:**   The consultants recommended a new method of shipping parts. This recommendation is the best alternative for the future.

Exercise

Correct these misused pronouns.

1. The company had high hopes for the new research program, but they encountered financial problems.

2. Neither the foreman nor the laborers want his pay reduced.
3. Everybody supported their union.
4. An instructor should encourage his students to ask questions.
5. Electrical engineering is an interesting field, and that is what I want to be.

Pronoun Case

Review the pronoun table. The personal pronouns and the relative or interrogative pronoun *who* have three forms depending on whether the pronoun is used as a subject, an object, or a possessive. Writers frequently encounter a few problems in proper case usage.

The object form of a pronoun is used after a preposition.

Incorrect: The work was divided between **he** and **I**.
Correct: The work was divided between **him** and **me**.

Incorrect: That is the data processor about **who** I have spoken.
Correct: That is the data processor about **whom** I have spoken.

In written English *than* is considered a conjunction, not a preposition, and it is followed by the form of the pronoun that would be used in a complete clause, whether or not the verb appears in the construction.

I am more experienced than **she** [is].

I like him better than [I like] **her**.

In general usage many educated people say "It is me" or "This is her," but standard English usage prefers the subject form after the linking verb *be*.

It is **I**.

This is **she**.

That is **he**.

It will be **I** who fail.

Although the distinction between *who* and *whom* is disappearing in oral communications, standard English usage prefers the distinction in writing. *Who* is the standard form when it is the subject of a verb; *whom* is the standard form when it is the object of a preposition or the direct object.

That is the professor **who** taught me chemistry. (Who is the subject of the verb taught.)

That is the woman **whom** I recommended for promotion. (*Whom* is the direct object of *recommended*.)

To **whom** are you speaking? (*Whom* is the object of the preposition *to*.)

Reflexive and Intensive Pronouns

The reflexive form of a personal pronoun is used to refer back to the subject in an expression where the doer and recipient of an act are the same.

He had only **himself** to blame.

I timed **myself** typing.

The same form is sometimes used as an intensive to make another word more emphatic.

The raise was announced by the president **himself**.

Safety **itself** is crucial.

In certain constructions writers mistakenly consider *myself* to be more polite than *I* or *me*, but in standard English the reflexive forms are not used as substitutes for *I* or *me*.

Faulty: Mr. Jones and **myself** attended the meeting.
Correct: Mr. Jones and **I** attended the meeting.

Faulty: The work was completed by Ms Burns and **myself**.
Correct: The work was completed by Ms Burns and **me**.

Exercise

Select the correct pronoun in each of the following sentences.

1.   From (*who, whom*) will we receive the instructions?
2.   The Director of Training assigned the project to Jones and (*I, me*).
3.   It is (*we, us*) who were to leave early.
4.   She was later than (*I, me*).
5.   Smith, White and (*I, myself*) were assigned to conduct the survey.

USAGE GLOSSARY

Many words in the English language are so similar that they cause confusion. Following is a brief glossary and exercise of such terms for you to review. (Words that are asterisked are corruptions of correct usage; they are not to be used in formal writing.)

accept, except

Accept means "receive" or "agree to."

Community colleges accept a wide variety of students.

As a preposition, *except* means "other than."

I did all of the work except your report.

As a verb, *except* means "exclude," "omit," "leave out."

If you except Mr. Jones, no other president has owned his own Lear Jet.

advice, advise

Advice is a noun meaning "guidance."

If I wanted it, I would ask for your advice.

Advise is a verb meaning "counsel," "give advice to," "recommend," or "notify."

I advise you to exercise stock options.

affect, effect

Affect means "change," "disturb," or "influence."

The rising cost of fuel has drastically affected the trucking industry.

It can also mean "feign" or "pretend to feel."

Although she knew she was to be promoted, she affected surprise when notified.

As a verb, *effect* means "bring about," "accomplish," or "perform."

She effected a perfect word-processed report.

As a noun, *effect* means "result" or "impact."

Her extra work had no effect on the vice-president.

all ready, already

Use *all ready* when *all* refers to things or people.

At noon the secretaries were all ready to lunch.

Use *already* to mean "by this time" or "by that time."

I have already typed that report.

all right, *alright

All right means "completely correct," "safe and sound," or "satisfactory."

My answers to the interviewer were all right. (The meaning is that *all* of the answers were *right.*)
Despite a few cuts, I was all right.

Do not use *all right* to mean "satisfactorily" or "well."

*Do not use *alright* anywhere; it is a misspelling of *all right.*

almost, *most all

Almost means "nearly."

By the time we reached Miami, the tank was almost empty.

*In formal writing, do not use *most all*; use *almost all* or *most.*

Almost all (or most) of the employees were eligible for vacation.

a lot, *alot

A lot of and *lots of* are colloquial and wordy. Use *much* or *many.*
*Do not use *alot* anywhere; it is a misspelling of *a lot.*

as, as if, like

Use *as* or *as if* to introduce a clause.

As I drove into the parking lot, my tire blew out.
He looked as if he had worked all night.

Use *like* to mean "similar to."

The logo looked like ours.

assure, ensure, insure

Assure means "state with confidence to."

I assure you that he will be hired.

Ensure means "make sure" or "guarantee."

There is no way to ensure that every policy is understood.

Insure means "make a contract for payment in the event of specified loss, injury, or death."

He insured the package for $100.00.

complement, compliment

As a verb, *complement* means "bring to perfect completion."

His red tie complemented his blue suit.

As a noun *complement* means "something that makes a whole when combined with something else" or "the total number of persons needed."

Practice is the complement of learning.

Without a full complement of workers, we cannot complete the task.

As a noun, *compliment* means "expression of praise."

He complimented the appearance of my report.

continual, continuous

Continual means "going on with occasional slight interruption."

At the office there is a continual humming of typewriters.

Continuous means "going on with no interruptions."

We have 24-hour guard service; surveillance is continuous.

different from, *different than

*Do **not** use *than* after different. Use *from.*

His management style is different from mine.

few, fewer, little, less

Use *few* or *fewer* with countable nouns.

We have fewer employees than we did a year ago.

Use *little* or *less* with uncountable nouns.

I have less experience than you on the word processor.

good, well

Use *good* as an adjective, but not as an adverb.

The proposal for staggered work hours sounded good to many employees.

Use *well* as an adverb when you mean "in an effective manner," "ably."

He did so well on the project that he was promoted.

Use *well* as an adjective when you mean "in good health."

She hasn't looked well since her operation.

***hopefully**

Use *hopefully* to modify a verb.

She looked hopefully at her boss as he scanned her proposal.

*Do not use <u>hopefully</u> when you mean "I hope that," "we hope that," or the like.

Incorrect: Hopefully, the company will make a profit this quarter.

Revised: The stockholders hope that the company will make a profit this quarter.

its, it's

Its is the possessive form of *it*.

I like this company because of its location and its benefits.

It's means "it is."

It's evident that we are an expanding company.

stationary, stationery

Stationary means "not moving."

The typewriter was on a stationary table.

Stationery means "writing paper."

We had to order more stationery from the printing department.

Exercise

Supply the correct word. You may have to change the tense of the verbs.

1. Everyone has _____ the invitation _____ Sam.
   (accept, except)
2. I _____ you to follow your instructor's _____ .
   (advise, advice)
3. The malfunctioning air conditioning _____ our tempers.
   The manager _____ a defiant look.
   The _____ of nuclear fallout are under study.
   (affect, effect)

4. Finally, the reports were xeroxed, and we were _____
    to begin the board meeting.
    The President had _____ left for lunch when I reported
    for our interview.
    (already, all ready)

5. It is _____ with me if you use correction tape.
    (alright, all right)

6. Winstons taste good _____ a cigarette should.
    (as, as if, like)

7. I _____ you that we can _____ your
    right to strike.
    (ensure, assure, insure)

8. If there are _____ members, it means _____
    work for the secretary.
    (fewer, less)

9. The departmental members work _____ together,
    and I feel _____ about their cooperation.
    (good, well)

10. Ace Company is an ideal employer because of _____
    benefits, and _____ improving _____
    stock option program each year.
    (its, it's)

Punctuation and Mechanical Conventions

INTRODUCTION

The professional or technical writer must be conscious and demanding of punctuation and mechanical conventions to prevent vagueness and misreading. Two practices of punctuation are prevalent today. A few businesses and industries adopt an open punctuation system, which favors only essential marks and omits those that can be safely omitted, such as the comma before *and* in a series (screws, nuts, and bolts). The majority of professional writers use standard, or close, punctuation conventions because these conventions promote greater accuracy. This appendix reviews close punctuation conventions.

One of the major characteristics of professional and technical writing is the extensive use of abbreviations, numbers, symbols, and other mechanics. This appendix reviews the general conventions that govern mechanics.

Both the punctuation and mechanical conventions are arranged in alphabetical order to help you edit your writing quickly.

PUNCTUATION

1.0 Apostrophe

1.1 Use an apostrophe to indicate the possessive case of the noun:

The company's product

Jack and Bob's office (joint possession)

Bill's or Jack's car (individual possession)

his sister-in-law's law practice

1.2 Use an apostrophe to indicate the possessive case of indefinite pronouns:

another's tools	neither's wrench
anybody's desk	one's customers
each one's station	somebody's computer

Do *not* use an apostrophe to indicate the possessive case of personal pronouns:

his schedule
Ours is the newest model.
The mistake was hers.
Its handle is steel.

1.3 Use an apostrophe to indicate the omission of letters in contractions:

> I'm   o'clock
> he'll   we're
> can't   you're

Do not confuse *they're* with *their* or *there*.

Their supervisor knows they're there.

Do not confuse *it's* (it is) with *its* (a possessive).

It's demonstrating its graphic function.

1.4 Use an apostrophe to indicate the plural of letters, numbers, symbols, and cited words:

Your *r*'s look like your *n*'s.

You use too many *and*'s.

Your *7*'s look like your *l*'s.

the 1980's

The *&*'s are broken on all of the typewriters.

2.0 Brackets

2.1 Use brackets within a quotation to add clarifying words that are not in the original:

Mr. Roberts stated, "They [computers] have revolutionized his business."

2.2 Use brackets within a quotation to enclose the Latin word *sic* ("so," "thus") which indicates that a misspelling, grammatical error, or wrong word was in the original:

He wrote, "Your [sic] selected to head the committee."

3.0 Colon

3.1 Use a colon after a formal salutation:

Dear Ms Benson:

Gentlemen:

Good morning:

3.2   Use a colon to introduce a phrase or clause which explains or reinforces a preceding sentence or clause:

Food processing consists of three main steps: selecting the blade, measuring the ingredients, and processing at the appropriate speed.

The position sounds attractive: the salary is high and the opportunities for advancement are excellent.

3.3   Use a colon when a clause contains an anticipatory expression (*the following, as follows, thus, these*) and directs attention to a series of explanatory words, phrases, or clauses:

The requirements for the position are as follows:
1.   a master's degree,
2.   three years experience, and
3.   willingness to relocate.

3.4   Use a colon to express ratios, to separate hours and minutes, and to indicate other relationships.

3:1	signal:noise
A:B	8:25 P.M.
Acts: 14:7	12:101–104 (volume 12, pages 101–104)

3.5   Use a colon between the main title and subtitle of a book:

Technical Writing: An Easy Guide

4.0   Comma

Refer to Table B.1 for a review of comma and semicolon usage in compound and complex sentences.

4.1   Use a comma to separate independent clauses joined by a coordinating conjunction.

The cursor shows where you are typing, and it moves across the screen as you type.

4.2   Use a comma after an introductory dependent clause:

If you have a two-drive computer system, you place your program diskette in drive A.

4.3   Use a comma after a conjunctive adverb introducing a coordinate clause:

This system is easy to use; however, we suggest that you read the directions carefully.

Table B.1 ***Comma and Semicolon Review for Compound and Complex Sentence Construction***

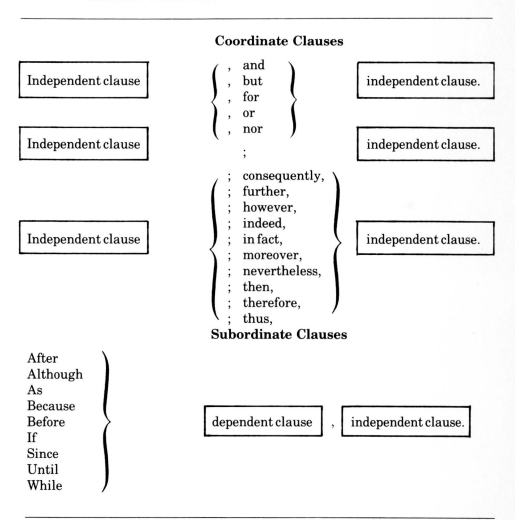

4.4 Use a comma to separate a nonrestrictive word, phrase, or clause from the rest of the sentence:

You should, however, make copies of your original diskette for safekeeping.

His goal, to become computer literate, is easy.

The cursor, which is a blinking square, shows where the entry will appear on the screen.

4.5   Use a comma to separate items in a series:

These instructions will teach you how to create, edit, or proof a file.

The Personnel Department will receive all letters of application, forward them to the appropriate search committee, and handle all correspondence.

The comma is often omitted in company names:

Jones, Smith and Scully

4.6   Use a comma to separate a series of adjectives or adverbs not connected by a conjunction:

Store your thin, sensitive, magnetic disks out of direct sunlight.

The computer blinked haphazardly, noisily.

4.7   Use a comma in a date to separate the day and year:

June 9, 1987

the April 15, 1985, deadline

Do *not* use a comma in the military or British form:

9 June 1987

4.8   Use a comma to separate city and state, state and county, county and state:

Fort Lauderdale, Broward Country, Florida, has twenty-seven electronic firms.

4.9   Use a comma to separate titles from names and to set off appositives:

Juan Murillo, M.D.

Julie Koenig, attorney-at-law

K. D. Marshal, Jr.

Robert H. Larsen, president

Jerry Noosinow, the PanAm pilot, checked the KAL log.

4.10 Use commas to group numbers into units of threes in separating thousands, millions, and so forth:

3,845

74,763

9,358,981

4.11 Use a comma after the salutation of an informal letter and after the complimentary close of most letters:

Dear Sally,

Very truly yours,

Cordially,

4.12 Use a comma to separate corporation abbreviations for company names:

Trolleys, Ltd.

Jones and Scully, Inc.

Ace Company, Inc.

4.13 Use a comma after expressions that introduce direct quotations:

President Dan Barker said, "We must double our profits."

If the phrase interrupts the quotation, it is set off by two commas:

"We must," said President Dan Barker, "double our profits."

5.0 Dash

5.1 Use dashes to set off emphatic and abrupt parenthetical expressions:

The idea of this program—it has been tested thoroughly—is to simplify spelling correction.

5.2   Use a dash to mark sharp turns in thought:

He was an arrogant man—with little to be arrogant about.

5.3   Use dashes to separate nonrestrictive material which contains commas from the rest of the sentence:

These manuals—*Guide to Operations, Disk Operating System, Word Proof,* and so on—are protected by copyright.

6.0 Ellipsis

6.1   Use the ellipsis (three spaced periods) to indicate any omission in quoted material:

Martin stressed, "The technical writer . . . must master punctuation." (The words *as well as the professional writer* have been omitted.)

6.2   Use four spaced periods to indicate the ellipsis at the end of a sentence.

The consultant stressed, "Write carefully . . . . " (The words *and edit endlessly* have been omitted.)

7.0 Exclamation Point

7.1   Use an exclamation point at the end of an exclamatory sentence to show emotion or force:

Shred the files!

We will not file bankruptcy!

7.2   Use an exclamation point at the end of an exclamatory phrase:

What a disaster!

8.0 Parentheses

8.1   Use parentheses to enclose an abruptly introduced qualification or definition within a sentence:

You may place your program diskette in drive A and your storage diskette (the one with your file on it) in drive B.

8.2   Use parentheses to enclose a cross-reference within a sentence:

The ellipsis (see Section 6.0) is used in direct quotations.

8.3 Use parentheses to enclose figures or letters to enumerate points:

To use this program (a) insert your DOS diskette in drive A, (b) turn on your computer, (c) type in the date, and (d) press the Enter key.

9.0 Period

9.1 Use a period to signal the end of declarative or imperative sentences:

Diskettes are sensitive to extremes of temperature.

Do not try to clean diskettes.

9.2 Use a period with certain abbreviations (see pages 418-20 for exceptions):

Dr.	Jr.	Nov.
A.M.	Mr.	J.C. Lewis
P.M.	Ph.D.	etc.

9.3 Use a period before fractions expressed as decimals, between whole numbers and decimals, and between dollars and cents:

.10	$3.50
3.6	$0.92 (or 98¢ or 93 cents)

9.4 Use a period after number and letter symbols in an outline:

I.
   A.
   B.
      1.
      2.

10.0 Question Mark

10.1 Use a question mark at the end of an interrogative question:

Do you own a personal computer?

Do *not* use one after an indirect question.

He asked me if I owned a personal computer.

10.2 Use a question mark in parentheses to indicate there is a question about certainty or accuracy:

This is the best (?) computer.

11.0 Quotation Marks

11.1 Use quotation marks to set off direct speech and material quoted from other sources:

Dr. William Haskell writes, "Before 1960 the thing rarer than a marathoner was a health professional trained to care for one. Most doctors," he points out, "forbade post-cardiac patients to do anything more vigorous than walk to the refrigerator."

11.2 Use quotation marks to indicate nonstandard terms, ironic terms, and slang words:

This is a "gimmick."

His "problem" was his genius I.Q.

He "got his act together."

11.3 Use quotation marks to indicate titles of articles, essays, short stories, chapters, short poems, songs, television and radio programs, and speeches:

I read the article "Ten Years of Sports Medicine" in *Runner's World*.

Do *not* use quotation marks around quoted material which requires more than four lines in your paper. Display a long quote by indenting it ten spaces from your regular margins and omitting the quotation marks.
Commas and periods are always placed *inside* the closing quotation mark:

"Yes," Ms Gloss said, "we have a swine flu epidemic."

He said "electrons," but meant "electronics."

Semicolons and colons are placed *outside* the closing quotation mark:

He said, "The trapped air bubble will leave honeycombs"; honeycombs are sections of little indentations.

He said, "The trapped air bubble will leave honeycombs": little indentations.

Question marks, exclamation points, and dashes are placed inside *or* outside the final quotation mark, depending upon the situation:

He asked, "Is the oscillator connected to the mixer?"

Did he say, "The assembly is constructed of heavy-gauge stainless steel"?

12.0 Semicolon

Refer to Table B.1 for a review of comma and semicolon usage in compound and complex sentences.

12.1 Use a semicolon between coordinate clauses not connected by a conjunction:

The new system will use low-powered transmitters; it is called a cellular radio.

12.2 Use a semicolon before a conjunctive adverb including a coordinate clause:

Retort pouches are like cans; however, they do not dent.

12.3 Use a semicolon before a coordinating conjunction introducing a long or loosely related clause:

Niobium, which is used primarily as an alloy, is a metallic element that resists heat and corrosion and hardens without losing strength; and it is widely available in Canada and South America.

12.4 Use a semicolon in a series to separate elements containing commas:

J. D. Smyth, member of the board; Carol Winter, president; Glenn Morris, committee chairperson; and I attended the conference.

13.0 Virgule (Slash)

13.1 Use a virgule to indicate appropriate alternatives:

Define and/or use the words in sentences.

13.2   Use a virgule to represent *per* in abbreviations:

    17 ft/sec   12 mi/hr

13.3   Use a virgule to separate divisions of a period of time:

    the April/May report

    the 1986/87 academic year

MECHANICAL CONVENTIONS

1.0 Abbreviations

1.1 Avoid the overuse of abbreviations. (See Table B.2 for a list of common technical abbreviations.)

1.2 Explain an abbreviation the first time you use it:

He has worked for the Department of Transportation (DOT) and the Office of Mental Health (OMH).

1.3 Omit most internal and terminal punctuation in abbreviations:

BTU	lb
psi	ft
DNA	rpm

1.4 If the abbreviation forms another word, use the internal and terminal punctuation:

in.	A.M.
gal.	No.

1.5 Use uppercase (capital) letters for acronyms and degree scales:

NASA   (National Aeronautics and Space Administration)
VHF   (very high frequency)
OEM   (original equipment manufacturer)
C (Centigrade)
F (Fahrenheit)

1.6 Use lowercase (small) letters for abbreviations for units of measure:

Table B.2   *Common Technical Abbreviations*

ac	alternating current	kw	kilowatt
amp	ampere	kwh	kilowatt hour
A	angstrom	l	liter
az	azimuth	lat	latitude
bbl	barrel	lb	pound
BTU	British Thermal Unit	lin	linear
C	Centigrade	long	longitude
Cal	calorie	log	logarithm
cc	cubic centimeter	m	meter
circ	circumference	max	maximum
cm	centimeter	mg	milligram
cps	cycles per second	min	minute
cu ft	cubic foot	ml	milliliter
db	decibel	mm	millimeter
dc	direct current	mo	month
dm	decimeter	mph	miles per hour
doz	dozen	No.	nummber
dp	dewpoint	oct	octane
F	Fahrenheit	oz	ounce
f	farad	psf	pounds per square foot
fbm	foot board measure	psi	pounds per square inch
fl oz	fluid ounce	qt	quart
FM	frequency modulation	r	roentgen
fp	foot-pound	rpm	revolutions per minute
fpm	feet per minute	rps	revolutions per second
freq	frequency	sec	second
ft	foot	sp gr	specific gravity
g	gram	sq	square
gal.	gallon	t	ton
gpm	gallons per minute	temp	temperature
gr	gram	tol	tolerance
hp	horsepower	ts	tensile strength
hr	hour	v	volt
in.	inch	va	volt ampere
iu	international unit	w	watt
j	joule	wk	week
ke	kinetic energy	wl	wavelength
kg	kilogram	yd	yard
km	kilometer	yr	year

gph   (gallons per hour)
cc   (cubic centimeters)
rpm   (revolutions per minute)
mph   (miles per hour)
bps   (bits per second)

1.7 Write plural abbreviations in the same form as the singular:

17 in
47 lb
 5 hr
30 gph
10 cc

2.0 Capitalization
   2.1 Use standard English conventions.
   2.2 Begin all sentences with a capital letter.
   2.3 Capitalize all proper nouns (proper names, titles which precede proper names, book and chapter titles, languages, days of the week, months, holidays, names of organizations and groups, races and nationalities, historical events, names of structures and vehicles, and so forth:

John Doe	Ace Construction Company
Professor Jane Doe	American Federation of Labor
Introduction to Nursing	Caucasian
French	Jewish
Monday	the Korean War
October	the Statue of Liberty
Labor Day	a Ford Mustang

   2.4 Capitalize adjectives derived from proper nouns:

English

Elizabethan

   2.5 Capitalize words like *street, avenue, corporation,* and *college* when they accompany a proper name:

Elm Street
Forty-second Avenue
Ace Company, Inc.
Yale University
Broward Community College

2.6 Capitalize *north*, *east*, *midwest*, *near east*, and so on when the word denotes a specific location:

the South
the Midwest
the Near East
101 Northwest First Street

2.7 Capitalize brand names:

Kleenex tissues	Xerox photocopies
Scotch tape	a Frigidaire
a Formica counter	the Astro-Turf field
a Polaroid camera	Sanforized

3.0 Hyphenation

3.1 Use a hyphen between some compound names for family relationships:

Hyphenated:	brother-in-law's company
One word:	my stepmother's portfolio
Two words:	my half brother was graduated

3.2 Use a hyphen in compound numbers from twenty-one to ninety-nine and in fractions:

thirty-seven cartons
forty-third year
four-fifths of the book
one-eighth inch

3.3 Use a hyphen after the prefixes *all-*, *ex-*, *self-*, and before the suffix *-elect:*

all-American
ex-president
self-contained
president-elect

3.4 Use a hyphen in some compound nouns:

kilowatt-hour
dyne-seven
foot-pound

3.5 Use a hyphen in compound adjectives when the latter precedes the word it modifies:

alternating-current motor
closed-circuit television
high-pressure system
easy-to-build model

3.6 Use a hyphen between a number and a unit of measure when they modify a noun:

6-inch ruler
12-volt charge
a 3-week-old prescription

4.0 Italics

4.1 Use italics (underline in handwritten or typed material) to indicate the names of books, magazines, newspapers, and other complete works published separately:

the book *Introduction to Nursing*
the magazine *Newsweek*
the movie *The Right Stuff*
Dante's *Divine Comedy*
Word Proof: A Manual

4.2 Use italics to indicate the names of ships and planes:

the H.M.S. *Ark Royal*

the U.S.S. *Independence*

4.3 Use italics to indicate words, symbols used as words, and foreign words which are not in general English usage:

The prizewinning orchids were *Alleraia* Ocean Spray, *Bloomara* Jim, and *Guantlettara* Noel.
coup d'etat
deus ex machina
The word *thrombosis* is derived from the Greek word *thrombos* which means "a clot" or "a clump."
Your *9*'s look like *7*'s.

Do not italicize foreign expressions which are established as part of the English language, such as:

a priori	bona fide	habeas corpus	pro tem
ad hoc	carte blanche	laissez faire	resume
ad infinitum	etc.	per annum	status quo
	ex officio	pro rate	

5.0 Numbers

5.1 Handle numbers consistently in any one report.

5.2 Write out single digit numbers from zero through nine when the number modifies a noun:

five disks	two printers
three word processors	nine keyboards

5.3 Use numerals for zero through nine when the number modifies a unit of measure, time, dates, pages, chapters, sections, percentages, money, proportions, tables, and figures:

2 inches	section 9
3-second delay	2 percent
5 gph	a 4% increase
9 years old	$50
2:40 A.M.	$0.05 or .05 cents
June 9, 1986	1:9
9 June 1986	4 to 2 odds
page 7	Figure 2
Chapter 1	Table 6

5.4 Use numerals for decimals and fractions:

0.6	1/4 or 0.25
3.341	7/16 in.
3/5 or 0.6	6½ lb

5.5 Use numerals for any number greater than nine:

10 psi	237 lb
97 employees	101,400 people

5.6 Write out numbers which are approximations:

a half cup of coffee
a quarter of a mile farther
a fifth of the energy
approximately three times as often

5.7 Place a hyphen after a number of a unit of measure when the unit modifies a noun:

7-inch handle
6-inch-diameter circle
10½-lb box
27-gal. capacity

5.8 When many numbers, both smaller than and greater than nine, are used in the same section of writing, use numerals:

Buy 4 sheets of 8-inch by 11½-inch paper, 15 sheets of 8-inch by 20-inch paper, and 7 manila envelopes.

Exception: If none of the numbers are greater than nine, write them all out:

The office contains eight desks, seven chairs, six file cabinets, and seven typewriters.

5.9 When one number appears immediately after another as a part of the same phrase, avoid confusion by writing out the shorter number:

nine 50-watt bulbs
two 4-inch wrenches
thirteen 20-pound packages
twenty-two 2,500-component circuit boards

5.10 Place a comma in numbers in the thousands:

1,000
17,276
427,928

5.11 Write numbers in the millions in one of two ways:

2,700,000 or 2.7 million
16,000,000 or 16 million
$1,500,000 or $1.5 million
72,110,427

5.12 Write numbers in the billions, trillions, quadrillions, and so on in numerals:

2,700,000,000
47,337,426,104,900

5.13 Do not begin a sentence with a numeral:

Fifteen inches of rain fell.
not
15 inches of rain fell.

6.0 Symbols
    6.1 Use symbols sparingly.
    6.2 Define symbols in your text. (See Table B.3 for common technical symbols.)

Table B.3 **Common Technical Symbols**

Symbol	Word
%	percent
°	degree
&	and
'	feet
"	inches
$	dollar
¢	cents
@	at (12 at $2.00 each)
+	plus
−	minus
×	times
÷	divide
‖	greater than or derived from
=	equals
F	Fahrenheit
C	Centigrade
Rx	take (on prescriptions)
θ	the Sun, Sunday
£	pound
#	number
Hb	mercury (the element)
☿	Mercury (the planet)
X	snow
↑	gas
Ω	ohm
S	Silurian soil

7.0 Spelling

7.1 Use a dictionary when in doubt about the proper and preferred spelling of a word. (See Table B.4 for a list of frequently misspelled words.)

Table B.4 *Frequently Misspelled Words*

accidentally	comparative	heroes	prominent
achievement	competitive	humorous	propaganda
acquaintance	consensus	immediately	psychology
amateur	contemptible	indispensable	pursue
analysis	convenience	irrelevant	questionnaire
anonymous	courageous	irresistible	receive
anxiety	criticism	knowledge	rhythm
appreciate	definitely	laboratory	schedule
arctic	descent	leisure	scissors
athletics	desirable	lieutenant	secretary
auxiliary	despair	lighting	seize
awkward	disappear	loneliness	separate
bachelor	discipline	maneuver	sergeant
beggar	efficient	meant	siege
beginning	eighth	medieval	similar
believe	eligible	minimum	sophomore
benefited	equipped	mortgage	souvenir
bookkeeper	exaggerate	necessary	subtle
breath	exercise	ninth	succeed
bulletin	exhausted	noticeable	successful
bureau	existence	ocasionally	surprise
business	familiar	occurred	synonym
calendar	fascinating	omitted	thoroughly
campaign	fatigue	opportunity	tragedy
caricature	fiery	parallel	twelfth
catastrophe	foreign	parlaysis	unforgettable
cemetery	forty	pastime	unmistakable
colonel	government	possibility	vacuum
coming	guarantee	privilege	vengeance
committee	height	procedure	weird

Index